MW00633149

WOMEN AND SLAVERY

VOLUME ONE

Africa, the Indian Ocean World,
and the Medieval North Atlantic

WOMEN AND SLAVERY

VOLUME ONE

Africa, the Indian Ocean World, and the Medieval North Atlantic

VOLUME TWO

The Modern Atlantic

Edited by Gwyn Campbell,
Suzanne Miers, and Joseph C. Miller

The editors wish to acknowledge the support of the Institute for American Universities, Avignon, and the Office de Tourisme, Courthézon, in organizing the conference "Women and Slavery" at which most of the papers appearing in these volumes were first presented; the discussants and participants at that conference; and especially Marianne Ackerman for creating an atmosphere that nurtured discussion and cemented friendships.

WOMEN AND SLAVERY

VOLUME ONE

Africa, the Indian Ocean World,

and the Medieval North Atlantic

Edited by

Gwyn Campbell

Suzanne Miers

Joseph C. Miller

OHIO UNIVERSITY PRESS

ATHENS

Ohio University Press, Athens, Ohio 45701
www.ohio.edu/oupress
© 2007 by Ohio University Press

15 14 13 12 11 10 09 08 07   5 4 3 2 1

Published separately: *Women and Slavery*, vol. 2, *The Modern Atlantic*

Earlier versions of three chapters in this volume—those on Mauritius by
Richard Allen, on Cape Town by Elizabeth Jordan, and on the Transvaal by Fred
Morton—appeared in the special issue of *Slavery & Abolition* on "Women in
Western Systems of Slavery" (volume 26, no. 2, 2005). The editors and Ohio
University Press gratefully acknowledge the courtesy of Gad Heuman, editor,
and Taylor and Francis, publishers of *Slavery & Abolition*.

Library of Congress Cataloging-in-Publication Data

Women and slavery / edited by Gwyn Campbell, Suzanne Miers, Joseph C.
Miller.
    p. cm.
Includes index.
ISBN-13: 978-0-8214-1723-2 (hc : v. 1 : alk. paper)
ISBN-10: 0-8214-1723-1 (hc : v. 1 : alk. paper)
ISBN-13: 978-0-8214-1724-9 (pbk. : v. 1 : alk. paper)
ISBN-10: 0-8214-1724-X (pbk. : v. 1 : alk. paper)
[etc.]
    1. Women slaves—History. 2. Slavery—History. I. Campbell, Gwyn, 1952– II.
Miers, Suzanne. III. Miller, Joseph Calder.
    HT861.W66 2007
    306.3'6208209—dc22

2007018274

To the memory of our friend,
colleague, and contributor,
Timothy Fernyhough

CONTENTS

A TRIBUTE TO SUZANNE MIERS

Martin A. Klein and Richard Roberts

It says a great deal about Suzanne Miers that she edited many of the chapters in this book, all of which originated as papers presented at a conference organized to honor her. This book was to be a Festschrift—but Suzanne seems to gain full satisfaction from working closely with contributors in refining their ideas and professes no desire to rest on her laurels and collect honors. At the conference that led to this book, whose subject she had suggested, she seemed almost embarrassed by the praise she received, presumably seeing herself as a modest trooper in the academic trenches.

Suzanne Miers is an American who has spent most of her life elsewhere. She was born in 1922 in Luebo, in the Democratic Republic of the Congo, where her father was a mining engineer. She spent most of her childhood in Belgium and England. She received a BA from the University of London in 1944 and an MA in 1949. She taught briefly at Bedford College for Women but, like many academic women of her generation, put any professional aspirations on hold to marry and have two children. When she followed her husband, Brigadier R. C. H. Miers, to Singapore, she taught for three years at the Singapore branch of the University of Malaya (1955–58). She returned to the academic world after the untimely death of her husband in 1962. In 1969 she received a PhD from the University of London. That dissertation, published in 1975 as *Britain and the Ending of the Slave Trade*,[1] opened up the subject of slavery and the slave trade as a theme in international relations and contributed to the upsurge of interest in African and comparative slavery. She has contributed significantly to that body of literature ever since, writing both about slavery in distant places and about the way governments have struggled with the often embarrassing question of human servitude. Only in the years when she was completing her dissertation did Sue return full-time to the United States, teaching several years at the University of Wisconsin and then spending sixteen years at Ohio University before retiring in 1992.

Important as Sue's scholarship has been, her most important contribution to the field of African history has been as a coeditor of four volumes on slavery, in two of which we collaborated with her. The most seminal was the first, *Slavery in Africa: Historical and Anthropological Perspectives* (1977), which she edited with Igor Kopytoff. Along with Claude Meillassoux's *L'esclavage en Afrique précoloniale* (1975), it launched what has since been one of the most important themes in historical research on Africa. Particularly important was the provocative eighty-page introduction, which advanced a powerful argument about the dynamics of incorporating slaves into African lineage systems. Not all specialists accepted Miers and Kopytoff's emphasis on integration, but whatever one's position on that point, it stimulated debate not only in African history studies, but more generally in slave studies, and made the understanding of slavery a central question for historians of Africa.

Her second collaboration was with Richard Roberts on *The End of Slavery in Africa* (1988). Central to this volume was the debate about whether the end of slavery in Africa was a smooth, virtually frictionless process or whether it ushered in a set of profound social, cultural, and economic changes. Sue was particularly interested, however, in the condition of women and child slaves. The model of African slavery as a mechanism of incorporating outsiders was primarily drawn from virilocal, patrilineal marriage patterns, where wives were married into their husband's lineages. Thus, the model of slavery in Miers and Kopytoff was taken to a large degree from female experiences. In editing *The End of Slavery*, Sue demanded that contributors address the specific situation of women and children slaves. She insisted that women and children had distinct vulnerabilities and that applying the gender-unspecific term *slave* or *freedman* obscured the significant differences between men, women, and children as they faced the choices posed by the ambiguous end of slavery. Sue Miers's interest in the gender-specific vulnerability of women in slavery, their agency in their escape from bondage, and her interest in comparative slavery led to her editing, with Maria Jaschok, *Women and Chinese Patriarchy: Submission, Servitude, and Escape*. Her own contribution to that volume was a study of a Chinese woman who had been sold in Hong Kong as a *mui ts'ai*, a servant girl. Sue's consistent concern with women slaves connects her early work to this current collection.

During the 1990s she and Martin Klein, together and separately, organized a series of panels on modern slavery at meetings of the African Studies Association. The central problem those panels addressed was why slavery or slavelike conditions had persisted so long in Africa. Whereas

The End of Slavery had principally examined the moment of emancipation, the new studies explored why emancipation took so long and why it followed such uneven courses in different parts of Africa. A selection of those papers appeared as *Slavery and Colonial Rule in Africa* (1999). Her own contribution to this volume was an essay on "Slavery and the Slave Trade as International Issues, 1890–1919."

Sue's work as a scholar was never a purely academic concern. It is very hard for those of us who study slavery to forget that slaves were human beings, but many historians of slavery see modern forms of slavery as different from traditional forms. In Sue's case, however, recognition of the commonalities of experience among those coerced to labor for others led to an involvement in modern forms of slavery. In 1980 she attended a meeting of the United Nations Working Group on Slavery. She describes in the preface of her most recent book, *Slavery in the Twentieth Century: The Evolution of a Global Problem* (2003), the "disheartening experience" of bored experts and officials going through the paces in a ritual that was like throwing a bone to some of the nongovernmental organizations trying to raise questions about modern forms. It was a ritual encumbered by the era's rhetoric of confrontation, East-West around the Cold War and North-South between the developed and developing worlds. For much of this meeting, Sue was the only spectator in the room. She was deeply disturbed and left Geneva determined to write on the politics of anti-slavery, but in the years since the meeting, the situation changed. A number of NGOs were successful in raising issues of forced labor, forced prostitution, debt bondage, child labor, and other abuses, and the Group of Experts was transformed into the Working Group on Contemporary Forms of Slavery. Sue Miers was often in the gallery, but also active in groups like Anti-Slavery International,[2] which were raising questions about modern forms of servitude and kept pressure on international bodies to act against both slavery and the continued trafficking in people. She was also a trustee of Anti-Slavery International and regularly attended meetings of its management board in London. The result was a series of articles, some historical, some descriptive, that provided scholarly substance to political struggles that are still going on. The end product of much of this research was her magnum opus, *Slavery in the Twentieth Century*, which traces the decline of formal slavery, a process that ended only in 1970, and the growing struggle to deal with more modern forms of coerced labor.

The two of us have sometimes disagreed with Sue Miers, starting with the introduction to Miers and Kopytoff's *Slavery in Africa*. But that has not really affected our relations with Sue. She is a gentle warrior, and a determined one, recognizing that debate and disagreement are the essence of academic life and demanding only that disagreement be polite. She has been a superb collaborator, well organized and with a network of connections. She always knew who was doing what and could be asked to do an article to fill some need. A generous person herself, she could usually get contributors to follow through on their commitments with only the gentlest hectoring. She is a meticulous and careful editor, open to discussion, easy to work with, but often very persistent. She keeps her eye on the goal and works hard to achieve it. And she gets results. It is hard to say no to a woman who is both gentle and firm. Both of us have been informed by her research, enriched by our collaboration with her, and enlivened by her friendship.

NOTES

1. For publication details of works by Suzanne Miers, see the chronological list of published works that follows.

2. Anti-Slavery International is the world's oldest antislavery organization, having been founded originally as the British and Foreign Anti-Slavery Society in 1839. We thank Michael Dottridge for filling us in on Sue Miers's work with Anti-Slavery International.

THE PUBLISHED WORKS OF SUZANNE MIERS ON SLAVERY

Britain and the Ending of the Slave Trade. New York: Africana, 1975.

and Igor Kopytoff, eds. *Slavery in Africa: Historical and Anthropological Perspectives*. Madison: University of Wisconsin Press, 1977.

and Richard [L.] Roberts, eds. *The End of Slavery in Africa*. Madison: University of Wisconsin Press, 1988.

"Humanitarianism at Berlin: Myth or Reality." In *Bismarck, Europe and Africa: The Berlin Africa Conference 1884–1885 and the Onset of Partition*, edited by S. Forster, W. J. Mommsen, R. Robinson, 333–45. London: Oxford University Press, 1988.

and Michael Crowder. "The Politics of Slavery in Bechuanaland: Power Struggles and the Plight of the Basarwa in the Bamangwato Reserve 1926–1940." In *The End of Slavery in Africa*, edited by Suzanne Miers and Richard Roberts, 172–200. Madison: University of Wisconsin Press, 1988.

"Britain and the Suppression of Slavery in Ethiopia" In *Proceedings of the Eighth International Conference of Ethiopian Studies*, edited by Taddese Beyene, 2:253–66. Addis Ababa: Institute of Ethiopian Studies, 1989.

"Diplomacy versus Humanitarianism: British and Consular Manumission in Hijaz 1921–1936." *Slavery and Abolition* 10, no. 3 (1989): 102–28.

Maria Jaschok and Suzanne Miers, eds. *Women and Chinese Patriarchy: Submission, Servitude, and Escape.* Hong Kong: Hong Kong University Press, 1994.

"Mui Tsai through the Eyes of the Victim: Janet Lim's Story of Bondage and Escape." In *Women and Chinese Patriarchy: Submission, Servitude, and Escape,* edited by Maria Jaschok and Suzanne Miers, 108–21. Hong Kong: Hong Kong University Press, 1994.

"Contemporary Forms of Slavery (review essay: [Anti-Slavery International], Sutton, *Slavery in Brazil;* Anderson, *Britain's Secret Slaves;* Sattaur, *Child Labour in Nepal;* Smith, *Ethnic Groups in Burma*)." *Slavery and Abolition* 17, no. 3 (1996): 238–46.

"Britain and the Suppression of Slavery in Ethiopia." *Slavery and Abolition* 18, no. 3 (1997): 257–88.

"Slavery and the Slave Trade as International Issues, 1890–1939." *Slavery and Abolition* 19, no. 2 (1998): 16–37.

and Martin Klein. Introduction to "Slavery and Colonial Rule in Africa." *Slavery and Abolition* 19, no. 2 (1998): 1–15.

and Martin Klein, eds. "Slavery and Colonial Rule in Africa." *Slavery and Abolition* 19, no. 2 (1998), special issue. Also published as *Slavery and Colonial Rule in Africa.* London; Portland, OR: Frank Cass, 1999.

"Contemporary Forms of Slavery." *Canadian Journal of African Studies/Revue canadienne d'études africaines* 34, no. 3 (2000): 714–47.

"Slavery to Freedom in sub-Saharan Africa: Expectations and Reality." *Slavery and Abolition* 21, no. 2 (2000): 237–64.

"Slavery: A Question of Definition." In "The Structure of Slavery in Indian Ocean Africa and Asia," edited by Gwyn Campbell, special issue of *Slavery and Abolition* 24, no. 2 (2003): 1–16. Also as "Slavery: A Question of Definition," in *The Structure of Slavery in Indian Ocean Africa and Asia,* edited by Gwyn Campbell, 1–16. London; Portland, OR: Frank Cass, 2004.

"Mue Tsaï à travers les yeux d'une victime: Histoire de l'asservissement et de l'évasion de Janet Lim." *Cahiers des anneaux de la mémoire,* no. 5 (2003): 15–32. Extract translated from *Women and Chinese Patriarchy: Submission, Servitude, and Escape,* edited by Maria Jaschok and Suzanne Miers. Hong Kong: Hong Kong University Press, 1994.

Slavery in the Twentieth Century: The Evolution of a Global Pattern. Walnut Creek, CA: Altamira, 2003.

"Slave Rebellion and Resistance in the Aden Protectorate in the Mid-Twentieth Century." *Slavery and Abolition* 25, no. 2 (2004): 80–89.

"Slavery and the Slave Trade in Saudi Arabia and the Arab States on the Persian Gulf, 1921–63." In *Abolition and Its Aftermath in Indian Ocean Africa and Asia,* edited by Gwyn Campbell, 120–36. London; Portland, OR: Frank Cass, 2005.

PREFACE

The essays that the editors present in this volume center on Africa and the western Indian Ocean, but they also include the medieval Norse Atlantic in a way that we find historically revealing. We have grouped the following chapters into categories that transcend the geographic and cultural frameworks conventional in studies of slavery and of women.[1] Why else would one group, as we do, medieval Iceland with the nineteenth-century Afrikaner republic in southern Africa, and also with a Frenchman's household in Cairo and its guest from the Antilles? Nor would most scholars think first of juxtaposing women's legal strategies in a French colony in West Africa with Muslim law and custom on Africa's Indian Ocean coast. Writers on nineteenth-century European commercial enterprise have seldom contemplated the full range of the trading towns and plantations that we have assembled here, from the Upper Guinea Coast to the Cape of Good Hope and on east to Mauritius, in the Indian Ocean. By presenting works by specialists on all these regions, and more, we hope to stimulate thinking about women and and about slavery alike in analytically historical and integrative terms.

Our calculatedly trans-culturo-geographic grouping of these chapters exposes similarities in women's experiences of slavery and uses of it as recurrent, parallel aspects of very broad processes of historical change. Women's gendered exclusion from the modern public realm of highly commercialized and legally framed forms of slaving that developed in the eighteenth century in the New World, centered on plantations and mines, developed in parallel with, and eventually replaced, the millennia-long, continent-spanning positioning of women, children, and others in private households centered on patriarchal extended families. It was there in the recent Americas that the stereotypical modern image of slaves became male, men imagined as toiling from sunup to sundown in fields and canebrakes, subject to sale at any time for the financial advantage of their owners. In this prevailing modern stereotype, women accompanied men only incidentally and were understood primarily as quasi (and often thereby deficient) units of male labor.

The studies of the earlier phases of this long-term process of commercialization presented here reveal complex domestic worlds—in Europe often seigneurial, but elsewhere patriarchal or kin-groups built around male elders and ancestors—in which dominant men surrounded themselves with women of many origins outside the group, including some acquired through capture or purchase, that is, as slaves. It is the distinctions within these groups deriving from the diverse origins of these domiciled women—in marriage, wardship, adoption, or through capture or purchase—that organize the following chapters. In these domiciliar contexts, the women who brought in through "marriages" had access to their families of origin to safeguard their welfare. Women who had entered households through capture or purchase—experiences equally and absolutely isolating—had no such protectors, occasionally—from their points of view—for the better but overwhelmingly often for the worse.

THE PRIVACY OF HOUSEHOLD SLAVERY

The enslavement of these females, unlike the highly legalized institutions of slavery in the Americas by the eighteenth century, was not a public affair in the modern sense. The public laws regulating the control of masters, or patrons, over their slaves of either sex, were limited to confirming their abilities to exchange them through acquisitions or disposal, usually among men, occasionally among widows or other women entering the public spaces of law and commerce. These regulations adapted general laws of property—inheritance and commerce—regarding transfers among men of rights over assets of any sort to the women slaves' humanity, and particularly to the potential consequences of their reproductive capacities. Since women brought into households through slaving had no relatives to protect them, the regulation of commercial dealings among mostly male strangers paralleled marriage law regulating exchanges of women as wives by male heads of households (or other aggregations of individuals). Further, the law was all about males' sexual potency, their prospective sons by different women, and these women's claims to the men's estates on behalf of their children.

The public regulations—before the modern civic state, really moral strictures more than laws—of such household slaving,[2] primarily of women, reminded the patriarchs that their untrammeled power within their domestic domains also brought correspondingly weighty moral responsibilities for the people thus rendered dependent on them. In the absence of outside protectors of the enslaved women they controlled, the respect they claimed among other men beyond the household depended on at least the appearance of beneficently honorable conduct within it. In the moral worlds of the universalistic Abrahamic religions, these injunctions came in the form of the familiar—and in this volume, oft-cited—Qur'anic injunctions along these lines; Christianity enjoined the same. The corporate kin groups of Africa, when confronted with collective threats from outsiders, closed ranks around even the most recently acquired slave women to similar protective effect.

Of course, the private household was also a concealed domain, making such responsible conduct no more certain in practice there than among planters in the Americas notorious for their failures to heed similar ideological expectations—sometimes expressed legally, sometimes religiously, sometimes as the personal honor of paternalism. In none of these cases could the many women whom irresponsible masters treated badly appeal to state or civil protections, but neither could legitimate wives appeal to outside authority against husbands who indulged base inclinations within the privacy of their homes. George Michael La Rue's reconstruction of the fates of African women slaves in nineteenth-century Cairo households—Muslim, Jewish, Christian alike—provides stomach-churning direct witness to the vulnerability of enslaved women there to human abuses as well as to the bacillary plagues that he also describes.

The public obscurity of women slaves in societies composed of family-centered households was no greater than the "social death" suffered by their counterparts in the modern civic polities—monarchies, then nations—that emerged in Europe and the Americas after the sixteenth and seventeenth centuries. In such contrastingly composite contexts, their principal recourse was flight to a more responsible counterpart, often religious institutions, or the creation of autonomous religious communities of their own, where refugees from abuse could cluster together, still apart from the secular "societies" that had no conceivable places for them. Christian missionaries in Africa sometimes offered enslaved women this option of escape, as we see in the studies presented here on Madagascar, Ethiopia, the Swahili regions, and at the Cape of Good Hope. In Islamic regions conversion to the Muslim faith brought parallel protections, as well as parallel limitations. The European colonial powers in Africa, as Richard Roberts documents, added a precisely parallel secular escape hatch by introducing civic protections, if—however oddly—selectively only for women enslaved, not for other women.

xviii JOSEPH C. MILLER

VALUE AND VULNERABILITIES OF WOMEN SLAVES IN HOUSEHOLDS

The dynamics of bringing women into these households through slaving hinged not only on their vulnerability to being assigned distinctively humiliating or arduous chores: everyone, and particularly women in general, worked very hard to support the family, except the very few in the most privileged circumstances. Women slaves certainly supplemented the basic female labor force of the domestic household, and the nameless woman who spun arctic hare fur into fine thread in Norse America (see chapter by Seaver) and her sisters across the globe and through the centuries exemplify the economic value of their skills in domestic artisanry. Differentiation in responsibilities for domestic chores within these households increased with commercialized forms of wealth. The chapters here on the Swahili areas of eastern Africa by Katrin Bromber and Jan-Georg Deutsch highlight the ways in which the humiliating exposure of slave girls and women on public streets enabled the seclusion of legitimately married women in "respectable" Islamic households.

But the greater value of the women acquired through slaving was the prospect of the exclusive loyalty of their children to their fathers, masters, and—in commercialized contexts—also owners. From the perspectives of the women enslaved the utter isolation distinguishing their entries into such households through slaving cut both ways. On the one hand, it made slave women particularly vulnerable to personal abuse, often and even primarily sexual by the men of the house. But on the other, it also made them valuable, even cherished, as potential mothers of heirs unencumbered by the ambitions of the in-laws that encumbered (as well as protected) legitimate wives. Wealthy and powerful men could vest their legacies through slave "wives," or "concubines" promoted to the status of "wife," by bearing sons implicitly recognized as heirs to their owner-husbands. Through sons by slave women, male household heads concentrated and controlled assets they had accumulated into at least the succeeding generation, without having to guard against jealous or grasping in-laws.

Beyond the apparently universal aggressive tendencies of males not held socially accountable for their behavior toward women, these men's domestic liaisons with the enslaved women in their households ranged from highly informal, even discreet, "concubinage" to which Christian monogamy consigned the African (and no doubt also Indian) women in the households of the planters of Mauritius, or the noble households of Christian Ethiopia, to the formally limited (to four wives) polygyny of Islamic households, to the indefinite numbers of women whose marriages to rulers drove lineage-structured politics in much of Africa. Catherine Coquery-Vidrovitch systematically highlights the structural formality of women slaves in the African political context of "lineages," but the same multiplicity of political marriages also forms the backgrounds of other chapters on Africa and Madagascar.

I also emphasize the varying degrees of competition with "legitimate" wives that slave women within these households provoked.[3] Fred Morton, Sharifa Ahjum, Elizabeth Jordan, and Richard Allen all allude to varying aspects of these domestic rivalries—on many levels, culturo-religious, deeply psychological, social and political, and demographic. Their studies range from the almost purely patriarchal domains of Dutch farmers in the South African Republic, held accountable for all the women in their monogamous domestic domains, to the much less responsible French planters in remote, sexualized, and exotic Mauritius. Expatriate French male planters there acquired women, along with many men, for commercial purposes, but the absence of European females allowed them to integrate some of the ones they found more attractive into their domestic households as companions in their loneliness and as outlets for their virile ambitions, even for competitive display of power over women. The legitimate wives and daughters, or the males' relatives, evident in Morton's account of taking in African girls in the South African Republic, were in positions to enforce greater responsibility.

Ahjum innovatively draws on Lacanian psychoanalytic theory to explore the deep human psychodynamics that slavery evokes within the reproductive and nurturing, and hence emotionally very intense confines of the patriarchal family. Using examples from studies of slavery in the Anglo-Dutch Cape Colony in southern Africa, she explains the distinction between slave women and legitimate wives by focusing on the socially constitutive role of the recognized "Father," denied to slaves of either gender by limiting their significant relationships to their enslaved "mothers." The same dynamic reduced slave "mothers" to their bodily functions, to physical property that could be possessed, sexually as well as by directing and claiming the benefits of their labors.

Beyond the incidental personalities always involved in specific cases, these domestic politics, or the politics of domesticity, revolved in significant part around the competing interests of the multiple women in the household in the futures of the children they might bear. That is, this competition among the women of these households was the female experience of their male heads'—husbands', patrons', owners', fathers'—

efforts to control their own legacies by bringing others in as mothers through slaving.

LONG-TERM TRENDS: COMMERCIALIZATION AND STATE INTRUSION

The contributions in this volume also illustrate a sequence of specific moments in a millennium-long process of increasing state intrusions on the private authority of household heads over the females within. Ultimately these political authorities external to the households—monarchical, or imperial, as phrased in the section heading we employ—became civic, or national, as British abolitionism loomed in the background of Ahjum's and Morton's contributions on southern Africa. It is also plausible to consider the possible—indeed likely—correlate of this process: that householders concentrated on holding females in slavery as one means of preserving their integrity and autonomy against the growing intrusions of military and political authorities operating in domains gendered male and not directly concerned with the standings of women of any background. With women thus excluded from the politics of these increasingly modern realms, transfers and consequent enslavement survived in private. In fact domesticity for all sorts of women may have thrived as the necessary correlate of the gendering of modern politics as male. Gender, in excluding women from participation in modern civic societies, became the equivalent of race in the Americas as an ideology shunting aside the males there freed from slavery.

In Africa profits from exchanges with the growing commercial worlds of the Indian and Atlantic oceans often paid for the high costs of political centralization, as has also been observed elsewhere around the world. During the relatively recent era studied in all but one of the contributions to this volume, and also toward the end of the much earlier Norse explorations of the North Atlantic, global economic integration both provoked and enabled consolidation of these new, often highly militarized monarchical domains.

Gwyn Campbell's study of slaving and women in the aggressively consolidating nineteenth-century Merina polity in Madagascar most clearly shows the intense and complex competition between local groups of kin and the looming imperial power over the women (and other slaves) that both desperately needed. Campbell emphasizes the value of slaves of both sexes as laborers in a contest between an underfinanced military regime reaching the viable limits of the plundering that had fueled its initial growth and small agricultural communities left struggling to feed themselves. Similar political contests over people between overlords and local householders were evident also in Ethiopia, as the late Tim Ferny-hough showed in the essay he left for us here. From another angle, Roberts's study of the enslaved women and wives who turned to the colonial courts of French West Africa before the First World War shows the vulnerability of the household authority of African men to a determined imperial power (incidentally, in this case, European), offering women access to public courts. Victorious invaders in the Americas, as throughout Africa, often undercut local power holders by luring members of their retinues away with offers of favorable treatment; where their followings were slaves, as in both the North American revolution and the American Civil War, manumissions and emancipation followed.

Similar political tensions divided both Zanzibari sultans and early European colonial regimes from the wealthy householders of the towns on the Swahili Coast, as planters and urban merchants brought thousands of enslaved women and men from the remote interior of the continent into the Islamic culture of the littoral and adjacent islands. The harem, as Martin Klein reveals it, was an extreme form of the sanctity of this domestic authority, intensely sexualized in the eyes of naive and fanciful European male voyeurs and no less acutely politicized in the eyes of the male patriarchs (household heads, kings, sultans, and others around the world). La Rue sets his reconstruction of the history of the slave (and other) women in a Frenchman's household in nineteenth-century Cairo against the Orientalist elaboration of this sexualized European fantasy particular to the Muslim world.[4]

Christianity reached the medieval Norse Atlantic, as Kirsten Seaver shows, at about the same time that slavery there for both men and women declined. She finds no direct consequences of Christianization in Iceland or Greenland for public law regarding slaves, but comprehensive monarchical law was barely emergent in the islands in the period about which she writes. Rather, the mitigating effects of Christianity on the privacy of Norse heroes' domestic domains may have taken more local forms by converting formerly private and ad hoc "marital" arrangements to a public sacrament of "marriage," with subsequent legitimation of their progeny through baptism. The public accountability brought by the Christian sacraments might well have imposed an increased degree of social responsibility on household heads and thus reduced the tactical utility of bringing women in as slaves. Supplies of such women in northwestern Europe declined with the creation there of monarchical, often Christian, political authorities with commitments to popular welfare that eroded the former privacy of the households of the heroic Norse of old in the name of protecting the people thus claimed as subject of benevolent monarchs.

It seems suggestive, at least, that the standing[5] of the children of the women enslaved repeatedly emerged at the cores of the initial monarchical laws regulating slaves—particularly in monogamous Christian cultures, but also in the Qur'anic background of polygynous Muslim households. Lovejoy's examination of the large majorities of males among the people sent into the Atlantic attributable to the Muslim regions of western Africa shows how seriously slaveholders there may have taken these injunctions of sharia (Islamic law). Ahjum's Lacanian psychodynamics also work through children and their social constitution as "signified" persons— that is, recognized in relational terms as human—to resurrect in analytic terms the Abrahamic religious focus on children.[6]

The underlying differentiation among the offspring of women of varying standings lurked in the Roman laws of slavery, which excluded all children of female slaves from standing in the recognized family. They were slaves by the female side of their heritage alone; their paternity did not matter. This legal framework prevailed in subsequent European canon (and eventually also civil) law, and it appears in this collection as imported to South Africa and Mauritius. Along the Upper Guinea Coast, inheritance of enslavement through the maternal line created a convenient distinction between the legitimate heirs, in Europe, of Portuguese and other expatriate traders there and their "local offspring" (as the Portuguese termed them, *filhos da terra*, or "natural children") thus left to the care, and eventual benefit, of the wealthy widows in the trading towns of the coast. By the by the late nineteenth century—as Philip Havik shows—these "country wives" often operated businesses in partnership with their (local) sons.

These women and others often surrounded themselves with enslaved women (and men) to enter the increasingly pervasive public sphere of commerce as traders, as several chapters in this volume demonstrate. Their commercial successes led them also into politics—as Havik emphasizes in the quasi-colonial sphere of Portuguese influence on Africa's Upper Guinea Coast and as Coquery-Vidrovitch also mentions for less commercialized regions of the continent. They turned to others enslaved more recently than they as the only people more marginal than themselves to the male-gendered public domains of commerce and politics.

Enslaved women thus enslaved other women to expand households of their own, often using them to develop artisan production for commercial purposes, to attract and marry male trading partners, even—as Coquery-Vidrovitch explains—in Africa to take culturally constructed "males" or as "female husbands" as "marriage" partners for themselves. Acquiring women slaves allowed women—even if themselves enslaved—otherwise dependent on men to build personal retinues entirely independent of male control, through whom they might overcome their exclusion from the gendered worlds of commerce and politics, as Klein has accented in other contexts.[7] Women tended to find opportunities in enslaving other women along the interstices between the otherwise solidly male domains of commerce in the Atlantic and Indian Oceans and of the land-based military polities of Africa and Asia.

THE ORGANIZATION OF THIS BOOK

The sections into which we have divided the chapters in this collection frame the domestic dynamics motivating, and then deriving from the consequences of, the presence of enslaved women in households found from the medieval north Atlantic to nineteenth-century tropical Africa and the Indian Ocean world. Households in those places at those times were engaging, in varying degrees, but were not subordinated to, transcending commercial economies and monarchical polities, often Islamic or Christian, but not yet modern and civic. Coquery-Vidrovitch provides the most extensive coverage of the dynamics of enslaving women in kin-defined communities (as well as other political frameworks), as they are known from Africa.

Klein considers the domestic household enlarged by power or by wealth in terms of the politics of the harem, Islamic and Asian. This largely productive, nonsexual, and nonreproductive political household contrasts with the multiple, and significantly reproductive, mother-children segments of polygynous households elsewhere, particularly in Africa.[8] Ahjum explores the ambiguous, contradictory, and ultimately profoundly disabling consequences of the singular authoritarian male that the enslavement of women enshrined for human development and social validation, that is, for viable personal identity in modern contexts, projected outward from the nuclear family to civic societies. These dynamics recurred across cultural and geographical regions.

The second section of the volume focuses on the domestic politics among the women in these compound households, slaves and wives, or thralls and queens in Seaver's phrasing of the core tension developed in this collection. Again transcending conventional cultural contrasts, we

offer Seaver's reconstruction of the medieval Norse Atlantic as a nominally European—but not modern—example of patriarchal households
that gathered women of varying backgrounds in ad hoc and often violent
ways, a world in which even "queens" could become thralls of a strong
man. The Norse in the medieval Atlantic recognized little law beyond
the dictate of the dominant male in the household. The ambiguity of the
civic standing of all women—in other words, the primacy of their domestic standings—is equally evident continents and centuries distant
in the households of all cultural backgrounds that La Rue reveals in
nineteenth-century Cairo. Similarly, patriarchal networks in the late-
nineteenth-century South African Republic gave places to daughters, enslaved female wards, and other women much more effectively than did
the kind of civic society that the British were importing to southern
Africa at the time.

The chapters in the third section offer two approaches—one historical, the other literary—to the differing ways in which strategies of enslaving women played out within the enmeshed but distinct domestic
(religious) and commercial (public, secular) frameworks generally characteristic of the Islamic world. Both focus on the Swahili regions of eastern Africa and were contextualized in the growing commercialism of the
late nineteenth century. One may see them as local manifestations of the
wealthy commercial households expanding elsewhere by incorporating
large numbers of women as slaves, as in near-contemporaneous Egypt
and in the background to the French colonial conquest of western Africa
in the 1890s.

The fourth section, perhaps in a surprising juxtaposition, considers
women in similarly patriarchal household domains across a range of
nineteenth-century moments of political consolidation—warlord/monar-
chical in style in Ethiopia and Madagascar and theocratic/warlords in
Sahelian/Sudanic western Africa. These regions are usually contrasted
culturally and religiously as Islamic, Christian, and other. However, our
focus on the women enslaved in households—rather than on males imported exclusively for commercial purposes and thus subject to culturally
derived legal frameworks, as in the Americas—illustrates the analytical
power of this volume's focus on women to transcend the conventional
confines of culture and associated frameworks of law.

The value of slave women in the struggles to preserve household autonomy in the face of new (or in the case of Ethiopia, resurrected) assertive "state" power is thus recurrently evident, in forms differing according to local circumstances. Islamic theocracies in western Africa

legitimated themselves by protecting women according to Qur'anic injunction; the competitive warlords of the Christian empire in Ethiopia
moved with entire populations from the regions they abandoned, and
the "autarkic" Merina kingdom in Madagascar struggled to replace its
base in military plundering with labor-intensive mining and agriculture.

The essays presented in the final section shift from households challenged by military regimes to adaptations to the fully commercial worlds
of the Atlantic and Indian Oceans through enslaving women. They pro-
ceed from the commercial towns, and eventual plantations, of the Upper
Guinea Coast, to the autonomous moments of the enslaved washerwomen in the urban environs of the Dutch East India "Company town"
at the Cape of Good Hope, and eventually to the Atlantic-style sugar
plantations of Mauritius.

Our focus on the women in slavery, and on women slavers, we hope,
highlights recurrent contexts of slaving around the world that transcend
the inhibitingly contrastive cultural and regional practices of treating
both women and slavery. We calculatedly transgress the contrast between
"West and the rest" still basic to historical thought, however lamented
and even muted. The slaving thus revealed calls attention to the underlying processual dynamics of households, polities, and religion and other
ideologies within all the regions from which our authors draw their studies—particularly including the seemingly familiar European and Christian areas presented here as local manifestations of trans-local dynamics.

The order of the sections also follows a historical logic, not one of
chronological time but rather one of processual dynamics, from significantly autonomous, older (but increasingly submerged or marginalized)
communities of kin, through large patriarchal households held increasingly accountable to transcending religious ethics, Islamic or Christian,
to the more secular intrusions of militarized political power, ranging
from its religiously legitimized formulations in Islamic sultanates and ji-
hadist caliphates and the Solomonic Christian empire of Ethiopia to
Madagascar, and—finally—to secular French colonialism. The blessings
of the Merina emperors and the French *mission civilisatrice* were, in their
own modern ways, no less religiously injunctive than the worldly man-
dates of what we think of as religion. The commercial profits that financed acquisition of the women who entered these households through
slaving supported predominantly commercial communities, here represented by the Portuguese Upper Guinea Coast and by Cape Town, on the
fringes of territorial political authority established on European military
or religious grounds.

The full flowering of commercial slavery in eighteenth-century mines and plantations in the Americas had Old World counterparts (not precedents) only on previously uninhabited (or depopulated) islands of the eastern Atlantic and the Indian Oceans, where military-political interests did not constrain private enterprise. Mauritius here provides the conceptual bridge from medieval Europe and from much of Africa to the following volume's focus on women enslaved in the remote, depopulated Americas, where institutionalized, public, legal modern slavery developed in a similar power vacuum. Women in slavery in the Americas, in terms of the historical processes framed here, worked in much more modern contexts, slowly taking shape through incremental steps marked by several of the contributions in that volume. Women in slavery in the Americas faced not only the brutalities of labor in gold mines, canebrakes, tobacco and cotton fields, and all the other sites of massive production at the base of American economies, they also faced new challenges of racial exclusion in the national civic polities taking form there and claiming to protect universal human rights.

Gender, primarily a matter of excluding women from commerce and from these politics of theoretical civic equality under early-modern monarchs and eventually within modern nations, played more personally in the (often but not always earlier) worlds of the households portrayed in this volume. Here men conducted both politics and trade less in public spaces gendered male and more through relations among patriarchal households filled with women, often enslaved, that they established and mediated through liaisons with the women in them. Hence the male strategies centering on children and the female competition swirling around them. Women became marginal to competition and negotiating among men only later, in the civic domains of modern states and commercial economics.

In this volume readers are invited to contemplate women and slavery in realms very unlike these familiar modern contexts and to consider potentially surprising implications of the slaving highlighted here for the deceptively well-known slaveries of the Americas. They may then turn to the companion volume in this set to find themes elaborated here followed through as they changed radically in the profoundly novel contexts of the modern Americas.

—Joseph C. Miller

NOTES

1. For an initial attempt to comprehend the concept of women on the scale of world history, finely balanced between regional specificities, general patterns, and theoretical considerations, see Bonnie G. Smith, *Women's History in Global Perspective*, 3 vols. (Champaign: University of Illinois Press, 2004).

2. I prefer *household* as a useful analytical term in this context, as its possible substitute, *domestic*, has too many connotations in the literature on modern American slavery to use effectively here; the concept of household, as a haven excluded from public affairs, offers intriguing parallels with the cult of domesticity that emerged together with the strengthening of civic citizenship in the late nineteenth-century North Atlantic.

3. The American counterparts are emphasized in several of the essays in the companion volume in this set, esp. Laura F. Edwards, "Enslaved Women and the Law: Paradoxes of Subordination in the Postrevolutionary Carolinas."

4. Background on this aspect of Victorian cultural and intellectual sexualization and domestication of women, Europeans as well as others, may be found in Henrice Altink, "Deviant and Dangerous: Proslavery Representations of Jamaican Slave Women's Sexuality, ca. 1780–1834," in the companion volume in this set.

5. Or sheer survival in Iceland, where infanticide was the issue.

6. Also, in the companion volume, see Felipe Smith, "The Condition of the Mother: The Legacy of Slavery in African American Literature of the Jim Crow Era," among other essays there highlighting slave women's manipulations of this rule.

7. Martin A. Klein, *Slavery and Colonial Rule in French West Africa* (New York: Cambridge University Press, 1998).

8. For theorization of this contrast between "production" and "reproduction," see Claire Robertson and Marsha Robinson, "Re-modeling Slavery as If Women Mattered," in the companion volume.

Africa, the Indian Ocean World,
and the Medieval North Atlantic

INTRODUCTION

WOMEN AS SLAVES AND OWNERS OF SLAVES

Experiences from Africa, the Indian Ocean World, and the Early Atlantic

JOSEPH C. MILLER

Only in the 1970s did historical slavery became the focus of serious academic study beyond its classical focus in the ancient Mediterranean and, more recently, the United States and other parts of the Americas. We now know that the practice had been widespread in medieval Europe, Africa, and the Indian Ocean region, as well as elsewhere throughout the world. In Africa, as elsewhere, historically low population densities, a paucity of capital, and a plentitude of land had resulted in the need to recruit labor in growing economies there by compulsion. However, research on slavery in all these areas remained centered on males, even after the emergence of women's history as a coherent field of study, also in the 1970s.[1] This volume and its companion, *Women and Slavery: The Modern Atlantic*, are intended to correct this imbalance by showing not only that women slaves outnumbered men in these earlier times but also that they played crucial roles in the politics of the men who brought them into their households, and sometimes also the economies of the women in them.

The chapters in this volume illustrate some of the many strategies of acquiring and the complex implications of holding women in slavery in Africa, in the western Indian Ocean region, and also—integrally, if also surprisingly by conventional measures—in the northern Atlantic in the era of medieval Norse explorations. Slaving in these regions ranged from the highly commercialized chattel variety that European settlers practiced in South Africa and Mauritius to the more domestic uses and abuses characteristic of Muslim societies and the diverse political and economic values that women in servitude had in Africa and Madagascar. Enslaved

I

women's experiences differed widely, then, as did the enslavers' purposes in acquiring them. Furthermore, women's experiences of slavery, as well as of redemption, manumission, and finally the often nominal emancipations of the colonial era, differed significantly from those of the less numerous men enslaved.

In these regions enslaved women were usually taken into domestic households of varying sorts rather than assigned the more public and commercially productive duties of enslaved men. However hard they worked, like other women not in slavery as well as all men, what distinguished them as slaves from their male counterparts was their ability to bear children, who then became slaves for or heirs to their masters rather than being able to claim descendants of their own or bear children for their families. Thus enslaved women and the children they had by their masters constituted potential challenges to legitimate wives' and children's interest in inheriting the father's wealth and position. They also had a distinctively female, if often limited, advantage, as objects of their masters' sexual desires, though one obtained often at the cost of great physical and emotional abuse. "Free" women, even when not themselves owners of slaves, were usually the primary beneficiaries of the labor of the women and others whom their husbands owned.

The collection of chapters, finally, illustrates how the many forms of female slavery, like the enslavement of men, changed over time and through the spaces of the many and contrasting cultures of Africa, the Indian Ocean world, and also Europe at the threshold of its Atlantic era. This introduction suggests how the intensifying global commercialization of the eighteenth and nineteenth centuries interacted—in Africa, in particular—with domestic economies that tended to emphasize reproduction, continuation of the community—rather than production of material surpluses as commodities for sale—and thus sought reproductive females through slaving. Global commerce also promoted the growth of trading towns and—in them—large, compound mercantile (and sometimes also political) households filled with women of varied origins, but particularly including those who arrived through the slaving that accompanied—and in the Atlantic world often overwhelmed—trade in commodities. Africa and the Indian Ocean world also produced and sold commodities in vast quantities, and—as in the Americas—the relatively limited commercially productive areas tended to favor men as workers.

This volume, and its introduction, therefore focus primarily on women and household slavery in the more commercialized centers of the regions discussed—Europeans in southern Africa and Mauritius, Afro-

Portuguese in Upper Guinea, Egypt engaged with Europe and Ethiopia
with the Muslim world, the Swahili cities and plantations of eastern Africa,
Saharan and Atlantic traders in Muslim western Africa, Merina efforts to
resist British and French merchants in Madagascar, and the early phases
of European investment in colonial rule. Though only one chapter on
Africa and this introduction refer explicitly to the rather larger domestic
economies that prevailed throughout these parts of the world, all the contributions to the volume implicitly acknowledge the households filled
with enslaved women that supported the accelerating tendencies toward
commercialization from the mid-eighteenth to the twentieth century.

THEORETICAL BACKGROUNDS PROBLEMATIZED

Either of the two conceptual fields drawn together here—women's history and slavery studies—might provide a viable theoretical framework
for this initial consideration of the chapters in this volume. However,
these introductory comments do not confine themselves to either field
individually, since the purpose is to engage both, to integrate each with
the other. Most of the authors writing here are historians of slavery and
not regular contributors to the important debates within the fields of
women's history and gender studies. I will therefore follow their implicit
grounding in questions regarding slavery, extending these perspectives to
consider where women have fit within the analytical structure of this
field rather than organizing the discussion around the no-less-important
debates about patriarchy, such as whether men valued women and tried
to possess them as slaves for their labor or for their ability to reproduce or
for sheer sexual satisfaction, to which most authors devote only intermit-
tent attention.

In the service of equal neglect of the structurally framed questions of
the conventional separate fields, I do not discuss the abstract nature of
"slave systems" either, or attempt systematic contrasts among the distinct
tendencies in the specific cultures of slaving encountered in the following pages. Rather, this essentially exploratory initiative presents historicized views on the vital, but underappreciated, female participants—
mostly enslaved, some enslavers, and others who benefited from the
efforts of the enslaved—of what may be one of the world's oldest experiences for women.

Women were majorities, perhaps large ones, among the enslaved, and
enslavement was a major, perhaps also a majority, experience of the women
in the portions of the world that enter this volume. The emphasis here

falls not on this generality but rather on the specificities of being female in and around pervasive slaving in particular times and places. The hope is that historicization of this sort will raise new questions for both of the relatively theorized and structural related fields.

WOMEN IN THE SLAVE TRADES OF AFRICA AND THE INDIAN OCEAN WORLD

Women and men moved in many directions through trades in slaves within Africa, around the Indian Ocean world, and also in medieval Europe, including the Norse Atlantic. On the African side, it is currently impossible to estimate with any precision the numbers of women or men displaced in Africa itself or sold into any but the Atlantic phases of exporting. The antiquity of trading there in slaves was too great, and the extant records are too limited, since—in contrast to slaving in the Atlantic—the people shipped out across the Indian Ocean and the Red Sea rarely constituted identifiable specialized cargoes. For the Sahara, as George Michael La Rue details, even where caravans were organized around moving captives, only scattered and incidental data on them survive.

In the Atlantic, between the sixteenth and nineteenth centuries European slavers carried an estimated twelve million Africans to the Americas, of whom fewer than 40 percent, or about five million, were women, mostly from West and West-Central Africa. It is much less clear how many other western Africans, including women, were exported over a longer period across the Sahara to predominantly Muslim markets in North Africa and the Middle East, starting in significant numbers by the eighth century. Also from these early Islamic centuries pilgrims from all over the Muslim world, including Africa, took along women and children to sell on their ways to Mecca (in modern Saudi Arabia) or at their destination, to pay for their journeys home. Some were slave girls sold off by their owners, others were daughters sold by their own parents or wives sold by their husbands. Still others were kidnapped and kept as slaves by Bedouins or residents of the other regions through which the caravans of pilgrims passed. As late as the 1950s Africans from as far away as Mali were reportedly tricked into embarking on the Islamic pilgrimage and sold in Arabia.[2]

Estimates for maritime exports of slaves from East Africa are hardly more precise. Significant numbers of people were taken from at least the eighth or ninth century to the Red Sea and Persian Gulf to serve the needs of the early Islamic regimes there. Approximate figures for the larger exports of the nineteenth century vary in the range of 1 to 2 million. Possibly one-third of these enslaved people were males and two-thirds (as many as 1.4 million) females. All told, if mortality through slave raiding in Africa and losses en route to the coasts are taken into account, the direct human costs of these exports in labor and reproductive potential to Africa could have exceeded 20 million people, perhaps two-thirds of them females.[3]

La Rue's examination of the Cairo slave market in the 1830s gives some idea of the enormity of the losses within Africa. The Egyptian pasha Muhammad 'Ali's military forces enslaved many Sudanese from the region of the Upper Nile in the 1820s and 1830s. They usually conscripted the fittest males to serve as soldiers near where they had been captured in the Sudan and cared for these conscripts reasonably well. The thousands of women and children they also seized they sent downriver to Egypt, where they flooded longstanding markets for slaves. Mortality rates en route across the desert were so high that when Muhammad 'Ali requisitioned ten thousand male slaves from Kordofan, his commanders seized fifty thousand people, five times the number demanded. Half were females, who cooked for and otherwise served the men who were driving them northward to Egypt on the long journey across the desert. At most twelve thousand of these enslaved—roughly a third—reached the gateway to Lower Egypt at Asyut. The violence and mortality along the trails to the Cairo market would not have far exceeded casualties sustained by other caravans destined for the Atlantic and Indian Ocean shores of Africa, which by the latter part of the eighteenth century were forming far inland at similar distances from the coasts.[4]

However large these numbers, they do not support the conventional belief, bolstered by a recent upsurge in interest in the global black diaspora, that most slaves in the history of the world originated in Africa.[5] The exaggerated emphasis on Africa as sole source of the enslaved of the world derives from the immediacy of the experiences of the enslaved Africans taken in modern times to the Americas, most from West and West-Central Africa, with others, but far fewer, also from southeastern Africa. In addition, significant numbers of Africans were among the slaves transported in modern times in other directions, including the Middle East, India, central Asia, and South and Southeast Asia. However, other active trades from central Asia, the Caucasus, and the Balkans had supplied the ancient and Renaissance Mediterranean, as well as later Ottoman provinces at least into the nineteenth century. Arabia and the Persian Gulf also imported slaves from India, Baluchistan, Indonesia, and possibly even China into the twentieth century. Large numbers of slaves were moved through eastern and southeastern Asia from early times, from a range of sources touching Japan and Melanesia and even sending some "Chinese" (as they were known) to sixteenth-century Mexico.

However large these global numbers, it is likely that still greater numbers of the people enslaved in both Africa and Asia were retained within the respective continents themselves and involved women in proportions even greater than among the flows of exports. In the nineteenth century slaves accounted for between 20 and 30 percent of the population of many regions in Africa, rising to 50 percent and more in the areas of most-concentrated commercial agriculture.[6] Women from the Balkans were imported as slaves into North Africa, and in the early nineteenth century Muhammad 'Ali imported Circassian and Greek women to Lower Egypt to serve as slave concubines.[7] The sultans of Zanzibar, like Muslim rulers elsewhere, included women from the Caucasus in their harems.[8] Moreover, as the following chapters by Gwyn Campbell (Madagascar), Elizabeth Grzymala Jordan (Cape Town), and Richard B. Allen (Mauritius) show, the western Indian Ocean islands were not only sources of the slaves sent elsewhere but also destinations for slaves from other regions around the entire circumference of the Indian Ocean. The Dutch settlement at the Cape of Good Hope, for example, imported slaves from Madagascar, Indonesia, and India as well as from southeastern Africa.[9]

The sex ratios in the different trades varied according to historical circumstances in the captives' areas of origin, as Paul E. Lovejoy's chapter examines in detail for the Atlantic and the Saharan trades from the western and central sudanic regions in West Africa. Males predominated in the transatlantic traffic, but women accounted for up to three-quarters of the mainly African imports of enslaved people across the desert. Lovejoy considers whether the majorities of males in the Atlantic trade resulted from American buyers preferring men or Muslim and other African exporters wishing to retain women. As he notes, New World planters wanted primarily males for agricultural labor but, because of their large investments in land and equipment that they had to keep operating, accepted women if men were not available. The numbers of females in the early days of the Atlantic trade almost equaled those of males, but in later centuries the proportion of males increased. However, Lovejoy concludes that the overall predominance of males was due, at least in part, to Muslims in western Africa who retained women or directed them to

Muslim markets in the Sahara and beyond because of ethical and political reluctance to send coreligionists, or potential converts to Islam, into the hands of the infidels who ran the trade in the Atlantic.

Another possible consideration motivating Africans to retain women would have been the growing demographic losses created by the rapid increase in numbers of people sold into the Atlantic. These aggregate numbers would, according to this hypothesis, have strained the reproductive capacities of the populations supplying the trade to the point that they concentrated increasingly on retaining girls and adult women of reproductive ages. They would not have done so only out of some purported effort to preserve viable levels of population in Africa, as demographic considerations like these are abstractions imaginable only to outside observers like modern historians; they explain nothing about why people anywhere acted as they did, including the hard decisions involved in releasing people to outsiders.

Rather, slavers in Africa faced much more particular challenges. Heads of innumerable small African communities sought to preserve their own populations, without regard for—or even at the calculated expense of—the people of their rivals and enemies. They sent more males, and increasingly younger ones, toward the Atlantic, reflecting successes in retaining reproductive women to bear children in numbers sufficient that they had enough youthful males on hand to select them for removal, as necessity or advantage might arise, without compromising the viability of their own communities. In general, as many studies show, commercial considerations like these came to prevail in West and West-Central Africa by the nineteenth century, as traders and raiders became more dependent on selling captives to Europeans and more calculating about maintaining their abilities to do so. However, business considerations did not always determine whether to keep or release people, and which ones, as Lovejoy suggests in showing that Islamic areas of West Africa preferred to export surpluses, in this case females, to Muslim buyers across the Sahara, or to keep them for local uses. Muslim areas of West Africa also were more likely to retain male coreligionists by ransoming them back to their kinsmen.[10]

In the absence of an overarching religious or political community like Islam in western Africa, households upset by conflict and the capture of personnel had other reasons to ransom captives rather than selling them. Redemption restored peaceful balances among themselves and might also bring premiums above the market prices of slaves from relatives or some other patron. In such cases, war captives were more like hostages held for ransom than like slaves. Group redemptions for cash (or fungible equivalents) corresponded to self-purchases in thoroughly commercialized cultures according primacy to individuals over their membership in the constituting groups, where slaves were theoretically left to redeem themselves by earning the money to buy themselves.

Since restoration of workable relationships would have been important on local scales, as distinct from hit-and-run raids on distant and unrelated communities, the apparent frequency of ransoming male captives in eighteenth-century western Africa may suggest the damaging degree to which pervasive slaving had by that time corrupted the regions just south of the Sahara. If so, Lovejoy's evidence may also suggest the tensions that were then building up to the early nineteenth-century mass conversions to Islam in the area, often attributed to popular efforts to seek security from capture under militant Muslim clerics.

Since the sex ratios in the Atlantic trade depended on local circumstances in Africa in these and countless other ways, they varied over time as conditions there changed. Thus in the late seventeenth century, nearly half the slaves sold into the Atlantic trade from the Bight of Biafra were women, apparently because men accounted for the bulk of the demand for agricultural labor in the region at that time, planting and harvesting large yams. When male Aro traders expanded into the area in the later eighteenth century, creating a need to retain women for wives, these local demands for heavy field labor diminished, at least relatively.[11] The sex ratios among the men and women sold to European buyers in this region in the nineteenth century then shifted toward larger proportions of males.

The diverse and changing demands for labor in Africa generally increased the numbers of women sold into all the export trades from the continent as local demands for male labor for commercial production rose. Philip J. Havik's chapter on the Portuguese-claimed domains along the Upper Guinea Coast and adjacent islands makes it clear that local slave owners, predominantly women traders of the coastal towns, built up their agricultural holdings employing more women slaves than males. When, in the nineteenth century, they replaced their previous sales of males overseas with exports of rice and peanuts, they retained more male slaves than females.[12] Though female slaves predominated in nineteenth-century Madagascar, male slaves outnumbered bondswomen on the island on commercial plantations on the eastern coast and in the heavy and mobile labor of porterage, once again in the more commercialized sectors of the economy.[13]

VIOLENCE AND THE ORIGINS OF THE WOMEN ENSLAVED

Slaves constituted only one of a number of sources of basic female labor in mostly self-sufficient "domestic" economies in non-Muslim Africa.[14] Under normal circumstances, that is—from the point of view of the small, often kin-based, communities of most of the continent—when they were capable of maintaining themselves through births and marriage alliances with neighbors, they reproduced themselves by defending claims to the children of the wives or sisters of the men at the core of these groups, both to bear infants and to sustain children by producing and preparing food. The competing claims of these kin-structured groups to the offspring of the women married into them were a kind of implicit, preemptive coercion reflecting the generally low levels of population relative to land. Since these groups calculated their collective success in terms of maintaining, or if possible increasing, their group's own numbers, or gaining influence over others by putting them in debt for women they loaned as wives, they supplemented these structured sources of female fecundity with other girls and women acquired from strangers when such opportunities presented themselves.

The conventional literature on slavery emphasizes violence as an, if not the, integral process of acquiring such women, through capture and enslavement. In Africa such captives had long been primarily females. With the introduction of the horse along the southern margins of the Sahara in the tenth or eleventh century, they were also the prizes of ensuing wide-ranging military campaigns, in which the males of the populations raided were often executed. This localized and temporary practice of seizing women as spoils of war and killing defeated males continued into the expansive military campaigns of the nineteenth century, such as those of the Merina of Madagascar and in Ethiopia covered in this volume.[15] The perpetrators of violence also included raiders and warriors specializing in assembling captives for the slave export trades, eventually in virtually every part of the continent. Force thus became the primary means of enslaving those destined for slave markets in the Americas from the late seventeenth century to around 1860, as well as those exported during the nineteenth and twentieth centuries from Sudanic and eastern Africa to Muslim markets in the Middle East and South Asia.

By the nineteenth century violence in Africa extended to kidnapping people from neighboring communities. For example, many thousands of the enslaved in nineteenth-century Egypt and Imerina (Madagascar) were captives taken in military campaigns launched against adjoining populations.[16] On the frontiers of the Ethiopian Empire slave raids on these local scales continued until at least 1935, as described in the contribution here of the late Timothy Fernyhough. Within the earlier Empire, its unpaid "officials", when transferred from the regions they controlled to weaken them as competitors to the imperial court, sought to secure their political futures by enslaving and taking with them as many as they could of the local population—men, women, and children. Departing governors and their retinues therefore often had to fight their ways out of the provinces they thus decimated as they left. Some of the people they seized, mainly women and children, were subsequently exported to Arabia, but most were kept for sale in Ethiopia, often into the cities there and in adjoining Muslim regions.[17]

Violence was not the only source of the women enslaved. Enslavement in Africa, like debt bondage in South Asia and elsewhere in the Indian Ocean world, also resulted from individuals seeking refuge from recurrent man-made and natural calamities—wars and droughts—frequently accompanied by disease and famine.[18] During such catastrophes parents and kin groups often voluntarily sold their children, usually girls, in efforts to guarantee the survival of the collective remainder.[19] Sometimes men offered themselves for sale, but children, especially girls or young women, were the most marketable.

Girls and women in Africa were also transferred temporarily as "pawns," in return for loans of trade goods or money. But creditor lineages retained female pawns not redeemed by their relatives as originally intended, or feigned.[20] Some became wives of the creditors. Others the creditors sold as slaves to realize their value in other forms. Young daughters and nieces transferred in marriage by male elders enjoyed no greater say in determining their fates. Women as well as men were paid as political tribute, or exchanged for ransom among enemy neighbors. Among the Ewe living along the banks of the lower Volta River in modern Ghana and Togo, relatives offered girls, even very young ones (trokosi), to a shrine in expiation of their sins. Thus abandoned, the girls became entirely subject to the priests of the shrine, and their children inherited their positions as de facto temple slaves.[21]

In open markets and in private negotiations, elders sold troublesome family members into slavery. The independent villages of the western African forests expelled difficult or mistrusted kinsmen by taking them to an oracle that settled their disputes by condemning and seizing the losing parties. While the men among these losers found themselves spirited away into the slave trade, the operators of the oracle   the so-called Aro—

kept the women as wives.[22] Arguably, the men whom the Aro sold brought the imported goods that financed the Aro's acquisition and retention of women, and through them the creation of a new ethnic community.

EMPLOYMENTS OF FEMALE SLAVES IN AFRICA AND THE INDIAN OCEAN WORLD

The captors found many advantages in having females as slaves. Girls and women were less likely to try to escape than young men or boys and easier to absorb into households. Unlike males, they were often trained for and accustomed to domestic as well as agricultural labor.

African employments of slaves, especially females, in their communities' entire array of tasks left them in a far wider range of capacities than the stereotype of field labor applied to their (implicitly male) counterparts in the New World. Agricultural labor prevailed, as production of food or agricultural commodities probably accounted for more than 90 percent of economic activities in Africa. In some areas the slave traffic itself increased demands for agricultural production to feed caravans and their prisoners, and thus for women slaves as cultivators. At the eighteenth-century peak of slaving in Angola, the Mbundu provided food for passing slave caravans by buying women from them to help their wives produce manioc and other crops. The result was a change in the sex ratios in the area from equal numbers of males and females to two women for every adult male.[23]

Though female slaves in Africa worked as agricultural laborers, they were also concubines, entertainers, prostitutes, domestics, brewers, washerwomen, and seamstresses. Close attention to the language of slavery bears out these occupations. For instance, recently arrived slaves on the Swahili coast were called *mateka* (captive), *mshenzi* (barbarian), or *mjinga* (ignorant, or "one who does not know how to do the washing or cooking")—hence implicitly female.[24] They also carried water, mined, wove textiles, and, as Philip Havik shows, cooked, baked, healed, traded, and served as go-betweens.[25] In the unusual case of Dahomey, women slaves incorporated into the royal household could become soldiers, military commanders, trading agents, governors, and trusted advisors to rulers.[26] Girls and young women who struck male purchasers as sexually attractive were universally prized.

Recognized wives and accepted concubines in the Muslim world were generally secluded in harems and concealed under scarves or behind veils when they emerged from the household, but slave women could move freely in public and were unveiled.[27] As Katrin Bromber and Jan-Georg Deutsch both point out, such women were particularly valued as petty traders selling harem-produced artisanry and food, as well as engaging in other business activities. They thus augmented the economic independence of their mistresses from their husbands and from rival wives within the household.[28] Unlike free women in respectable seclusion, they could also be used as field hands or hired out as prostitutes.

WOMEN RETAINED IN HOUSEHOLD SLAVERY

Women brought into kin-structured African societies as slaves were arguably valued above all for their progeny. The greater the numbers of female slaves and their offspring, the greater their patrons', or sponsors', influence within the community or power in political contexts.[29] Ownership in the sense of holding a transferable individual title to the person enslaved was a relatively muted aspect of masters' authority, since the purpose was to keep or distribute these women among clients and relatives rather than to sell them. Men with enslaved women distributed them to individuals with superior status, to "host" kin groups, or to political authorities created in return for protection, blessedness, and material largesse from the more powerful and respected. In matrilineal societies slave women were in special demand, as their children by men of the lineage belonged to their fathers' kin groups, whereas the children of free women belonged to the lineages of their mothers and were responsible to their maternal uncles.[30] Moreover, the men who took these slave women as "wives" incurred no obligations to in-laws, since these women, as slaves, had no relatives or other protectors.

Much of the literature on females enslaved in the Islamic world draws on Orientalizing tendencies to romanticize Muslim male sexual appetites and equates women slaves with concubines. However, as George Michael La Rue and Martin A. Klein show in this collection, this European sexualization of the harem greatly oversimplifies female slavery in Islamic cultures.[31] Harems in fact housed wives, concubines, children, female dependents, and slave servants, and in large numbers they enhanced the status of the male owners at the heads of large households. Only the most favored of the females imported became concubines in the modern sense of regular sexual partners.

As Katrin Bromber shows with regard to the Muslim Swahili Coast in eastern Africa, the modern sense of "concubine" is an inadequate translation of the local term designating such women, in this case *suria*.

There, the slave woman who became a mother of her owner's child was a highly respected member of the household, who could not be sold or divorced. Though perhaps acquired through purchase and initially subject to sale as chattel, she had acquired the security of a form of publicly acknowledged marriage.[32] In accordance with the sharia (Islamic law), concubines who bore their masters' children might be freed before or on the deaths of their owners. If so, their children were recognized as legitimate heirs to the household estate. These manumitted women and their progeny tended to remain clients of their former owners and their descendants in perpetuity, though as family dependents rather than as slaves.

The number of female slave servants in the households of wealthy men might run into the hundreds, and the senior wives and concubines might be attended by retinues of slave girls of their own.[33] In poorer households a single female slave might double as her master's concubine and drudge or even, if household finances otherwise failed, be hired out for prostitution. Those who became the wives or concubines of nomadic Bedouins in the deserts shared the harsh lives of their owners without particular distinction. La Rue, writing on Cairo, notes that life in Muslim domestic female slavery, contrary to the Victorian-era scholars' romanticization of the harem as luxurious, was usually harsh, that rates of reproduction were low, and that mortality among the infants and children born there was high. Many female slaves were raped in childhood; few survived into their forties.[34]

The most prized concubines in Muslim southwestern Asia and northern Africa came from regions that varied according to supply and demand. For instance, when the supply of Circassian and Georgian girls to Arabia declined in the nineteenth century with Russian expansion into central Asia, Baluchi and "red" (Oromo and Sidamo) Ethiopian girls become the concubines of choice. Black African slave women in Arabia were used mainly as servants, not for sexual purposes.[35] In the twentieth century, slaving ships from eastern Africa captured in the Red Sea contained mostly young women or girls and boys rather than adult men.[36] Women and children were easier to train and integrate into the households of the Middle Eastern markets for which most were destined.

At the opposite extreme of the continent, the "slave lodge," or barracks of the VOC (Verenigde Oostindische Compagnie, or Dutch East India Company) at the Cape of Good Hope, kept bondswomen in numbers as great as those of the men enslaved there and employed them in the same types of labor, including mining. This elaborately documented

Dutch corporate "household," while the creation of a European company, demonstrates the general—and largely female—dynamics of building up operationally independent mercantile establishments in African and Indian Ocean commercial contexts, regardless of cultural or religious backgrounds. Philip Havik, while focusing on the women who characteristically headed the commercial "houses" of the Portuguese trading towns along western Africa's Upper Guinea Coast, demonstrates the parallel reliance on enslaved women in "Christian" contexts.

The culture-transcending historical dynamic behind these corresponding tendencies in the enslavement of women in the Indian Ocean and African worlds of the eighteenth and nineteenth centuries was that of male merchants building trading capacities at the nodes of contact between rapidly growing global commercial integration centered on Europe—in this volume mostly African, but secondarily also central Asian.[37] Households filled with women acquired through trade, and thus without kin to protect them or to claim the legacy of the house for their children, allowed rapid intergenerational accumulation, concentration, and transmission of the wealth derived from trade.

CHATTEL SLAVERY IN AFRICA AND THE INDIAN OCEAN WORLD

More abstract forms of legal and political authority prevailed, or at least were asserted in the many more-commercialized parts of the eighteenth- and nineteenth-century worlds presented in this volume. In Western law a slave is defined commercially, not personally, as a chattel, that is, as fungible, transferable at the will of an "owner." That the person so enslaved lacked the rights guaranteed by civic governments or could hold property of his or her own under law, and could be punished at the owner's whim are all incidental to the fundamental quality of being disposable, through sale. Though these highly proprietarial aspects of slavery existed also in Arabia, Egypt, and the rest of North Africa, in Ethiopia, and on relatively commercialized—often also Muslim—parts of the eastern African coast, they were relatively limited moments in the lives of both the enslavers and the enslaved. Slavery, as distinguished from the transactions involved in slaving, was a protected status within households. La Rue's love triangle in Cairo and the elaborate Swahili vocabularies denoting degrees of integration into households demonstrate this assimilative emphasis.

The areas of Africa subject to European rule in the eighteenth and nineteenth centuries, and also the European plantation islands of Mauritius and Réunion (Mascarenes) in the Indian Ocean, formed particularly commercial enclaves characterized by a Caribbean-style sugar plantation economy with full chattel slavery.[38] Omani Arabs established other nineteenth-century cash-crop plantations to grow cloves, sesame, coconuts (for copra), and grain on the Swahili coast of eastern Africa, and sugar, on more limited scales, on the eastern littoral of Madagascar. These uses of slaves for production added commercial counterparts to the fundamentally household slavery on the mainland described by Bromber and Deutsch. In Bissau in Upper Guinea indigenous women and their Portuguese or mixed-blood husbands employed slaves in chattel-like conditions to cultivate commercial peanuts and rice.[39]

Still, except for males in Mauritius, these proprietarial aspects of employing slaves for commercial production did not overwhelm the personal autonomy of the captives. Women slaves earned money for themselves, as Deutsch notes for the Swahili coast, where the most fortunate women slaves had personal plots of land or cooked foodstuffs and sold them or home-brewed beer in public markets. Some lived with husbands and families separately from their owners and effectively, if not legally, became clients of their masters, or even sharecroppers.[40] Even in the (relatively limited) plantation sector of the Swahili-Omani region, not all slaves experienced the regimentation and other controls, or the vulnerability to arbitrary disposal through sale, characteristic of sugar slavery in the Caribbean region.[41] The difference, as the companion volume on women and slavery in the Americas suggests, lay in the more profoundly commercialized economies, and hence greater indebtedness, of the faster-growing mines and plantations of the Americas, less inhibited by the religious obligations of Islam or—for that matter—late-medieval Catholicism.

Except for the Cape of Good Hope and the Mascarenes, where European law formally and effectively applied, the chattel aspects of the legal standing of slaves in Africa and the Indian Ocean world were also tempered by local legal and ethical codes, in Muslim societies by the Qur'an (and the various schools of the sharia law derived from it) and in Christian Ethiopia by a medieval legal code known as *festa negath,* or the Law of Kings.[42] Within the public transactions governed by the commercial laws of these regions, quite distinct from the political and religious charters governing residential households, "trade" slaves had no rights and were often treated very badly by the merchants who dealt in them. However, as elsewhere, once they found a buyer they might acquire some of the domestic protections, if not also rights, mentioned in the Qur'an or the *festa negath*. Even in nineteenth-century Madagascar the monarch protected slaves with limits on punishment—owners could punish but not kill them—and respected their marriages. Such legal recognition, it could be argued, meant that slaves were not true outsiders, as one classic definition of slavery would make them, because they had entered into the dominant society's system of reciprocity, at least with regard to the king.[43] It could also be argued that monarchical regimes, as well as Muslim clerical interests, had every interest in intruding on the privacy of household heads' relations with their slaves that might otherwise limit the otherwise absolute authority of monarch and clerics.

Beyond the inclusive Muslim community of the faithful, strong family and patron-client ties obligated men wealthy and powerful enough to have women to manumit to demonstrate their prestige through piety, to protect the humble of all backgrounds, including enslavement. A slave's origins in the marketplace, or by birth to a women acquired through purchase, thus did not contrast dichotomously with the civic freedom of modern states but rather integrated the slave woman into the quasi family of dependents of many sorts, mostly female, in Muslim patriarchal households.

In all these monotheistic cultures, underlying relatively assimilative, "domestic" dynamics coexisted with tendencies of monarchical rulers (sultans, "kings," and so on) to claim direct political authority over all the people within their domains—including slaves. The intrusive strategies that made monarchs the singular authorities they claimed to be also appear in this volume in the background to Kirsten A. Seaver's chapter on the medieval Norse in the North Atlantic. The first Scandinavian rulers on the mainland built their authority by delimiting and then suppressing large, potentially competitive retinues of slaves in the hands of erstwhile political rivals.

In the nineteenth century merchants got on with the brutal business of slaving within quite separate public legal spheres of commercial law. Multiplicities of legal environments, not integrated and comprehensive single "systems" of law of the sort imagined in the nineteenth-century Americas (though in practice never achieved there either), prevailed.[44] The enslaved suffered the overwhelming vulnerabilities of arbitrary disposition as chattel property in the process of capture and sales, sometimes repeatedly, but others—and particularly women taken in as "wives"—managed to claim the limited protections afforded them by the doctrines of patriarchal domestic responsibility and comprehensive monarchical patronage.

OPPORTUNITIES FOR AGENCY DISTINCTIVE TO ENSLAVED FEMALES

Female slaves were human assets with more potential uses than men, particularly in capacities close to their possessors or protectors. They thus found themselves with opportunities to exploit the dependence on them of men, or women, who had—after all—made significant efforts to acquire them, presumably because they needed them. Male heads of households valued enslaved women for their reproductive capacities, for nurturing the masters' own families as wet-nurses and nannies, for their domestic skills in their masters' households, and for sexual services. Male slaves, on the other hand, were valued predominantly for their physical strength, as laborers or warriors, and were relatively isolated from their acquirers, anonymous, and disposable. Discussions of slave agency have traditionally focused narrowly on male slaves' occasional open resistance and infrequent revolts, but the chapters following add to a growing literature exploring the more subtle ways in which females created dynamic spaces of their own within the environments that also exploited them as slaves. Women, more often than men, also found ways to move into the households where they resided or, in more commercialized environments, to buy their ways out of proprietarial slavery.

Revolt was a gendered reaction of male slaves to generalized exploitation and the relative isolation of their employments. By far the largest number of those who rebelled, or who fled and established maroon communities in the Cape, Mauritius, and elsewhere, were men.[45] Women seldom joined them voluntarily. Moreover, owners exercised greater surveillance over women, particularly in situations with pronounced divisions of slave labor by sex, such as Cape Town, that left men in relatively unsupervised locations but kept the women living in the households of their owners.[46] Thirdly, women, often with children and committed to other enslaved kin or friends, tended not to abandon these relationships through flight or revolt.

Maroon life was harsh and unappealing, since these fugitive bands of young adult males took refuge in inaccessible—and also inhospitable— areas. In order to survive they were obliged to raid nearby plantations, and they remained constantly on alert to fend off harassment by authorities there. Even so, few established a viable independent existence. The men in these renegade communities therefore sometimes resorted to kidnapping women from nearby plantation or urban areas for sexual services and for companionship, as well as for field labor and other tasks. Few women found much appeal in the deprivations and vulnerabilities of living thus on the edge.

Rather than fleeing enslavement, women enslaved in households tended to protect themselves within through subtle forms of evasion, passive resistance, and manipulation. One example of such subversion from within, sometimes attributed to commercial plantation environments, often costly to their owners, may have been enslaved women's reluctance to bear children. Unable to avoid the field labor to which they were driven, they might have refused to undertake the additional labor of child-bearing or to create offspring who would be burdened with the hardships to which birth as slaves would condemn them.[47] This idea, derived primarily from the extreme brutalities of mid-eighteenth-century sugar plantations in the West Indies,[48] would have applied in the Indian Ocean region most directly to women enslaved in Mauritius, less so to most women slaves at the Cape, and still less to those in the much more domestic circumstances elsewhere, in both Muslim and non-Muslim contexts. However, reproduction rates among women enslaved in Africa appear to have been lower than those of their legitimately married sisters. Although unsanitary conditions and lethal disease environments contributed to universally low rates of fertility and high rates of infant mortality there, it might be argued from this differential that women enslaved in Africa thus similarly subverted the purposes of the males who acquired them to ensure or increase the size and influence of their lineages through reproduction.[49]

But slave women bore children nonetheless, even in the West Indies. Feminist scholars have focused on undoubted, even constant, instances of the rape and other violence that must have accounted for some of these births. However, for women unable in so many ways to protect themselves it is possible to sense the pride and accomplishment they might have felt from protecting children of their own. The satisfactions of family must also have relieved the essential isolation of their enslavement. Richard Allen shows that the women enslaved on the plantations of Mauritius developed strategies of using their owners' interest in their sexuality to raise the life chances of the resulting offspring, and—with luck—also themselves as elderly mothers supported by children favored by their white fathers.

The fecundity of the women enslaved on these remote plantation islands was relatively easy for masters to accept.[50] The mostly European men directing them were lonely as well, far from whatever families they may have had in France or England. Enslaved women became concubines of their owners, who freed the most fortunate, sometimes with their children, and also sometimes left them property to support themselves and their families. Many succeeded in founding matrifocal families of their own. Some of those who became wealthy bought other slaves, often females, as a way of overcoming the legal disabilities imposed on "freed-persons" among the freeborn by controlling the labors of newly enslaved people even more marginal than they.[51]

This tendency of enslaved females to turn companionship, and their sexuality, into comfort and respectability developed primarily, even exclusively, where European wives were absent, again like in the West Indies. Females enslaved in these more commercialized environments seem to have focused their energies on protecting their children.[52] But they faced enormous obstacles. Where slaves were cheap and easily replaced and where their owners' short-term financial survival depended on putting pressure on slave women as producers, planters found little incentive to promote natality, particularly since effective medical and sanitation techniques to do so were virtually nonexistent. In bearing and protecting children, enslaved females not only affirmed themselves, as women, but also defied the antinatalist interests of their owners, at enormous risk to their own physical well-being. The paradoxical possibility thus emerges that the lower rates of reproduction attributed to female slaves in the contexts of reproductive communities of kin in Africa and enslaved women's strategies of bearing and using children in the anti-natalist contexts of commercial plantations both bear witness to efforts, with inevitably varying degrees of success and at potentially great cost to themselves, to assert themselves against the contrasting wishes of the men who sought to control them for other purposes not theirs.

Where women slaves living in urban areas congregated in numbers sufficient to collaborate among themselves, although normally isolated in separate households, they exploited the humiliating tasks assigned them outside the households to form communities of their own. In this volume, Jordan has used historical archaeology to interpret items found in pools along streams above Cape Town to reconstruct how late eighteenth- and early nineteenth-century slave washerwomen there forged bonds among themselves and with other lower status groups in the city, free and slave. They had gained enough (presumably undetected) access to their owner's crockery, food, and alcohol to use a furtive commensality to build these connections. Moreover, they appear to have brought up their infants in this alternative culture of their own.[53] Sharifa Ahjum once again, in the same place and more or less at the same time, shows the exclusionary dynamics of households that left slave women to turn their laboring responsibilities into moments of companionship to affirm themselves.

Enslaved females everywhere took advantage of their proximity to, if not also intimacy with, their masters to manipulate their owners' cultural values to attempt to improve their living and working conditions. Their efforts, often expressed in household food rituals, dress and adornment, and religion, produced the results often observed sociologically as "assimilation," thus attributed to the groups rather than to the women who accomplished these feats of cultural adaptability and adaptation. For example, in nineteenth-century Madagascar, many slaves sought religious roles as "traditional" ancestral mediums.[54] Those who fled in nineteenth-century Africa to the Christian mission churches, including in Madagascar, adopted parallel tactics of utter and elaborate devotion to win the favor of their missionary sponsors.[55]

Girls who arrived as children and young adults had distinct advantages in these terms, since they learned local languages/dialects more easily and also often welcomed the religious ideologies of the slaveholders as means of integrating themselves. Fred Morton notes that children from the surrounding African societies absorbed as slaves and brought up by the Dutch settlers in the South African Republic usually lost all ties with their own kinsfolk, to whom they rarely returned when freed, and regarded Dutch civilization as superior, or at least personally preferable.[56] Their preferences for the Christian culture in which they had been raised survived manumission. Though acculturation was an essential strategy for all slaves, females particularly might then transmit the masters' beliefs and value systems to their children. Richard Allen states that prosperous freed "persons of color" in nineteenth-century Mauritius, female and male, not only themselves owned slaves but also viewed them as inferior no less than did whites.[57] However, the masters' ideologies—whether Muslim, seventeenth-century Christian as in the case of the Calvinist Dutch at the Cape and in the South African Republic, Ethiopian, or the communalism of most Africans—in turn always justified their enslavement.[58]

In composite polities in Africa, multiple women of varied backgrounds in households were normative, indeed sought after and celebrated when attained. Large political systems were often constructed through multiple "marital" alliances of the ruling male with women from the groups of kin comprising the "state." The "kings" built up large households of local, politically connected women and kinless female slaves, and these became the primary domains of politics, as Catherine Coquery-Vidrovitch outlines in her contribution to this volume. Within these compound royal households, open female politics among co-wives—senior and junior, married and slave—prevailed in place of the ambiguity and denial that characterized the ideally monogamous families of the Europeans.

Neither sort of domain was harmonious, as intense competition among in-laws or political factions built around kinship and marriage alliances converged in both, but these dynamics promoted the women, including those of slave origins, into positions of great prominence, culminating in the famed "queen mothers" of Dahomey and in other well-known African polities of the eighteenth and nineteenth centuries. The aims of most female slaves in the politics of these households, including royal compounds, centered on securing relatively protected niches for themselves and their children, to improve those positions over time and, if eventually granted (nonslave) status in the broader religious communities of Islam and Christianity, or in the emergent civic polities of European colonies, to construct new identities in their adopted cultures.

Enslaved women thus sought to overcome the isolation of their capture and removal into enslavement by belonging, by creating and exploiting the relationships available to them within slavery, and—for women uniquely—as sexual partners of their male masters and, more importantly, as potential mothers of their heirs. These distinctive strategies of enslaved females constituted counterparts of the processes often characterized (sociologically, that is in Western, i.e., modernist, individual, and civic terms) as "assimilation" to the communal ethos prevalent in more collective African contexts.

DISTINCTIVE OPPORTUNITIES FOR WOMEN IN OWNING SLAVES

Women subject to patriarchal subordination in public venues reclaimed a degree of personal autonomy not by seeking so dubious a "freedom"— that is, exposure to unforgiving military rulers or to commercial markets—but rather by accumulating other enslaved women within households. Women slaves were the primary individuals available who were sufficiently dependent, or not otherwise claimed by men, to allow them to build up networks of their own, both within their households and for public commercial endeavors. As Deutsch points out for the Swahili coast, the wife or wives of the male heads of households directed the daily lives of the slaves within them, although the masters could always interfere with the domestic authority of their wives by demanding personal services, including sexual ones, from their enslaved females.[59]

The wealthy slave-owning and slave-trading Luso-African women in Philip Havik's narrative of the Portuguese-linked trading towns of the

Upper Guinea region—like their counterparts among the so-called *signares* (*ñaras*, *nharas*) everywhere along that coast, including Luanda in Angola[60]—acquired even males as slaves, similarly excluded from the public domain as "men who did women's work." The *ñaras* ran these towns, staffed them with dependents and slaves, and controlled the export trade in slaves through family connections to African chiefs and kinsmen in the interior. When their slave trading ended in the mid-nineteenth century, they then used these connections to acquire land and to pioneer production of rice and groundnuts for export, using male slaves as labor.

They also used the enslaved female strategy of informal "marriages" with lonely European men far from home, as well as the resulting children, to build considerable estates for themselves. The *ñaras*, though as marginal in the male-dominated world of European trade as their sisters elsewhere on Africa's Atlantic coast, succeeded also through serial domestic and business relationships with passing traders and officials from Europe. When their male marital and business partners returned home, or died (and many did, in regions known wryly but accurately as "the white *man's* grave"), they inherited their deceased or departed partners' local assets, including real estate and the large numbers of domestic slaves needed to maintain these properties. They then employed the slaves to develop the commercial elements of their inheritances. Local partners were often themselves of mixed blood, some of them the adult children of other wealthy women of the coast.[61]

Havik concentrates on the most successful of these women, at a time in the nineteenth century when the ending of exports of slaves forced traders everywhere along western Africa's Atlantic coasts to shift their interests in slaving from selling men and keeping women to investing mostly in men to produce commodities, rather than human beings, for exports.[62] The material wealth and even local political power of these women slavers, themselves descendants of enslaved women, and their children embodied the threat to legitimate heirs avoided elsewhere by the European rule excluding the children of female slaves as slaves themselves.

POLITICS OF SLAVE WOMEN IN MONOGAMOUS HOUSEHOLDS

Although communities that maintained themselves through kinship and descent generally wanted children as descendants, and accordingly valued the reproductive capacities of women,[63] enslaved girls and women had far fewer opportunities where European women lived in monogamous families. Urban households in the Dutch colony at the Cape, as Jordan shows, often valued older, postmenopausal women as domestic servants and child minders because of their maturity and experience, and possibly also because they were less likely to arouse the sexual interest of the white males in the household and could not threaten domestic dissension by bearing their children.[64]

This "legitimist" protection of the recognized "white" family was a highly sensitive issue also in the Dutch Calvinist settlements on the high grasslands of southern Africa that Fred Morton discusses. In the South African Republic, public acknowledgement of cohabitation of a white owner and his female slave could ruin an otherwise honorable white male partner's reputation, and thus career. The Dutch families of this small community captured African girls in childhood and brought them up as "apprentices" to be "freed" on reaching physical maturity. In the name of such "freedom," Dutch patriarchs offered these girls as wives to their African business partners, the heads of cattle-owning Tswana lineages, in exchange for cattle paid as bride-wealth. By this exchange Dutch former owners turned their investment in potentially troublesome female human livestock into bovine assets more manageable, and salable. The parallel was close with Africans' exchanges of livestock for wives among themselves; however, differences arose from the Africans' intent to assimilate the women they acquired into polygynous compound households, in contrast to the incompatibility of multiple women of reproductive ages, of any standing, within the strictly monogamous households of the Calvinist Dutch.

Dutch patriarchs also disposed of others of these young female potential rivals of the matriarchs of their families by marrying them off in respectable Christian monogamy to male Africans who, like the girls, had been captured as children and raised in the monotheistic and monogamous values of the Dutch homestead. Still others they handed over to British Christian missionaries as "students" and converts.[65] All these transfers of nubile young women captives out of the pious Dutch households lessened opportunities for their (former) owners and their sons to take them as concubines. These varied transfers also consolidated the networks of patronage and clientage among the Dutch patriarchs, Tswana lineage heads, and the missionary advance guard of the growing British presence in southern Africa, very much as senior African males elsewhere exchanged female dependents broadly to strengthen relationships among themselves.

A slave woman married to a white man in the Dutch Reformed Church was generally "freed," together with her (their?) children, to the authority of her new husband, as elsewhere in the Dutch empire from which the progenitors of these Calvinist patriarchs had come. This rule, which prioritized the prevailing bonds of family in these communities over the muted legal or civic standing of "slave," paralleled the same preference in Islam of the domestic domain of the household over the legal world of the commercial market.

Young Dutch men in the South African Republic tended to select their brides from among half-breeds, and so the enslaved African females who were left to seek husbands among male slaves sought impregnation by passing European male visitors, often even with the encouragement of their enslaved mates, to create the opportunity of mixed parentage for any girls they might bear. With the "white" father thus absented, the mothers lessened the risk of losing such children to a legally favored local free man. They subsequently inscribed the names of their half-breed children in the baptismal records of the Dutch Reformed Church, giving daughters the opportunity to obtain freedom, or local respectability, through Christian marriage to a local Dutch man. Elsewhere in Dutch southern Africa, newly arrived European male settlers in Cape Town, lacking access to the daughters of the tightly linked local Dutch families, also often married such women, freed them and their children, and thus contributed to the growing "coloured" population of the city.[66]

These enslaved women thus converted their Dutch masters' rule of maternal inheritance of the status of slave to the prospective advantage of their own progeny. The Dutch rule was intended to exclude the children of slave concubines from competing for their father's estates against the "legitimate" children of the white women whom they had married legally. These African women used the partial identification of their daughters—but not their sons—with their white fathers to enhance their prospects for assimilation through marriage into the patriarchal families who composed the South African Republic.

Sharifa Ahjum's highly innovative application of Lacanian insight to the psychodynamic implications of these absent—whether figuratively or legally—"(white) father[s]" to the patriarchal dimensions of Dutch (though not English, and to their bafflement) slavery at the Cape demonstrates the emotional power of these contradictions and ambiguities of standing—both emotionally at the level of the existential family and ideologically at the level of its societal manifestations, for the enslaved and the enslavers alike. Enslaved females of a white household bore children who were in fact members of a polygynous interracial—but deeply denied—"family." Ahjum reveals the usual abstraction of "slavery" contemplated as a civic "institution," an exclusionary inversion of inclusive modern national laws of citizenship, into the overwhelmingly—and for her, deeply distortingly—formative and agonistic personal experience that it was. This contradiction of excluding progeny by declaring them "property" appeared most clearly throughout the region at the margins of the commercial world, where Ahjum chooses to examine it. Trade in maritime ports like the Cape made it possible to introduce slave women in large numbers into worlds still centered around large patriarchal households.

One might extend Ahjum's argument to wonder whether the image of the slave as "male" in modern Western culture might reflect a similar need to obscure the agonizing contradictions of attempting to dehumanize people as "property"—most intensely and unavoidably one's own offspring by women held in slavery. The mothers, or potential mothers, were demonized as scheming "Jezebels," as Ahjum explains here. In the Americas, the ability of enslaved males to challenge the purity of "white" descendants of legitimate white wives became a threat of proportions sufficient to justify, indeed demand, lynchings of any slave—or later simply black—man suspected of lusting for a respectable female.

THE LIMITED RELEVANCE OF MODERN CONCEPTS OF SLAVERY AND FREEDOM TO ENSLAVED WOMEN IN HOUSEHOLDS

The modern Western concept of a free individual enjoying rights of citizenship, or civic standing, within a comprehensive and inclusive national community had very limited relevance in the times and places considered in this volume.[67] It is the rights guaranteed by modern civic states that enable anyone's security of person and personal property, as well as at-least-theoretically autonomous choices of occupation and lifestyle. In the civic ideologies of modern nations, slaves were thus dichotomously excluded as chattels held by individuals entitled civically as "owners" in lifelong and hereditary bondage These owners of the enslaved could punish, sell, or transfer their human property at will, separating mothers from their children, husbands, or male companions, and they controlled both the productive and reproductive capacities of the women they owned. Hence the status of property that their children inherited, regardless of paternity, in public spaces—but not in the households at the center of this volume—as well as the denial of their value as bearers of family legacies and their reduction to ungendered commercial units of labor, regardless of their sex.[68]

Compared to the heavy emphasis in modern Western political theory on the ideal of civic freedom, African societies gave little importance to individual liberty or personal autonomy. Rather, they embedded individuals in social hierarchies, wherein each person had a unique status defined by a multiplicity of obligations as well as protections that they had built up throughout their lives. In the absence of mutually exclusive legal categories of slave and free, as in all the places presented in this volume, enslaved individuals instead moved along continua of whatever personal connections they might establish in whatever communities they found themselves. All women tended to occupy places at the marginal and contingent ends of these social continua, because of their removal from their communities of birth (or birth families) through transfers as tokens of relationships among men. However, they moved toward the centers of their husbands' families or communities as they became mothers. As Catherine Coquery-Vidrovitch shows, a female of slave origin might at different times be a child in a free household, a trade slave, or an enslaved concubine, and—if she were extraordinarily fortunate—eventually find a place for herself as a wife, even of a powerful and prominent man. For women, the social membrane separating slave and "free" was more permeable than for men, so long as they made places for themselves.[69] As Coquery-Vidrovitch further suggests, it made relatively little practical difference to women whether they were slave, that is, without significant local networks of their own, or well and deeply connected as sisters, nieces, and wives, since all lived—and worked very hard—under the generalized patriarchal control of fathers, husbands, and brothers.

While females of both legitimate and slave (outsider) origin often did the same work, the key distinction between their positions lay in wives' access to responsible kin, to whom they could appeal for protection if they were ill treated.[70] By appealing to their kinsmen, they effectively played off the competitive patriarchs in their lives, fathers (or uncles), brothers, and husbands, one against another. Some free women exploited their multiple patriarchal relationships to acquire assets to build up trading networks of their own. By contrast, slave women, as Deutsch suggests, had no comparable opportunities to divide those who otherwise dominated them in order to survive. Even when married to their owners and mothers of their children, in hard times they would be the first to be sold to passing caravans.[71]

In larger and more centralized polities, a sovereign theoretically owned all the persons subject to him, in the senses both of his ultimate responsibility for them and their complementing obligations to him. In the Indian Ocean world such rulers commanded corvée labor, and it could be argued that state corvée, imposed on individuals dignified as subjects of such a ruler but not applicable to slaves, fits some authors' definition of slavery as property performing "compulsory labor."[72] Nineteenth-century Merina rulers' continuous demands for *fanompoana*, as Gwyn Campbell shows, made people subject to these demands prefer the less intense labor demands of most private slavery. Females in the families constituting the Merina state formed the core targets of some of the rulers' massive labor drafts, notably when young males fled to escape the imperial dragnet.[73] Thus the labor obligations restricted in the Americas to the enslaved in Madagascar fell, when conquests and plundering no longer sustained the military power of the state, to subjects nominally protected by sovereign authorities. Enslavement was an assertion of privacy for the masters, and it protected their people, increasingly slaves, from the competing demands of the monarchy. In a polity created to support a warrior regime, the state was the exploiter of its people rather than its protector, as guaranteed—at least theoretically—by modern constitutions. The slaves' protectors were their owners, though more in their own interests against the intrusive state than in the interests of the enslaved. Enslavement was a refuge, manumission was a threat, and "emancipation" into the status of subjects of so oppressive a regime was at times a crushing burden.

In more commercialized, urban environments women with standings beyond the households where they resided—that is, not enslaved—also could face circumstances worse than those of females attached to them as slaves. In nineteenth-century Egypt, for instance, a "free" female domestic servant had no market value and might be given "coarser" work than the slave women, who represented an investment worth protecting.[74]

For most African populations, security in the form of a viable, close community or a strong and responsible patron, rather than the modern abstract concept of civic "freedom," was the primary aim. Liberty, in the sense of individual freedom from acquired relationships and their associated protections and obligations, would have effectively destroyed the webs of reciprocity that offered protection from dangers both man-made and natural.[75] Women and men slaves, who lacked connections most closely approximating the modern premise of individualism, sought slaves to overcome their isolation and vulnerability. Contrasting concepts of slave and free as permanent, inherited statuses are of limited analytical utility in societies built, like most of those discussed in this volume, around belonging.

MANUMISSION FOR WOMEN SLAVES

Owing to the opportunities of belonging to the patriarchal households and composite political systems of Africa, the Indian Ocean world, and the medieval Norse Atlantic, manumission was less a privilege sought by slaves of either sex than it had been—for men—in ancient Rome or than it became for all the enslaved in modern monarchical or national civic states. These more comprehensive civic states entitled the person "freed" from a master's private control to the "liberties" that monarchs guaranteed their subjects or the "rights" that constitutional governments accorded to their citizens. But the remote and nonintrusive rulers—or where intrusive, often abusive—in the backgrounds of the studies in this volume left the route to personal security, even comfort and in rare cases privilege, for the enslaved running through female cultivation of wealthy and powerful men as responsible masters, patrons, or husbands.

The frequency of manumission for women thus increased in cultures where an overarching legal authority—secular or religious—offered some promise of protection against the arbitrary abuses to which irresponsible or hard-pressed masters resorted all too often.[76] In the kin-based regions of Africa, release from an abusive relationship often took the form of a slave woman seeking an alternative master in a way that gave offense to the abusive owner or that invoked the intervention of a powerful third party or interventionist political authority.

In the regions studied in this volume, Muslim societies offered the most developed legal apparatus for both manumission and assimilation into the overarching, and theologically protective, community of the Islamic faith. According to the sharia, gratis manumission of slave converts was meritorious to their owners as piously honorable patrons. Further, slaves who converted to Islam could redeem themselves through contracted purchase arrangements with their owners. Though female slaves might redeem themselves by self-purchase, this public strategy was more accessible to men than to women, largely confined within households.

The degrees to which Muslim masters were able to act according to these ideals of course varied among Islamic societies and over time and—doubtless much more—among individual masters. Within Africa the jurisdiction of clerical authorities to enforce rulings along these lines varied with the prominence of Islam in particular regions, from its marginality along the Upper Guinea Coast (Havik) through its much more pervasive presence in the central Sudan (Klein, Lovejoy, Roberts) to Egypt (La

Rue) and the Swahili regions of eastern Africa (Bromber, Deutsch), and even in Cape Town (Jordan) and in parts of Madagascar (Campbell). In the absence of a state premised on civic equality, individual manumissions and spiritual inclusion posed no threat to the general practice of slavery. The dignity and respect and limited personal responsibility that manumission attested acted as an important individual incentive to dutiful assimilation and provided a psychological safety valve—attained through raising a son in accord with the aspirations of the slave woman's master—that helped the enslaved woman recover from the trauma of the isolation she had suffered through her enslavement. These manumissions encouraged further imports of young girls to replace the women "freed," stabilizing the practice by perpetually renewing the population of new, vulnerable enslaved females. The women enslaved in turn had no choice but to learn to please and thus repeat the cycle of assimilation and—with any luck—survive to a respectable old age as mothers of their masters' heirs.[77]

The practice of granting manumission more readily to slaves, predominantly women in their owners' households, and particularly to those with children by their owners, appears as a general tendency in the predominantly female slaveries throughout Africa and the Indian Ocean world—including European planters in Mauritius and Dutch families at the Cape—rather than an exotic cultural or religious peculiarity of Muslims.

WOMEN IN DOMESTIC HOUSEHOLD SLAVERY AND THE CONSOLIDATION OF MODERN MONARCHICAL AND NATIONAL POLITICAL AUTHORITY

The nineteenth century everywhere in the world was an era of consolidation of modern military states, in Africa and the Indian Ocean region often warlords, but in Europe and the Americas modern civic "nation states." These theoretically homogeneous political entities, composed of citizens or subjects directly and equally accessible to central authorities, necessarily intruded on the former privacy of the household domains sheltering dependents of every sort, prominently—if not also increasingly—including enslaved women.

A desperately centralizing political authority like the Merina monarchy—or its less-threatened earlier counterparts in formative Scandinavian kingdoms, or a nineteenth-century Portuguese state seeking to recruit local allies against stronger British and French rivals in Upper Guinea—

also created "free" subjects whom it could recruit, or created them in order to recruit them, as highly involuntary ("unfree") corvée laborers. On the other hand, the military authorities of imperial Madagascar also needed to defend against the intrusions of merchants wielding debt as a weapon to capture the loyalties of peasants, and so it also defended local debtors from enslavement by private creditors. In Madagascar it was considered meritorious to manumit *zazahova* (local Merina with whom slave owners shared a common cultural heritage) enslaved chiefly for indebtedness—men, women, and children alike. Such political assimilation did not apply to non-Merina taken in military campaigns on the island, mostly women who often spoke dialects of Malagasy largely incomprehensible to the Merina, or to slaves of mainland African origin, all of whom were of understandably dubious loyalty.[78]

Colonial regimes, like all central authorities intruding on autonomous and fully viable networks of households, including their enslaved residents, thus found it effective to staff their initial infrastructure by "redeeming" the enslaved in these communities. The French and Belgian administrations regularly conscripted enslaved men to serve as soldiers in their early colonial armies by purchasing them and then gave them the women they captured in battles fought in the service of the colonial rulers. The French settled the slaves of both sexes whom they "freed" in West Africa in so-called Freedom Villages (*villages de liberté*) and then used them as a labor pool to build the initial infrastructure of their colonies.[79]

The early colonial powers, weak as they were on the ground in Africa before World War I, offered manumission—at least in the eyes of the colonial regimes—to slave women in order to undermine the African heads of strong households where they lived. In this volume, Richard Roberts shows how aggrieved slave wives used the early French colonial courts to obtain divorces or authorization to leave their husbands—and escape the intense workloads imposed on them. Their petitions peaked seasonally during the harvest, when work demands on these women were most intense.[80] In the eyes of the petitioning women, the French may have seemed to offer the prospect of patronage, protections, and places to belong less abusive than the men who had "married" them. The responsibilities of a modern state to its citizens, or the French Republic to its subjects in its colonies, paralleled the theoretical duties of Muslim, or Christian, masters to the slaves in their households. The degree to which the patrons in either case, private or public, lived up to these ideals also varied similarly.

The opportunities for manumission that the colonial regimes brought to Africa made a difference to the enslaved. In small and intensely communal kin-based societies, such as the Giryama in British East Africa, where slaves were initiated into a kin group upon arrival and given new names reflecting their integrated standings, the idea of releasing them was unthinkable. They had nowhere else to go, and no one to redeem them. They became integrated as "brothers" and "sisters" of the free, although they were not necessarily treated as well as other members of deeper local ancestry and hence more numerous and more influential potential protectors.[81] However, in the late nineteenth and early twentieth centuries, when word got out that the European colonial rulers—particularly the British and French—did not recognize slavery within the administratively uniform, or civic, legal spaces they were creating, many slaves—even these "brothers" and "sisters"—abandoned their masters to seek colonial patronage, or protection. Or, if they remained at home, they used their access to alternative standing as colonial subjects to negotiate improved terms of service. These women tended to leave in small family groups or with a male partner. In contrast, the Germans in East Africa recognized African domestic slavery, with the result that some indigenous owners encouraged their slaves to buy themselves out of their enslavement instead, for cash.[82]

Early European missionaries in East Africa similarly redeemed slaves of both sexes to settle around their first mission stations in family units. Even when they decided that evangelism was served better by proselytizing among the free and respected, these slaves and their descendants nevertheless remained to maintain the facilities of the missions.[83] The first missions and the early colonial authorities alike saw themselves as bringing civilization to Africa, including the strong ethical and political commitments to personal faith and individual liberty of the Age of Emancipation in Europe. They also needed local recruits more or less knowledgeable in the cultures they claimed to civilize in order to staff programs intended to do so. Individual Europeans, even before formal colonial rule, sometimes bought slaves as the only people on whom they could count to assist them in projects calculatedly disruptive to local communities that anyone with better prospects in them could ignore.

La Rue notes a variant of the same dependence of isolated European civilizers in the intricate networks of households in Africa and Asia. French doctors in early-nineteenth-century Egypt bought enslaved Ethiopian and Sudanese women in the market to train them as midwives, since in this Islamic culture male doctors were barred from attending women.[84] Missionaries in nineteenth-century Madagascar maintained their missions by hiring slaves from the Merina elite or redeemed them to serve as household maids and man-servants to overcome the acute shortages of local labor created by the draconian recruitment of the Merina state.[85]

A CONCLUDING NOTE ON HISTORICAL CONTEXTS

The chapters in this collection frame enslaved women's experiences of slavery in historical contexts very unlike the modern slavery that generated the stereotypical slave as a laboring male. Slavers sought and kept women according to parallel contexts of households, varying relatively incidentally across the many particular cultures of this region—Islamic, Christian, African, European, or any other. The strong and free-wheeling patriarchs of the households of the early Norse Atlantic turn out to bear intriguing resemblances to the household heads in similarly composite societies and polities throughout nineteenth-century Africa and in much of the Indian Ocean world. Women in all these times and places were numerous among the enslaved, and certainly dominant within the large households where everyone of any standing at all struggled to find places for themselves. Their enslavement was not the anonymous exclusionary institution that slavery became in the commercial economies and civic polities of the eighteenth- and nineteenth-century Americas and Western Europe. The intimate worlds of households examined in this volume, where women, slave or not, had central places, turned the abstract categories of gender, race, and slavery in the modern world inside out.

Slaving in Africa, the early Atlantic, and the Indian Ocean world, as also in the modern Americas, was a means of recruiting outsiders sufficiently controllable for those who brought them in to achieve strategic purposes of their own at their expense. Slave women worked, of course, but their backgrounds in enslavement (not a permanent categorical "status") limited only some of them, usually the newest, to menial and despised tasks, even in the largest and most differentiated households. Their distinctive strategic value as slaves to their masters, patrons, and sometimes husbands lay in their vulnerability to control, and therefore sometimes—perhaps often, even ubiquitously—to abuses, sexual and otherwise.

But as women, their sexual availability also made them vehicles for producing children similarly not subject to the claims of in-laws or other potential protectors and thereby controllable by their fathers or his sons or clients of the household. For men, the value of women brought into households through slaving thus turned on their reproductive capacities. The children resulting from their sexual allure in the eyes of men these

enslaved women in turn forged into a classic weapon of the weak, seeking both recovery from enslavement's quintessential isolation and also
eventual self-fulfillment by focusing on the prospects of their offspring,
particularly those fathered by their masters.

Assertions of individual autonomy, or quests for modern sorts of civic
freedom, were available to them in Islamic and Christian communities of
religion in ethical, but only marginally legal, forms. Escape meant taking
the risk of finding another patron of unknown character or ability to
shelter. Rather, enslaved women sought fulfillment inwardly. In urban
contexts, women slaves used their moments outside the respectable
seclusion of the households where they lived to create autonomous, if
only momentary and always furtive, voluntary associational communities
of their own around their work or in ritualized dance societies. But most
primarily sought security, the fundamental quest of anyone radically and
traumatically uprooted through enslavement, ways to belong within the
more accessible domains of the households where they lived. Some even
succeeded in making places of their own.

The value of female slaves as producers, rather than as reproducers,
accrued mostly to other women, otherwise themselves burdened with the
toilsome and often unpleasant responsibilities of making households
work, whether as nurturing spaces for children or as havens of comfort
for their husbands and masters. The primary route open to women to enter
the otherwise male domains of commerce, expanding steadily throughout the eras studied in this volume, lay in enslaving others. Within
households, although the female sharing of the work of maintaining them
transcended the male-centered competition over the prospects of their
children, the politics of polygyny often allowed legitimate wives to devolve
the most offensive and humiliating chores on the newest of the enslaved.
The conflicts of slavery in compound domestic contexts thus ultimately
divided the multiple women in these households, thereby reinforcing the
manipulative control of the patriarchs in charge, except when women in
them managed to escape these confines by creating autonomous followings of their own through slaving.

NOTES

Gwyn Campbell composed the original draft of this introduction, and Suzanne
Miers contributed additional material and arguments; I have developed it themati-
cally and thus assume full responsibility for the ways in which it presents the import
of the chapters in the volume. Credit for the initial conference from which all but
one of these chapters have developed goes to Campbell, Avignon Conference on

Slavery and Forced Labour, "Women in Slavery—In Honour of Suzanne Miers," 16–18 October 2002.

1. With the noteworthy exception of Claire C. Robertson and Martin A. Klein, eds., *Women and Slavery in Africa* (Madison: University of Wisconsin Press, 1983).

2. Suzanne Miers, *Slavery in the Twentieth Century: The Evolution of a Global Problem* (Walnut Creek, CA: AltaMira, 2003), 348–49.

3. Helge Kjekshus, *Ecological Control and Development in Eastern Africa* (Nairobi: Longmans, 1979), 14–16; Gwyn Campbell, "Abolition and Its Aftermath in the Indian Ocean World," introduction to *Abolition and Its Aftermath in Indian Ocean Africa and Asia*, ed. Campbell (London: Routledge, 2005), 5.

4. George Michael La Rue, "African Slave Women in Egypt, ca. 1820 to the Plague of 1834–35," in this volume.

5. See, for example, Isidore Okpewho, Carole Boyce Davies, and Ali A. Mazrui, eds., *The African Diaspora: African Origins and New World Identities* (Bloomington: Indiana University Press, 1999); Emmanuel Akyeampong, "Africans in the Diaspora: The Diaspora and Africa," *African Affairs* 99, no. 395 (2000): 184–86; Darlene Clark Hine and Jacqueline McLeod, eds., *Crossing Boundaries: A Comparative History of Black People in Diaspora* (Bloomington: Indiana University Press, 1999); Vincent B. Thompson, *Africans of the Diaspora: The Evolution of African Consciousness and Leadership in the Americas* (Trenton: Africa World, 2000). See also Graham W. Irwin, *Africans Abroad* (New York: Columbia University Press, 1977); Joseph E. Harris, *The African Presence in Asia: Consequences of the East African Slave Trade* (Evanston: Northwestern University Press, 1971).

6. Igor Kopytoff and Suzanne Miers, "African 'Slavery' as an Institution of Marginality," in *Slavery in Africa: Historical and Anthropological Perspectives*, ed. Kopytoff and Miers (Madison: University of Wisconsin Press, 1977), 60–61; Anthony Reid, "Slavery and Bondage in Southeast Asian History," introduction to *Slavery, Bondage, and Dependency in Southeast Asia*, ed. Reid (St. Lucia: University of Queensland Press, 1983), 12, 29; Gwyn Campbell, "Slavery and Fanompoana: The Structure of Forced Labour in Imerina (Madagascar), 1790–1861," *Journal of African History* 29, no. 2 (1988): 474–75.

7. La Rue, "African Slave Women."

8. Richard B. Allen, "The Mascarene Slave Trade and Labour Migration in the Indian Ocean during the Eighteenth and Nineteenth Centuries," in *The Structure of Slavery in Indian Ocean Africa and Asia*, ed. Gwyn Campbell (London: Frank Cass, 2004), 33–50; Edward A. Alpers, "Flight to Freedom: Escape from Slavery among Bonded Africans in the Indian Ocean World, c. 1750–1962," in Campbell, *Structure of Slavery*, 51–68; Pedro Machado, "A Forgotten Corner of the Indian Ocean: Gujerati Merchants, Portuguese India and the Mozambique Slave Trade, c. 1730–1830," in Campbell, *Structure of Slavery*, 17–32; Nigel Worden, "Indian Ocean Slavery and Its Demise in the Cape Colony," in Campbell, *Abolition and Its Aftermath*, 29–49.

9. Gwyn Campbell, "Female Bondage in Imperial Madagascar, 1820–95"; Richard B. Allen, "Free Women of Color and Socioeconomic Marginality in Mauritius, 1767–1830"; Elizabeth Grzymala Jordan, "It All Comes Out in the Wash: Engendering Archaeological Interpretations of Slavery," all in this volume.

10. Paul E. Lovejoy, "Internal Markets or an Atlantic-Sahara Divide? How Women Fit into the Slave Trade of West Africa," in this volume; Gwyn Campbell, *An Economic History of Imperial Madagascar, 1750–1895: The Rise and Fall of an Island Empire* (Cambridge: Cambridge University Press, 2005), 42. See also anon., "Indian Slaves in South Africa: A Little-Known Aspect of Indian-South African Relations," www.anc.org.za/ancdocs/history/solidarity/indiasa3.html.

11. See Claire Robertson and Marsha Robinson, "Re-modeling Slavery as if Women Mattered," in *Women and Slavery*, vol. 2, *The Modern Atlantic*, ed. Gwyn Campbell, Suzanne Miers, and Joseph C. Miller (Athens: Ohio University Press, 2008; hereafter referred to as the companion volume in this set), quoting G. Ugo Nwokeji.

12. Philip J. Havik, "From Pariahs to Patriots: Women Slavers in Nineteenth-Century 'Portuguese' Guinea," in this volume.

13. Campbell, *Economic History*, chs. 5, 9.

14. For discussion of this term, see Lovejoy, "Internal Markets."

15. Gwyn Campbell, "Madagascar and the Slave Trade, 1810–1895," *Journal of African History* 22, no. 2 (1981): 203–27; Jack Goody, "Slavery in Time and Space," in *Asian and African Systems of Slavery*, ed. James L. Watson (Oxford: Basil Blackwell, 1980), 20–21; Timothy Fernyhough, "Women, Gender History, and Slavery in Nineteenth-Century Ethiopia," in this volume.

16. See, for example, Fernyhough, "Women, Gender History"; Campbell, "Female Bondage."

17. Miers, *Slavery in the Twentieth Century*, 66–88. For slavery in Ethiopia, see Fernyhough, "Women, Gender History."

18. See, for example, La Rue, "African Slave Women."

19. This is stated classically by Moses I. Finley, "Slavery," *International Encyclopedia of the Social Sciences*, ed. David L. Sills, 19 vols. (New York: Macmillan/Free Press, 1968), 14:307–13; it is elaborated by Orlando Patterson, *Slavery and Social Death: A Comparative Study* (Cambridge, MA: Harvard University Press, 1982). Also see Martin A. Klein, "Modern European Expansion and Traditional Servitude in Africa and Asia," introduction to *Breaking the Chains: Slavery, Bondage, and Emancipation in Modern Africa and Asia*, ed. Klein (Madison: University of Wisconsin Press, 1993), 11.

20. Kopytoff and Miers, "African 'Slavery' as an Institution of Marginality," 10–11.

21. In Ghana, although illegal, this continues today; see "Ritual Slavery in Ghana," *Anti-Slavery Reporter*, July 2005 (http://www.antislavery.org/archive/reporter/reporter%20july%202005%20articles.htm).

22. See, for instance, Victor C. Uchendu, *The Igbo of Southeast Nigeria* (New York: Holt, Rinehart and Winston, 1965), 100.

23. Jan Vansina, "African Society and the Slave Trade c.1760–1845," *Journal of African History* 46, no. 1 (2005): 1, 14.

24. Jan-Georg Deutsch, "Prices for Female Slaves and Changes in Their Life Cycle: Evidence from German East Africa," in this volume.

25. Havik, "Pariahs to Patriots." Male slaves were also employed in a wide range of activities, from agricultural labor to craftwork, commerce, transport, fishing, domestic service, stewardship, bureaucratic service, soldiering, and diplomacy.

26. Edna G. Bay, "Servitude and Worldly Success in the Palace of Dahomey," in Robertson and Klein, *Women and Slavery in Africa,* 340–67.

27. See Katrin Bromber, "*Mjakazi, Mpambe, Mjoli, Suria:* Female Slaves in Swahili Sources"; Deutsch, "Prices for Female Slaves"; Klein, "Sex, Power, and Family Life in the Harem: A Comparative Study"; La Rue, "African Slave Women," all in this volume.

28. Deutsch, "Prices for Female Slaves"; Bromber, "*Mjakazi.*"

29. The relative valuation of women as slaves for their labor, production, or reproduction (through bearing children) has been a continuing debate in the specialized literature on Africa, though not elsewhere. For the initial framing of the debate, see Robertson and Klein, *Women and Slavery in Africa;* Kopytoff and Miers, "African 'Slavery' as an Institution of Marginality," make the classic case; for a fully theorized refutation, see Claude Meillassoux, *The Anthropology of Slavery: The Womb of Iron and Gold,* trans. Alide Dasnois, foreword by Paul E. Lovejoy (Chicago: University of Chicago Press, 1991)—originally *Anthropologie de l'esclavage: Le ventre de fer et d'argent* (Paris: Presses Universitaires de France, 1986).

30. See Mary Douglas, "Is Matriliny Doomed in Africa?" in *Man in Africa,* ed. Douglas and Phyllis M. Kaberry (Garden City, NY: Anchor, 1971), 124–37.

31. Ibid.; Martin A. Klein, "Sex, Power."

32. Bromber, "*Mjakazi.*"

33. Klein, "Sex, Power."

34. La Rue, "African Slave Women."

35. Miers, *Slavery in the Twentieth Century,* 89, 165, 304–5, 308–9. For the Circassian girls' view see, for example, Ehud Toledano, *The Ottoman Slave Trade and Its Suppression, 1840–1890* (Princeton: Princeton University Press, 1982), 18.

36. Lovejoy, "Internal Markets."

37. Robert C.-H. Shell, "Rocking the Cradle: The Women of the Slave Lodge, 1671 to 1793," paper presented to the Avignon Conference on Slavery and Forced Labour, 16–18 October 2002.

For seventeenth- and eighteenth-century North American parallels, see Juliana Barr, "Womanly Captivation: Native American Enslavement in Comparative Perspective," paper presented at the annual meeting of the American Historical Association, 6–9 January 2005, Seattle; published as Barr, "From Captives to Slaves: Commodifying Indian Women in the Borderlands," *Journal of American History* 92, no. 1 (2006): 19–41; Barbara Krauthamer, "A Particular Kind of Freedom: Black Women, Slavery, Kinship, and Freedom in the American Southeast," in the companion volume in this set.

A comparable sexualization of these wealthy and powerful women marked eighteenth-century European male depictions of them, particularly those of the British and French; George E. Brooks Jr., "The *Signares* of Saint-Louis and Gorée: Women Entrepreneurs in Eighteenth-Century Senegal," in *Women in Africa: Studies in Social and Economic Change,* ed. Nancy J. Hafkin and Edna G. Bay (Stanford: Stanford University Press, 1976), 19–44.

38. Jean Mas, "Scolies et hypothèses sur l'émergence de l'esclavage à Bourbon," in *Fragments pour une histoire des économies et sociétés de plantation à la Réunion,* ed. Claude Wanquet (Saint-Denis: Université de la Réunion, 1989), 109–58.

39. Frederick Cooper, *Plantation Slavery on the East Coast of Africa* (Portsmouth, NH: Heinemann, 1997); Abdul Sheriff, *Slaves, Spices and Ivory in Zanzibar* (London: James Currey, 1987); Campbell, "Slavery and Fanompoana"; Havik "Pariahs to Patriots."

40. Deutsch, "Prices for Female Slaves."

41. Even in the United States, slavery took a number of forms that included slaves, with their own families, working and living away from their owners—see the companion volume in this set.

42. Margery Perham, *The Government of Ethiopia* (Evanston: Northwestern University Press, 1969), 138–42.

43. Angela Schottenhammer, "Slaves and Forms of Slavery in Late Imperial China (Seventeenth to Early Twentieth Centuries)," in Campbell, *Structure of Slavery*, 143–54; Bok-rae Kim, "Nobi: A Korean System of Slavery," in Campbell, *Structure of Slavery*, 155–68.

44. For this important emphasis on multiplicity of legal (and cultural and so forth) environments, see Lauren Benton, *Law and Colonial Cultures: Legal Regimes in World History, 1400–1900* (New York: Cambridge University Press, 2002).

45. Edward Alpers, Gwyn Campbell, and Michael Salman, eds., *Slavery and Resistance in Africa and Asia* (London: Routledge, 2005).

46. Jordan, "It All Comes Out"; Shell, "Rocking the Cradle."

47. Robert C.-H. Shell and Parbavati Rama, "Breeders or Workers? Slave Women in the Cape Colony, 1823–1830," Avignon Conference on Slavery and Forced Labour, "Women in Slavery—In Honour of Suzanne Miers," 16–18 October 2002; Gwyn Campbell, "The State and Pre-colonial Demographic History: The Case of Nineteenth Century Madagascar," *Journal of African History* 32, no. 3 (1991): 415–45.

48. For critiques of this argument, see Kenneth Morgan, "Slave Women and Reproduction in Jamaica, ca. 1776–1834"; Richard Follett, "Gloomy Melancholy: The Reproductive Lives of Louisiana Slave Women, 1840–60," both in the companion volume in this set.

49. A differential claimed for Africa, though on the basis of very scattered evidence, in the distinct sense of attributing low female slave birth rates to the harshness of the labor imposed on women slaves, seen exclusively as producers and not reproducers; see Robertson and Klein, *Women and Slavery in Africa.* Meillassoux, *Anthropology of Slavery*, defines slavery as a population worked beyond its ability to reproduce itself, thus replaced by captures (the "iron" of the book's subtitle) and by purchases (the "gold") of people belonging to others rather than by bearing children of its own.

50. And also in the West Indies; but for the resulting denials see Henrice Altink, "Deviant and Dangerous: Proslavery Representations of Jamaican Slave Women's Sexuality, ca. 1780–1834," in the companion volume in this set.

51. Allen, "Free Women of Color."

52. For accents on maternity and slavery, see Jennifer Morgan, *Laboring Women: Reproduction and Gender in New World Slavery* (Philadelphia: University of Pennsylvania Press, 2004).

53. Jordan, "It All Comes Out."

54. See Gillian Feeley-Harnik, *A Green Estate: Restoring Independence in Madagascar* (Washington, DC: Smithsonian Institution Press, 1991); Michael Lambek, *The Weight of the Past: Living with History in Mahajanga, Madagascar* (New York: Palgrave Macmillan, 2002); Gwyn Campbell, "Unfree Labour and the Significance of Abolition in Madagascar, c. 1825–97," in Campbell, *Abolition and Its Aftermath*, 66–82; Campbell, "Crisis of Faith and Colonial Conquest: The Impact of Famine and Disease in Late Nineteenth-Century Madagascar," *Cahiers d'études africaines* 32, no. 3 (1992): 409–53.

55. Campbell, *Economic History*, esp. ch. 5.

56. Fred Morton, "Female *Inboekelinge* in the South African Republic, 1850–80," in this volume.

57. Allen, "Free Women of Color."

58. Nineteenth-century missionary Christianity in Madagascar, among English and Scots Protestants at the Cape and elsewhere in eastern Africa, adamantly opposed slavery and was an expression of North Atlantic abolitionism; the stations of these missions became refuges for slaves fleeing hardships in all the communities surrounding them, as several authors in this collection note.

59. Deutsch, "Prices for Female Slaves."

60. Joseph C. Miller, *Way of Death: Merchant Capitalism and the Angolan Slave Trade, 1730–1830* (Madison: University of Wisconsin Press, 1988), 290–95; Douglas Lanphier Wheeler, "Angolan Woman of Means: D. Ana Joaquina dos Santos e Silva, Mid-Nineteenth Century Luso-African Merchant-Capitalist of Luanda," *Santa Barbara Portuguese Studies* 3 (1996): 284–97.

61. Havik, "Pariahs to Patriots."

62. The transition has been studied widely; for the core literature, see Anthony G. Hopkins, *An Economic History of West Africa* (Cambridge: Cambridge University Press, 1972); Robin Law, ed., *From Slave Trade to "Legitimate" Commerce: The Commercial Transition in Nineteenth-Century West Africa* (New York: Cambridge University Press, 1995).

63. Joseph C. Miller, "Domiciled and Dominated: Slaving as a History of Women," in the companion volume in this set; Goody, "Slavery in Time and Space," 20–21.

64. Jordan, "It All Comes Out."

65. Morton, "Female *Inboekelinge*."

66. Shell, "Rocking the Cradle."

67. See the companion volume in this set, *The Modern Atlantic*, whose thematic structure is shaped by the gradual emergence of these modern economic, then ethical, and eventually political contexts, as well as slavery in its public, institutionalized form.

68. For an exploration of this process in Lacanian psychodynamic terms, see Sharifa Ahjum, "The Law of the (White) Father: Psychoanalysis, 'Paternalism,' and the Historiography of Cape Slave Women," in this volume.

69. Catherine Coquery-Vidrovitch, "Women, Marriage, and Slavery in Sub-Saharan Africa in the Nineteenth Century," in this volume. See also Deutsch, "Prices for Female Slaves."

70. Kirsten A. Seaver makes a similar point about the women—some "thralls," others "queens"—whom Norse pioneer mariners in the North Atlantic took with them to settle Iceland and Greenland in the eleventh and twelfth centuries. Seaver, "Thralls and Queens: Female Slavery in the Medieval Norse Atlantic," in this volume.

71. Deutsch, "Prices for Female Slaves"; Havik, "Pariahs to Patriots."

72. See James L. Watson, "Slavery as an Institution, Open and Closed Systems," introduction to Watson, *Asian and African Systems of Slavery*, 7.

73. Gwyn Campbell, "Gold Mining and the French Takeover of Madagascar, 1883–1914," *African Economic History* 17 (1988): 1–28.

74. Gabriel Baer, "Slavery in Nineteenth Century Egypt," *Journal of African History* 8, no. 3 (1967): 419.

75. Gwyn Campbell, "Slavery and Other Forms of Unfree Labour in the Indian Ocean World," introduction to Campbell, *Structure of Slavery*, vii–xxiii; Peter Boomgaard, "Human Capital, Slavery and Low rates of Economic and Population Growth in Indonesia, 1600–1910," in Campbell, *Structure of Slavery*, 83–96; Suzanne Miers, "Slavery and the Slave Trade in Saudi Arabia and the Arab States on the Persian Gulf, 1921–63," in Campbell, *Abolition and Its Aftermath*, 120–36; Michael Salman, "The Meaning of Slavery: The Genealogy of 'an Insult to the American Government and to the Filipino People,'" in Campbell, *Abolition and Its Aftermath*, 180–97. All the preceding also appeared as a special issue of *Slavery and Abolition* 24, no. 2 (2003).

76. See Alpers, "Flight to Freedom"; Campbell, introduction to Campbell, *Abolition and Its Aftermath*.

77. Miers, "Slavery and the Slave Trade"; Abdul Sheriff, "The Slave Trade and Its Fallout in the Persian Gulf," in Campbell, *Abolition and Its Aftermath*, 66–82; Gwyn Campbell, "The African Diaspora in Asia," in *Encyclopedia of Diasporas: Immigrant and Refugee Cultures around the World*, ed. Melvin Ember, Carol R. Ember, and Ian Skoggard, 2 vols. (New York: Kluwer Academic/Plenum, 2005), 1:13–15; Gwyn Campbell, "The Afro-Asian Diaspora: Myth or Reality?" in *The African Diaspora in Asia*, ed. Shihan de Silva Jayasuriya and Jean-Pierre Angenot (Leiden: Brill, forthcoming).

78. Ch. Poirier, "Un 'Menabe' au coeur de la forêt de l'Est," *Bulletin de l'Académie Malgache* 25 (1942–43): 122–24; Gwyn Campbell, "The History of Nineteenth Century Madagascar: 'Le royaume' or 'l'empire'?" *Omaly sy anio* 33–36 (1994): 331–79.

79. Denise Bouche, *Les villages de liberté en Afrique Noire Française, 1887–1910* (Paris: Mouton. 1968); Martin Klein, *Slavery and Colonial Rule in French West Africa* (Cambridge: Cambridge University Press, 1998), 84–88.

80. Richard Roberts, "Women, Household Instability, and the End of Slavery in Banamba and Gumbu, French Soudan, 1905–1912" and "The End of Slavery in the French Soudan, 1905–1914," both in *The End of Slavery in Africa*, ed. Suzanne Miers and Richard Roberts (Madison: University of Wisconsin Press, 1988), 282–307.

81. Justin Willis and Suzanne Miers, "Becoming a Child of the House: Incorporation, Authority and Resistance in Giryama Society," *Journal of African History* 38, no. 4 (1997): 479–95.

82. Deutsch, "Prices for Female Slaves"; Suzanne Miers and Martin Klein, introduction to *Slavery and Colonial Rule in Africa,* ed. Miers and Klein (London: Frank Cass, 1999), 9.

83. Roland Oliver, *The Missionary Factor in East Africa* (London: Longmans, 1952), 22–23, 50–81.

84. La Rue, "African Slave Women."

85. Gwyn Campbell, "The Role of the London Missionary Society in the Rise of the Merina Empire, 1810–1861" (PhD diss., University of Wales, Swansea, 1985).

1

Women in Domestic Slavery

across Africa and Asia

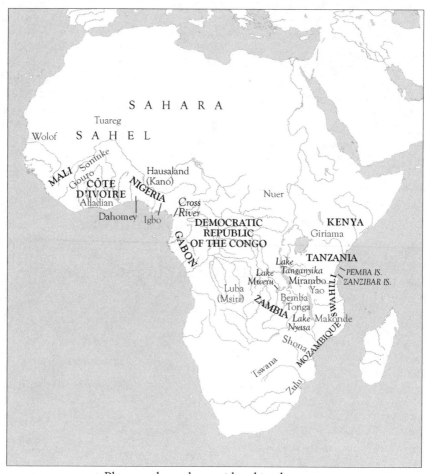

Places and people considered in chapter 1

1

WOMEN, MARRIAGE, AND SLAVERY IN SUB-SAHARAN AFRICA IN THE NINETEENTH CENTURY

CATHERINE COQUERY-VIDROVITCH

Particularly in the most patriarchal of the patrilineal societies, the function, if not also the status, of a free wife differed little from that of a slave. I develop here a few cases on the specific topic of slave women's evolving status and suggest from these comparisons a few comprehensive conclusions on gender relations in sub-Saharan Africa. To begin, let us agree that this status may be broadly defined by two main features: first, to be looked at as a commodity—let us say as a tool when monetarization did not yet exist; this utilitarian position is the point I will stress. Second, since most of the time individuals were not recognized apart from their kinship relationships, a slave was uprooted (i.e., taken out or away from his or her "normal" kin ties and milieu). This isolation was, at least on a small scale, also the case for female spouses: most marriages were patrilocal, and most wives were foreign to the villages where they had to live after marriage. Moreover, most wives were further isolated since they came from varied home villages. Many of them were—at least to some degree—uprooted.

This chapter, based on multiple sources, most of them case studies from all over Sub-Saharan Africa, draws on my book on the history of women in Africa, *African Women: A Modern History* (Boulder: Westview, 1997). One may find in this book a comprehensive bibliography of the references used to review the question, of course before the date of publication. Rather than burden this essay with bulky notes, my intention here is—most of the time using other researchers' fieldwork—to suggest how fruitful comparisons may be on a continental scale.

MARRIAGE: A POLITICAL AND SOCIAL ORDER CONTROLLED BY MEN

The usually complex process of marriage in African societies has been frequently described. In rural societies, where monetarization was unknown or barely developed, most exchanges were interregional or international—the so-called long-distance trade. This trade was more or less strictly controlled by chiefs or kings. Matrimonial exchanges were part of the core of economic and social balancing and hence an important part of political relations within rural societies. Marriages were organized and concluded by the elders—the senior heads of extended families.[1] They were concluded with families whose alliance was wanted, either because they brought some reward or because they established links with dependent lineages. The prospective husband had to give the bride's family prestige goods such as cattle, copper plates or rings, and cloth. The fact that cattle were so often part of the deal shows that the bride's family benefited from the exchange at least as much as the bridegroom's.

The bridegroom, usually a young man, did not as a rule possess the goods needed for the dowry. He depended on the good will of his social group—normally the senior chief of his lineage. Sometimes, all he could offer was his labor. This was often the case in central and southern Africa, as well as the rain forest in, for example, Igboland in modern southeast Nigeria. Sometimes he even became a virtual slave of his mother-in-law.

As for the new wife, she was welcomed not only because she was expected to be a prolific mother but because she provided labor (agricultural, domestic, trading tasks) more valuable than a man's. Men seeking wives sought to know the fertility of a woman before marrying her. In a few areas, such as western Africa (for example for Wolof people in modern Senegal),[2] virginity was required, for it was shameful for a girl to become pregnant before marriage, and young unmarried expectant mothers were sometimes expelled from their villages. If a woman proved infertile later, she was repudiated. In other societies, such as in coastal Gabon, a girl had to prove she was fertile before marriage. If her first child was a boy, the bridegroom's family waited for a girl before beginning to pay the dowry, because only at that moment had the bride proved that her fertility was of the best quality.[3] Thus, unlike in India or China, the birth of a girl, even if it was not as much appreciated as that of a boy, was well received by her parents because a girl held promise of future wealth: the bridewealth to be received from her husband's household in return for the labor and children she would provide them.

Marriage was at once an economic, social, and political question. Its negotiation was the business of the elders. It was they who were responsible for negotiating alliances and for controlling the resulting wealth. If a wife, for one reason or another, fled from her husband and came back to her own family, the contract had been broken, and her family, having regained her labor power, had to reimburse the husband's family for the dowry. They usually raised the necessary wealth by immediately negotiating another marriage for her. We cannot say that the wife was actually marketable—at least not more than she was in a premodern marriage in the West (although it is true that there were areas where the value of the dowry was sometimes more symbolic than real). Nevertheless, African women were everywhere regarded as wealth to be used and exchanged. The social and political significance of the exchange was lost only after the Western market economy introduced monetarization. Then marriage turned into a mere financial operation, a sense captured well in the terminology that anthropologists used to describe the practice: *bridewealth* turned into *bride price*.

FREE WOMEN AND MARRIAGE: A KIND OF SLAVERY?

This process of marriage was the way it worked when the bride was a free woman, whether the union was endogamous (within the same lineage) or exogamous. But we may well ask whether any pubescent female torn against her will from her home and family as part of a complex series of financial and territorial arrangements really came within the dichotomy of slave versus free woman. As a female, her status was part of a complex structure in patriarchies in which all women were subordinate, but some more so than others: young women were submitted to all—elders, younger men, and also senior women. In polygamous marriages, the younger wives had to obey the first wife, who herself had to obey the shared husband's mother, their mother-in-law. Although a senior woman might enjoy power more or less similar to men's once her reproductive years had passed, all women knew (and still may know today) whether they reached their present standing through free or slave descent; in former times they had to remain acutely conscious of their social status.

Status in turn was highly differentiated, between chief-linked ranking families—let us call them parts of local *aristocracies*—which were often developed in pastoral societies around wealth in cattle (the best examples were the Tuareg in the north and the Tswana people in the south,[4] and more generally in the Muslim Sahel[5]); *common people* (let us call them free people); *casted people* (endogamous kin groups mostly devoted to valuably skilled professions—artisans or storytellers and singers—thus passed on from generation to generation, especially in western Africa); and *slave people* (allowing for the variety of meanings of this disputed denomination). But did all this ranking among groups, at a public level, make much difference for women within the various groups? In a number of patrilineal societies, whatever their social level, girls, who were married very young without being consulted, most often without any possibility of refusal or resistance and unable to come back to their own families, were totally in the power of their own fathers (or their uncles—their mothers' brothers—when matrilinearity was the rule), then of husbands and their families. Were they not, practically speaking, made slaves by marriage just because they were women?

We are led to think so by missionaries' descriptions of young Tswana girls married by force, whose husbands' families could even murder them if they resisted. Even if we have to be cautious in interpreting missionaries' accounts, their reports to this effect are so many, come from such diverse nineteenth- and early-twentieth-century contexts, and are so often confirmed by local courts after colonialism began that there is little reason to doubt them.[6] In the mid-twentieth century, things had not changed so much when Christina Sibiya, a former spouse of a Zulu chief, told her sad story.[7] At first she was the only spouse in her husband's compound, a beloved one; but soon she was relegated, without any possibility of resistance, to anonymous membership in the chief's harem. She was desperately miserable, abandoned, without the right to flee, and entirely subject to the will of her spouse. He ordered her to move from remote village to remote village, taking her children out of her reach, and finally abandoned her in poverty.

In Tswanaland, women appear to have been actual beasts of burden.[8] Their subordination was exaggerated because of strict patrilineal rule. A wife had to obey both her husband, who decided everything for her, and her own mother, whose house usually was close to hers. The mother stored her daughter's share of crops and decided how to use them. Therefore the young one was doubly dependent and twice forbidden to enjoy the fruits of her own labor, having nothing more at her disposal, at best, than the one or two head of cattle that her father had given her when she married.

Tswana women had a negative image of themselves, resulting from society's refusal to recognize them as individuals. They were brought up to be humble and to think it normal that their entire existence was devoted to labor. The whole of the domestic economy depended on their labor power, and they worked longer days than men. Of course they assumed responsibility for cultivation, housekeeping, and child care. Besides this they had to build and repair houses and granaries, which was not usually the case elsewhere. Missionaries described the extreme privations they endured. Men and boys were given priority over women and girls, especially when food was scarce. Alarmed outside observers may have overemphasized some of the hardships Tswana women endured, but the reports are consistent enough to be convincing. From the age of five or six, while boys were beginning to roam the pastures with cattle and playing with their first weapons, girls were at work in fields with their mothers.

In their harsh childhood they were taught to be docile and to submit to men. No social sanction limited a father's or husband's right to beat the women dependent on them. The apex of their identities as objects of men's purposes for them was their initiation, which essentially consisted of verifying the girls' virginity. Intercourse outside marriage meant bad luck for the community as a whole, potentially keeping away rains, and therefore requiring purification rites. A girl's training aimed at teaching her role as a wife and mother. As it was described, the first phase of initiation was the deflowering of the girl with a tuber shaped like a phallus (the Makonde in northern Mozambique used a phallus made of clay). The girl was taught her sexual role by an older woman, preferably a widow, and then violently beaten to give her a sense of the pains of childbirth to come. The whole of the affair was enough to teach passivity and to idealize subordination. During the first month of the ceremony, the girl was given to a poor family to be treated like a low-caste servant, requiring daily carrying of water and wood and a beating on her return. Nevertheless, this period ended with a public ceremony during which the girls insulted men, and accused them of laziness and failing to work for their kin group. This assertive moment gave them an opportunity to emphasize their own merits as beasts of burden. Their servile status was reinforced during the second month, when girls had to put on cloth woven of wet grasses that rubbed their skin raw as they dried. A missionary went so far as to state that the final trial consisted of making the initiate grasp a piece of burning metal in order to show that "her hands were ready for the hardest labor."[9]

Missionaries probably exaggerated. Yet this climate of passive feminine obedience, pushed to its extreme among the Tswana, was hardly better among other ethnic groups, especially in central, eastern, and southern Africa. Yao and Shona sexual habits made women similarly submissive to men and trained them primarily to give men pleasure.[10]

SLAVERY AND MARRIAGE

The above information applies to free women. A number of societies also captured women from other people or bought them for marriage. Wife capture or purchase was widespread in the kinship-based societies (the Ani, Guro, Alladian, and others) of what is today southern Ivory Coast.[11] These practices were splendidly demonstrated a few years ago by several anthropologists, among them a brilliant Ivorian social scientist, Harris Memel-Foté.[12] These groups, ranging in size from only a few thousand to tens of thousands of people, lived in the rain forest or on its edges and along the coastal lagoons. From at least as early as the nineteenth century (one can only guess at earlier times), high death rates threatened their survival and their productive capacities. The genealogies of their dominant lineages reveal that succession to positions of authority was often a problem because of a lack of surviving children.

Seeking slave women from outside, through force or purchase, was necessary both to increase their reproductive capacities (although this hope was not always realized) and, especially in matrilineal societies, to strengthen the father's line. Continuity through descent was necessary to assert his lineage's superiority over competing lineages, and the children of a female slave belonged unquestionably to their father's family. Slave women, in contrast to free women, were not allowed to leave their husbands or to have extramarital relations. Similar customs have long prevailed in some of the small kinship-based societies of central Nigeria (the Cross River basin), where as late as the 1930s, and perhaps much earlier, because of extreme poverty, the Obubra captured children and purchased slaves.[13] During colonial times, to avoid being prosecuted for buying slaves, their usual pretext was that they were paying bride price for early marriages. In 1944 a girl cost about £30 and a boy only £25. The children came from large, poor families in nearby districts (Okigwe and Bende). The custom was favored by the native authorities, who saw it both as a way to balance the decline in population due to labor migration and as a defense against the frequently unstable marriages of free women in their matrilineal society.[14] Other societies, such as in south-central Africa, also took female slaves but forbade formal marriage between free men and slave women, a luxury they could probably afford because of their steady population growth.[15]

As for aristocratic Sahelian societies, they radically opposed "mixed" marriages between free males and women acquired as slaves. At best, a female slave was a concubine. Other female slaves were less reproductive than free women, first because these women slaves were looked on solely as commodities or were used for labor and not as vehicles to found families, and second because they lived in such harsh conditions that they were not enabled to give birth to, or rear, children.[16] As a result, infanticide was frequent among them, and they often abandoned their babies. Women slaves were wanted all but exclusively for their productive capacities rather than for their fertility.

Female slaves, whether wives or not, played important roles in exchanges among the men of the kin groups of the countryside. Their daughters were often pawned, either as security for a debt to another lineage or as compensation for a crime. Girls especially were pawned because their status in the lineage was inferior to that of boys and, above all, because they were more likely to provide labor for the receiving lineage.[17] When the pawn was not redeemed, which was usual, her children belonged to her new family, who thus acquired a hereditary line of slaves or dependents.

In the often very hierarchical societies of western Islamized Africa, there were various categories of female slaves. In Soninke country (now Mali), there were, on one side, slaves belonging to the royal families and, on the other side, ordinary slaves. The former were relatively well integrated into the royal lineages. They were often used for domestic tasks, such as watching the children of the elite, weaving, carrying water, or even serving as traditional singers, and they sometimes enjoyed special privileges.[18] In the northern Nigerian sultanates women were practically the only slaves likely to be manumitted and thus to enjoy all the social and political rights of a free person. Manumission was particularly a possibility for concubines who bore children to their masters. Nevertheless, their origin in slavery was seldom forgotten; it was a kind of family secret, and it remains so today.[19] A "free man" is even now not ready to agree to his daughter marrying a man of maternal "slave" descent, and in the past it was quite unusual for a free woman to enter such a marriage, although it was not necessarily forbidden. However, in this case children were born free because "they have sucked milk from a free woman," as Baba of Karo, who was born in a northern Nigerian emirate around 1897, explains.[20] The marriage of a female "slave" and a free man, however, was, and is, more acceptable.

Generally speaking, women slaves were less likely than males to be sold, offered as gifts, or killed for two reasons: their labor value, and their ability to produce children. Even when a female slave was given to a male slave, she was not really married, because no dowry was paid for her: formerly, to be bought, kidnapped, or given (as a female slave) was not synonymous with being exchanged (as a free spouse) for bridewealth. Hence the slave father had no rights over his children, even if he could buy back his spouse and progeny, which was unusual because the cost was equivalent to nearly all the food crops produced by the entire slave family. Therefore, more frequently, like cattle, in the Sahel the female's fruits belonged to her master. Theoretically, in Senufo country (Mali), children of slaves were not sold. They were circumcised when twelve or thirteen years old, then became "privileged" slaves, or *woromo*, often closely linked to the master's lineage. The male slave was a stallion (*komo-yugo ni kawadi si i*)[21] and his children "followed the milk side" (belonged to their mother's owner).[22]

Usually, sexual intercourse was allowed between female domestic slaves and the master and his dependents. A young free man was taught by a specialized slave how to work and was sexually initiated by the slave's wives or daughters. If the slave discovered this, he was allowed only to strike him symbolically with his fist.[23] The perpetuation, from generation to generation, of a female slave's status was frequent but diversely applied according to the society. It was stronger in matrilineal societies because women transmitted their own status to their daughters, whereas in patrilineal societies, a free man frequently bought a slave spouse in order to incorporate their children, without any other lineage affiliation, into his own. In these aristocratic societies, younger free women lived among many slaves. Baba of Karo describes how, because her mother was a secluded spouse, she was cared for by a slave nurse. Every man in her family possessed at least twenty slaves. The cost of a woman was twice the price of a man.

Things differed on the coast, where children born from a free man and a slave mother were usually free, because (even in a matrilineal society) they belonged to the father's line and descent. This was, for example, the case in the kingdom of Dahomey, or in the Alladian or Ani societies in the modern Ivory Coast.[24] A possible explanation is that, in societies where infant death rates were very high, the only possibility to avoid population decrease was to acquire slave women from all around so as to adopt their descendants.[25]

Female slaves probably outnumbered male slaves in Africa. The hypothesis that this mainly resulted from the higher demand for males in the Atlantic slave trade is disputable, as recent studies have shown: it depends on the period. The sex ratio of the slaves who were exported was probably more balanced before the eighteenth century, when plantation labor was little gendered, because American planters were rather indifferent as to the sex of the workers they bought: probably the model was similar to women's use in Africa, where women were in charge of most agricultural tasks.[26] From the eighteenth century at least, according to the Western model, male slaves became in greater demand in the Americas, and women accounted only for one third of the total. Later, possibly when the Atlantic slave trade was forbidden by the British at the beginning of the nineteenth century, women and children were again valued for purposes of staffing American slave labor forces through reproduction. As for Africa, even in areas where cultivation was mainly man's work, as in Hausaland, where free women were cloistered, wealthy families might possess several hundred slaves, most of them working in the fields, regardless of their gender.

SLAVE WOMEN IN CENTRAL AFRICA: A FEW BIOGRAPHIES

In the nineteenth century, eastern and south-central Africa especially experienced unprecedented growth in the slave trade with the lands surrounding the Indian Ocean in exchange for increasingly sought-after firearms and Western manufactured products imported by Arab and Swahili traders. Insecurity caused by slave raids was even greater here than in the Sahel, where Baba of Karo described pillagers attacking women and girls and the despoiled husbands having to pay high ransoms for them if they could find them. In the case Baba of Karo describes, the man paid four hundred thousand cowries for a woman, four hundred thousand for each of three children, and four hundred thousand for a child in the womb.

People in these areas, prey to aggressive slave trading, also began to use slaves much more intensively themselves. Men began taking slave wives. Among the Bemba of what is now Tanzania and southern Congo, historian Marcia Wright collected various life stories of female slaves from this period. A matrilineal ideology and the absence of expensive dowries explain why free women in this area enjoyed, according to chiefs and missionaries, "excessive freedoms": "Recently Chief Mporokoso, after touring his villages, told me that the women of the country were growing out of hand, and that the results were becoming apparent in a decrease in the birth-rate. The character of the Wemba woman must be borne in mind. . . . Always notably independent—more or less a shrew—and prone to unfaithfulness."[27]

Using slaves as wives meant stability because the women could not be taken back, since no bridewealth had been paid for them. The vagaries of their status caused them to be sold in times of need and made them veritable walking hoes, with each protector getting the most from them every time they were acquired.

Bwanikwa, for example, was sold and married ten times between 1886 and 1911.[28] Her tribulations had three phases. The first was during the reign of Msiri, a great trafficker in slaves in the modern southern Democratic Republic of Congo (DRC, formerly Zaire), who died in 1891. The second was in a period of turbulence and insecurity in which male protection was an absolute necessity, and the final phase came after a Christian mission took her in. Born in the early 1870s in Luba country (central Congo), she was sold into slavery by her father, a man with twelve wives, when he was required by the in-laws of a deceased wife to pay three slaves in order to marry her younger sister. He could come up with only two. In adding Bwanikwa to make three, he promised to come back for her, but he never found the money to do so. Bwanikwa was sold again, this time for a package of gunpowder. Traded from man to man several times because she was too young to serve as a wife or to work in the fields, she ended up in Msiri's capital city, Bunkeya, as the wife of a slave trader there, who kept her for himself (apparently because she was beautiful). Msiri's death threw his empire into disarray and left the capital in ruins. Bwanikwa's master fled east to Kazembe on the upper Luapula River, where the chief, Mukoka, managed to acquire her, only to sell her again to a band of slave traders from the western coast. Bwanikwa escaped and married a man who worked as a mason for missionaries settling on the banks of Lake Mweru, but he too sold her to Arab traders, this time from the eastern coast.

Escaping again, Bwanikwa took refuge with an old civil servant from Msiri's government who had converted to Christianity and entered the service of the mission. He bought her for the price of a gun and then married her. She became the trusted assistant of a missionary's wife and worked making pottery and raising chickens until she could buy her freedom by repurchasing the gun. The author of this account, a missionary, notes that from that point on, as a free woman, Bwanikwa went to the fields at her husband's side, rather than walking respectfully behind him, and ate at the same time he did, rather than subsisting on remainders. "They sat and chatted together on the veranda of their house, and speaking of each other to outsiders there was the tone of deference and respect formerly lacking."[29]

Bwanikwa must have been a woman of remarkable energy and intelligence. Yet having suffered from her status as a slave for more than twenty years, and believing in, and adhering to, native customs, she did not regard herself—and was not regarded by others—as free until she had paid for herself. This self-purchase was common in the region in the early twentieth century, according to missionary and police accounts and the reports of the British judiciary. The most disturbing case was that of a woman who repeatedly sought permission from the British authorities to buy her freedom when no one was asking her to pay. However, her case was exceptional. In the corridor from Lake Nyasa to Lake Tanganyika (east-central Africa) we know that women whose lives had been disrupted by being sold or taken prisoner were sometimes able to return to their homes. Some ran away and found their way back from distances of sixty miles or more. Narwimba, Chisi, and Meli were three women taken from their families at young ages.[30] They had many masters and husbands before ending up at the mission. In their cases, networks of neighbors and kin spread word about their whereabouts, despite the turbulence of the region. Hence each of them was finally found by her first protector and went voluntarily to end her days with him, so intense was their need to remain part of their society of origin. Once home, they picked up the agricultural and domestic tasks that had always been their lot. Permanently submissive, despite the energy with which they had fought adversity, they showed a kind of social conformism not untinged with fatalism.

In contrast, in such hard times, young men who were uprooted had other paths open to them. They found new opportunities for work within the colonial world. Basically, they felt group pressure less because they had the power to found new lineages, albeit inferior ones. Women were denied even that modest freedom; slaves or not, they always belonged to someone—their lineage, their husband, or their master.

We see this clearly in the life of Narwimba, who was born in the mid-nineteenth century to a family of chiefs in what is now western Tanzania, but whose noble birth did not spare her the enslavement common to women from her region. Thus marked by extremes, her life began in the normal way for a chief's daughter. She was married to a man to whom she gave six children, one of whom survived. Widowed when still young, she became the wife of her deceased husband's nephew, Mirambo. Decades later, Mirambo became one of the main slave-trading chiefs in the area. Narwimba again had six children, of whom two survived. Mirambo grew less interested in her as she grew older (she was about forty), and she came to be among the captives of a neighboring chief, who tried unsuccessfully to sell her. After making the rounds from man to man several times, she was given back to Mirambo, though without her children, who remained in slavery. As an old, neglected woman, her social status became more and more delicate, and she could marry her daughter only to a slave. She managed with great difficulty to keep her granddaughter from being pawned to Mirambo as compensation for a peasant dispute. In despair, she took refuge in her natal village, where she was barely tolerated, because she had no man able to clear a plot of land for her to cultivate. Her isolation was why she eventually came to the mission to live out her life and, incidentally, to tell her story as we now know it.

Chisi, born around 1870 in Nanwanga (modern western Tanzania), had an even harder life. Captured with her elder sister when she was just a child, she was sold several times as a slave and passed from man to man in the Swahili caravans passing through Nanwanga country. She escaped and was hidden and taken in by a chief who gave her to an adoptive father who eventually married her. Mistreated by his other wives, she refused to follow the family when it sought protection with a nearby chief. Of course, she had to leave her children behind, but she managed to get them back again later. On her ex-husband's death, she married a peddler. His frequent absences allowed her to live more independently but were also a hardship because she had no protector. At one point she was penalized with a heavy fine and her only recourse was to seek protection within her second husband's family. She spent her last days between the mission and one or the other of her children.

Meli belonged to the generation following Chisi's. At five she was captured during a raid by Bemba as revenge against her father, a petty local chief. The group of women with whom she was captured abandoned their children when they managed to flee. Now motherless, she embarked on the hard life of a child female domestic slave. She was finally sold to a Swahili elephant hunter for four pieces of ivory. Resold several times for ivory or cloth, she went from caravan to caravan. At about age ten she was freed by whites and brought to the mission. A passing woman, hearing her name, made contact with the men in her kin group. Married at the turn of the century by the missionaries (who received her bride price), she was baptized in 1910. Eventually she returned to her society of origin when she was recognized by her paternal family and adopted by her husband's family. Yet the latter meant to profit from this and applied customary law with the result that, on the death of her husband, she was successively married to two of his relatives. The second husband was polygamous, but she lived with him for over ten years before her death.[31]

In practice, the distinction between the duties of a free woman and those of a slave was tenuous. Therefore I completely support Claire Robertson and Martin Klein's conclusion that the statuses of free and slave women were not very different in the past.[32] Women's statuses were blurred to the point that almost all the first travelers, missionaries, and explorers referred to slaves as male. "True slavery"—servile work and lack of inheritance rights—was a male condition. Men in slavery, deprived of free ancestors, free wives, and children and thus unable to father a lineage, had neither manhood nor adulthood. They could even be required to perform such female-gendered tasks as carrying water. A slave man was an individual made to do a job that a woman would normally do. There is no clearer way to describe the condition of women, slave or free, at the dawn of colonization.

A slave woman's status was usually defined as domestic. She was more a member of the family, or at least was more able to become a member, because of a certain ambiguity in the different tasks she was called upon to perform. For this reason, her position was far less difficult socially than the male slave's. Among the Nuer, anthropological observations that, no doubt, were transmitted from long ago show that an adult man asserted his superiority and independence by keeping a certain distance between his real needs and his role as master of production.[33] For example, he controlled cattle, but women milked them. His separation from manual labor allowed him to retain his prestige. Because of women's function as providers of foodstuffs, it may be suggested that women were thought to be mediators between men and their animals, between men and nature, and between men's social dignity and their physical needs.

Female slavery increased all over Africa during the nineteenth century. In the west, the dwindling Atlantic slave trade led to a glut of captives retained, and many of the women among them were then sent across the western Sudan by conquerors' armies. Other women slaves remained as tools of production in a slave-operated cloth-weaving artisan industry, and in the forest areas in harvesting the new export products that had replaced slaves, mainly palm kernels. A parallel shift occurred in eastern Africa with the development of Arab and Swahili plantations on the coastlands, encouraged by the Zanzibar sultans' clove plantations on the islands of Zanzibar and Pemba, as well as sugarcane plantations on the coasts of what are now Kenya and Tanzania.[34] On the eve of colonial conquest at the turn of the century, slaves probably formed at least a quarter of the population of western Africa and were even more numerous in eastern and central Africa.[35] The majority may have been women, although the earliest Western observers showed little interest in them, and traditional African sources did not mention them.

Fortunately, recent work has thrown light on the impact on the status of women of the ending of legal slavery as the colonial period began, around 1900. Not only were slaves of both sexes able to claim their freedom, but colonial development produced a great demand for labor for government infrastructure and private enterprises. As a result, many free men and former slaves left the land to take up wage labor. Interestingly, when the first "villages de liberté" (freedom villages) were created by the French colonizers to receive former slaves, more women than men fled there as refugees.[36] Slaves also left their owners to establish their own farms and households. In the rural areas former owners faced a labor shortage and so demanded more work from their wives and junior members of their households. In Tonga in Nyasaland (now Malawi), Margo Lovett noted that freeborn women began to equate themselves with slaves as a result of the burdens that this male labor emigration left to them.[37] Moreover, the colonial cash economy not only thus increased the female work load but it also changed husbands' attitudes toward their wives as they came to regard them like (male) slaves—as an economic investment. Richard Roberts notes that in the French Soudan (now Mali) this increase in the female workload led to an increase in the number of divorce cases that wives brought to the colonial courts.[38] When the British in Kenya ceased to recognize slavery and stopped returning fugitives, the Giriama there simply bought more wives. It made little difference, they said, since women and slaves did the same work.[39] In Muslim areas women retreated into more rigorous seclusion to escape increased demands of colonial labor markets. Some slave women, who had not previously been secluded, moved into purdah once they were freed for the same reason, and also to raise their social standing.[40]

Until very recently the trend in studies of Africa was to concentrate on the export slave trade while minimizing the prevalence of slavery in Africa. However, Claude Meillassoux's and Memel-Foté's work, and that of Suzanne Miers and Igor Kopytoff, followed a few years later by Robertson and Klein's studies of female slavery, as well as Paul Lovejoy's synthesis, have revised this view.[41] This chapter suggests that the study of female slaves turns up many more sources than expected. Therefore, we need to beware of received wisdom.

The fact is that many scholars still have a tendency to speak of peasants and of slaves without differentiating among either by gender. Meillassoux was the first to initiate a change, with his seminal study published in 1975.[42] He underlined the major role of women in rural Africa and in agriculture—a fact that is nowadays well known—pointing out their double exploitation, first as producers (in a subsistence economy) and second as reproducers (thanks to their fertility). Meantime, in the Western world, Victorian and bourgeois ideologies focused on women exclusively as reproducers, keeping them in the domestic sphere, which in Europe meant at home. Since then, literature on African women's history has proliferated in the anglophone world but has been slower to develop in France. Nevertheless, in France a relatively early study on African women emerged as early as the late 1930s, written by a female observer, at the time of the Popular Front government.[43] The first scholarly study on African women was edited by Denise Paulme as early as 1960.[44] Nowadays gender studies in Africa have multiplied.[45]

Meillassoux once more challenged the norms of French scholarship in the early 1980s to study not just the slave trade but rather slavery itself, and besides that, slavery in Africa. He developed his ideas further, connecting and contrasting, for example, slavery and kinship, slavery and power, and slavery and commerce. He showed how slavery was interconnected with war, sometimes promoting it and sometimes preventing it. He documented his case primarily in the Sahel, at the same time (1988) when an Ivorian scholar, Memel-Foté, did the same for the rain forest. Thus, in African societies in the nineteenth century, people of power were using slaves as the main tool of labor and production. Meillassoux did not hesitate to describe this as a "slave mode of production."

He made it clear that African slavery was predominantly a female phenomenon. Male slaves were condemned to do what free men regarded as female jobs. As for female slaves, they were de-gendered. They were supposed to do every kind of labor, men's as well as women's, including work that respectable free women were not allowed to do. For example, in Hausaland, they worked in the fields, while free Muslim women were cloistered. Female slaves were more useful for production than male slaves. Nevertheless, as Meillassoux shows, female slaves were more efficient as producers than as reproducers.[46] They gave birth to fewer children. This low natality was truer in the forest area than in the Sahelian belt: Emmanuel Terray and Claude-Hélène Perrot calculated that the demographic deficit in the forest area was high.[47]

Many questions still remain to be answered about female slavery in Africa, and this essay merely suggests some of them. One conclusion is certain: whatever has been written about women in the past, especially in the 1950s and 1960s, when a number of anthropologists had a tendency to idealize the precolonial past as a golden era, and again in the 1980s, when the first serious historical gender studies sometimes exaggerated the deterioration of women's status during colonial times, the condition of most women in Africa grew harder and harder in the nineteenth century, owing to the political and social disturbances all over the continent. Possibly, as already suggested, the transitional period at the beginning of colonialism increased the inequality of status between former male and female slaves still further, as colonizers recruited liberated males as workers or miners, therefore as wage earners, a capacity denied to women, left to manage by themselves.

Women—former slaves or not—were able to react only when the colonial administration grew aware of this major discrepancy and slowly began to support their efforts to lessen it. Previously, historical gender relations in Africa had been similar to the rest of the world: based on minimal status and power for women, and this deficit was still truer for females who were slaves. Of course, it would be misleading to assume freedom (which originated as a Western concept) to be the natural antithesis of slavery. Indeed, for women, marriage, and slavery in nineteenth-century sub-Saharan Africa, it becomes difficult—if not impossible—to draw any meaningful practical—and by extension analytical—distinction between freedom and slavery. The day-to-day reality of women's lives in the most patriarchal systems collapsed together those who occupied the meanest social and political position, by virtue of their sex, more than by virtue of their "official" status.

NOTES

1. Internal lineage relationships between elders and youth, and the political and social role of matrimonial exchanges between lineages, were first and cleverly theorized by Claude Meillassoux in 1960. Meillassoux, "Essai sur l'interprétation du phénomène économique dans les sociétés d'autosubsistance," *Cahiers d'études africaines* 4, no. 1 (1960): 38–67.

2. Abdoulaye Bara Diop, *La famille Wolof: Tradition et changement* (Paris: Karthala, 1985).

3. Personal interview.

4. For gender's relations in Tswanaland, see details below.

5. As shown, among others, by Claude Meillassoux, "État et conditions des esclaves à Gumbu (Mali) au XIXe siècle," *Journal of African History* 14, no. 3 (1973): 429–52, reprinted in *L'esclavage en Afrique pré-coloniale*, ed. Claude Meillassoux (Paris: Maspéro, 1975), 221–51.

6. For detailed sources and reports, see Coquery-Vidrovitch, *African Women*, 13–15.

7. R. H. Reyher, *Zulu Woman: The Life Story of Christina Sibiya* (1947; New York: Feminist Press, 1999).

8. Margaret Kinsman, "Beasts of Burden: The Subordination of Southern Tswana Women, ca. 1800–1840," *Journal of Southern African Studies* 10, no. 1 (1983): 39–54. See also Iris Berger, "'Beasts of Burden' Revisited: Interpretations of Women and Gender in Southern African Societies," in *Paths toward the Past: African Historical Essays in Honor of Jan Vansina*, ed. R. W. Harms, J. C. Miller, D. S. Newbury, and M. D. Wagner (Atlanta: African Studies Association Press, 1994).

9. Robert Moffat, *Missionary Labours and Scenes in Southern Africa* (London: John Snow, 1843), 250.

10. Cf. *Ethnologie régionale*, vol. 1, *Afrique, Océanie* (Paris: La Pléïade, 1972).

11. I mainly refer to the relatively recent era just before or on the eve of colonization, when kinship-based rural societies still functioned beyond the Western (commercial) sphere.

12. See Claude Meillassoux, *Anthropologie économique des Gouro de Côte d'Ivoire: De l'économie de subsistance à l'agriculture commerciale* (Paris: Mouton, 1964); Harris Memel-Foté, *L'esclavage dans les sociétés lignagères d'Afrique noire—Exemple de la Côte d'Ivoire précoloniale, 1700–1920*, 3 vols. (thesis, Université Paris-5/CNRS, 1988).

13. Gloria Thomas-Emeagwili, "Class Formation in Pre-Colonial Nigeria," history department, Ahmadu Bello University, Zaria, c. 1985, in *Nigeria and the International Capitalist System*, ed. Toyin Falola and J. Ihonvbere (Boulder: Lynne Rienner, 1988).

14. Benedict B. Naanen, "Itinerant Gold Mines: Prostitution in the Cross River Basin of Nigeria, 1930–1950," *African Studies Review* 34, no. 2 (1991): 57–79.

15. Marcia Wright, "Technology, Marriage and Women's Work in the History of Maize Growers in Mazabuka, Zambia," *Journal of Southern African Studies* 10, no. 1 (1983): 55–69.

16. Claude Meillassoux, *The Anthropology of Slavery: The Womb of Iron and Gold* (Chicago: University of Chicago Press; London: Athlone, 1991); published in French as *Anthropologie de l'esclavage: Le ventre de fer et d'argent* (Paris: Presses Universitaires de France, 1986).

17. Paul E. Lovejoy and Toyin Falola, eds., *Pawnship, Slavery, and Colonialism in Africa* (Trenton, NJ: Africa World, 2003).

18. M. Diawara, "Femmes, servitude et histoire: Les traditions orales . . . dans le royaume de Jaara du XVe au milieu du XIXe siècle," *History in Africa* 16 (1989): 71–96.

19. Mary Smith, *Baba of Karo: A Woman of the Muslim Hausa* (London: Faber and Faber, 1954).

20. Ibid., 41.

21. Meillassoux, *Anthropology of Slavery*, 110–29.

22. Smith, *Baba of Karo*, 41.

23. Ibid.

24. See, among others, Memel-Foté, *Esclavage*.

25. This practice has been studied for the nineteenth century by Cl.-H. Perrot, *Les Ani-Ndenye et le pouvoir aux 18e et 19e siècles en Côte d'Ivoire* (Paris: Publications de la Sorbonne, 1982).

26. David Eltis and Stanley L. Engerman, "Was the Slave Trade Dominated by Men?" *Journal of Interdisciplinary History* 23, no. 2 (1992): 237–57; Eltis and Engerman, "Fluctuations in Sex and Age Ratios in the Transatlantic Slave Trade, 1663–1864," *Economic History Review* 46 (1993): 308–23.

27. Marshall, "Notes on the Bamba" (1910) (Marshall Papers, Livingstone Museum), quoted in Marcia Wright, *Strategies of Slaves and Women: Life-Stories from East/Central Africa* (London: Lillian Barber, 1993), 153.

28. A detailed biography of Bwanikwa appears in Wright, *Strategies of Slaves*, ch. 7.

29. Dugald Campbell, *Ten Times a Slave but Freed at Last: The Thrilling Story of Bwanikwa, a Central African Heroine* (Glasgow: Pickering and Inglis, 1916), quoted in Wright, *Strategies of Slaves*, 168.

30. All three life stories in Wright, *Strategies of Slaves*.

31. Marcia Wright, "Women in Peril: A Commentary on the Life Stories of Captives in 19th century East-Central Africa," *African Social Research* 20 (1975): 800–819.

32. Claire C. Robertson and Martin A. Klein, eds., *Women and Slavery in Africa* (Madison: University of Wisconsin Press, 1983).

33. Sharon Hutchinson, "Relations between the Sexes among the Nuer, 1930," *Africa* 50, no. 4 (1980): 371–88.

34. See, for example, Fred Cooper, *Plantation Slavery on the East Coast of Africa* (New Haven: Yale University Press, 1977).

35. For West Africa, see Meillassoux, *Anthropology of Slavery*; for East Africa, see, among others, Jonathon Glassman, *Feasts and Riot: Revelry, Rebellion, and Popular Consciousness on the Swahili Coast, 1856–1888* (Portsmouth, NH: Heinemann, 1995).

36. Marie Rodet, "Frauen im Spannungsfeld des 'Droit colonial' in Afrique Occidentale Française: Zwei Fallbeispiele aus der Region Kayes, Soudan Français (1918 und 1938)," *Stichproben, Wiener Zeitschrift für Kritische Afrikastudien* 7 (2004): 89–105. From the same author, "La migration des femmes du Soudan (Mali) des débuts de la colonisation à la suppression du travail forcé (1900–1947)" (PhD diss., Vienna, 2006).

37. Margot Lovett, "Gender Relations, Class Formation, and the Colonial State in Africa," in *Women and the State in Africa*, ed. Jane L. Parpart and Kathleen A. Staudt (Boulder, CO: Lynn Rienner, 1989), 30.

38. Richard Roberts, "Women, Household Instability, and the End of Slavery in Banamba and Gumbu, French Soudan, 1905–1912," in this volume.

39. Suzanne Miers, pers. comm., March 2004, based on interviews in Kenya, 1972–74.

40. B. A. Cooper, "Reflections on Slavery, Seclusion and Female Labor in the Maradi Region of Niger in Nineteenth and Twentieth Centuries," *Journal of African History* 35, no. 1 (1994): 61–78.

41. Suzanne Miers and Igor Kopytoff, eds., *Slavery in Africa: Historical and Anthropological Perspectives* (Madison: University of Wisconsin Press, 1977); Robertson and Klein, *Women and Slavery*; P. Lovejoy, *Transformations in Slavery: The History of Slavery in Africa* (Cambridge: Cambridge University Press, 1983).

42. Claude Meillassoux, *Maidens, Meal, and Money: Capitalism and the Domestic Community* (Cambridge: Cambridge University Press, 1981); published in French as *Femmes, greniers et capitaux* (Paris: F. Maspéro, 1975).

43. The original archive report was published in full: Denise Savineau, *La famille en AOF et la condition de la femme: Rapport présenté au gouverneur général de l'AOF en 1938*, introduction by Pascale Barthélémy, Institut National d'Études Démographiques, Dossiers et recherches, no. 102 (Paris: INED, 2001): 1–211.

44. Denise Paulme, ed., *Women of Tropical Africa* (Berkeley: University of California Press, 1963).

45. For a bibliographical survey of colonial gender in Africa, see Sophie Dulucq and Odile Goerg, "Le fait colonial au miroir des colonisées: Femmes, genre et colonisation: Un bilan des recherches francophones en histoire de l'Afrique subsaharienne (1950–2003)," in *Histoire des femmes en situation coloniale: Afrique et Asie, XXe siècle*, ed. Anne Hugon (Paris: Karthala, 2005), 43–70; on colonial and postcolonial African gender, see Catherine Coquery-Vidrovitch, "Des femmes colonisées aux femmes de l'indépendance, ou du misérabilisme au développement par les femmes: Approche historique," in *De la "condition des femmes" à l'emprise du genre en Afrique*, ed. Thérèse Locoh, Cahiers de l'INED, no. 160 (forthcoming 2007).

46. Meillassoux, *Esclavage en Afrique*; Meillassoux, *Anthropology of Slavery*.

47. Emmanuel Terray, *Une histoire du royaume Abron de Gyaman: Des origines à la conquête coloniale* (Paris: Karthala, 1995); Perrot, *Ani-Ndenye*.

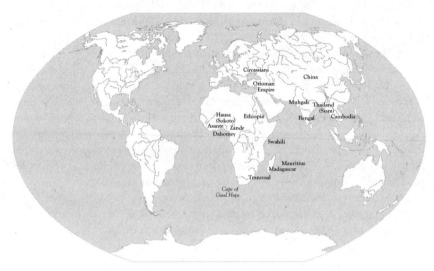

Locations of royal and imperial harems and sources discussed in chapter 2

2

SEX, POWER, AND FAMILY LIFE IN THE HAREM

A Comparative Study

MARTIN A. KLEIN

In 1863 the French established a protectorate in Cambodia. Not interested in undertaking the full expense of direct administration, they administered Cambodia for most of the next eighty years through the king.
In the early years, this involved constant struggle over boundaries of authority. One of the French complaints about King Norodom was that the
cost of his harem was more than half the budget of the kingdom. To be
sure, Norodom had other pleasures. He smoked opium, often provided by
the French, and enjoyed drinking and smoking with his acolytes.[1] The
harem, however, was a central institution. It contained women given to
him by powerful families interested in currying favor. Norodom had,
however, spent a period of exile in Thailand and liked Siamese girls, whom
he purchased through a representative in Bangkok.[2] Security in the
harem does not seem to have been as tight as it was in most Muslim states.
His women had occasional love affairs, or at least, he feared that some of
them had lovers. That fear cost several women their heads, and when
one of them fled to Saigon, the colonial state had to decide whether to
return a woman to almost certain death.

A WIDESPREAD INSTITUTION

The harem as an institution was found throughout much of Asia and
Africa, where it is of great antiquity.[3] It is often seen in the West as a

I thank Suzanne Miers and Beverly Mack for their comments on earlier versions of
this paper.

Muslim institution, but harems existed long before Islam and in many other societies. This chapter will be primarily concerned with royal or imperial harems, but it is worth noting that other powerful men often had harems. Royal harems differed from those of other wealthy and powerful men both in scale and function. Those of kings and emperors contained hundreds, and in some cases, more than a thousand women. The Mughal emperor, Akbar, is reputed to have had five thousand women in his harem, each with a separate apartment.[4] In some cases, the royal harem was filled largely with free women offered to the king. In others, all or a vast majority were slaves.

There are some differences between Islamic and non-Islamic harems, but given the limited amount of information on what went on behind harem walls, it is sometimes difficult to be precise on those differences. One is probably that Islam limited the role outside the harem walls of any but the most powerful, usually postmenopausal, woman. Another is that most slave concubines in Muslim harems came from non-Muslim areas, though the Hausa recruited local women and there were some favored sources within the Muslim world, like the nominally Muslim Circassians of the Caucasus. The Qing dynasty in China chose women for the emperor and his sons from among Manchu and Mongol women, generally at an annual ceremony, in which the thirteen- and fourteen-year-old daughters of select noble families were presented and the emperor or senior court officials took their choice. Marriage to Chinese women was forbidden.[5] Relatively few of these girls became imperial consorts and many were married off after a period of service. Nine Qing emperors had anywhere from three to fifty-four consorts who were honored by being buried in a consort's tomb.[6]

In Kano there were three categories of women in the harem. The wives—Islam allowed each man up to four—were free women chosen from other elite families. There was a much larger group of concubines, chosen from among the daughters of royal slaves, prisoners of war, and women given to the emir. They were secluded and held major administrative functions. There was also a larger group of slave women, who did most of the manual labor within the palace and could be sent out of the palace on errands. A slave woman could be promoted into the ranks of the concubines, but most were married off to male slaves or given away after a period of service.[7]

We have more information on Ottoman harems than on any other, thanks in part to Leslie Peirce's detailed account, which used Ottoman archives and abundant written accounts.[8] Islamic law limited a male—

king or commoner—to four wives, but he was authorized to have as many concubines as he could support. The Ottoman sultans, unlike the emirs of Kano, generally did not marry and had only slave concubines in their harems. Kings, emperors, and sultans generally had little difficulty supporting their harems, though such support may have been a burden on the tax-paying peasant or worker. Harems were usually lavish institutions. Within a harem, the difference between a slave and a free woman was important, though not always determinant. In most harems, important positions were held largely by women who came from other important families, but a slave, a serving girl, or other low-status woman could become powerful if her master valued her. A woman's status depended on attracting the eye of her royal master, and then, of producing a son. Cixi (Tz'u Hsi in the old orthography), the powerful empress dowager of China, originally entered the Forbidden City as a lowly consort of the sixth rank, but she produced an heir.[9] In Qing China, 16 percent of the imperial consorts were originally palace maids. Of the eleven Qing emperors, only one was the son of an empress.[10]

The word harem comes from two closely related Arabic words, haram (forbidden, unlawful) and harim (sacred, inviolable place). Mecca and Medina, as sacred places, were "haram,"[11] places to which access is limited. Fatima Mernissi describes a harem as "a traditional household with locked gates that women were not supposed to open."[12] For her grandmother, it was a prison, but it was also the site of family life. At Topkapi, the Ottomans had two harems. The first, where the sultan transacted much public business, was peopled by slave boys, who worked as pages and were being trained to enter the bureaucracy, where some would rise to the highest offices in the empire. This harem had no sexual function. It was concerned only with the administration of the empire and the reproduction of the slave elite that ran it.[13] The second was where the sultan's family lived—his mother, aunts, concubines, sisters, minor children, and their servants.

Other societies used different terms, but generally there was a controlled area for the ruler's wives and concubines. In Bangkok it was the Nang Harm, the Inner Palace.[14] In Beijing the Forbidden City was the administrative headquarters of the empire, but there was an inner court barred to all but a select number of princes and high officials. Security was tight and every worker's entry was tightly recorded. In the Sokoto caliphate the emir's palace was enclosed by a wall and was guarded by royal slaves or by older women. In Kano the women's area was called the stomach.[15] Powerful Zande rulers each had a large enclosed area, in some cases covering several square miles. Each wife had her own hut, granary, and gardens.[16] In Asante some of the royal wives represented the Asantehene in villages, but most lived in an enclosed area behind the palace. Men entering the city of women had to be careful because the penalty for seeing an Asante royal wife naked was castration.[17] In almost all cases, the ruler's apartments were within the enclosure, which meant that access to him was limited when he was there.

In general, harems were surrounded by tight security. In Dahomey, a force of women guarded the palace and provided the bodyguard for the king.[18] The Siamese court in Bangkok was also guarded by women. In Muslim harems, security was maintained by eunuchs, slaves, and powerful older women, though the Mughal harem also had a force of female bodyguards skilled with bow and arrow.[19] In Kano the harem was guarded by older women, who locked the gates at night.[20] In Topkapi, the Ottoman palace, eunuchs guarded the gate, but were reinforced by other guards outside the walls. The apartments of the sultan lay between the two wings of the palace. Most of the time, the only male authorized to enter a harem was the royal master, though in some non-Muslim harems select high officials had access and confinement was less rigid. Harems were occasionally visited by female European visitors, by market women, or by others, particularly by daughters or concubines, who had been married off outside the harem. Chinese concubines were allowed to see their parents when they were pregnant or the parents were elderly.[21] In the Ottoman harem the palace dwarf was often brought in to divert women in labor, and in the eighteenth century, French dancing masters and musicians were allowed supervised access. Much of the French influence may have come from a concubine named Nakshedil. She was originally Aimee Debucq de Rivery, born in Martinique and a cousin of Josephine Bonaparte. She was captured by corsairs and sold to the dey of Algiers, who gave her to Sultan Abdulhamid I.[22] European doctors were sometimes brought into harems to see sick women, though in the Mughal harem they were often not allowed to actually see their patients.[23]

The Mughal court often traveled and the Ottomans sometimes had carefully supervised outings.[24] The king of Siam had a country palace and the emperor of China had his Summer Palace. When they moved to a temporary residence, it was generally with a select but large group of royal women.[25] Kano royal women rarely left the palace except to go to a clinic or to make the pilgrimage to Mecca, and then with supervision.[26] Before the Sokoto jihad, slave women in Kano seem to have handled tax collection, but afterward, their role was more circumscribed.[27]

Much of the abundant literature on the Ottoman harem is based on visits to Ottoman harems by European women during the eighteenth and nineteenth centuries.[28] There is also some writing from the descendants of its residents. This is largely the result of the abrupt abolition of the Ottoman harem in 1909. Many of the harem women married educated men and raised educated daughters and granddaughters, who often were interested in their maternal heritage.[29] Of course, the break was not always as sharp. There is also a small but significant literature on life in the harems of the middle class and lesser nobility.[30] There is also a growing literature from China, but mostly on the gentry household and concubinage, some of it from granddaughters exploring the experiences of their grandmothers, but relatively little on the imperial household.

AUTHORITY AND STATUS

Harems generally had clear lines of authority. Though many courts had a queen or empress, the most powerful position in most harems was the ruler's mother or a senior woman from his family. She administered the harem but also often played a role in the larger political arena.[31] In China, there was an empress, who participated in court life, but the harem was generally run by the widow of an earlier emperor, who was known as the empress dowager.[32] Such a woman in the Ottoman harem was the *valide sultan*, the mother of the sultan, or an older woman from his family. If there was no royal mother, the top authority would be another senior woman or the woman who had nursed the sultan as an infant. Called the *daye khatun*, these women often returned to the harem if widowed. The milk tie created an intimate link to the prince. In Muslim India, this authority was the begum. She was in charge of the harem and often exercised great power at court. The Mughal harem had as elaborate a hierarchy as the Ottoman one.[33] In many African kingdoms, a key title-holder was a similar senior woman of the ruler's family. In Dahomey, she was the *kpojito*.[34]

There were also a variety of other administrative positions. Anna Leonowens writes, "Every harem is a little world in itself, composed entirely of women—some who rule, others who obey and those who serve."[35] In the Ottoman court, there was a laundry mistress, a treasurer, and a bath mistress. Others ran the baths, supervised storerooms, made sherbet, sewed, or took care of jewels. In many courts, the manager of the kitchen was important. In Bangkok there were even female judges, who administered justice within the palace. There were also great differences in roles.

King Mongkut had eighty-two wives, but the palace was a city of eight to nine thousand people, the vast majority of them women.[36] These women included large numbers of servants, but also the guards, merchants, and a range of artisans, particularly jewelers.

In the Qing harem there were eight different ranks for imperial consorts. In the Qing court, there was a population that numbered at times over three thousand, but relatively few consorts. The consorts, the emperor's daughters, and other senior women were served by an army of ladies-in-waiting, palace maids, bondservants, and state slaves. The empress dowager Cixi had twenty maids.[37] Most left after a term of service to get married. In other harems, excess women were given away as wives. Among the Zande, where large royal harems left a shortage of women for other men, the distribution of wives guaranteed the royal court the support of young men.[38]

In nineteenth-century Kano the most important concubine was the Master of the Grain Silos. She supervised grain tax collection, the storage of grain, and its distribution. Another maintained the emir's rooms and summoned concubines for him. Others collected and distributed milk and ran the palace kitchens, which usually fed about a thousand people at every meal. Slave women worked under their direction. They did the laundry, pounded grain, cooked, and often tended garden plots.[39]

When a new girl was brought into the Ottoman harem, the valide examined her for imperfections. Once the transaction was approved, she supervised the training of the new girl in palace etiquette and Islamic culture. There was a similar process at the Qing court. Most of the girls entering a harem did so very young. They had to be taught courtly etiquette and were often trained to dance, sing, play musical instruments, sew, and embroider. They were given religious training and sometimes a literary education. Training in dancing or playing a musical instrument was also important in Siam, Bengal, the Mughal Empire, China, and probably in most large monarchical societies.[40] The valide often gave the sultan a slave girl on the occasion of a major festival. Similar gifts came in from provincial governors. The same was true in many royal courts.

There were also sharp differences in the perquisites of office. The Asante queen mother had her own palace and the senior women in the Siamese harem had their own houses. In Topkapi, the valide had her own spacious apartment and her own courtyard. The favorites also had their own apartments, their own courtyard, and often a barge and a carriage. Some sultans had a *haseki*, a principal concubine. Others had several *kadin*, regular partners of the sultan. Below these *kadin* were a number of aspirant concubines called *ikbal*. Both the valide and the favorites had servants. Most of the other women lived in dormitorylike rooms. There were four hundred rooms in Topkapi, but in later centuries, they were home to over one thousand women. Ottaviano Bon reported that "in the women's lodgings, they live just as nuns do in great nunneries. . . . Their bed-chambers hold almost a hundred of them apiece."[41] In the Chinese Forbidden City, consorts all had their own apartment. Many harem women never slept with their royal master. Others had only a brief window of opportunity to bear him a child. Cixi's early success was based on her success in getting into the emperor's bed and her luck in producing an heir. The master of a harem could have hundreds of children, but few concubines had more than a single child.[42] A woman entering a harem had different potential directions. She could enter the dynastic family as a lover and mother, she could be promoted to the administrative hierarchy of the harem, or she could remain a worker and servant. Many women were manumitted and married off to high-ranking officials, themselves often of slave origin. In Bengali harems, women were servants, took care of carpets and tents, prepared the *huqqa* for smoking, and were midwives and wet nurses.[43]

The organization of harem life had important implications for the raising of sons. It has been argued that in the Chinese dynastic cycle, the vigor of the founders and their sons was gradually sapped as sons were raised in a harem atmosphere surrounded by women and eunuchs anxious for their favor. This was even more evident when the ruler was a child, as was frequently the case in China. Bernardo Bertolucci's film *The Last Emperor* has depicted the indulgent treatment of the last Manchu emperor, Pu Yi, who inherited the throne as an infant.[44] James Fernandez has suggested that this has important psychological implications. The Oedipus complex of Freudian psychoanalysis, Fernandez argues, is a product of the European monogamous family.[45] In a polygamous family, the child spends his earliest years in constant contact with his mother. The father is a distant figure, even more so in a harem, where the father has dozens of children. The problem for the harem culture is producing a transference to the father, his values, and the sense of lineage or dynasty. At puberty, there is a second problem. The sons must be removed from the harem to keep them from competing with their fathers. Imperial cultures made a conscious effort to deal with these problems, perhaps mostly in the way they educated potential heirs. Chinese princes lived with their mothers until the age of six, when they entered school and moved into a boy's house.[46] In Muslim states, Koranic education and religious training were important.[47] In Kano, the adolescent male offspring of the emir generally lived with and were trained by royal slaves, whose careers were often based on loyalties forged during this period.[48] Of course, the link to the mother or in Pu Yi's case, to his wet nurse, usually remained important, as the British found out in Bengal, when they tried to separate the nizam (the ruler of Hyderabad state) from his harem, underrating the political importance of the harem, and particularly, the importance of the nizam's mother.[49]

SEX IN HAREM LIFE

Ehud Toledano has written that the harem was not about sex. It might be more accurate to say that it was about more than sex.[50] Certainly, rulers sought sexual pleasure in their harems and young women were trained to give pleasure, but this has been much exaggerated by many Western writers, particularly those who have written about Muslim harems.[51] Western painters have often depicted beautiful, firm-breasted odalisques lounging by pools or lying expectantly in lavishly furnished boudoirs. Many of those who have written about harems have reacted against the image of the harem as a place of unimaginable sexual delights.[52] Croutier's beautiful coffee-table book argues against this image, but contains two contrasting types of illustration. On one hand there are the beautiful reproductions of highly erotic paintings of Ingres, Gérôme, Delacroix, and other Western artists.[53] On the other hand, there are photographs actually taken in harems that depict women fully and modestly clothed in elegant embroidered garments. Mernissi is more decisive that the harem is family place, a place where the master comes to relax. It is also "a densely populated place where everyone is always watching everyone else." In Muslim harems, she writes, even married men and women have great difficulty finding a private place in which to caress each other. As for the married women in the harem, sexual gratification is difficult since they must share their men with hundreds of frustrated "colleagues."[54] Peirce also focuses on the family: "It was not sex, however, that was the fundamental dynamic of the harem, but rather family politics. That is not to say that sex—sexual desire, the sexual act—was absent as an animating force within the harem, but it was only one of several forces, and for most of the period examined here, one of relatively little importance."[55] This was also underlined by Beverly Mack: "I have lived long enough in the Kano harem to know that it is all about sons, sons, sons, not sex, sex, sex. One needs a big offspring pool from which the kingmakers choose if the kingship is to be kept in the family."[56]

The harem was also a place where female family members lived, as well as older women, servants, and children. Many widows connected to the royal family moved back into the harem. The emir of Kano complained that he was feeding over one hundred old women, many of them not from his family, but rather women offered shelter in the harem.[57] In the 1990s, the Kano palace still housed about twelve hundred persons, which included only three wives and twenty-five actual and former concubines.[58] Findly suggests that the Mughal harem included "stray women of all classes brought in under a variety of circumstances for stays of indeterminate length."[59]

Mernissi sees the harem as a place where women resist and seek to transcend their powerlessness.[60] Scheherazade, who used her storyteller's art to defuse a bloody-minded sultan, is her prime example. She also argues against the whole image of what is erotic. The sex act, she writes, is most satisfying when set in elaborate interaction. For Mernissi, the sexual game is an intellectual game and the mind is as important as the body, perhaps more so. Her harem women are storytellers, poets, philosophers, chess players, women of art and learning. Other literature supports these notions. The harem was a place of relaxation. One sultan enjoyed playing chess with the witty elderly woman who had been his wet nurse. Findly also talks about the intellectual and artistic activities of harem women.[61]

The harem was also a major political arena. It was where the dynasty reproduced itself and trained its young. The Ottoman Empire was unusual in its total reliance on slaves, though African states tended to fill their harems with women taken in slave raids and also used male slaves as soldiers and officials. In the first centuries of Ottoman expansion, soon after Mehmet II's troops seized Constantinople, the Ottomans felt that there were no ruling houses they wanted to marry with. Their daughters were thenceforth married to slave officials, as it were, incorporating these officials into the imperial family as sons-in-law. Also, from the middle of the fifteenth century, only slave women were brought into the harem. Because enslavement of Muslims was prohibited by Islamic law, most concubines did not even speak Turkish when they entered the harem; however, the abler ones proved quick learners. Policy was that the sultans did not marry. Of course, one advantage of slave women was that they had no family ties outside the royal palace.

It was also Ottoman policy that a concubine ceased to be a sexual partner once she bore the sultan a son. At this point, her future was tied to that of her son. Her role shifted from the sultan's lover to that of teacher and advisor of a potential heir. She trained her son and promoted his career. Up into the seventeenth century, young princes were sent into the provinces as governors, usually in their adolescence. The prince was accompanied by his mother, who managed his household, and by a tutor appointed by his father. The tutor's job was difficult. The sultan expected him to prevent the son from threatening his father's power, but if the young man was successful, the tutor often rose to high office. The mother's task was simple. The single-son policy meant that she did not have divided loyalties. Many princes had quite substantial households, replicating on a small scale imperial households. One prince in 1513 had a harem of seventeen, including two laundry women. Sixty years later, another prince went out with a party of two thousand. The one problem with this was that some princes became too powerful. For centuries, the only way a sultan could deal with his brothers was to have them all murdered. When this policy was rejected, it became necessary to keep all the princes at home.

The mother's role remained the same. The mother who became a valide sultan thus had years of political experience before she ascended to that office. Older women were also freer in their movements because they were postmenopausal and no longer capable of conceiving a child. In general, they were the only women who could deal with men outside the harem, though in the Ottoman harem, they often did so veiled.[62] The powerful women in a harem were politically active in many ways. They generally had the ruler's ear, but they also had access to information. They acted and received information through manumitted slaves, through their princess daughters, and through in-laws—all categories of women who had access to the harem. This could be a deadly game. Those who killed or injured their rivals often lost out in the process, but if a woman planted stories that a son was plotting revolt, it could cost that son his life. Suleyman the Magnificent executed two sons and three sons-in-law during the course of his forty-six-year reign.[63] In both the Ottoman and the Mughal empires, many of the senior women had great wealth and engaged in Muslim forms of public charity, building mosques, creating gardens, and freeing slaves. The powerful Mughal women had properties and trade interests, for which they had managers.[64]

A contrast to Ottoman policy was that of Mongkut, the king much maligned by the writings of Anna Leonowens and the movie Anna and the King of Siam. Leonowens depicted him as capricious, brutal, and autocratic, organizing her book The Romance of the Harem (1873) around a series of totally fictional tales of women who were brutally tortured and killed for seeking love affairs.[65] In fact, Mongkut gave his wives and con-

cubines the option of leaving the palace, and twelve of them accepted
the offer. One married a humble boatman. Mongkut had been a celibate
Buddhist priest for twenty-six years before becoming king. He had about
a hundred wives and concubines, of whom thirty-five produced eighty-
two children in the sixteen years he reigned. He was not a brutal man
and never burned anyone at the stake.[66]

THE FAVORITE

If harem history has anything to say about male sexuality, the most interesting institution is the royal favorite. In a situation where he had a choice
of beautiful women eager to please him, the royal master often fell in
love and had a favorite. These favorites were often not the most beautiful of the harem's inmates, but were generally interesting and intelligent
women. The emir of Kano told Beverley Mack that he did not want a
harem, but his mother reminded him of the obligations that attended his
office. I then asked her if he had a favorite. She responded that such things
were not openly discussed, but his relationship with his third wife was
clearly loving and respectful.[67] One powerful royal favorite was Nur Jehan,
wife of the seventeenth-century Mughal emperor Jehangir.[68] A woman in
her mid-thirties with a daughter, she was the widow of a Turkish soldier
who had served the Mughals. She was not a slave, but was first taken into
the imperial harem as a maidservant. In 1611 she met Jehangir and cap-
tivated him. Within months they were married. Almost from the first,
she took over the running of the government, installing her father as
grand vizier and other relatives in key positions. With Jehangir spending
much of his time with alcohol and opium, she managed the finances of
the empire, minted coins, traded with foreign merchants, and was a patron of the arts. She had no children with Jehangir, and when he died in
1627, she was unable to hold on to power. Her image in Indian history is
one of a patron of the arts, a politically skilled ruler, and a powerful in-
tellect. Her influence was all the more striking in that the sex life of most
women in the Mughal harem was finished by age thirty.[69]

If Nur Jehan was able to shape Indian history because of her husband's
weakness, Hurrem, or as she was known to Europeans, Roxalena, capti-
vated Suleyman the Magnificent (r. 1520–66), a forceful sultan, who extended the Ottoman Empire to its greatest size. Suleyman inherited the
throne at age twenty-six.[70] As a young prince, Suleyman was known as a
vigorous young man with a taste for the pleasures of the harem. About
the time he ascended the throne, he met Hurrem, the daughter of a

Ruthenian priest, who had been captured by Tatar raiders. She bore him a son in 1521 and then, in violation of Ottoman custom, they had three more children over the next three years. In 1524, Suleyman violated another Ottoman custom by marrying her and then marrying off many of the eligible concubines in his harem. Hurrem did not accompany any of her sons to their provincial governorships and remained Suleyman's companion until her death in 1558. The Venetian ambassador described her as "young but not beautiful." Her letters to Suleyman, who was often on tour, are love letters, full of family information, but also with political information and advice. In her early years, they were clearly written by a harem scribe, but with time her mastery of Turkish enabled her to write directly.

Suleyman's immediate successors also had favorites as well as close relationships with their mothers. The next period of Ottoman history is often known as the sultanate of the women. Selim II (r. 1566–74), Suleyman's son, also had a favorite, a Venetian named Nurbanu. He had four children with her, though only one son, and seems to have married her. Selim's son, Murad III (r. 1574–95), was monogamous as a prince, and while he eventually had numerous concubines and forty-seven children, he relied heavily on his mother, Nurbanu, and his favorite concubine, Safiye. Ahmed I (r. 1603–17) also had a favorite, a Greek woman named Kossem, who seems to have borne all his children. Each of Hurrem's successors outlived their royal mates and played a crucial role as valide. Widowed young, Kossem dominated the palace for a turbulent half-century, marked by short reigns, several erratic sultans, and the interference of eunuchs and Janissaries. There were, to be sure, often conflicts between the valide and various imperial favorites. When Kossem's son Ibrahim was removed for mental incompetence, the only candidate was her seven-year-old grandson, Mehmed. Since his mother, Turhan, was only twenty-five, a faction of the administration tried to keep Kossem as valide, but she was killed in a palace coup and Turhan became regent.[71]

Regencies often enabled women who had risen within the harem to exercise power. The most powerful such woman in recent centuries was Cixi (Tz'u-hsi in the old orthography), empress dowager of China. Born to a good Manchu family that had provided a number of mid-level officials in preceding generations, she entered the harem in 1852 as a lowly consort of the sixth rank. Even after producing an heir in 1856, she was only promoted to the third rank. It is not clear that she was a favorite, but the birth of a son gave her the opportunity she needed. In 1861, when the reigning emperor died, her five-year-old son inherited the throne and she became, along with his wife, the empress dowager. There was a regency council of eight generals and senior councillors, but all edicts were to be endorsed by the two empresses. Cixi, the prince's mother, had the support of the chief eunuch and a key general with whom she had a love affair. In a coup, she seized power and eliminated the regency council.[72] When her son, the Tongzhi emperor, died in 1874, soon after achieving his majority, she installed her nephew, once again acting as regent, this time until 1887.[73] In 1898, after a period of reform, which she and many of the more conservative bureaucrats opposed, she seized power again, imprisoned the emperor, and controlled China until her death in 1908.[74] There is a long tradition of powerful women in Chinese history, in part because a preference for father-son succession often led to young emperors. The Northern Sung dynasty lasted 166 years, of which twenty-five were under female regents. There were five empress dowagers who governed.[75]

There are numerous other examples of close relationships to favorites. Thus, Mack has written of Hajiya Ma'daki, the daughter of the emir of Kano and a slave concubine, who was married to the emir of Katsina. From an early date, her husband took her with him on trips through the countryside and then to England and to Mecca. Clearly someone the emir relied on, she played a key role in the founding and running of a girls' school.[76] Even where a royal master had children by numerous women, there was often a favorite. Mongkut had children by thirty-five women, but he had ten of them with Thiang and presumably had a close relationship with her.[77]

For most harem women, it was a barren existence. The women were physically confined, and almost all were denied the satisfaction of a loving relationship. In the larger harems, most women never bore children. For example, two-thirds of Mongkut's wives and concubines bore no children. The percentage would have been much larger in the harems of the Ottoman or Mughal emperors. Many harem women never had sexual relations. Some courts like those of Zande, Dahomey, Kano, or China either gave surplus women to men who served the state or, after a period of service, released them to marry. Harem women spent their lives in a confined world of women. The situation often produced suspicion of affairs, sometimes with eunuchs, sometimes with men who entered the harem clandestinely, sometimes with royal offspring.[78] As in Norodom's Cambodia, punishments were often severe. For example, a woman in the Mughal harem who was seen kissing a eunuch was buried up to her armpits, where the hot sun could kill her slowly. And when their royal master died, the women often lost what little privilege they had. In the

Ottoman Empire, wives of a deceased sultan were sent to the Old Palace, also known as the Palace of the Unwanted Ones, or the House of Tears.

In most, perhaps all, premodern states wealth extracted from peasants and workers permitted a small number of people to live in tremendous luxury. Where they existed, harems were a major part of that luxury. They involved the expenditure of large amounts of money on a very private and secluded world. When I undertook this chapter, it was because I found the harem a supremely irrational institution. It lay at the heart of much of the slave trade into the Arabic and Turkish core lands of Islam, which forbade the enslavement of Muslims. That prohibition was violated from time to time, but it had the effect of pushing the demand for slaves to peripheral parts of the Muslim world. Slaves in these areas were also rarely used as agricultural labor. The dominance of women in the Middle Eastern trade suggests that women for the harems, not only of rulers but also of other members of political and commercial elites, were the most important part of the trade that shaped Arabic and Turkish economic relationships with both Africa and eastern Europe. This contrasted sharply with the American or the Indian Ocean trade, which focused on labor.

When I have articulated skepticism about the value of the harem, friends have often said that it was about prestige. This argument has been made by Gerda Lerner: "The ready availability of captive women for private sexual use and the need of kings and chiefs, frequently themselves usurpers of authority, to establish legitimacy by displaying their wealth in the form of servants and concubines led to the establishment of harems."[79] If that were so, then why did they confine their harems behind walls? Why did most rulers not show off their women? Is it about sex? Of course, it is about sex. Women were acquired for their beauty and were trained to make love. They used their sexuality and their eroticism to attract, but whatever alpha male instinct pushed some royal males conflicted with a desire for a stable continuing relationship. We do not know much about the details of the sex lives of various ruling dynasties because for the most part, it was not something that was talked about. In the Chinese Forbidden City, the concubine chosen for the emperor's bed was brought to him secretly—on the back of a eunuch lest her feet get dirty. Among the Ottomans, a eunuch also quietly ushered the woman selected to the ruler's bed. It is clear that sex was important, but Mernissi, Peirce, and Mack are certainly right that it was not the greatest concern of the harem.

The harem met several basic needs. First, it was a place where the dynasty reproduced itself. It did not need hundreds of women. It did, however, need to guarantee heirs. The women the harem also produced, both the daughters and the unwanted concubines, were useful in creating ties to men who served the dynasty. Second, it was often the place where princes were trained to rule. Sometimes, as with the weak sybarites of late-Qing China, they learned the wrong things, but a major function was educating potential rulers. Mongkut's involvement in the education of his children produced a very able successor, Chulalongkorn, revered by many as the greatest Thai ruler, and a number of children who participated in the modernization of the Thai state. In addition, the harems of the Ottomans, the Mughals, and the Qing produced politically sophisticated women capable of guiding their sons and, in some cases, of controlling them. The large number of sons meant that most dynasties had to cope with controlling ambitious sons. By contrast, European ruling dynasties, constrained by official monogamy and primogeniture, often had to cope with either the absence of heirs or the problem of an idiot king. Third, the harem was where the ruler relaxed. Depending on his tastes or his mood, that could involve music, dance, sex, a game of chess, or just good conversation. Finally, because the harem involved many powerful people, it was a central political institution. Power is lonely—everywhere and all the time. The ruler needs people he can talk to and can trust. Rulers are generally surrounded by self-interested men. Even those groups created to be loyal—slave soldiers, officials, and eunuchs—sometimes act independently, often when their interests are threatened or when the ruler is acting irrationally. And his sons sometimes get impatient for a crack at his throne. The ruler can trust two women, his mother and his wife or favorite. They become in many states a pillar of the regime, certainly people he consulted.

Why then do harems sometimes get so large? I think there were two processes at play here. First, the top people at court generally had large entourages. What ruler would not offer his mother or his favorite the same privileges available to senior males? If Anna Leonowens is to be believed, a newly acquired concubine who caught the king's eye had the services of her own slaves. And with a large and rather privileged assemblage, there were important services to provide. They had to be fed, clothed, and bathed. Harems in general had large infrastructures. Second, there was, I think, often a process that was hard to control. Families that wanted to curry favor offered the ruler a daughter. Or if the harem was limited to slaves, officials that wanted to curry favor offered him a slave girl. Finally, the alpha male instinct was not always absent. A conqueror, for example, often took control of and distributed the harem of the defeated. How often was it tempting to keep the prettiest or the most aristocratic for himself? That was not, however, what most shaped the administration of the harem. Furthermore, a significant number of rulers chose to age together with a woman who provided sex, offspring, and companionship.

NOTES

1. Resident to Governor General, 12 December 1881, Archives Nationales, Section Outre-Mer, Fond des Amiraux, no. 142, 10169.

2. Resident to Governor General, 18 March 1880, 20 May 1882, Archives Nationales, Section Outre-Mer, Fond des Amiraux, 10169.

3. On that antiquity, see Leila Ahmed, *Women and Gender in Islam* (New Haven: Yale University Press, 1992), ch. 1. See also Gerda Lerner, *The Creation of Patriarchy* (New York: Oxford University Press, 1986).

4. Ellison Banks Findly, *Nur Jahan, Empress of Mughal India* (New York: Oxford University Press, 1993), 95. One Sassanian king is reputed to have had a harem of twelve thousand women. Ahmed, *Women and Gender*, 14.

5. Evelyn Rawski, *The Last Emperors: A Social History of Qing Imperial Institutions* (Berkeley: University of California Press, 1998), 131.

6. Ibid., 141.

7. Heidi Nast, "The Impact of British Imperialism on the Landscape of Female Slavery in the Kano Palace, Northern Nigeria," *Africa* 64 (1994): 34–73; Nast, "Engendering 'Space': State Formation and the Restructuring of the Kano Palace Following the Islamic Holy War in Northern Nigeria, 1807–1903," *Historical Geography* 23 (1993): 62–75; Nast, "Islam, Gender, and Slavery in West Africa circa 1500: A Spatial Archeology of the Kano Palace, Northern Nigeria," *Annals of the American Association of Geographers* 86 (1996): 44–77.

8. Leslie Peirce, *The Imperial Harem: Women and Sovereignty in the Ottoman Empire* (Oxford: Oxford University Press, 1993); Barnette Miller, *Behind the Sublime Porte: The Grand Seraglio of Stambul* (New Haven: Yale University Press, 1931); Norman Penzer, *The Harem* (London: Harrap, 1936).

9. Rawski, *Last Emperors*, 127. Marina Warner puts her in the fifth rank, but she started out low in the hierarchy. Warner, *The Dragon Empress: Life and Times of Tz'u-hsi, 1836–1908, Empress Dowager of China* (London: Weidenfeld and Nicolson, 1972).

10. Rawski, *Last Emperors*, 131–34.

11. Peirce, *Imperial Harem*, 4. See also Beverley Mack, "Harem," in *Macmillan Encyclopedia of World Slavery*, ed. Paul Finkelman and Joseph Miller, 2 vols. (New York: Simon and Schuster Macmillan, 1998), 1:374–76.

12. Fatima Mernissi, *Scheherazade Goes West: Different Cultures, Different Harems* (New York: Washington Square, 2001), 1.

13. On the role of slaves, both male and female, in the Ottoman state, see Ehud Toledano, "Ottoman Concepts of Slavery in the Period of Reform, 1830s–1880s," in *Breaking the Chains: Slavery, Bondage, and Emancipation in Modern Africa and Asia,*

ed. Martin Klein (Madison: University of Wisconsin Press, 1993); Ehud Toledano, *Slavery and Abolition in the Ottoman Middle East* (Seattle: University of Washington Press, 1998), esp. ch. 1. For a different royal slave system, see Sean Stilwell, *Paradoxes of Power: The Kano "Mamluks" and Male Royal Slavery in the Sokoto Caliphate, 1804–1903* (Portsmouth, NH: Heinemann, 2004).

14. Anna Leonowens, *Siamese Harem Life* (1873; New York: E. P. Dutton, 1953); Leonowens, *The English Governess at the Siamese Court* (London: Trubner and Co., 1870).

15. Beverly Mack, "Royal Wives in Kano," in *Hausa Women in the Twentieth Century*, ed. Catherine Coles and Beverly Mack (Madison: University of Wisconsin Press, 1991), 109–29; M. G. Smith, *The Affairs of Daura* (Berkeley: University of California Press, 1978); Nast, "Impact of British Imperialism," 44–45.

16. E. E. Evans-Pritchard, *The Azande: History and Political Institutions* (Oxford: Clarendon, 1971), 177–78; C. R. Lagae, *Les Azande ou Niam-Niam: l'organisation zande, croyances religieuses et magique, coutumes familiales* (Brussels: Vromant, 1926); Jan Czekanowski, *Research in the Nile-Congo Region*, trans. Human Relations Area Files (Leipzig: Klinkhardt and Biermann, 1924).

17. Robert Rattray, *Ashanti Law and Constitution* (Oxford: Clarendon, 1929). See also Eva Meyerowitz, *The Early History of the Akan States of Ghana* (London: Red Candle, 1974), 281.

18. Edna Bay, *Wives of the Leopard: Gender, Politics, and Culture in the Kingdom of Dahomey* (Charlottesville: University of Virginia Press, 1998), 67–69.

19. K. S. Lal, "The Mughal Harem," *Journal of Indian History* 53 (1975): 415–30.

20. Nast, "Impact of British Imperialism," 44–45.

21. Rawski, *Last Emperors*, 133.

22. Alev Lytle Croutier, *Harem: The World Behind the Veil* (New York: Abbeville, 1989), 121–23.

23. Findly, *Nur Jahan*, 105–6.

24. Croutier, *Harem*.

25. Leonowens, *Siamese Harem Life*, ch. 22.

26. Mack, "Royal Wives," 115.

27. Nast, "Engendering 'Space.'"

28. See especially Lady Mary Montagu, *The Letters and Works of Lady Mary Wortley Montagu* (1794; New York: AMS, 1970). But the European fascination with the Ottoman harem is an old one. See the seventeenth-century account of Ottaviano Bon (1552–1623), *The Sultan's Seraglio: An Intimate Portrait of Life at the Ottoman Court* [1650], trans. John Withers, introduced and annotated by Godfrey Goodwin (London: Saqi Books, 1996). B. Miller, *Sublime Porte*, ch. 1, reviews the success of select European men in getting a very limited access.

29. Croutier, *Harem*, preface. Croutier's grandmother was the daughter of a gun maker who was married to a scholar friend of her father at age fourteen. When her husband died, she was taken into the harem of his brother, where she spent most of the rest of her life. See also Leila Hanoum, *Souvenirs de Leila Hanoum sur le harem impérial au XIXe siècle* (Paris: Calmann-Lévy, 1925); Yeshim Ternar, *The Book and the Veil: Escape from an Istanbul Harem* (Montreal: Véhicule, 1994).

30. See for example, Croutier, *Harem*; Melek Hanum, *Thirty Years in the Harem* (London: Chapman and Hall, 1872); Huda Shaʻrawi, *Harem Years: The Memoirs of an Egyptian Feminist (1879–1924)* (London: Virago, 1986); Fatima Mernissi, *Dreams of Trespass: Tales of a Harem Girlhood* (New York: Addison-Wesley, 1994); Mary Smith, *Baba of Karo: A Woman of the Muslim Hausa* (London: Faber and Faber, 1954); Sarah Mirza and Margaret Strobel, eds. and trans., *Three Swahili Women: Life Histories from Mombasa, Kenya* (Bloomington: Indiana University Press, 1989). See also Maria Jaschok, *Concubines and Maidservants: A Social History* (London: Zed, 1988).

31. On Bengal, see Indrani Chatterjee, *Gender, Slavery, and Law in Colonial India* (New Delhi: Oxford University Press, 1999), 57–73.

32. Rawski, *Last Emperors*, 137.

33. Findly, *Nur Jahan*, ch. 5. See Findly also for frequent references to the role of Marymuzzamani, the mother of Jehangir.

34. Bay, *Daughters of the Leopard*, 71–80.

35. Leonowens, *Siamese Harem Life*, 90.

36. W. G. Bristowe, *Louis and the King of Siam* (London: Chatto and Windus, 1976), 13.

37. Rawski, *Last Emperors*, 166–71.

38. Czekanowski, *Nile-Congo*, 55; C. G. Seligman, "The Azande," in *Pagan Tribes of the Nilotic Sudan*, by C. G. Seligman and Brenda Z. Seligman (London: George Routledge and Sons, 1932).

39. Nast, "Impact of British Imperialism," 37–42; "Engendering 'Space,'" 65–68.

40. Chatterjee, *Gender, Slavery, and Law*, 65–66.

41. Bon, *Sultan's Seraglio*, 47.

42. Chatterjee, *Gender, Slavery, and Law*, 102.

43. Ibid., 66–68.

44. See also Edward Behr, *The Last Emperor* (London: Macdonald, 1987).

45. James Fernandez, "The Shaka Complex," *Transition* 29 (1967), 10–14.

46. Rawski, *Last Emperors*, 117–20.

47. Mack, "Royal Wives," 121.

48. Sean Stilwell, "'Aman' and 'Asiri': Royal Slave Culture and the Colonial Regime in Kano, 1903–1926," in *Slavery and Colonial Rule in Africa*, ed. Suzanne Miers and Martin Klein (London: Frank Cass, 1999); Stilwell, *Paradoxes of Power*.

49. Chatterjee, *Gender, Slavery, and Law*, 59–65.

50. Toledano, *Slavery and Abolition*, 28–32. For a good critique of my earlier reticence to deal with sexuality and female slavery, see Paul Lovejoy, "Concubinage in the Sokoto Caliphate," *Slavery and Abolition* 11, no. 2 (1990): 159–89.

51. But see also Leonowens, *English Governess; Siamese Harem Life*.

52. See, for example, Billie Melman, *Women's Orients: English Women and the Middle East 1718–1918: Sexuality, Religion and Work* (London: Macmillan, 1992), chs. 1–5.

53. Croutier, *Harem*.

54. Mernissi, *Scheherazade*, 8. Some of her ideas are also presented in Fatima Mernissi, *Êtes-vous vacciné contre le "harem"? Texte-test pour les messieurs qui adores les dames* (Casablanca: Editions Le Fennec, 1998).

55. Peirce, *Imperial Harem*, 3.

56. Mack, pers. comm. upon reading an earlier version of this chapter.

57. Mack, "Royal Wives," 116.

58. Nast, "Islam, Gender," 71.

59. Findly, *Nur Jahan*, 93.

60. Mernissi, *Scheherazade*.

61. See also Najma Khan Majlis, "Women Painters during the Time of the Emperor Jahangir (1605–1627 A.D.)," *Journal of the Asiatic Society of Bangladesh* 31, no. 2 (1986): 51–55.

62. In 1331, Ibn Battuta was received by the wife of the sultan, the sultan himself being on a military campaign. There is little evidence of such activity later. B. Miller, *Sublime Porte*, 28.

63. Peirce, *Imperial Harem*.

64. Findly, *Nur Jahan*, 96.

65. Leonowens's inaccuracies are summed up briefly in Bristowe, *Louis and the King*, ch. 2, "Anna Unveiled," and in Abbot Low Moffat, *Mongkut, the King of Siam* (Ithaca: Cornell University Press, 1961), appendix 4, "Anna as a Historian." *The Romance of the Harem* was reissued as *Siamese Harem Life*.

66. Bristowe, *Louis and the King*, 13. For a discussion of Thiang and of Wad, a wife of Mongkut, who supervised the palace under his successor, Chulalongkorn, see Lysa Hong, "Of Consorts and Harlots in Thai Popular History," *Journal of Asian Studies* 57 (1998): 333–53.

67. Beverly Mack, pers. comm.

68. Findly, *Nur Jehan*.

69. Ibid., 101.

70. Peirce, *Imperial Harem*, 58–65; Croutier, *Harem*, 113–18.

71. Findly, *Nur Jahan*, 144.

72. Rawski, *Last Emperors*, 127, 136–37; Frederic Wakeman Jr., *The Fall of Imperial China* (New York: Free Press, 1975), 179–81.

73. Wakeman, *Fall of Imperial China*, 187–88.

74. Ibid., 214–16.

75. Priscilla Ching Chung, "Power and Prestige: Palace Women in the Northern Sung (960–1126)," in *Women in China: Current Directions in Historical Scholarship*, ed. Richard Guisso and Stanley Johannesen (Lewiston, NY: Philo, 1981), 99.

76. Beverley Mack, "Hajiya Ma'daki: A Royal Hausa Woman," in *Life Histories of African Women*, ed. Patricia Romero (Atlantic Highlands, NJ: Ashfield, 1988).

77. Hong, "Consorts and Harlots," 337–39.

78. Findly, *Nur Jahan*, 99–104.

79. Lerner, *Creation of Patriarchy*, 133.

3

THE LAW OF THE (WHITE) FATHER

Psychoanalysis, "Paternalism," and the
Historiography of Cape Slave Women

SHARIFA AHJUM

Historically, many processes of representation[1] have rendered slaves as property and deprived them of their capacity to signify as human. I link the Lacanian psychoanalytic with slavery, as depicted in literature on the Cape Colony of Southern Africa, to suggest how the mechanics of representation and signification construct and buttress relations of power in this context. My theoretical framework, therefore, gestures at the interrelation of the psychic, the social, and the economic as it is delineated within the psychic operations of representation and signification.

This chapter began with a query about the curious similarity, and yet difference, between the slaveholding, paternalist discourse of "family" at the Cape of Good Hope and its theoretical oedipal counterpart: that is, in their masculinist structurations of power. The slave owner's infantilization of slaves there seemed to mirror, as well as to unsettle, the dynamic of power and desire that emerges from the core oedipal relation of son to desired mother and son to feared father. I suggest that the selective law of uterine descent for slaves, or the slave matronymic,[2] as I shall refer to it, foregrounds the ambiguities through which a paternalist discourse of power operates, while also emphasizing the limitations of a gendered psychoanalytic paradigm. This focus on the matronymic demonstrates slave women's central role in these operations of power,[3] thereby challenging the conventional notion that the ideology of power on which slavery rests is essentially defined by the emasculation of slave men, or what is termed castration in a psychoanalytic idiom, vis-à-vis an autonomous slaveholding masculinity. When I encountered historiographical debates about

Cape slave "paternalism,"[4] my interest was piqued by the (dis)connections between the slave matronymic designation and the infantilization of slave women in the paternalist rhetoric of Cape slave owners.[5] Also, I wondered what and how the slave matronymic would signify within an oedipalized and therefore masculinist trajectory of power and desire. The matronymic exception to the normative patronymic indicates the ideological function of paternalist discourse: it foregrounds the latter's status as discourse. This positioning of the slave mother is 'fictional', as it produces the marginalization of slaves from the dominant patronym, or the Name of the Father, in a Lacanian idiom. It therefore underlines the ideological workings of a supposedly universal psychoanalytical narrative of gender.

POWER, REPRESENTATION, AND THE OEDIPAL

In the Lacanian reframing of Freud, the Name and the Law of the Father describe the patriarchal logic by which gender differentiation is organized. This Lacanian rereading of the oedipal positions the phallus as the master signifier of the Father's Law, in relation to which masculine and feminine positions are assumed. The phallus, as the embodiment of power that is neither simply anatomical nor simply metaphorical, governs the exchange of desire by which one becomes a speaking subject, by which one becomes intelligible within representation. By *exchange*, I mean that the subject acquires the linguistic designation of 'I', a self, in exchange for renunciation of the incestuous desire for the mother described in the Oedipal.

In the Lacanian psychoanalytic register to which I refer, the oedipal complex describes the resolution of the male child's incestuous desire for the female parent, which is the condition for intelligibility in the Symbolic, the domain of language and signification.[6] The male child relinquishes his desire for the mother under the fear of castration, which comes with his recognition of her own 'castrated' condition. In exchange he receives the Name of the Father. This process of subjectification,[7] very simply, depicts the transition that directs the male child away from the mother as the desired object, or the (m)other. In the Symbolic, the realm of sociality, the phallus functions as a substitute for this loss of the maternal object; and it is in this sense that the desire for the mother is transformed into the linguistic, social operation of desire that is governed by the phallus, as the representative of the Father's Law. The irretrievable loss of the (m)other is the enabling condition for both signification of others and *subjectification* of self: the dynamic of both is structured by the desiring mechanism. Desire mediates the subject to itself through the lack initiated by the loss of the maternal object, the (m)other. Difference, in this schema, becomes an effect of the desire for the other: the metonymic displacement of one object for another in an attempt to cover up the constitutive lack. The phallus, as the master signifier, the term by which the exchange of meaning is installed, is the vehicle by which this difference is encoded, and from which it derives its value. How one signifies as a subject is determined by how one is encoded by desire. The phallus, thus, regulates the patriarchal circulation of desire in which social relations are ordered by the Proper name. The oedipal injunction against incest institutes a domain of representation and language that is grounded on the debased positioning of the feminine, through the Law and the Name of the Father.

Fundamentally, meaning operates through a phallus-castration binary in which anatomical difference determines how one is orientated toward the phallus. Masculinity is defined by its 'having' the phallus, due to the illusory association of the physical penis with the metonymic phallus, while femininity, as a consequence of its condition of 'castration', is resigned to 'being' the phallus.[8] That is, while a woman cannot 'have' the phallus, she mediates it or reflects it to a man. In this sense femininity is defined by its negative relation to masculinity: women come into gendered being only as mirrors for male self-recognition. Masculine autonomy (which is itself an illusion) is predicated on the negated status of femininity while femininity in such a schema cannot be represented autonomously: it exists only as an Other to the masculine self. The relation between the masculine and the feminine is therefore regulated by their differentiated positioning vis-à-vis the desire for the phallus. Both men and women desire the phallus, although in different ways. As Grosz writes, "it is insofar as he *has* the phallus that the man is the object of the woman's desire; and it is insofar as she *is* the phallus that a woman is a man's object of desire."[9] This exchange or circuitry of desire thus describes the subject's entry into the domain of language and representation via sexually differentiated relations to the phallus.

The matronymic designation of slavery suggests implicit and unacknowledged racialized coordinates that deflect this Lacanian heterodynamic of subjectification.[10] This dynamic shows how the matronymic exception to the general rule of patrimony in the context of slavery regulates the miscegenation taboo. It regulates the well-known and oft-repeated hierarchy of negative difference, in which white femininity and slave men are both Othered in relation to an autonomous white masculinity.[11] The matronymic, thus, excludes slave women from this set of relations by its veiling of their relation to white masculinity. Slave women's remaining sole relation to slave men in this schema of difference therefore makes them an Other's Other. It is white femininity's specific positioning as phallic object that mediates relations between autonomous and white masculinities: that is between 'sons' and 'fathers'. Theoretically slave men have the anatomical potentiality to partake in this desiring exchange. Slave women, bluntly put, do not have a relation to the phallus, either in its theoretical capacity that slave men may signify in terms of their anatomy or in the mediating role ascribed to white femininity. The phallic rationale for self-representation therefore precludes any parallel psychical-social relation between white femininity and slave women. In other words, an autonomous white masculinity, whose 'possession' of the phallus corresponds to its positioning at the apex of colonial hierarchies of power and difference, is predicated on the 'exchange' of white women among white men as mothers and wives, while slave women and men function, in different ways, solely as use value. That is, excluded from the humanizing imperative of desire, slaves exist in a different order of being: that of dehumanized property, as opposed to a gendered order of masculine mobility vis-à-vis a passive femininity installed by the patronymic Proper name.

The racialized pattern of kinship that results from the Lacanian dynamic thus excluded slaves from any relation of kin and the usual laws of the patronymic Proper name that govern it. As an inversion of the normative, humanizing process of gendering, the matronymic 'rule' institutes the slaves' condition of illegitimacy vis-à-vis the Proper name, the defining or organizing Name of the Father, and in the realm of representation thus produces their condition of signification as property. The impotence of the slave father, whose legal and discursive, if not always literal, effacement produces an absence of the patrilineal symbolic for the slave that stands in sharp contrast to the normative primacy of the Father's Law.[12]

The matronymic rule, then, suggests slave women's pivotal inscription in the organization and proliferation of colonial power. Slave women are positioned as the medium by which the slave's mark of property, as opposed to the interpellative mark of gender required for subjectivity, is inaugurated and endures.[13] Elision of the patronym along with fictional naming of the slave mother attests to a lesser, negative operation of intelligibility as human than that enshrined in the standard gendered psychoanalytic paradigm. This naming is fictional and strategic because of its function and status as ideology. In other words, the process by which gender is conflated with humanness, the hegemony of whiteness as humanness, is enabled by the marginalization of colonized, enslaved Others. In sum, the slave matronymic constitutes the limit of representation, or the limit of what is able to be represented within the gendered psychoanalytic paradigm. It institutes the symbolic processes by which slaves are made representationally mute or, in Orlando Patterson's sociological parlance, are rendered "socially dead."[14]

My primary object in reading the paternalist discourse from the Cape against or within the Lacanian psychoanalytic paradigm is to rethink the terms of the debate about paternalism in Cape slave historiography. This debate has turned on the question of the actual extent of a paternalist ethos at the Cape: on whether it is possible to characterize Cape slave owners properly as paternalist. I argue the discrepancy between slave women's representational erasure via the matronymic and their hypersexual reinscription in colonial discourse gestures toward a way of refiguring this question. It is not simply that the reality of slave women's sexual exploitation by their owners disproves the efficacy of the paternalist ideology, in its occlusion of them. This paternalist discourse is itself elaborated in the apparent discontinuity between the slave matronymic designation of exclusion and the simultaneous hypersexual embodiment of slave women as property.

By this I mean that a normative, autonomous (free, white) masculinity is defined by the utter negation of slave women. The slave matronymic, its specific exclusion of slave women from the desiring circuit underpins the colonial, masculine imperative of power, subjectivity, and domination. My argument here is fundamentally informed by the premise that identities at the Cape were secured hierarchically and relationally. The disavowed relation between white masculinity, representing the pinnacle of colonial power, and slave women, positioned at its base, psychically structured this colonial order. Secondarily, centering on the slave matronymic necessarily emphasizes the gendered condition of intelligibility in the Lacanian Symbolic.

While this theoretical insight may seem marginal to the primary focus of this paper on specific circumstances at the Cape, it is crucially entwined with the question of the slave matronym. The slave matronymic implies that slaves are not privy to the gendering process required for intelligibility within the Symbolic domain of representation and language. Within a Lacanian schema of representation, exclusion from the Symbolic realm of sociality results in psychosis. The condition of social death, within this logic, is impossible, untenable. The question addressed here is, therefore, if the Law of the Father represents an overarching position from which there is no escape—in the sense that it is the only means by which one becomes an intelligible subject—what does one make of the colonial exclusion of slaves from the humanizing imperative of desire? The matronymic deviation from the Father's Law suggests another, lesser order of existence in which slaves are constituted as being outside representation. Slaves, thus, come into the sphere of representation only as bodies. Their bodily visibility is a function of slaves' status as property, and hence it results from the matronymic exclusion. Since gender is a precondition for this process of becoming intelligible within representation, slaves' dehumanization stems from their exclusion from the dominant gendered paradigm, signaled by the matronymic exception.

SOCIAL DEATH:
GENDER AND THE UNMAKING OF THE HUMAN/SUBJECT

Given that the relation to the phallus is depicted as the inescapable route to socialization in the Symbolic, feminist theorists have long used this rationale to engage with the debased positioning of the feminine.[15] By this dynamic the girl-child's problematic positioning within the heteronormative, patriarchal dictates of the Oedipal produces an ambiguous and fraught relation to the Maternal. The girl-child is required to forgo her desire for the mother in order to identify with the mother's condition of castration and take up her feminized position as 'being' the phallus. Feminist theorists have generally underscored the lack of an autonomous feminine identity.[16]

However, these accounts have largely failed to engage with the unacknowledged manner in which gender is constructed as a cultural normative. Brian Carr develops this line of enquiry by addressing the links between "degendering" and "subalternity," and by bringing the racialized nonsubject to bear on the ahistoricity of the psychoanalytic narrative of gender.[17] He asks, "If psychoanalytic narratives of subjectivity provide a useful model for understanding the formation of the human subject, do they not also harbor a tale of that subject's de-formation? Do they not, that is, explain something of the mechanics of a subject's symbolic designification?"[18]

In his analysis Carr frames the representational economy of the film *Blade Runner* within the history of slavery in the United States, suggesting that discourses of race appear as the underside of the Lacanian het-

erosexual injunction "to desire."[19] He suggests that the process of gendering by which the category of human is constituted is underpinned by a
concomitant, but implicit and unacknowledged, process of dehumanization. The process by which one is able to signify as human, is the same by
which slaves are dehumanized—thus the process of this "desymboliza-
tion" is the underside of subjectification. He suggests, therefore, that the
human-seeming but emotionless "replicant" Rachel gains a fictive human
identity solely as a result of her potential to signify as feminine through
her romance with the human Deckard. Conversely, for Carr, the process
of a "subject's de-formation" stems from exclusion from any oedipalized
circuit of desire and, as a consequence, an inability to garner a reciprocal
relation to a desired Other. The (phallic) operation of heterosexual desire demarcates the limits of the human through the hegemonic mechanisms of gender: "It is not that Rachel first signifies 'human' and *then* she
can enter into sexual normativity. Rather, what the film makes clear is
that sexual normativity constitutes the hegemonic field of the human's
intelligibility as such."[20]

Carr's interrogation of the elision of the human within the psychoanalytic gendered subject discloses the modalities of exclusion that occur
within the Symbolic. In this way he distinguishes the subaltern's condition
of symbolic death from psychosis, otherwise the logical and inevitable outcome of exclusion from the Symbolic. His analysis, therefore, elaborates on
how the colonial operation of desubjectification of the enslaved may occur
within a psychoanalytic schema that only "*appears* to have nothing to say
about race."[21] Within Carr's theoretical frame, therefore, Patterson's notion of social death describes how death operates contradictorily within
the social, how bodies excluded from the gendered imperative of subjectivity are rendered "dead at the level of socio-symbolic signification."[22]

In an American context, Hortense Spillers's infinitely sophisticated engagement with Lacanian discourse explains the exclusion of the enslaved
from its phallocentric-gendered paradigm of desire by asserting the
slave's orientation to the Father's Law as disjunctive and alienating.[23]
Evoking the isolating horrors of the transatlantic passage within the gendered prerogative of Lacan's Symbolic, she both inflects and deconstructs
the cultural ascendancy of the Father's Law. She shows how the brutality
of slave traders desymbolizes captive bodies, wrenched from their own
cultural systems of gendering, and renders them merely dehumanized
"flesh."[24] The crucial difference between the enslaved body/flesh and the
normative desired, and therefore human subject of the Father's Law is
crystallized in this process of degendering.

The body of the slave, as Carr makes apparent, and that of the slave woman in particular as flagged by the slave matronymic, cannot be reconciled to a feminist revision of psychoanalysis. The transformation from human to property familiar to historians as the res (thing)/persona (human) split, the prevailing condition of the enslaved, is precisely accomplished through the signifying practices of the "ruling episteme," which is organized by the Father's Law.[25]

> In effect, under conditions of captivity, the offspring of the female does not "belong" to the Mother, nor is s/he "related" to the "owner," though the latter "possesses" it [the offspring], and in the African-American instance, often fathered it, *and,* as often, without the benefit of patrimony. In the social outline that Meillassoux is pursuing, the offspring of the enslaved, "being unrelated both to their begetters and to their owners . . . find themselves in the situation of being orphans. . . ." In the context of the United States, we could not say that the enslaved offspring was "orphaned," but the child does become, under press of a patronymic, patrifocal, patrilineal and patriarchal order, the man/woman on the boundary, whose human and familial status, by the very nature of the case, had yet to be defined.[26]

This commodification of slaves leads Spillers to question the feminist emphasis on the recuperation and revaluation of reproduction, family, and mothering as self-constitutive for slave women. The historical conditions of captivity and the representational matrix in which slaves signify as property they produced make the meanings of kinship and family, derived necessarily from Father's Law, questionable in the case of slaves and their descendants. The relation of property undermines any signifying relation in the familial sense for slaves, rendering their otherwise humanizing familial ties perpetually vulnerable to commerce. It is this vulnerability wrought and perpetuated through the degendered condition of the mother as slave that splinters the domestic from its otherwise hegemonic inflection.

Where Luce Irigaray, for instance, accepts the mother-daughter relation as a site for positive intervention, given its problematic nature within a phallocentric gendering schema, Spillers rejects that possibility for the enslaved by asserting slavery's destruction of kinship ties and the meaninglessness of "blood" relations as the determinative outcome for all slaves. She thus sets the pathologization of all slave relations against Irigaray's reworking of mother-daughter relations as crucial for negotiating a maternal link, a genealogy that counters the disavowal of the mother in the phallocentric Lacanian Symbolic.[27]

The mark of property makes slave women's wombs little more than breeding sites and binds their destinies to those of their daughters in a relation that Spillers herself does not address. Elizabeth Abel has suggested that Spillers's neglect of Irigaray's mother-daughter nexus stems from its contradictory implications for her degendering thesis.[28] According to Abel, since the slave daughter's maternal legacy differentiates her from her enslaved male counterparts, it therefore heralds a difference of gender within slavery. I suggest that the condition of the mother could be considered a dimension of those very ideological mechanisms that produce slaves' degendered condition. That is, the degendered status, which produces the objectification of slaves as property and hinges on the matronymic designation, may intimate something of the implicit contradictory underside of this dynamic. In other words, the degendered condition of slaves in relation to the Law of the Father also necessitates a strategic (and perhaps unacknowledged) genderedness. The necessity of a matronymic designation in itself connotes this genderedness.

This implicit genderedness suggests that the degendering, paradoxically, cannot operate without a gendered point of articulation. The paradoxical manner in which slaves enter into the dominant representational domain through their nullification in it corresponds here to Patterson's oxymoronic "social death." In the Cape context, for instance, slaves were referred to as *lijfeigene* (lit., body property) and yet were also known by gendered designations both infantilized and bestial.[29] Robert Shell notes that in the period of Dutch East India Company rule (1652–1796) slave women were referred to as *wijven* (which is a bestial, gendered designation), as opposed to the more normative term *vrou* (wife); additionally, and more generally, slaves were commonly addressed by the infantilized *meid* (girl) and *jong* (boy). Clearly, these differentiations from normative (human) gendered designations institute a distinct (nonhuman) order of being. It is precisely this exclusion that makes the notion of slave gender something of an oxymoron, at least within the hegemonic terms of the gendered rationale for becoming intelligible in the Symbolic. The 'lower' order of slave gender, by its difference from its normative counterpart, nullifies the very precepts for gender in its sense of constituting humanness.

There need be no contradiction per se between theorization of the degendered condition of enslavement and its matronymic delineation: the two are intrinsically related mechanisms of an ideology that must strategically affirm gender in order to render its effacement for slaves so powerfully

exclusionary. Irigaray's concern, thus, with the implications of the exchange of women among men that occasions, and is occasioned by, the
sexual dynamic of representation, cannot account for the matrix of power,
difference, and differentiation in slavery. It serves only as a jarring reminder of the extreme disavowal of slave women in the representational
schema of slavery and the realm of the unintelligibility to which it reduces
them. Spillers reflects on the transatlantic slave trade as marking a violent
historical encounter between radically different significatory systems.
The hegemony of the Symbolic, she makes clear, is enforced through torture that literalizes the captive body, making it emblematic of "a cultural
text whose inside has been turned outside,"[30] the dehumanization that
produces the slave as body, as lacking interiority or consciousness.

This degendered condition of slaves, then, reflects their negation, their
lack of a normative (human) subject status within the gendered dictates of
representation. In the context of Cape slavery this differentiation of
(human) subjects from slaves is strikingly foregrounded in the ambiguities
of slave owners' infantilization of slaves. Instead of the effort in the current historiography to ascertain or refute its presence, I suggest that it may
be precisely the contradictions through which this discourse is constituted
that need to be deconstructed. That is, the hypersexualization of slave
women and their sexual use by male slave owners needs to be considered
in terms of the slave matronymic, and the incestuous implications of slave
owner's paternalist rhetoric it signals. The very incongruity of the matronymic designation with such a paternalist discourse points to larger questions about how power and difference are configured through, and reso-
nate within, the symbolic and representational domains. Moreover,
emphasizing these (dis)connections between slave matronymy and an ambiguous paternalism at the Cape sheds a different light on the colonial ob-
session with miscegenation and its dynamics. My contention here is that
the well-documented colonial fixation with miscegenation is not solely
symptomatic of an anxiety about racial boundaries but that it is also perhaps an anxiety about the discursivity of race: that is, the idea that whiteness can be unmade.[31] In other words, the dimensions of race itself are not
a biological given but are acquired and fashioned through the dictates of a
gendering hegemony located in the slave matronymic designation.

MISCEGENATION, MATRONYMY, AND THE DESIRING RELATION

The matronymic signals that the difference in the positionings of slave
women and white femininities with respect to the phallus, and thus to

subjectivity and representation, is secured via the relation to desire. A normative colonial white masculinity is circumscribed through the restriction of humanizing desire to white femininity, as the mediator of the phallus. The prescription to 'be' the phallus produces white femininity's construction as matter, in its barest sense. This is what I mean by white femininity's particular embodiment in relation to white masculinity. White masculinity is thus defined by the quality of its disembodiment or abstraction from its physicality, or what feminists have described as its escape into the ideal sphere of consciousness.[32] The 'having' of the phallus signifies a white masculine agency characterized by its active and exclusive positioning vis-à-vis the feminine. Miscegenation is thus an explicit threat to the sociosymbolic power associated with the phallus. It disputes the exclusive claims to autonomy of colonial, white subjectivities. It also shows up the ideological workings of that power: that is, the phallic rationale for the proscription or the sanctioning of desire by which a white masculine subjectivity is constituted. Gwen Bergner states, "In a colonial context, the operative 'law' determining the circulation of women among white men and black men is the miscegenation taboo, which ordains that white men have access to black women but that black men be denied access to white women. Both incest and miscegenation taboos enforce culturally dictated categories of permitted and prohibited sexual relations."[33]

It is this patriarchically ordained restriction of sexual desire, as Bergner makes clear, that enforces and delimits racial difference. The status of whiteness is fixed in white women's embodiment and, conversely, also in white men's abstraction, within a phallic desiring schema. The sexual activity of white men with black women can go virtually unheeded, as the illusion of authenticity is perpetuated through white women's bodies: hence, white women's crucial role in the circumscription of desire via the phallus. It is the 'mixing' of whiteness, not of blackness, that counts, as slave women's bodies do not have the same subjectifying import as white women's. Since it is women, of both races, who bear the stain and the outcome of the polluting act, it is women's bodies that are 'defiled', not men's: miscegenation is defined by the site of the womb. White women's wombs may be defiled, while the defilement of black women's wombs is not of equal concern.

The sexual transgressions of white male slave owners are in this way accommodated by a phallocentric operation of desire in which white masculine subjectivity is abstracted vis-à-vis the particular embodiment of slave women as property: that is, a relation that differs from that mediated by a normative white femininity strictly limited by the Law of the Father. Sexual relations between a slave woman and a white man do not signify the kind of miscegenation that counts, as it is the slave woman's body and therefore blackness that is 'polluted'. The white woman's womb, conversely, is the 'seat' of whiteness and is, therefore, prohibited to slave men. White male agency, and the potential for slave men to enact a similar agency, comes about through the relation to the feminine lack, yet slave men cannot partake in the same masculine symbolic discourses enacted through sexual access to women. Ideologies of race purity and colonial power as the exclusive preserve of male whites are, in this way, configured around the conceptualization of both white and slave women's bodies, as passive receptacles, as phallic lack.

The essentialization of slave women, as opposed to that of white femininity, however, is configured through their exclusion from the patriarchic rule of desire. In sum, within the logic of the normative heterosexual desiring regime, miscegenous relations between white men and slave women are metaphorically/symbolically outside the bounds of patriarchy, as signified by the Law of the Father. Slave women's identity as physical subjectivity is in this way paradoxically constructed through their erasure from the phallic dynamics that constitute gendered humanity.

To put it differently, slave women become intelligible solely through the contradiction engendered by their corporeal desirability, on the one hand, their visibility as body, and on the other hand by their erasure in the phallocentric economy of desire. Pamela Scully, in her examination of the post-Emancipation (1838) labor regulations in the Cape, has suggested that their cultural accommodation of black women who lived with or married white men within the legal defines of whiteness indicates that race was determined culturally rather than biologically.[34] She specifically discusses the manner in which the preamble to an 1839 draft of what became the Masters and Servants Ordinance of 1842 allowed for these black women to be absorbed into white communities but made no such concessions for white women in opposing circumstances. Scully thus notes the draft's "latent hostility" to the association of white women with black men.[35] Her observation that the preamble protected the status of white men testifies to the representational dictates by which whiteness signifies in the gendered mechanics of miscegenation. It demonstrates white femininity's principal function as bodily receptacle within a phallic organization of desire. By this I mean the relation of passivity and lack that stems from white femininity's having to 'be' the phallus, which, conversely, defines white masculinity's 'possession' of it.

THE FATHER'S WORD: 'PATERNALISM' AT THE CAPE?

As I have indicated, while historians have debated the extent to which Cape Dutch slaveholders could properly be described as paternalist, they have not considered the representational import of the term as I deploy it here: that is, in its invocation of the familial as an ideological aspect of power to conceptualize relations of power between slaves and their owners. I do not imply that slaves were actually incorporated into the slaveholding family. While Patricia van der Spuy makes the important distinction between patriarchal Dutch slave owners and the state paternalism of the British, my use of the term *patriarchy* denotes the Lacanian-inflected mechanics of difference in the symbolic sphere by which masculinities and femininities signify and which governed the gender systems of both British and Dutch.[36]

Also, I am not attempting to ascertain the actual extent of paternalist sentiment at the Cape. Rather I am concerned with the symbolic resonances of the *familial* as slaveholders used it: with what it says about the ambiguous manner in which they sought to fashion their identity as slaveholders, and with what the ambiguities in that construction of paternalism say about the power relations between slaves and slaveholders.[37]

The ambiguities of these relations precisely indicate the status of paternalism as ideology. They give the lie to its claims to familial intimacy, mutuality of responsibility, and inclusivity, which appear to define the relation of owner to slave. The slave matronymic designation thus exists as the underside of such a paternalist discourse. Although debate about Cape paternalism has turned on its effectiveness in terms of the extent to which it organized owners' and slaves' perceptions of their obligations to each other, within my analytic schema it is not so much a matter of proving or disproving this sense of moral community. Rather, what interests me is what and how this matronymic exclusion of the slave signifies within the frame of the paternalist familial and what this matronymy suggests about the paternalist ethic. Within my theoretical purview, it is not so much that the paternalist rhetoric veils the harsher realities of slavery but rather that the matronymic delineation facilitates a particular phallocentric configuration of power that centers on slave women's exclusion from the hegemonic Law of the Father.

Rachel van der Voort's readings of slave women's complaints to the British Protector of Slaves[38] in the 1820s about their sexual abuse by their owners, for instance, presupposes the existence of a "paternalist code" that links slaves and their owners in a system of mutually binding obligations.[39]

Her analysis of these cases is thus grounded in an understanding that Cape paternalism operated through an ethos of "reciprocal obligations" and that these sexual encounters were a "violation" of an understood and operative "paternalist code" and were for this reason, she concludes, rare. Her proposed code of honor echoes Wayne Dooling's argument that individual slave owners' behavior was censured through recourse to a moral economy constituted through the slave-owning community's public shaming of excessive behavior that exceeded its own norms.[40]

For van der Voort, these excesses, as exceptions that prove the rule of the paternalist relation at the Cape attest to its prevalence: as such, they substantiate her thesis that owner-slave relations were shaped by the familial. She writes, for example, that "each case of sexual manipulation or coercion demonstrates a failure within the paternalist system. . . . Slave owners, restricted by the 'moral community' and the 'incest' taboo of paternalism, were not willing to risk their reputations by having sexual relations with their slave women. This proves that paternalism was at the core of all domestic relations."[41] She further comments that "reciprocal obligations within paternalism allowed them [slave women] to make their owners accountable for unjust or inappropriate behaviour."[42]

Contra van der Voort's relatively benign position, I suggest that the reported "low frequency of sexual acts from 1830–1834,"[43] at least as documented in the available records, by no means indicates that these sexual encounters were exceptional. To make that assumption would be to risk mimicking the limits of colonial comprehension or knowledge as it is produced in the archives: taking the records at face value. Whereas van der Voort sees the infrequency of such reports as evidence of the success of an incest-inhibiting paternalism, it is perhaps precisely the ideology as such that both masked and thereby allowed for proliferation of sexual relations between slave women and male slave owners. Rather than demonstrating a paternalist success due to a moral censure, sexual relations between male owners and female slaves may be indicative of the success of the familial metaphoric to censure reporting. In other words, the effectiveness of a paternalist operation of power in this case is produced through its overt denunciation of sexual intimacy with slaves.

Van der Voort suggests that the incestuous overtones of such relations, given what she takes as the paternalist moral community of the slave owners, operated as taboo to inhibit such encounters.[44] Thus, again taking paternalist rhetoric at face value, she also literalizes the incest taboo, understanding it to be an effect of the paternalist "ethic" of male honor. When she briefly broaches the subject of incest, she uses it only to indicate the extremes that deviate from a presumed paternalist norm. That such relations amount to incest, within the frame of her argument, signifies the terms by which, and the extent to which, this honor code is violated: "As father-like figures to these women, owners should never have engaged in sexual activity with them, but instead served as their protectors, the same taboo they observed towards their daughters."[45]

For me, the contradiction signaled by the notion of incest does not so much affirm a Cape paternalist ethos through its assimilation of slaves into the slaveholders' familial domain but instead problematizes exactly the supposed similarity of slave women to daughters of the family. For me, this contradiction in these encounters with women slaves marks, on the one hand, the rift between slave women's desirability as signified by the sexual predations of their slave owners, ascribed to their "excessive" sexuality, the major part of their construction in Cape society, as other slave societies, and on the other hand, their supposed filial protection by their owners. Van der Voort briefly discusses the depiction of slave women as libidinally charged, but she does not link this in a systematic manner to their complaints to the Protector of Slaves against their masters or to the implications of these complaints for slave women's positioning in paternalist discourse. She notes for example:

> Though slave/settler connections were acknowledged they were not always sanctioned. Some owner/slave connections may have been eased by what historian Elizabeth Fox-Genovese described as the characteristics of "Jezebel" in the U.S. South. A "Jezebel" was a slave woman who was "free of the social constraints that surrounded the sexuality of white women. She thus legitimated the wanton behaviour of white men by proclaiming black women to be lusty wenches in whom sexual impulse overwhelmed all restraint." This eased the consciences of white men.[46]

In van der Voort's argument, then, the hypersexualization of female slaves similarly "may have justified sexual coercion on the part of the owner,"[47] though she does not specifically link its rationale for slave women's sexual exploitation to her ethos of paternalism. In fact, this discourse of hypersexuality appears to have marked a difference from that ethos, since she argues for the latter's efficiency on the basis of the paternalist code's sense of filial and parental duty. There is, then, an unwitting contradiction within her argument, since the "success" of paternalism means that its incest taboo effectively deters such transgressions, yet the hypersexualization of slave women, derived from the matronymic designation, also sanctions them.

In contrast, van der Spuy argues against the paternalism thesis, citing a criminal charge of adultery against a slave woman and her master as evidence that paternalism could not have been the defining idiom at the Cape, since sexual intercourse between the two was not legally defined as incest. She writes of the legal construction of the circumstances: "There is no sense of incest, which might have been the case had the ideology included slave women in the slaveholding family."[48] In making the important point that any notion of familial intimacy between slaves and their owners should not be taken at face value, van der Spuy inadvertently underscores my point that paternalism be considered in terms of its status as representation.

The arguments of van der Spuy and van der Voort thus, despite their opposing positions about the actual existence of a Cape paternalist discourse, both partake in and rely on it. Neither author considers the function and status of paternalism as a discursive construct that enables a particular organization of power. It would be as facile to suggest that the slaves were actually incorporated into slaveholding families, as the slave owners' benevolent notion of inclusion claimed, as to imply that slaves considered themselves to be literally included in their owners' personal familial domains. The paternalist discourse of slave owners should be regarded less as a given than as a discursive operation constituting the symbolic dimensions of a normative worldview.

Consequently, while the contradiction in van der Voort's formulation of sexual relations between male slave owners and their female slaves essentially defines them as a failure of paternalism, for me it expresses the ambiguity of slave women's construction in Cape colonial discourse. It reflects the contradictory positioning of slave women as desirable and visible as body, and yet as elided from representation by their matronymic exclusion. The hypersexualization of slave women is emblematic of the strategic circumscription of desire by which white femininity is defined from its slave counterpart. The same process that constitutes white femininity also erases the latter from the gendered order of representation. Van der Voort implies that slave women's hypersexuality results from their colonial construction as "free from the constraints of sexuality" imposed on white women. However this analytic schema suggests that the construction of whiteness and its correlating hegemony of power is facilitated through slave women's dual constitution, within the phallic circulation of desire, as both desirable and invisible.

In the personal accounts of Samuel Hudson, a slave owner at the Cape, for instance, it is the perceived excessive sexuality of slave women, amplified in the figure of the miscegenated female slave that threatens the paternalist ethic. While Hudson reproaches those Europeans who engage the sexual services of slave women and who should know better, according to his own paternalist logic, the roots of their moral erosion are firmly affixed to the slave woman's immoral libidinousness. Yet he also notes with abhorrence that these men make little attempt to free the children of these liaisons but only "look with indifference on the fruits of this shameful prostitution," whose enslavement is ensured through their matronymic designation.[49] The practical conveniences of such practices to slave owners do not escape him, with Hudson asserting that these owners "encourage these connections to improve their breed of live-stock."[50] He recounts a tale of one, in particular, who took these eugenic measures to the very extreme:

> I know one Gentleman—if he can by such conduct deserve the name—that at the time I left the Colony was considered among the richest of the Inhabitants, held one of the first situations in the English Government, was generally respected. Yet this very Man at his first outset was in possession of a white (or nearly so) Slave. He had children by this Woman, several which as they grew up from their color were considered very valuable. The connection continued with her own children and even with his Grandchildren. . . . This is a well established fact and it was re-marked Mister W——'s Slaves were considered the finest in the Colony and were brought to the Hammer would fetch extrava-gant prices. . . . Many of them had all the features of Europeans not with[out] a tinge of their Ancestors [sic] complexion.[51]

Slaves, being outside the domain of the Father's Name are not subject to the prohibition against incest, as the actions of this particular slave owner suggest. Their exclusion undoes or overrides any blood lineage and the usual laws that govern it, and legitimizes the sexual use of slave women. Despite the function of Hudson's story as a kind of hyperbolic anomaly, it enacts the exclusionary rationale of the slave matronym as it takes the commodification of slave bodies to its logical conclusion: 'ex-clusion' from the phallic circuit of desiring severs all relations of kinship. What surfaces in this anecdote, moreover, is how the commodification of slave women produces their hypersexualized inscription and how the latter is accentuated in the desirability (and consequent profitability) of the light-skinned slave woman. It makes explicit the link between the sexualization and commodification and of slave women, underscoring the manner in which the politics of desire, as circumscribed by the matronymic, allow for this reduction of slave women, on one level, to an explicitly sexual function.

I am not referring here to the sexual mandate that the matronymic exclusion produces for white men, the mechanisms of which I have just outlined. Instead I emphasize how the sexual nature of slave women's purely physical embodiment within the matronymic schema normalizes their exploitation, rendering it the 'natural' consequence of that embodiment. In other words, the construction of slave women as 'naturally' promiscuous and immoral is a function of their delineation as sexual objects. They become essentially objects with a purely sexual function and were essentially defined by this sexual function.

With the light-skinned products of these miscegenous (and in this case also incestuous) relations valued so highly in a commercial sense, the perceived sexual immorality of slave women conveniently coincides with the entrepreneurial efforts of their owners. Lady Anne Barnard, one of the better known residents at the Cape, notes that "virtue in a female slave was considered to be a most unproductive quality and as such is discouraged by the Mistress."[52] Robert Percival, a contemporary of Hudson, remarks similarly,

> The Dutch ladies have no reluctance to their slave girls having connections with their guests, in hopes of profiting by it, by their being got with child. I myself know instances where they have been ordered to wait on such a gentleman to his bedroom; what followed does not require to be mentioned. One of my friends, whose veracity I have not the least doubt of assured me that a very engaging slave girl, to whom he paid his addresses, and who seemed exceedingly coy and reserved, was one night pushed into his room by the mistress of the house, who locked the door and left her with him.[53]

These instances of forced sex with white males additionally underscore how this discourse of miscegenation reproduces or transmits the slave's status as property. The allure of the slave girl mentioned in Percival's story is contradicted by (and I think sits rather uneasily with) the "seemed" which qualifies it, as if her reserve is mere pretence. It may be, as has been suggested to me, that Percival's phrasing indicates her innocence, to emphasize the travesty of what followed. Whether or not she was innocent, this narrative illustrates the burden on her of preconceptions imposed by the discourse of hypersexuality: how she was expected to behave. That any such reserve on the part of a woman slave should be deemed feigned, as perhaps denoted by the "seemed," reflects on slave women's sexually charged construction in Cape society.

The high value ascribed to the miscegenated 'product' perhaps further testifies to the rationale for race underpinning the gendered mechanics of miscegenation. That is, the authenticity or purity of race that produces and, at the same time, is produced by a rationale of miscegenation cannot help but alert us to the discursivity of race itself. I refer here to the disjunction that the physical whiteness of these slave women makes them most attractive and valuable, yet this embodiment does not signify as white precisely by their being slaves. The appearance of whiteness among slaves, their resemblance to Europeans that so startled visitors to the colony, shows up the ideological mechanisms by which whiteness is constituted in the first place. Consider, for example, Hudson's "white (or nearly so)" in the quoted passage, in which the "or nearly so" occurs almost like an afterthought: one that inserts a crucial difference between the original, authentic whiteness and its deceptive imitations.[54]

In terms of my argument, then, the symbolics of incest as they are produced within a paternalist frame of meaning do not signal a violation per se but rather draw attention to the manner in which the prohibited, the taboo, constitutes power. Juxtaposition of the Lacanian-inflected Oedipal with the idiom of paternalism shows up the disjunction between the rhetoric of family and the matronymic 'exclusion' of slave women. It is in and through the colonial inflection of incest that this paternalist operation of power is elaborated.

Van der Voort cites an instance of a slave owner having sexual relations with his own slave offspring as "a true form of incest,"[55] but it is perhaps the inflection of the Oedipal by the paternalist discourse that suggests that the slaveholding familial domain may be conceptualized with reference to slaves, and vice versa. That is, the patriarchal domestic discourse is elaborated via a racialized topos, just as the servile positioning of slaves is configured through the familial. Those instances cited by van der Voort to affirm the existence of Cape paternalist sentiment, as for instance a slaveholder's comment, "Yes, we chastise our own blood, *and* are the slaves better than that?" then asserts the difference of slaves through its postulation of a familial similarity.[56] The similarity normally denoted by the term *and* acknowledges and institutes difference by its very attempt to displace or efface that difference. It signifies a kind of surplus of meaning that an economy of equivalence cannot accommodate.[57] The analogous relation of slaves and children in this remark (i.e., our "own blood") then operates through a paradigm of difference rather than of similarity.

CAPE "PATERNALISM" AND THE OEDIPAL:
MISCEGENATION AND THE "FAMILY ROMANCE"

The paternalist representation of slaveholder-slave relations as benign and reciprocal and the erasure of slave sexuality this implies is fissured by its oedipal double. The denial of slaves' sexuality in paternalist discourse, only to reinscribe them as also sexually threatening or desirable, exemplifies their invisibility in the Lacanian Symbolic, which leaves them visible only as body. In this way the narrative of heteronormative desire overwrites the infantilized inscription of slave women in Cape paternalist discourse. If white femininity is inaugurated through its thwarted desire for the Father, the lack by which its positioning as 'being' the phallus is constituted, the infantilization of women slaves is constituted via their symbolic exclusion from the realm of that subjectifying desire.

The paternalist representation of the slave woman as child, then, is interrupted or contradicted by the oedipal story's depiction of the girl-child's desire for the father, both veiling and revealing the slaveholding 'father's' tabooed desire for slave women. The incest taboo mirrors that of miscegenation, or rather the miscegenation taboo is ideologically reconfigured through that of incest to erase the material realities of slave women's sexual exploitation. This configuration of male power and desire has its inverse in the equally forbidden desire of the boy for the mother and the supposed, and even more forbidden, desire of the male slave—jong, or 'boy'—for the white woman, or 'mother'. The contradiction between the male slave as child, thus as emasculated, and the boy's desire for the mother in the oedipal signals slave men's positioning outside the phallic desiring circuit; that is, the manner in which their anatomical potentiality is curtailed by prohibition of their desire. In the colonial context, the colonial, paternalist family reflects the oedipal family and is also an inversion of it. The oedipal narrative of power and difference is thus replicated and inverted. This is what I mean by the parodic doubling of the Oedipal.

It is through the naming of both the Father and the Mother that the incest taboo ensures that social relations are regulated or ordered (and legitimated) through the Name of the Father: the injunction against incest in the Oedipal is necessary for representation in the social sphere. The miscegenation taboo, then, maintains colonial order through its denial of the colonized subjects' relation to an Other and its restriction of the heterosexual circuit of desire according to the patriarchic inscription of racialized difference. Thus, the organization of racialized identities pivots on the exclusion, but only on a representational level, of slave women from that circulation of desire. The disavowed relation between slave women and white men in the paternalist deployment of power necessitates its inverse in the proscription of desire between slave men and white women. While the Oedipal is driven by the injunction against the boy's desire for the mother, the paternalist articulation of colonial power reverses this formulation: its discourses of power are driven by the incest taboo against the (slaveholding) father and the (slave) daughter. The dynamic of power and violence depicted in the Oedipal then ruptures Cape paternalist representations of relations between slaves and slaveholders. My point is that the matronymic elision gives rise to a proliferation of power centered on the disavowed relation between white masculinity and slave women's negated positionality vis-à-vis the Proper name. In this way Cape paternalist discourses of power were constituted by, and through, the discontinuities and silences they produced.

NOTES

1. Working within contemporary assumptions of the term, I use *representation* to refer to the processes of signification by which reality is ordered—that is, through which we structure our perceptions of the world, of ourselves, and of our relations to others. Thus, it describes the process of a re-presentation, rather than a simplistic mimetic process.

2. I use the term *matronymic*, as opposed to *matrifocal* or *matrilineal*, to denote its specific implications in the dynamics of representation, vis-à-vis the patronym, or the Name of the Father, as it functions in Lacanian discourse. I do not suggest that slaves are literally excluded from the Symbolic realm but rather I attempt to address the manner in which the social and symbolic domains of Cape slave society may be organized by this (fictional) naming of the slave mother.

3. Patricia van der Spuy, for instance, writes that "the ideology of slavery rested on the denial of slave manhood." Van der Spuy, "A Collection of Discrete Essays with the Common Theme of Gender and Slavery at the Cape of Good Hope with a Focus on the 1820s" (MA dissertation, University of Cape Town, 1993), 42. While for van der Spuy this ideology operates through the polarity of "man versus slave" and "emasculation versus masculinity," I ask how the slave matronymic positions slave women in such a schema of power. In my doctoral thesis I elaborate on this

question, as it forms a major part of my engagement with the representational implications of the slave matronym. I ask why there seems to be no term parallel to *emasculation* that defines the negated condition of slave women. This linguistic lacuna,
thus, is emblematic of slave women's negation in a phallic order of representation

4. I enclose the term paternalism in quotation marks to foreground its contested
nature in the historiography of Cape slavery.

5. For the terms of this debate, see van der Spuy, "Discrete Essays"; John Edwin
Mason, "'Fit for Freedom': The Slaves, Slavery, and Emancipation in the Cape
Colony, South Africa, 1806 to 1842," 2 vols. (PhD diss., Yale University, 1992);
Robert C.-H. Shell, *Children of Bondage: A Social History of the Slave Society at the
Cape of Good Hope, 1652–1838* (Hanover, NH: Wesleyan University Press, 1994);
Jody Sarich, "Wet-Nurses, Wives and Witnesses: Domestic Slavery in the Stellen-
bosch District, South Africa, 1829–1834" (MA diss., University of London, 1999);
Nigel Worden, *Slavery in Dutch South Africa* (Cambridge: Cambridge University
Press, 1985). Mason's thesis has subsequently been published as *Social Death and Res-
urrection: Slavery and Emancipation in South Africa* (Charlottesville: University of
Virginia Press, 2003).

6. The Symbolic is, in such a formulation, the domain of social and linguistic
order, what amounts to the order of Logos, as opposed to the pre-oedipal, prediscur-
sive Imaginary, as the chaotic instinctual realm of the maternal. This problematic
valorization of the domain of culture—intelligibility and sociality as paternal—has
been engaged by several feminist theorists, most notably Judith Butler, *Bodies That
Matter: On the Discursive Limits of "Sex"* (London: Routledge, 1993); see also Butler,
Gender Trouble: Feminism and the Subversion of Identity (London: Routledge, 1990).

7. By *subjectification* I mean the processes of power through which the subject is
constituted. In that sense my use of the term, inflected by both feminist, psychoanalytic and Foucauldian conceptualizations of power, denotes the multiple and interconnected modalities of power through which the gendered and racialized subject is
made or unmade.

8. Radhika Mohanram notes that Lacan's relation between the sexes is "derived
from Freud's description of heterosexual relations in 'On Narcissism: An Introduction,' [which] suggests that women *are* the phallus as men *have* them. By this he
means that both sexes desire the phallus in the same way. The girl's greatest realiza-
tion in her heteromaturation process is that, though herself castrated, she can accede to the phallus via the man, by becoming the object of his desire, by reflecting
and representing male desire; in short, by becoming the phallus." Mohanram, *Black
Body: Women, Colonialism and Space* (St. Leonards, NSW: Allen and Unwin, 1999),
84. For an explication of the relation between the penis and the phallus, see Elizabeth Grosz, *Jacques Lacan: A Feminist Introduction* (London: Routledge, 1990), 116.

9. Elizabeth Grosz, *Sexual Subversions* (Sydney: Allen and Unwin, 1989), xx (emphasis in original).

10. While my association of 'slaveness' with race may appear problematic in the
context of the Cape, I am in no way suggesting that the divide between slave and
free was strictly contiguous with the racialized designations of black and white. Cape
historians have generally emphasized this slave-free divide as the determinative

one at the Cape. While I acknowledge the fluidity of racial identities, especially in early Cape society, I believe that there remains a racialized economy of difference, of blackness, broadly conceived, that hinges, in part, on the potentiality of being enslaved.

11. Fanon's analysis, for example, outlines a similar pattern: white men are set into opposition with their black, colonized counterparts, while white women are presented, uncritically and problematically in this schema, as the signifiers of whiteness. Most famously Fanon states of "the black woman," "I know nothing about her." Fanon, *Black Skin, White Masks*, trans. Charles Lam Markmann (1967; New York: Grove, 1991), 179–80. Perhaps this void corresponds, in part, to the matronymic's erasure of slave women.

12. My use of the term *symbolic* is intended to invoke the meanings and relations associated with, and instituted by, the paternal function, rather than the Lacanian Symbolic itself. In a Lacanian frame, though, the symbolic of the paternal is necessarily tied to the overall domain of the Symbolic.

13. I follow Judith Butler's (*Gender Trouble*) gendered inflection of Althusser's concept of interpellation; that is, as the process by which an individual recognizes and accepts the terms of his of her socialization. Hence, the 'mark of gender' is the visual recognition of castration that, ultimately, determines one's positioning in relation to the phallus.

14. Orlando Patterson, *Slavery and Social Death: A Comparative Study* (Cambridge: Harvard University Press, 1992). Both van der Spuy and Shell have qualified Patterson's concept for its applicability at the Cape. Van der Spuy suggests that the concept "can only strictly apply to imported slaves," given the nature of creolization and the demographics of importation at the Cape. Van der Spuy, "Discrete Essays." Shell writes, "[C]ape slaves were never regarded as socially dead [rather] they were offered hope of life," which he proposes as the basis for their infantilized incorporation into slaveholding families. Shell, *Children of Bondage*, 402. An emphasis on the representational implications of the slave matronymic suggests that such readings of social death may be indicative of an inadequate attention to the symbolic domain. Also, while this reflects slaves' negation in the domain of representation, it should be remembered, as Mohanram notes, that the agency of black bodies becomes visible only in "the everyday-ness of space," in their daily existence. Mohanram, *Black Body*, 22.

15. I am thinking specifically of Luce Irigaray's redeployment of the feminine and the maternal. See Irigaray, *Speculum of the Other Woman*, trans. Gillian C. Gill (Ithaca, NY: Cornell University Press, 1985); Irigaray, "Women on the Market," in *This Sex Which Is Not One*, trans. Catherine Porter with Carolyn Burke (Ithaca, NY: Cornell University Press, 1985).

16. In "Women on the Market," for instance, Irigaray asserts that it is the circulation of women according to the dictates of the Father's Law that organizes relations between men. In the phallocentric order installed by the incestuous injunction, women are reduced to commodities, having no relation to themselves and to each other. How slave women signify, in this configuration of capitalism, the Proper name and the quality of property by which Irigaray defines the feminine, is intimated by their matronymic designation.

17. Brian Carr, "At the Thresholds of the 'Human': Race, Psychoanalysis, and the Replication of Imperial Memory," *Cultural Critique* 39 (1998): 140.

18. Ibid., 122.

19. Set in a futuristic America, the Ridley Scott film depicts the efforts of Deckard, a detective, to hunt down and destroy a group of androids, known as replicants. These replicants have escaped a labor colony and have integrated with the human population, from whom they are virtually indistinguishable in appearance.

20. Carr, "Thresholds," 134; emphasis in original.

21. Ibid., 129; emphasis in original.

22. Ibid., 126.

23. Hortense Spillers, "Mama's Baby, Papa's Maybe: An American Grammar Book," *Diacritics* 17 (1987): 65–81.

24. Ibid., 67.

25. Ibid., 68.

26. Ibid., 74; emphasis in original. Spillers refers to Claude Meillassoux, "Female Slavery," in *Women and Slavery in Africa,* ed. Claire C. Robertson and Martin A. Klein (Madison: University of Wisconsin Press, 1983), 49–67.

27. For a discussion of this aspect of Irigaray's project, see Grosz, *Sexual Subversions.* As the feminine remains caught within a phallocentric desiring schema, the principal impetus of Irigaray's project involves the "reorganisation of desire itself" (125), in order for women to be positioned alternatively toward the maternal.

The positioning of the repressed mother as a counterorigin to the primacy of the paternal in the Symbolic finds a peculiar parallels Felipe Smith's discussion of the literary engagement with the condition of the mother in Pauline Hopkins and Charles W. Chestnutt. There it produces a motif of return, as the slave mother comes to represent the transmission of African origins in the "one drop" rule. The repressed maternal, in this case, describes the denial of the black mother and of slave origins: "if one drop of black blood could spawn the birth of a atavistic, regressive 'pure African,' then the source of that one drop, the womb of the original black slave mother, could never be escaped. The atavistic child was the essence of that slave mother herself, subject to innumerable returns to reclaim her descendants for the descent line begun in Africa." Smith, "'The Condition of the Mother': The Legacy of Slavery in African American Literature of the Jim Crow Era," paper presented at the Fourth Annual Conference on Slavery, "Women and Slavery," Avignon, October 16–18, 2002, p. 5.

28. Elizabeth Abel, "Race, Class, and Psychoanalysis? Opening Questions," in *Conflicts in Feminism,* ed. Marianne Hirsch and Evelyn Fox Keller (London: Routledge, 1990), 190.

29. Robert C.-H. Shell, "The Lodge Women of Cape Town, 1671 to 1795," paper presented at the Fourth Annual Conference on Slavery, "Women and Slavery," Avignon, 16–18 October 2002. See also Shell, *Children of Bondage,* 397–98.

30. Spillers, "Mama's Baby," 67.

31. I have noted in another arena how colonial discourses of degeneration, for instance, betray this anxiety about the constructedness of race. The British discourse of the degeneracy of the Dutch Boers, for instance, describes how whiteness may be

unmade in its colonial context. Ahjum, "*Othello* and Cape Slavery: Stories about Identities," paper presented at the North Eastern Workshop on Southern Africa, Burlington, Vermont, 2000.

32. See, for example, Mohanram, *Black Body*.

33. Gwen Bergner, "Who Is That Masked Woman? Or, the Role of Gender in Fanon's *Black Skin, White Masks*," *Proceedings of the Modern Language Association* 110 (1995): 81.

34. Pamela Scully, *Liberating the Family? Gender and British Slave Emancipation in the Rural Western Cape, South Africa, 1823–1853* (Portsmouth, NH: Heinemann, 1997).

35. Ibid., 86.

36. I use the term *paternalism*, thus, for the way in which it connotes the familial, which is lacking in *patriarchy*. Consequently, my deployment of these concepts is not intended to contradict that of van der Spuy's (8–9). British paternalism and Dutch patriarchy, as defined in her frame of analysis, are different historical configurations of the abstract concept of patriarchy; that is, both are informed by an underlying patriarchal economy of meaning.

37. It has been suggested to me that a major flaw of this chapter is "its use of English sources to analyze the Afrikaner mind." First, I think the idea of an "Afrikaner mind" highly problematic. I am generally concerned with the discourses by which slaveholding identities are constructed and mobilized. In my doctoral thesis, for instance, from which this paper derives, I also address the mechanics by which a British masculine slaveholding identity is relationally secured through a discourse of restraint and respectability. Second, since the Cape was under British rule for some time by the 1820s, largely the focus of this chapter, the archival records I accessed were mostly in English.

38. The British Protector of Slaves was an official authorized to hear slaves' complaints of abuses by their masters according to amelioration policies decreed in 1826 by Parliament for all British slaveholding colonies. The records of the Protector provide a rare viable approximation of slaves' own voices and have been used widely by recent historians of slavery at the Cape. See esp. Mason, "'Fit for Freedom.'"

39. Rachel Elizabeth van der Voort, "Daughters of Bondage: Paternalism and Slave Women in the Cape Colony, 1830–1834," MA thesis, Princeton University, 1993.

40. Wayne Dooling, *Law and Community in a Slave Society: Stellenbosch District, South Africa, c. 1760–1820* (Cape Town: Centre for African Studies, University of Cape Town, 1992).

41. Van der Voort, "Daughters of Bondage," 67.

42. Ibid., 84.

43. Ibid., 61.

44. She does write, however, "[T]hough slave-owners were violating their analogous role as 'father,' they also capitalised on it because of the dependency of their female slaves, whom many of them claimed to consider 'children.'" Van der Voort, "Daughters of Bondage," 63.

45. Ibid., 61.

46. Ibid., 62, citing Elizabeth Fox-Genovese, *Within the Plantation Household: Black and White Women of the Old South* (Chapel Hill: University of North Carolina Press, 1988), 292.

47. Van der Voort, "Daughters of Bondage," 63.

48. Van der Spuy, 72, n74.

49. Robert C.-H. Shell, "Introduction to S. E. Hudson's 'Slaves,'" *Kronos* 9 (1984): 9.

50. Ibid., 52.

51. Ibid., 68.

52. Lady Anne Barnard, *The Cape Journals of Lady Anne Barnard, 1797–1798*, ed. A. Robinson, with Margaret Lenta and Dorothy Driver, 2nd series, no. 24 (Cape Town: Van Riebeeck Society, 1994), 41.

53. Shell, "Introduction," 52.

54. Mason's discussion of miscegenation in accounts by residents and visitors is prefigured with the statement, citing Hudson, that "many of the women were 'perfectly white,' and yet they were 'black.'" Mason, "'Fit for Freedom,'" 204. He does not, however, follow up on the disjuncture here or consider its symbolic resonances.

55. Van der Voort, "Daughters of Bondage," 64.

56. Ibid., 40; emphasis added.

57. In this respect the slaveholder's comment exemplifies David Lloyd's observation about the operation of difference in the metaphor: "The constitution of any metaphor involves the bringing together of two elements into identity in such a manner that their differences are suppressed. Just so the process of assimilation, whether in bringing two distinct but equivalent elements into identity, or in absorbing a lower into a higher element as by metastasis, requires that which defines the difference between the elements to remain over as residue. Hence although it is possible to conceive formally of an equable process of assimilation in which the original elements are entirely equivalent, the product of assimilation will always necessarily be in an hierarchical relation to the residual, whether this be defined as, variously, the primitive, the local or the merely contingent." Lloyd, "Race under Representation," *Oxford Literary Review* 13 (1991): 72–73.

2

Women in Islamic Households

Swahili area of Eastern Africa, including the Mrima Coast, ca. 1870–1915

4

MJAKAZI, MPAMBE, MJOLI, SURIA

Female Slaves in Swahili Sources

KATRIN BROMBER

Nikaoa kijakazi, mke wa pili nyumbani
Nayo anayo marazi, yesiyotoka mwilini
Si marazi ya mzizi, wala dawa madukani
Nimwache mke gani katika wawili hawa.

Then I married a slave, the second woman of the household.
But she has an illness which does not come from the body.
It is neither an illness for the root nor is there a medicine in
    the shop.
Of those two, which woman should I leave?

With this stanza Shaaban Mfaume from Dar es Salaam starts his complaint about his second wife, a *kijakazi* (female slave), whom he describes
as a thief and disloyal to her husband and patron.[1] Similar negative descriptions of slaves, both male and female, with metaphors of incom-
pleteness and sickness, are not only part of the stylistic repertoire of
Swahili poetry but also especially common in aphorisms. Apart from the
content of the poem, its most surprising aspect is the date and place of its
publication. Shaaban Mfaume, who worked at a high school in Temeke,
Dar es Salaam, sent his poem to the Tanganyika Broadcasting Corpora-
tion, which broadcast it in January 1963.

But what does the poem reveal? Is it further proof that slavery continued in East Africa, or more precisely Tanzania, far beyond its official abolition at the beginning of the twentieth century? Or is the equating of a

disloyal wife (of perhaps lower standard) with a slave women merely a stylistic form of Swahili poetry? Both possibilities have to be left open, since the actual context is unknown. However, they show that the extensive research of the last three decades on women and slavery in central and East Africa is relevant for the more recent history of East Africa and the study of Swahili literature.

This chapter, which deals with the depiction of female slaves in various Swahili literary genres, is based on a research project entitled "Gendered Slavery—A Study on the History of Slavery Based on Swahili Sources."[2] This study did not merely contrast the lives of female and male slaves; rather it considered gender in a much broader sense including age, social status, and race.[3] Apart from written historical texts, this chapter is based on interviews with descendants of slaves and slave owners in Bagamoyo, collected in July 2000. It is divided into three sections. The first introduces the sources according to genre. The second explains the terms for female slaves found in the sources. The third describes what these texts reveal about slave women—the violence against them, their labor, their marriages, their role as concubines, and their public behavior, as well as the female solidarity binding them together.

METHODOLOGICAL CONSIDERATIONS AND SOURCES

Reports on female slaves can be found in poetic descriptions, travelogues, indigenous ethnographies, autobiographical accounts, letters, newspaper articles, and official colonial documents. This heterogeneity naturally raises the methodological question of how to construct an image, or to put it more modestly, a mosaic of the life of these women from sources spanning more than seven hundred years—if the Reverend W. E. Taylor, an Anglican missionary and one of the most prominent Swahili experts at the turn of the century, is correct in dating the poem about Liongo's slave Saada to the thirteenth century.[4] Admittedly, most of the source material stems from the late nineteenth and early twentieth centuries. Faced with such a diversity of sources and a lack of contextual knowledge, I have used Siegfried Jäger's concept of discourse as "flows of stocks of social knowledge through time"[5] and Jürgen Link's theory of "collective symbols." By "collective symbols" Link understands the totality or sum of images about a social group produced by their culture—including allegories, metaphors, comparisons, analogies, examples, and emblems.[6] These develop into cultural stereotypes (topoi) that are transmitted and applied collectively.[7] Hence, the result of a study based on different kinds of sources, which cannot be fully placed in their individual contexts and which cover a long span of time, is a set of collective symbols. The following brief introduction shows which topics arose in each of the different kinds of sources.

Poetry

The first mentions of female slaves are found in poems. *Song of the Slave Woman Saada* and *Serenade to the Coconut-Girl*, both of which are ascribed to the early legendary hero Fumo Liongo, mark the beginning of poetic accounts in which female slaves are described as servants in a noble house,[8] as the beloved of their masters,[9] as wives,[10] or as a means of payment.[11] In contrast, the numerous aphorisms that represent social concepts in a nutshell use "the slave" as a negative mechanism of disassociation from other groups of the East African population but contain no gender specificity.[12] Since both poetry and aphorisms are highly conventionalized genres, they have the highest potential to fix and transmit collective symbols through time.

Travelogues, Indigenous Ethnographies, and Autobiographical Accounts

Safari za Wasuaheli, the series of travelogues by East African authors published by Carl Velten at the turn of the century, contain information on the enslavement of women in the southern coastal hinterland,[13] the duties of a concubine kept by the Wazaramo, who live in the hinterland of Dar es Salaam, the rights of inheritance of children stemming from the liaison of a "free" Mdoe[14] with his concubine, and the restrictions on using women of the family as compensation for blood guilt.[15]

The most detailed description of slavery as it existed around the turn of the century in East Africa can be found in Velten's editions on the customs and traditions of the Swahili.[16] This account pays due attention to the particularities of male and female spheres of life. One could even go so far as to describe this report, which was produced by different authors and jointly edited by Carl Velten and Mtoro bin Mwenyi Bakari, as the first gender-specific work on slavery in East Africa.[17] The indigenous ethnographies which can be found in Carl Velten's *Prosa und Poesie der Suaheli* (Prose and Poetry of the Swahili) do mention slavery, but female slaves play no role. The same is true of the majority of the ethnographic reports produced under British rule. Only Ntiro's *Desturi za Wachagga* (Customs of the Chaga People) contains some gender-specific remarks about the slave trade in the interior.[18]

The sources summarized as autobiographical accounts include the autobiography of Hamed bin Muhammed el Murjebi (Tippu Tip), James Mbotela's *Uhuru wa Watumwa* (Liberation of the Slaves), and the memoirs of Kaje wa Mwenye Matano.[19] While Murjebi's and Mbotela's writings mention female slaves only marginally, Kaje's account provides an example of the role of female slaves in a Mombasa household at the turn of the century.

Letters and Documents

C. G. Büttner's *Swahili-Schriftstücke in arabischer Schrift* (Swahili Manuscripts in Arabic Script) includes documents about the sale of female slaves,[20] their release and mutual support, references to continued clientele relationships, concubinage, and the mortgaging of enslaved women to pay off debts.[21] The manuscript collection of the colonial official Gustav Neuhaus contains private letters and official documents in Arabic script sent to the district office in Pangani. They deal with the abuse and killing of a female slave, the release of a pregnant slave from prison, concubinage, and renewed enslavement.[22] Ahmed bin Muhammed bin Ahmed, of Mombasa, refers to the kidnapping and resale of his female slave in a letter to the Reverend Taylor.[23] As these sources indicate, colonial officials and European missionaries were often called on for support in legal cases, since particularly the former had the authority to reach a final verdict that had to be accepted by the African litigants on both sides.

Interviews

In July 2000, as part of a research project on the delimitation of local communities in Zambia and Tanzania,[24] a series of interviews was done in Bagamoyo, a coastal town fifty-four miles north of Dar es Salaam, and Madera, an outpost of the Spiritan mission on the outskirts of Bagamoyo. For historical reasons, slavery developed as an important topic. In the nineteenth century, Bagamoyo was the starting point and end of the central caravan route to the interior. It had a small local slave market, although the majority of slaves passing through were shipped on to Zanzibar. The Spiritan Mission had established a Freedom Village where freed slaves were settled near its compound.[25] By 2000 the local population was still sensitive to the topic of slavery, partly because of numerous projects run by the Mission Museum, the Department of Antiquities, and the Bagamoyo Art College.[26] Lukas Kadelya and I interviewed thirteen descendants of slaves and five members of former patronage or slave-owning families. Four of the interviewees were women.

Authors

It is commonly believed that the gender of a source's author has a great influence on its content. For the Swahili sources on slavery in general and female slaves in particular the overwhelming majority of the authors are male. This explains why both written and oral sources depict primarily male spheres of life. This does not necessarily point to any disparagement of women; rather, in my opinion, it seems to indicate that men usually did not publicly discuss female spheres of life. This courtesy is also reflected in the interviews.

TERMS FOR SLAVERY

The following paragraph attempts to show how the Swahili language developed a distinct terminology that reflects gender as social category in its combination with the institution of slavery. The sources contain a surprising diversity of terms to describe enslaved women and men. This situation not only points to the complexity of the social phenomenon slavery as such, it also reveals the linguistic productivity of a language that does not render grammatical gender as feminine, masculine, or neuter, as in other languages. Instead the Swahili noun classes, as a distinctive system of grammatical gender, attribute connotations like "big," "small," "good," or "bad" to a lexical item.[27] Furthermore, Swahili seems to possess no unambiguous pair of opposites for master/mistress versus male slave/female slave. The word *bwana* (master) refers to the head of the family, which includes the slave owner as well the husband. The women who use the slaves are called *bibi* (mistress). As can be seen from the memoirs of Kaje wa Mwenye Matano from Mombasa as well as the documents of sale and hire, it was usually men who bought the slaves and were thus considered to be their owners, or patrons. But the texts also demonstrate that it was chiefly the bibi who made use of the slave women's labor. The word pair *mwungwana* (noble person) and *mtumwa* (slave) does not seem to form a dichotomy either. Instead, a basic dichotomy between civilized (*kiungwana*) and barbarian (*kishenzi*) is assumed, mediated by the concept of slavery/service (*utumwa*).[28] In poetry, this transitional state is often exemplified by attributing *uungwana* (nobility) characteristics to slaves:

Kauye, mwana wa ezi, mwana masiwa kwa ngoma,
Kauye ni mjakazi, alipita waungwana.[29]

(Kauye, is a noble child, like the great siwa-horn[30] for the celebration.
Kauye is a slave, but she surpasses the noble citizen.)

The intermediate position is plausible to the extent that the slaves, who mostly came from the hinterland, frequently adopted the culture and religion of their owners and often regarded the way of life in the areas of their origin as uncivilized (kishenzi) and an obstacle to advancement in the social hierarchy of the slaves.[31] The term mswahili (pl. waswahili)—which, according to Jonathon Glassman's observation in Pangani and preindependence newspaper debates on Zanzibar, was a fashionable means to mask slave descent—does not occur in the texts.[32]

The following explanation of terms focuses on references to slave women.[33] In descriptions that include the capture and the march to the coast, slave women are either subsumed under the ungendered term mtumwa (slave) or referred to as wanawake (women). Their identity and thus the term used to refer to them does not change until they are sold—that is, until a specific function within the economic and social structure of their owners has been assigned to them. The sources suggest two possibilities: a slave woman either became a servant in the domestic sphere or a concubine. The first is referred to as mjakazi (female servant) or ki-jakazi (young slave woman).[34] Whereas the class marker m- (pl. wa-) assigns maturity, the class marker ki- (pl. vi-) indicates infant or dependent social status. Ethnographic accounts contain expressions in which kijakazi is also aligned with the pronominal concordant of the nominal class 7/8.[35] Normally, nouns of persons, which have the ki- (pl. vi-) class marker, behave syntactically exactly like nouns of class 1/2, which subsumes human beings. Thus, expressions with a change in concordance as mtu hununua kijakazi, akakiweka nyumbani, kikafundishwa kupika, na kulla desturi ya nyumba (a person buys a female slave, then he brings her home, she is taught cooking and all the customs of the household)[36] intensify the dependent character that was ascribed to slave women.

Female slaves with whom their owners had sexual relations, but whom they did not marry, were referred to as suria (pl. masuria), which is usually translated as concubine. However, Abdallah Khalid casts doubt on the adequacy of this translation: "The 'abd [Arabic: slave] who gave birth to a child from her 'master' was placed by this act into the legal category of suria which was a form of marriage and not the European 'concubinage.' The master could no longer sell her, which also means that he could not divorce her as his suria, and she became free at his death."[37] This evident criticism of "European" thinking with regard to an element of Swahili culture implies that the phenomenon of usuria, which was legally regulated by Islam, was fully valid on the East African coast and practiced there accordingly. But usuria was not equally handled in the various legal systems of Islam. The Shafi'ite legal norms, which are prevalent on the East African coast, handled usuria much more restric tively than the Malikite legal tradition, which was applied on the Comoros, or the Ibadite legal school, which was introduced into the legal system of Zanzibar. Additionally, one has always to be aware of a certain tension between the legal norm and an accepted social practice. Thus, from a linguistic point of view, the question arises whether certain terms referring to cross-cultural phenomena such as concubinage have universal meanings. The specifics of a number of cultures influenced by Islam permit at least the suspicion that there were differences between usuria on the East African coast and similarly named institutions in Arab countries. However, once a suria gave birth to a child, she became an *umm al-walad* (mother of a child) and this raised her social status.[38] The complexity of the usuria institution is only one example to show how difficult or even impossible it is to speak of an accepted norm and social practice in a clearly defined "Swahili culture." In a short poem originating in the nineteenth century, the author complains about the escape of *wajawa kenda* (my nine slaves).[39] *Wajawa* is the combined form of the noun *waja* (sg. *mja*, creature) and *wangu*, the possessive pronoun in the first person singular. The context indicates that these women were masuria.

The word *hadimu* (pl. *wahadimu*) refers to freed slaves who maintained a client relationship with their former owners. *Hadimu* is grammatically gender neutral; the context clarifies whether it refers to a woman or a man. One exception is the concluding formula of a letter in the Büttner collection in which the Arabic feminine plural variant *hadimat* is used.[40] In preindependence Zanzibar, the wahadimu as a social group were a hot topic of political discussions. While the British officials classified them as "original" inhabitants of Zanzibar,[41] the Afro-Shirazi Party mouthpiece *Afrika Kwetu* pointed to the negative connotation of the term (of slave descent) to prove the opposite.[42]

The last term for a slave woman to be discussed here is *mpambe* (pl. *wapambe*). This word, which is derived from the verb *pamba* (to adorn), appears in the *Habari za zamani za Kilwa Kisiwani,* in the authors' description of the procession of the ruler Mrimba.[43] Carl Velten, who edited this account, translates *wapambe* as "bejewelled slave girls." Charles Sacleux reserves the word for those young women who accompany the bridegroom to the bride on the wedding night and take care of the guests.[44] A combination of both meanings was found in Hemedi bin Abdallah El-Buhuriy's *Habari za Mrima.*[45] The author explained that in times of slavery the mpambe were young slave girls, who had to fan the bride. Moreover, he argued that a noble person from the coast would

rather have died than have been called mpambe. In time the word under-
went a semantic change. Its current meaning is "bodyguard."[46]

In reports about marriages in which both partners are of slave status,
the bride is referred to as *mjoli,* although the term seems to be gender
neutral.[47] Later, it was also applied to descendants of freed slaves.[48]

SPHERES OF LIFE

The above-mentioned terms for slave women do not always permit an
unambiguous reading. However, the contexts in which they are used can
help. The next section is an attempt in this direction. As indicated in
the first section, the sources provide information about slave women
only in the domestic sphere. Below, I will classify the descriptions of
women's experiences of violence, labor, concubinage, and marriage, as
well as their public behavior and solidarity.

Violence

In Swahili ethnographies, violence—understood as the use of force to
change the circumstances of someone's life—began with the capture of
people and their transformation from members of a community called by
ethnic or clan names into *watumwa* (slaves), or isolated individuals.
Mtumwa was a gender-neutral term used not only in descriptions of capture but above all in accounts of the grim march to the slave markets and
cities of the coast. This gender neutrality underlines the loss of identity
suffered by people in this transitional state, when they had already been
torn from their previous social structure but had not yet been assigned a
place in a new social system. In James Mbotela's autobiographical account, the description of women separated from their children and husbands was used stylistically to convey a vivid image of immense suffering.[49] Women are referred to as *mwanamke* (woman) and *mama* (mother).
Terms such as *kijakazi* or *mjakazi* do not appear. In Tippu Tip's life story,
"free" women in caravans as well as the wives of his slaves were also
called mwanamke.[50]

Aside from the letters that have been preserved, the sources are silent
about violence practiced on slave women after they were bought. As is
known from other works on slave women, their relationship to their
owners was itself a relationship based on force, which found vivid expression with each further sale. The manuscript collections of the colonial official Gustav Neuhaus and of the Reverend William E. Taylor
contain letters documenting the capture and sale of already freed slave

women, a practice clearly different from the accepted norm.[51] Abdul Sheriff also found this practice in the Persian Gulf and on the Benadir coast, where it was considered a criminal act and a ground for manumission when substantiated.[52]

According to Velten's *Desturi za Wasuaheli* (Swahili Traditions), the mortgaging of slaves was permissible not only for the owner. Married slaves were also allowed to offer their wives as security for debts they contracted.[53] That this latter practice was an established one is questionable, since the owner of the slave woman, not the male slave husband or his owner, retained control of her even after marriage. However, it points to the potential worsening of the conditions of a slave woman's life through marriage to another slave. Documents for the sale and hire of female slaves not only fix the price or the agreed period of hire but also include the reasons for which they could be sent back to their bwana, usually for disobedience or fatigue.[54] The only account of physical abuse leading to death is the complaint of Binti Salima to the district office of Pangani, in which she accuses Hemedi bin Abdallah of having killed her slave for whom she had paid forty rupees.[55]

Labor

The sale of the women meant their integration into a new social structure. As Swahili sources refer only to family settings, the *watumwa wanawake* (female slaves) now became *wajakazi*, *vijakazi*, or *masuria*, according to their new functions in the household. The tasks of the wajakazi and vijakazi included primarily domestic activities such as cooking, clearing away and washing dishes, washing laundry, weaving mats, fetching water, shopping, and field work.[56] In part, these tasks were performed together with the bibi or under her supervision. Activities outside the household such as trade and business were supposed to be performed by the wajakazi on their own, insofar as this was possible. Subjected to the seclusion required by Muslim law, "free" women used female slaves as an extended arm to preserve their economic independence. This is at least suggested by the memoirs of Kaje wa Mwenye Matano and the poem to Saada, which talk about slave women who were entrusted with important responsibilities.[57]

The further duties of the wajakazi included guaranteeing the well-being of the bwana by anointing and massaging his body as well as washing his feet. However, the consent of the bibi was required for these activities. The same seems to have been true for the offering of betel, which was sometimes prechewed by the women as a proof of ardent affection.[58]

Concubinage and Marriage

In an earlier version of this chapter I classified the position of a suria as labor or service, since the relationship between her and her bwana was fundamentally based on force. I doubted the romantic image painted in Velten's *Desturi za Wasuaheli*, which portrays the masuria as respected figures within the household, who upon the birth of a child advanced to highly regarded members of the community.[59] However, the respected status of many of these women has now been confirmed by numerous interviews. In contrast, a suria could quite well be married off to someone else and would thus cease to be a suria, as can be seen in Velten's first edition on the customs and traditions of the Swahili, and confirmed in a letter from the Neuhaus collection. In the case mentioned in the letter, doubt was cast upon the paternity of her child, and it would be interesting to know what happened to her. Was she sent back? Did the former owner care at all? Who accepted paternity for the child? Although the outcome of the case is unknown, the importance of the matter is indicated by the fact that it was legally solved by the colonial government.[60] However, numerous discussions drew my attention to the variety of circumstances under which a female slave became suria and the legal obstacles preventing a "free" man from taking a particular slave as his suria. In Islamic law, Muslim men were permitted to have intimate relations only with Muslim, Christian, or Jewish slaves. The Shafi'ite legal school was even more restrictive, as it confined a Muslim man to Muslim slaves only. Since most of the slaves were from the hinterland or remote areas and thus not (yet) converted to Islam or Christianity, it could be argued that deviations from these legal norms were the prevalent social practice.

As the *Desturi za Wasuaheli* shows, a man's relationship or marriage with a suria was much less onerous than if he took a "free" wife, since he had no obligations toward the woman's family. Under Islamic law a marriage between a male or female slave and a "free" man or woman was not permitted because of their unequal social status.[61] This legal norm could be ignored if the "free" person was not yet married (and was thus eligible to have extramarital relations) and if the slave was Muslim. This marital practice was quite common in the case of "free" males marrying female slaves whom they had to free before marriage.[62] However, a document from the Büttner collection indicates that "free" parents took care not to marry their daughters to men of slave status, stating in the marriage contract, "Wa kathalika na zamani yatokeapo bwana wangu kama ni mtumwa, mke talaka" (Furthermore, the married women is also divorced if the husband has been a slave).[63]

Arguably, the lack of kinsmen to protect the suria was one reason she often did not enjoy the same position as a "free" woman. In general, masuria were often seen as having inadequate upbringings. The poetic dialogue from Pemba found in the Whiteley Collection, in which the question of a suitable wife is discussed, characterizes masuria as women without a sense of shame, conveyers of bad luck, people who would not know what to do with their freedom.[64] And, ultimately, a suria remained a slave woman. The following lines of a song from Zanzibar make this presumption a certainty:

> suria mtumwa we, suria mtumwa we,
> usithanie utalalia godoro ya Bwana,
> suria mtumwa we.[65]

> Suria, you slave! Suria, you slave! Don't think that you can make yourself comfortable on your master's mattress. Suria, you slave!

In contrast, the autobiography of Princess Salme, daughter of Zanzibar's Sultan Seyyid Said, points out that although Azze bint Seif, the sultan's wife, was the undisputed head of the harem, his seventy-five masuria were highly respected women.[66] Furthermore, as oral accounts from Bagamoyo indicate, the suria often reared the children of the household.[67] Swahili poetry discloses both affection and love for masuria[68] as well as disappointment at their behavior.[69]

Accounts of marriages between male and female slaves state that the male slave usually informed his bwana about his intention to marry a *mjoli fulani* (a certain female fellow slave) after she had consented. He paid one reale[70]—the *kilemba* (turban)—to his bwana. The *mahari* (bridewealth) was five reale and was paid by the slave to the bwana of the female slave. The latter usually married the couple, but there are reports that in the early twentieth century such couples were also married by religious authorities.[71] Marriage celebrations are not reported. The *Desturi za Wasuaheli* further asserts that if the bridegroom was a hadimu (freed slave), he usually consulted his "patron"—a practice that applied to all important matters. According to Bibi Kajeri, who is descended from a slave-owning family of Bagamoyo, such consultation between the descendants of their former slaves and herself or her family still continues.[72]

Public Behavior

As indicated in the remarks on slave women's labor, they were mostly not subject to the seclusion requirements, which also included a dress code. While "free" women wore the *ukaya* (veil) if they wanted to be considered virtuous (*mwenye heshima*), slave women were not permitted to cover their heads and shoulders.[73] One reaction to this dress code was the invention of the *kanga*. This long, flowing garment was worn chiefly by former slave women of less affluent families who thus imitated the costly embroidered clothing of the "free" woman and the *masuria* of richer households.[74]

An additional public sphere in which slave women were involved was that of festivals. Reference has already been made to the bejewelled slave girls, the *wapambe*, who took part in the procession of Mrimba (elder) from Kilwa. Velten also mentions that the *wajakazi* danced with the male *waungwana* (nobility) on festive occasions, while the female *waungwana* celebrated in the house or in the courtyard.[75]

Aphorisms, which often ascribe negative characteristics to women in general, also show very clearly that not only were the *watumwa* not bound to the code of honor (*heshima*), they were literally excluded from it.[76] In contrast, there are numerous cases, especially with regard to male slaves, that prove the contrary. One very famous, but male, example is Sheikh Ramiya from Bagamoyo—a former slave of the el-Lamky family. He was not only entrusted with important economic transactions but also received higher Islamic education, which led to his appointment as imam of Bagamoyo. In 1918 he even became the town's *liwali* (headman).[77]

Solidarity

Solidarity among African women under the extreme conditions of slavery on the Gold Coast has already been discussed by Adam Jones.[78] According to the memoirs of Kaje wa Mwenye Matano from Mombasa, female slaves lived in harmony with their *mabibi* and were supported by them. Islamic law also stipulates that the bwana or the bibi must take good care of their slaves.[79] Collections of aphorisms and travelogues equate slaves with children (*watoto*): *Baa pia hutokanana vijana na watumwa* (Misfortune is usually brought by children and slaves).[80] The manuscript collections of Neuhaus and Büttner contain letters that may point toward mutual support among women. The document from the Neuhaus collection is a petition from Kuzi binti Kisimiya addressed to the German district office in Pangani, requesting the release of her ki-jakazi, who is held in prison there, so that she can bear her child at home.[81] The child would automatically become her slave and be a *mza-lia* (one born into the household), which would provide the basis for a stronger loyalty toward the bibi. A different matter is the case of Fatima, a freed slave of Muhammed bin Seleman al-Hadrami. She claims to be a mwungwana, and on this basis attempts to gain the release of her mother and two aunts.[82] For a better assessment of the effectiveness of such petitions, it would be interesting to know the outcome of this and similar cases.

NOTES

1. Shaaban bin Mfaume, *Nimwache mke gani katika wawili hawa* (Of those two, which woman should I leave), Whiteley Collection, School of Oriental and African Studies, Private Papers MS (hereafter abbreviated SOAS, PPMS) 42, S/30, 91.

2. The project lasted nineteen months (1999–2000) and was financed by a scholarship from the Berlin City Government, Department of Women, Youth and Work, to whom I am very grateful. A travel grant from the German Research Council facilitated the field research in Bagamoyo in July 2000. I also thank Abdul Sheriff, Zanzibar, and Thilo Schadeberg, Leiden, for their useful comments on an earlier version of this chapter.

3. For a discussion of this broader approach, see Heike Schmidt, "Geschlechter-verhältnisse: Gegenstand und Methode," in *Geschichte in Afrika: Einführung in Probleme und Debatten*, ed. Jan-Georg Deutsch and Albert Wirz (Berlin: Das Arabische Buch, 1997), 175–78.

4. Taylor Collection, SOAS, PPMS 53495, 29.

5. Siegfried Jäger, *Kritische Diskursanalyse: Eine Einführung* (Duisburg: DISS, 1999), 132.

6. Jürgen Link, *Versuch über den Normalismus: Wie Normalität produziert wird* (Opladen: Westdeutscher Verlag, 1997), 25.

7. Axel Drews, Ute Gerhard, and Jürgen Link, "Moderne Kollektivsymbolik: Eine diskurstheoretische Einführung mit Auswahlbibliographie," *Internationales Archiv für Sozialgeschichte der deutschen Literatur, Sonderheft Forschungsreferate 1* (1985): 265.

8. Liongo Fumo wa Bauri, "Shairi kwa kiyakazi Saada," Taylor Collection, SOAS, PPMS 53495, 29; Liongo Fumo wa Bauri, "The Song of Sada," in *Four Centuries of Swahili Verse*, ed. Jan Knappert (London: Heinemann, 1979), 92; Liongo Fumo wa Bauri, "The Serenade to the Coconut-Girl," in Knappert, *Four Centuries*, 99; "Das Lied vom Sklavenmädchen," in *Prosa und Poesie der Suaheli*, ed. Carl Velten (Berlin: by author, 1907), 424; "Allegorical Verse Celebrating the Rise of Zanzibar over Pemba," Whiteley Collection, PPMS 42, S/20.

9. "Liebe zu einem Sklavenmädchen," in Velten, *Prosa und Poesie*, 421.

10. Shaaban bin Mfaume, *"Nimwache mke gani"*; Abdallah bin Salim el-Busaidi, *"Paka Shume,"* Whiteley Collection, SOAS, PPMS 42, S/21, S/26; *"Nyimbo,"* Taylor Collection, SOAS, PPMS 193290.

11. Hemedi bin Abdallah el-Buhriy, *Utenzi wa Vita vya Wadachi Kutamalaki Mrima,* suppl. to the *Journal of the East African Swahili Committee* 25 (1960): 58.

12. S. S. Farsi, *Swahili Sayings from Zanzibar,* Book 1, Proverbs (Dar es Salaam: East African Literature Bureau, 1958); Casimiri Kuhenga, *Methali na nahau* (Arusha: Eastern Africa Publications, 1978); S. Y. A. Ngole and L. N. Honero, *Fasihi-Simulizi ya Mtanzania: Methali: Kitabu cha Pili* (Dar es Salaam: Taasisi ya Uchunguzi wa Kiswahili, 1982); M. Abudu and A. Baruwa, *Methali za Kiswahili: Maana na Matumizi* (Nairobi: Shungwaya, 1993); William E. Taylor, *African Aphorisms; or, Saws from Swahili-Land* (London: Society for Promoting Christian Knowledge, 1891); Jan Knappert, *Swahili Proverbs* (Ndanda: Ndanda Mission, 1997).

13. Selim bin Abakari, "Safari yangu ya Nyassa," in Carl Velten, *Safari za Wasuaheli* (Göttingen: Vandenhoeck and Ruprecht, 1901), 99.

14. The Wadoe are an ethnic group residing in the hinterland of Pangani.

15. Mtoro bin Mwenyi Bakari, "Safari yangu ya Udoe hatta Uzigua na khabari za Wadoe na mila yao," in Velten, *Safari,* 128, 215, 218.

16. Carl Velten, *Sitten und Gebräuche der Suaheli* (Berlin: Reichsdruckerei, 1898); Carl Velten, *Desturi za Wasuaheli na khabar za desturi za sheria za Wasuaheli* (Göttingen: Vandenhoeck and Ruprecht, 1903), 253–65.

17. Mtoro bin Mwenyi Bakari, "Khabari za utumwa," in Velten, *Desturi za Wasuaheli,* 253–65.

18. S. J. Ntiro, *Desturi za Wachagga* (Nairobi: East African Literature Bureau, 1953), 23–24.

19. Heinrich Brode, ed., "Autobiographie des Arabers Schech Hamed bin Muhammed il Murjebi, genannt Tippu Tip," *Mitteilungen des Seminars für orientalische Sprachen* 5 (1902): 175–227, 6 (1903): 1–55; James Mbotela, *Uhuru wa Watumwa* (Nairobi: East African Literature Bureau, 1956); Kaje wa Mwenye Matano, in *Wanawake watatu wa Kiswahili,* ed. Sarah M. Mirza and Margaret Strobel (Bloomington: Indiana University Press, 1991), 8–48.

20. Apart from the Swahili sources on slavery in Arabic script, there are also Arabic documents about the sale and hiring of slaves in the Neuhaus Collection of the Staatsbibliothek Preussischer Kulturbesitz at Berlin (hereafter StPK), Hs. or. 10527.

21. C. G. Büttner, *Suaheli-Schriftstücke in arabischer Schrift* (Berlin: W. Spemann, 1892), 46, 48–49, 51–53, 85.

22. Neuhaus Collection, StPK Hs. or. 698–5, Hs. or. 689–1, Hs. or. 772–15.

23. Taylor Collection, SOAS, PPMS 53489.

24. The research project was directed by Achim von Oppen and pursued at the Center for Modern Oriental Studies, Berlin, 1996–2000. A substantial part of the results went into Achim von Oppen's unpublished habilitation thesis on "Bounding Villages. The Enclosure of Locality in Central Africa, 1890s to 1990s," Humboldt-University Berlin 2003.

25. Further information about the foundation and development of the mission is provided by J. A. Kieran, "The Holy Ghost Fathers in East Africa" (PhD thesis, University of London, 1966).

26. The latest project is to establish a Slavery Museum in the Old Karawan Serai.

27. For a detailed discussion, see Rose-Marie Beck, "Perceptions of Gender in Swahili Language and Society," in Gender across Languages, ed. Marlis Hellinger and Hadumod Bussmann (Amsterdam: Benjamins, 2002), 311–37.

28. Carol M. Eastman, "Service, Slavery ('Utumwa') and Swahili Social Reality," Afrikanistische Arbeitspapiere 37 (1994): 87.

29. "Liebe zu einem Sklavenmädchen," in Velten, Prosa und Poesie, 421.

30. The siwa is a large, ornately carved horn that belongs to the set of instruments exclusively played in festive rites. For further information, see Jonathon Glassman, Feasts and Riot: Revelry, Rebellion, and Popular Consciousness on the Swahili Coast, 1856–1888 (London: James Currey, 1995), 155–56.

31. This is indicated in Mbotela's Uhuru wa Watumwa and in the life story by Kaje wa Mwenye Matano.

32. Glassman, Feasts and Riot, 95; "Furnish Us with the Zanzibar History," Afrika Kwetu, 17 June 1955, 1.

33. For a good collection and discussion of terms on slavery, see Abdulaziz Y. Lodhi, The Institution of Slavery in Zanzibar and Pemba (Uppsala: 1973); Eastman, "Service, Slavery," 88.

34. For a very eloquent bantuistic etymology of mjakazi, see T. Schadeberg, "Mjakazi" — The Female Slave, manuscript, Leiden, 2000.

35. Ntiro, Desturi za Wachagga, 23; Velten, Desturi za Wasuaheli, 262.

36. Velten, Desturi za Wasuaheli, 262.

37. Abdallah Khalid, The Liberation of Swahili from European Appropriation (Nairobi: East African Literature Bureau, 1977), 95.

38. For a detailed description, see H. A. R. Gibb and J. H. Krammers, eds., Shorter Encyclopedia of Islam (Leiden: Brill, 1961), 601–3.

39. Taylor Collection, SOAS, PPMS 53826, 3.

40. Büttner, Suaheli-Schriftstücke, 51–53.

41. This ethnological classification was fixed in the Zanzibar census of 1948.

42. "Furnish Us with the Zanzibar History," 1.

43. Akida Said bin Bushiri, Mohamed bin Nwenyi Mkuu, and Osmani bin Ahmed, in Velten, Prosa und Poesie, 245. Regarding Mrimba, see G. S. P. Freeman-Grenville, The Medieval History of the Coast of Tanganyika (Berlin: Akademie Verlag, 1962), 74, 81.

44. Charles Sacleux, Dictionnaire Swahili-Français (Paris: Institute d'Ethnologie, 1939), 583.

45. Hemedi bin Abdallah el-Buhriy, "Habari za Mrima," Mambo Leo 144 (1934): 103.

46. Kamusi ya Kiswahili-Kiingereza: Swahili-English Dictionary (Dar es Salaam: Taasisi ya Uchunguzi wa Kiswahili, Chuo Kikuu, 2001), 216. I am grateful to Sauda Barwani, who drew my attention to this linguistic change.

47. Velten, *Desturi za Wasuaheli*, 260–62.

48. Ibid., 205.

49. Mbotela, *Uhuru*, 12, 34.

50. Brode, "Autobiographie Tippu Tip," 217.

51. Neuhaus Collection, StPK Hs. or. 772–3, Taylor Collection, SOAS, PPMS 53489.

52. Abdul Sheriff, pers. comm., 22 August 2002.

53. Velten, *Desturi za Wasuaheli*, 264.

54. Neuhaus Collection, StPK Hs. or. 10527, 1–3; Büttner, *Suaheli-Schriftstücke*, 84–87.

55. Neuhaus Collection, StPK Hs. or. 698–5. This price was rather low compared to the 80 rupees mentioned in Velten, *Prosa und Poesie*, 158.

56. Velten, *Sitten*, 35; Velten, *Desturi za Wasuaheli*, 257; Velten, *Safari*, 128; Mirza and Strobel, Kaje wa Mwenye Matano, 18.

57. Liongo, *Shairi kwa kiyakazi Saad*.

58. Velten, *Desturi za Wasuaheli*, 257; Knappert, *Four Centuries*, 99; Whiteley Collection, SOAS, PPMS 42 S/20.

59. Velten, *Desturi za Wasuaheli*, 262

60. Velten, *Sitten*, 36; Neuhaus Collection, StPK Hs. or. 1592–2.

61. Gibb and Krammers, *Shorter Encyclopedia*, 2.

62. Ibid., 3; see also Velten, *Prosa und Poesie*, 262.

63. Büttner, *Suaheli-Schriftstücke*, 87.

64. Whiteley Collection, SOAS, PPMS 42 S/21, 26.

65. Taylor Collection, SOAS, PPMS 193290–93.

66. Emily Ruete, *Ein Leben im Sultanspalast* (Frankfurt am Main: Athenäum, 1991), 23. For an English translation, see Emily Ruete, *Memoirs of an Arabian Princess from Zanzibar* (Princeton: Markus Wiener, 1995).

67. Mzee Pima, interview by author, Bagamoyo, 27 July 2000; Abasi Bukheti, interview by author, Bagamoyo, 29 July 2000.

68. Velten, *Prosa und Poesie*, 421; Taylor Collection, SOAS, PPMS 53826,

69. Taylor Collection, SOAS, PPMS 193290–93, 53826; Whiteley Collection, SOAS, PPMS 42/30/91; Velten, *Prosa und Poesie*, 424–25.

70. One reale was equal to five Maria Theresa thalers. The reale was used before the introduction of the rupee.

71. Velten, *Desturi za Wasuaheli*, 261.

72. Interview with Bibi Kajeri, Bagamoyo, 23 July 2000.

73. Velten, *Sitten*, 35.

74. I am grateful to Rose-Marie Beck for pointing me to this fact. For dress and slavery, see Laura Fair, "Dressing Up: Clothing, Class and Gender in Post-Abolition Zanzibar," *Journal of African History* 39, no. 1 (1998): 63–94; Laura Fair, *Pastimes and Politics: Culture, Community, and Identity in Post-Abolition Urban Zanzibar, 1890–1945* (Athens: Ohio University Press, 2001).

75. Velten, *Sitten*, 35.

76. For women in African aphorisms, see Ruth Mukama, "Gender Stereotyping in African Languages," in *Theoretical Approaches to African Linguistics*, ed. Akinbiyi Akinlabi (Trenton, NJ: Africa World, 1995), 375–92.

77. For further details, see August H. Nimtz Jr., *Islam and Politics in East Africa: The Sufi Order in Tanzania* (Minneapolis: University of Minnesota Press, 1980), 120.

78. Adam Jones, "Female Slave-Owners on the Gold Coast," in *Slave Cultures and Cultures of Slavery*, ed. Stephan Palmié (Knoxville: University of Tennessee Press, 1995), 100–101.

79. H. A. R. Gibb, ed., *Encyclopedia of Islam*, 7 vols. (Leiden: Brill, 1960), 1:32.

80. Taylor, *African Aphorisms*, 8.

81. Neuhaus Collection, StPK Hs. or. 772–15.

82. Büttner, *Suaheli-Schriftstücke*, 48.

Swahili area of Eastern Africa, including the Mrima Coast, ca. 1870–1915

5

PRICES FOR FEMALE SLAVES AND CHANGES IN THEIR LIFE CYCLE

Evidence from German East Africa

JAN-GEORG DEUTSCH

This chapter shows how changes in the price of female slaves in German East Africa before the outbreak of war in 1914 reflected changes in their life cycle. A number of works on women as slaves in Africa have appeared since the publication of Claire Robertson and Martin Klein's seminal work *Women and Slavery in Africa* (1983), notably Marcia Wright's study *Strategies of Slaves and Women: Life-Stories from East/Central Africa.*[1] However, the question of how the social position and commercial value of female slaves changed during the course of their lives has received comparatively little attention. In this connection it is worth noting that the "typical" life cycle of a female slave in the 1870s and 1880s, when slavery was widespread in East Africa, particularly in the area that today encompasses Tanzania, was different from that of a female slave some twenty or thirty years later, during the early colonial period, when slavery was coming to an end.

FEMALE SLAVERY IN EAST AFRICA

At the end of the nineteenth century most slaves in East Africa were women and girls.[2] Most resided in the countryside, where they were employed as agricultural laborers. Almost all lived in distinctly patriarchal

This chapter is based on research carried out for a *Habilitationsschrift* at Humboldt-University at Berlin, a revised version of which appeared under the title *Emancipation without Abolition in German East Africa, c. 1884–1914* (Oxford: James Currey, 2006).

societies, in which their legal positions, social rights, and economic opportunities were on the whole even more severely restricted than those of male slaves, especially in terms of self-employment, social mobility, and domestic affairs, as in marriage and inheritance. These are, of course, sweeping generalizations. Some female slaves, as "wives" of local notables like the sultan of Zanzibar, could achieve a very high social status.[3] But the perhaps overdramatic statement made by a contemporary observer that female slaves in East Africa represented the "sum of human degradation, the lowest creature on God's earth" may not be far off the mark,[4] although it does not explain why younger slave women and female slave children seem to have commanded consistently higher prices in slave markets than their male counterparts of the same ages.[5]

Broadly speaking, there were two modes of social incorporation for female slaves at the time—clientage and lineage slavery.[6] The former was practiced on the East African coast and the adjacent islands. In these areas a sizeable proportion of the female slave population did not share the same household with their owner. Most of these slaves were "foreigners," brought to the coast as children or young adults. They lived in the rural areas, often in their own villages, and mainly worked as agricultural laborers. Together with their slave husbands they often maintained their own households. They were bound to their owners by a more or less distant but very durable patronage-clientage relationship, some remnants of which have survived to this day.

In the vast hinterland, extending inland from the coast as far as Lakes Tanganyika and Victoria, the situation was markedly different. Here fictive or real lineage affiliation was probably the predominant pattern of incorporation. Over time female slaves, especially younger girls, though also mainly employed as agricultural laborers, became firmly attached to the households of their (male) owners and through marriage or child bearing became part of it. In periods of political turmoil or ecological crises, they were the first to be sold to passing caravans, but otherwise their social position was not radically different from the free female members of the slave-owning household. As on the coast, the social rights and economic opportunities of female slaves in the hinterland were far more restricted than those of male slaves.

There has been considerable disagreement in the literature as to whether slave women were valued more for their productive or for their reproductive capacities.[7] This debate has not been resolved, probably because the various participants employed mutually exclusive definitions of such fluid categories as slavery, patriarchy, or dependency. For the purpose of this chapter, it is sufficient to point out that both the reproductive and productive capacities of women shaped the social lives of female slaves within specific households and communities and that their relative importance changed during the life cycle of the female slave and over time.

Historical knowledge about the life cycles of female slaves in East Africa is severely limited. Except for the autobiographical literature,[8] which has its own problems and distinct agenda, female slaves are mentioned in official documents only when they appear in the market or in legal disputes between owners or between the owner and the colonial state. "Authentic" female slave voices have yet to be found in official archives. Moreover, there are no ethnographic accounts of slaves' lives and the changes in them over time. Finally, it appears that the geographical coverage of archival documents is highly uneven. Most of the sources deal with the coastal areas, and far less is known about the hinterland and the interior. The following account will largely focus on the coast of Tanzania, which in the early colonial period belonged to German East Africa.

SOCIAL DIVISIONS AMONG SLAVES ON THE EAST AFRICAN COAST

The number of slaves resident on the coast was first estimated by European observers in the 1890s. It is not known how the German district officers arrived at the figures they gave, but according to their reports, the coastal districts harbored around 125,000 to 200,000 slaves. By district there were 4,673 slaves in Tanga; 17,500 in Pangani; about 2,000 in Bagamoyo; about 2,000 in Dar es Salaam; 9,313 in Rufiyi; between 40,000 and 50,000 in Kilwa; and between 50,000 and 100,000 in Lindi.[9] Most of them lived in or close to coastal towns, while the coastal hinterland was reported to have comparatively small resident populations of slaves. In the south, most slaves, probably as many as two-thirds, were women, whereas the gender proportions in the northern part of the coast were more equal. There is no way to establish the accuracy of these figures. Nevertheless, even allowing for mistakes, they indicate that large numbers of slaves were resident on the coast in the late 1880s, accounting in certain places, such as the town of Lindi or Mafia Island, for more than half the local population.

The generic term for slave in kiSwahili is *mtumwa* (one who is sent or used; pl. *watumwa*). From the owners' perspective, slaves were regarded more or less as dispensable personal clients, owing to the personal nature

of their ties to their owner. The number of the owner's dependents determined the degree of honor and respect they could command in their respective communities.[10] Yet the term *mtumwa* covered a whole range of
different social realities and conditions. The lives of slaves on the coast
not only varied—as one would expect—in different places and periods,
but they also varied significantly according to the gender, age, religion,
personal reputation, profession, and birth place—whether they were
born on the coast or elsewhere— of the individual slaves. These qualify-
ing markers reflected the general hierarchical divisions of Swahili urban
society, which were reproduced in its slave segment. In daily life these
divisions denoted differing degrees of personal autonomy and were
probably as vital to the slaves as the distinction between owners and
slaves itself.

Slaves who had arrived on the coast only recently were called *mateka*
(booty, captive; sing. and pl.), *mshenzi* (barbarian; pl. *washenzi*), or *mjinga*
(ignorant or stupid person; pl. *wajinga*) in kiSwahili.[11] According to one
source, after their arrival the adult mjinga slaves, "who do not know how
to do the washing or to cook"[12]—pointing to the fact that these slaves
were predominantly women—were given a few pieces of cloth and a hoe
and brought to a plantation or garden plot. They also received a new
kiSwahili name. Owners sometimes took younger mjinga slaves, especially girls, into the house, where they were taught by older female slaves
to do household work. According to Richard Burton, mjinga slave boys
were sometimes given an Islamic education and professional training.[13]
In later life these boys would usually work as "self-employed" artisans and
craftsmen (in kiSwahili *fundi*; pl. *mafundi*).

A second category included the people born into slavery on the coast.
They were called *mzalia* (pl. *wazalia*), which usually implied that their
mothers or both parents had been slaves.[14] In general, the social status of
mzalia slaves was higher than that of slaves who had arrived on the coast
only recently, not least because they spoke kiSwahili, had some knowledge of the teachings of Islam, and frequently had respectable urban professions in the service sector, such as skilled artisans. Because of the prevailing gender division of labor, most of these skilled slaves were men.
The economic relationship with their owners was often reduced to a
monthly or annual payment of a previously fixed amount of money or
a specified portion of their earnings. These payments varied a great deal
between the northern and southern coast. It was reported that in the
1890s in Lindi, for example, slaves kept half their earnings, whereas in
Pangani for the same period the amount was probably less than a third.[15]

Both mjinga and mzalia slaves were expected to show deference and respect in public to their owners. They were supposed to walk behind them, or, if they met them in the street they were to remove their caps immediately. "The slaves could not use their master's wells, nor might they look up when they passed their master's house, nor swing their arms" states one source.[16] In some areas, slaves were not allowed to cover their heads at all, a stipulation that meant female slaves had to walk around town unveiled. In the eyes of more pious Muslims this marked them as women with whom social contact should be avoided at all costs.[17]

The social lives of slaves thus differed according to the division between those "imported" and the locally born, as well as between slaves who worked in the fields and those whose duty was to conduct household work. Most of the latter were young women born into slavery on the coast.[18] In the market, they not only fetched higher prices than unskilled male slaves of the same age group but also higher prices than older women. In kiSwahili they were known as *kijakazi* (pl. *vijakazi*).[19] In the more well-to-do households they carried out ordinary household tasks, such as fetching water, cooking, cleaning, doing the washing, and looking after the children, basically relieving the owners' wife or wives of their usual chores. In less affluent households, the owners' wife or wives and female slaves shared these duties. Moreover, female slaves could venture outside the house, whereas "free" women were prevented from doing so by the more pious Muslim household heads, who insisted on the strict observance of Islamic doctrines and beliefs regarding the proper behavior of women in public. In any case, female slaves delivered messages, purchased mundane supplies in the markets, and ran errands for their mistresses.[20]

Finally, female slaves sold food and other commodities in the streets—such as bread, cakes, fried fish, and mats—that had been produced in the house by the "free" women. The earnings were usually shared between the female "free" members of the household and the female slaves.[21] Thus, although female household slaves were owned as a rule by the male household head, it was his wife or wives who directed their work in daily life. Female slaves also accompanied their mistresses through the streets to marriage ceremonies and other festivities. In the case of elite families, the *kijakazi* was expected to carry an umbrella to protect her mistress from both the sun and male curiosity.[22] In general, these female slaves received food, housing, and clothing but no wages, except for the occasional gift of small amounts of money. According to one report, they earned some extra money by selling foodstuffs and vegetables, which they grew in small garden plots.[23]

The slave owner's concubine, locally known as a *suria* (pl. *masuria*), occupied a special position in the house. Masuria were the most expensive slaves and therefore found only in the more affluent households. According to Islamic law and practice on the coast, Muslim men were allowed to marry up to four wives, but they could possess as many concubines as they liked—and could afford.[24] Like other female household slaves, masuria had to provide sexual services to the male household head, even against their will. Both female household slaves and masuria who refused to cohabit with their owners were evidently put to work in the fields as a punishment. According to a contemporary observer, there was a popular kiSwahili saying on the coast at the time which ran: *kijakazi kina meno, chauma / Sikitaki tenna, kipileke shamba / kikalime.* Roughly translated it meant: "The slave girl has teeth, she bites. / I do not want her any longer, send her to the fields / to do agricultural work!"[25]

Those who worked in the fields did so either on the plantations or on plots of land they had been given to farm on their own. In the latter case, they had agreed to pay their owners a specified sum of money at regular intervals or to hand over part of their crop.[26] The amount received by the owner was known in kiSwahili in some areas as *ijara*, in other areas as *taja*, irrespective of whether such dues were paid in kind or in money. For the 1880s and 1890s, such taja arrangements were found more often in the southern than in the northern part of the coast.[27]

Slaves working on plantations did not usually earn "wages" but received food, housing, and clothing from their owners instead. Clothing for women consisted of a "gift" of two *kanga* (pieces of patterned cloth) twice a year; at the same time male slaves received a *kanzu* (a long-sleeve, straight cotton gown), a *kofia* (a white needleworked cap), and perhaps a few pieces of cotton cloth.[28] The typical work of a coastal agricultural slave consisted of cleaning and weeding coconut plantations, harvesting and cutting the nuts, and extracting the white meat (copra) of the fruit. After drying, the meat would be boiled to extract the valuable coconut oil, which was locally used for cooking. The length of the working day on the plantations varied enormously, even within a particular locality.[29] The majority of plantation slaves were new arrivals, most of whom were women.[30] They were allowed to work their own garden plots for an agreed period during the week, usually two or three days, which always included Friday, the day of Islamic prayer.[31] Like the slaves who were left to work their own fields, plantation slaves sold part of the produce from their garden plots at urban markets.[32] Finally, there were the vast numbers of slaves who neither worked their own fields nor the plantations under supervision but rather on their own accounts as wage laborers and skilled artisans.[33] The great majority of these were men. As already mentioned above, they "shared" their wages with their owner or had to pay him a fixed sum of money each month.

There were two groups of urban laborers: First, there were the petty traders such as hawkers and unskilled menial workers such as day laborers, porters, stevedores, builders, and—in the case of women—cleaners, water carriers, and sex workers.[34] In the coastal rural areas "self-employed" slaves worked chiefly as casual plantation labor. They did the most unrewarding and tiresome work such as digging up and cleaning gum copal, a resinous substance used in Europe and elsewhere in the industrial production of varnish. It is therefore hardly surprising that many of them, dissatisfied with rural life and their meager incomes, were drawn to the coastal towns in search of more lucrative employment.[35] There they "could be found lurking at the waterfront," as Glassman poetically phrases it.[36] In kiSwahili this type of slave was called kibarua (pl. vibarua), and vibarua formed a significant part of the local slave populations almost everywhere on the coast.[37] Second, there were those slaves who worked as "self-employed" artisans or skilled workers, some of whom had previously worked as day laborers but had learned a more lucrative trade. They worked as sea captains, fishermen, sailors, rope makers, tailors, shoemakers, potters, mat makers, wood-carvers, weavers, palm wine tappers, carpenters, metalworkers, bricklayers, and masons.[38] Others joined caravans as porters, petty traders, and itinerant artisans, some even as caravan leaders and guides.[39] In addition, there were those who worked as professional soldiers, or rather, mercenaries.[40] Women were generally excluded from these professions, but some female slaves managed to become small foodstuff sellers, buying cheap meat or fish in the market, for instance, putting it on small wooden sticks, grilling it, and then selling the sticks in the streets and local markets. A number of female slaves also engaged in beer brewing, evidently a highly profitable undertaking.[41]

These "self-employed" slaves were the elite among the servile. Some of them earned substantial amounts of money. They had their own families, and their children were frequently regarded as free, although their fathers or mothers had not yet been formally manumitted. They were respected for their knowledge and thus commanded exceedingly high prices in the market, but they were rarely for sale. With almost the same status as "freed slaves," a number of them actually owned small garden plots, and occasionally even slaves.[42] Because of the strict gender division of labor on the coast, the category of self-employed slaves probably included few women. In this connection it is probably worth noting that German colonial sources have little to say about high-class female prostitution, and that as far as the slave records are concerned female slaves are not mentioned in this context at all.

FEMALE SLAVE PRICES

Growing up and getting old are natural processes for the human species. However, at the same time, they are social processes, since society attaches different values and attributes to different age groups, and these affect—though they do not necessarily determine—individual behavior, especially within social institutions such as the family, the household, or the place of work. Stages in the life cycle are often associated with particular age groups and rituals. The term *rites of passage* signifies different stages of life such as childhood, puberty, adulthood, and old age. Despite being almost universal, the values and characteristics attributed to different age groups as well as their delineation are locally defined—determined by culturally specific configurations of the social setting such as race, class, and age and gender relations. Moreover, these tend to change over time and not necessarily in the same manner or direction.[43]

The sources for female slave prices in East Africa are rare and widely scattered throughout the contemporary literature and archival documents. Even for relatively well documented areas, like the East African coast and the nearby islands of Zanzibar and Pemba, comprehensive lists are not available. The best precolonial, nineteenth-century source is Richard Burton, who reports for Zanzibar town that the following prices were applicable in the late 1850s:[44] boys before puberty (MT$15–30); youths (worth less than boys), men in their prime (MT$13–20); older men (MT$10–13), educated slaves (MT$25–70), trading agents ("fancy prices"). He also states that prices for female slaves were one-third higher than those for male slaves.[45]

More detailed information for the coast can be found in the sales tax records and official documents regarding the redemption of slaves, which were kept by the German colonial authorities. The reason for keeping such records was that German colonial law recognized slavery. Under official supervision slaves could be freely bought and sold locally. However, slaves had the legal right to redemption. This often took the form of third-party redemption, in which someone else redeemed the slave in exchange for a promise from the slave that he or she would work for the redeemer for a specified period, varying from six months to two years according to the perceived value of the slave. Slaves could also redeem themselves. Both self-redemptions and third-party redemptions were regulated by the local district officer, who fixed the redemption prices according to the local market prices of slaves. He was also required to issue a certificate of emancipation, the *Freibrief,* to the slave. This certificate contained the slave's name, age, gender, and origin, or location of birth. Sometimes it also included the slave's profession and the price the redeemer had to pay to the slave's owner. Copies of these certificates were kept in the district office, and their particulars were entered into the Freibrief register. Some of these registers have survived because they were sent to the colonial authorities in Berlin. Arguably, they provide a glimpse into the gender, age, and price structures of slaves in coastal East Africa in the early colonial period.[46]

At first glance, a clear pattern seems to emerge, arguably representing the "commercial" value of slaves in their childhoods, young adulthoods, mature adulthoods, and old ages. In general, coastal slaves fetched higher prices than up-country slaves.. It also appears that slave prices in the northern part of the coast were higher than in the south. Moreover, it seems that individual factors, such as the slave's profession, had a considerable influence on price. Taking all these considerations into account, the records show that younger female slaves were more highly valued at the turn of the century than their male counterparts in the same age group. Those aged from one to ten fetched medium redemption prices, about fifty rupees a head. Those between ten and twenty-five were much more highly valued, commanding maybe eighty to ninety rupees a head, while females between twenty-five and thirty-five were redeemed for about seventy rupees. Older females were apparently redeemed at a discount, fetching only about twenty-five rupees a head. In this oldest age group the differences in the prices between male and female slaves narrowed considerably (table 5.1).

This pattern of a steep rise in the price of female slaves followed by a gradual decline, with the peak in puberty and early adulthood, suggests that the socioeconomic estimations of the productive and reproductive capacities of female slaves reinforced each other. Arguably, there was a basic estimation of the surplus production capacity of female slaves that was "topped up" in the relevant age groups by other considerations, such as the actual or expected future reproductive capacity of female slave children and young adults.

However, and perhaps not surprisingly, things were more complicated than that. First, the evidence regarding age group prices for female slaves

Table 5.1. Slave redemption prices on the East African Coast, 1894–96 (in rupees)

AGE	MALE SLAVES			FEMALE SLAVES			ALL SLAVES	
	No.	Range	Mean	No.	Range	Mean	No.	Mean
0–5	4	32–50	37	2	37–80	58	6	48
6–10	8	14–50	33	11	25–80	45	19	39
11–15	9	20–90	42	17	40–160	88	26	65
16–20	24	25–150	58	30	20–160	90	54	74
21–25	5	58–200	88	10	30–200	80	15	84
26–30	3	40–100	80	3	60–80	70	6	75
31–35	4	60–140	100	2	36–105	71	6	86
over 35	3	30–40	36	2	12–35	24	5	30
Totals	60		68	77		75	137	72

Source: BAB RKolA 7410–7412, "Sammlung der zur Mitteilung an das Spezialbüro bestimmten Nachweisungen," October 1892–November 1901. In the preparation of this table I was greatly helped by Vincent Ovaert (Berlin).

Note: In 2005, one rupee was worth about £5.

In 1895 the Mikindani district officer applied a flat redemption rate of Rs 50 for male slaves and Rs 55 for female slaves, irrespective of their age, origin, or profession. Overall, sixty-two slaves were redeemed in this way in that year. Their details were not included in the table. See BAB RKolA 7412: 10, "Verzeichnis der im Jahre 1895 erteilten Freibriefe des Bezirksnebenamtes Mikindani," n.d. [January 1896].

The data in the table are slightly at odds with those provided by August Leue, the district officer of Dar es Salaam in the later 1890s and early 1900s. According to Leue, young slave women fetched Rs 80 to Rs 100, while younger men sold for only Rs 60 to Rs 80. Older slaves could be bought more cheaply, he states, but buyers had to pay "fancy" prices for concubines and highly skilled (male) artisans. Leue, "Sklaverei," 618.

is highly uneven. As already pointed out, most of this data comes from the urban coastal centers of East Africa and the adjacent islands. Little is known about the redemption prices of female slaves in the vast coastal hinterland or in the East African interior except that they were on the whole much lower.[47] The question as to whether or not the rise and decline pattern outlined above for the coast represent a wider East African phenomenon cannot be answered on the basis of the available evidence, nor can it be assumed that female slave redemption prices followed exactly the pattern of urban slave redemption prices.

Second, redemption price variations within age groups overlapped with the variations between age groups. In the ten-to-twenty-five-year age group the lowest prices were paid for redeemed female agricultural slaves and probably the highest redemption prices for masuria, the religiously sanctioned concubines of wealthy Muslim slave owners.[48] Household slaves, both female children and adults, occupied the wide middle ground. Third, the composition of these groups changed drastically within age cohorts. There were, for instance, no masuria in the childhood or old age group and few household slaves in the childhood and early adult group. It also appears that comparatively few locally born slave girls and young adults sought redemption. They tended to stay in their owners' households. As associated family members, they had probably little to gain from official manumission through redemption. Moreover, owners refrained from having slave children redeemed, since so much prestige was invested in having large numbers of clients, and dividing families through partial redemption was considered by many owners to invite trouble. Occasionally whole slave families or mothers and daughters were redeemed together, but such respect for personal ties was an exception rather than the rule.

Finally, and perhaps most important, the social composition of the age groups reflected the relative attachment of female slaves to their owners' household. Those with the strongest ties were least likely to seek redemption, and thus the picture that emerges from the age group price pattern may be highly biased against locally born household slaves who do not appear in the sales tax records and only rarely in the redemption register. Moreover, a number of female slave girls who had been brought to the coast from the interior, became members of their owners' households. They were also less likely to seek redemption. In the event that these younger slave women had children by their owner or one of his sons, they were themselves no longer regarded as slaves, though they were not necessarily considered free. They appear only rarely in archival documents. Consequently, those female slaves who were sold in the market tended to be agricultural slaves, who had only weak ties to their owners' household.

It thus appears that a life cycle analysis based on female redemption prices has to be interpreted with great caution. These figures reveal the social value of female slave age groups only if they appeared in the market. Outside the market, the social estimation of age groups followed the general patterns of the societies in which female slaves lived. Thus, for instance, older female slaves were sometimes highly regarded for their knowledge or their specific position in the owners' household, but such prestige was based on the general position of elderly women rather than specific ideas about the honor of elderly female slaves.[49]

NEW OPPORTUNITIES IN THE PERIOD OF ABOLITION

The biographical literature about female slaves in the 1880s reveals that their lives were largely dominated by the quest for greater personal security.[50] Slave women and children were particularly vulnerable in this period, especially in the areas close to the coast and in trading centers in the interior, such as Tabora. Local conflicts, ecological crises, and the activities of commercial slave traders procured a steady stream of female slaves destined for distant markets. In this situation, female slaves in different age groups employed distinct strategies to gain greater protection against resale. As in many areas flight was not a viable alternative; younger slave women sought to become more firmly attached to the households of their owners even if their social positions in these households as spouses or dependents were precarious in the extreme. Older female slaves sought the protection of their children, many of whom were regarded as free—that is, unsalable—by their "host" societies.

In the later 1890s and the early 1900s, during which slavery drastically declined in East Africa, the strategies of female slaves changed as they now embarked on a quest for greater personal autonomy. Because of greater security of movement provided by the establishment of colonial rule, flight, and, to a lesser extent, redemption became more common. Younger female slaves in particular seem to have taken to flight, seeking employment in the growing wage sector of the colonial economy, often far away from their previous places of residence. In contrast, older female slaves often remained with their owners, seeking greater autonomy within the household rather than outside it. Many of them had children by their owners, and they probably did not wish to leave them behind. But they too sought wage labor as a means of generating independent incomes, often against the will of their owners. Wage employment was possible only if such income opportunities existed near their places of residence.

Faced with loss of their authority to control the movements of their female slaves, many owners seem to have offered them greater personal autonomy as a means of binding them more closely to their households. Those owners who did not see the advantage of such a strategy apparently suffered the consequences. Like their male counterparts, female slaves simply ran away if they felt the demands of their owners had become too great a burden.

This fundamental transformation is reflected in a number of descriptions regarding changes in attitude and everyday behavior. Several contemporary observers noticed that after the colonial conquest, female

slaves no longer displayed the kind of respect or obedience to their owners that they had previously shown. For instance, they gradually appro-
priated the outward signs of authority and status. They began to wear
clothing previously reserved for the "better" classes. Writing about Dar es
Salaam, the district officer, Bezirksamtmann August Leue, thus noted
that slave women began to proudly wear the *ukaya*—a headscarf made
of blue cotton cloth—which according to him was the sign of "freeborn" women.[51]

NOTES

Abbreviations

BAB   Bundesarchiv, Abteilungen Berlin
RHO   Rhodes House Library, Oxford
RKolA   Reichskolonialamt
TNA   Tanzania National Archives

1. Claire C. Robertson and Martin A. Klein, eds., *Women and Slavery in Africa*
(Madison: University of Wisconsin Press, 1983); Marcia Wright, *Strategies of Slaves
and Women: Life-Stories from East/Central Africa* (London: James Currey, 1993). For
an overview of slavery in Africa, see Paul E. Lovejoy, *Transformations in Slavery: A
History of Slavery in Africa* (Cambridge: Cambridge University Press, 1983), 223–30.
    2. Robertson and Klein, *Women and Slavery*, 1.
    3. See, for instance, the autobiography of Salme (Emilie Ruete), the daughter of
the Sayyid Barghash, *Memoiren einer arabischen Prinzessin* (Berlin: Luckardt, 1886).
For an English translation, see Emilie Ruete, *Memoirs of an Arabian princess from
Zanzibar, with a new introduction by P. W. Romero* (New York: Markus Wiener, 1989).
    4. For this statement, see Dugald Campbell, *Ten Times a Slave but Freed at Last*
(Glasgow: Pickering and Inglis, 1916), 12, quoted in Wright, *Strategies*, 152.
    5. For mid-nineteenth-century slave prices, see Richard Burton, *The Lake Regions
of Central Africa, a Picture of Exploration* (London: Longman 1860), 520. See also
Verney Lovett Cameron, *Across Africa*, 2 vols. (London: Daldy, Isbister and Co.,
1877), 1:144. For the early colonial period, see Carl Velten, ed., *Desturi za Wasuaheli
na khabari za desturi za sheri'a za Wasuaheli* (Göttingen: Vandenhoeck and Ruprecht,
1903), 310; August Leue, "Die Sklaverei in Ostafrika," *Beiträge zur Kolonialpolitik und
Kolonialwirtschaft*, 1900/1901, 606–8, 617–25. The main archival sources for slave
prices in colonial East Africa can be found in BAB, RKolA 7382/27: 42–115,
"Berichte der einzelnen Verwaltungsstellen in Deutsch-Ostafrika über die Sklaverei,"
"Anhang zu den Berichten der einzelnen Verwaltungsstellen in Deutsch-Ostafrika,"
1 October 1901; BAB RKolA 7410–7412, "Sammlung der zur Mitteilung an das
Spezialbüro bestimmten Nachweisungen," October 1892–November 1901; RHO,
Afr Micr R.8/MF 19, Mafia District Book, "Domestic Slavery in German East Africa"
by N. King, Mafia, April 1915: 12; TNA G38/7, "Verzeichnis der Sklavenkäufe und
Verkäufe, 1911–1914," n.d. [April 1914].

6. This paragraph is a broad summary of chapter 3 ("The Social Life of Slaves, c. 1860–1890") in Deutsch, *Emancipation without Abolition*, pp. 53–96, which in turn draws heavily on Justin Willis and Suzanne Miers, "Becoming a Child of the House: Incorporation, Authority and Resistance in Giryama Society," *Journal of African History* 38, no. 3 (1997): 479–95; Jonathon Glassman, *Feasts and Riot: Revelry, Rebellion, and Popular Consciousness on the Swahili Coast, 1856–1888* (London: James Currey, 1995); Igor Kopytoff and Suzanne Miers, "Introduction: African 'Slavery' as an Institution of Marginality," in *Slavery in Africa: Historical and Anthropological Perspectives*, ed. Miers and Kopytoff (Madison: University of Wisconsin Press, 1977), 3–81.

7. Claude Meillassoux argues that in Africa female slaves were exclusively used as agricultural workers. This might be a matter of classification, since he also states that the moment female slaves became kin, they were no longer—by definition—to be regarded as slaves. Meillassoux, *The Anthropology of Slavery: The Womb of Iron and Gold* (London: Athlone, 1991), 14–15, 99–100.

8. Wright, *Strategies*, 10–16. See also Edward A. Alpers, "The Story of Swema: Female Vulnerability in Nineteenth-Century East Africa," in Robertson and Klein, *Women and Slavery*, 185–219.

9. For these numbers, see BAB, RKolA 7382/27: 42–93, "Berichte der einzelnen Verwaltungsstellen in Deutsch-Ostafrika über Sklaverei," esp. BAB, RKolA 7382/27: 42 Tanga, n.d. [1899], BAB, RKolA 7382/27: 48 Pangani, n.d. [1899], BAB, RKolA 7382/27: 57 Bagamoyo, n.d. [1898], BAB, RKolA 7382/27: 60 Dar es Salaam, n.d. [1899], BAB, RKolA 7382/27: 63 Rufiyi, n.d. [1899], BAB, RKolA 7382/27: 65 Kilwa, n.d. [1900], BAB, RKolA 7382/27: 68 Lindi, n.d. [1900].

10. Randall L. Pouwels, *Horn and Crescent: Cultural Change and Traditional Islam on the East African Coast, 800–1900* (Cambridge: Cambridge University Press, 1987), 78. See also Glassman, *Feasts and Riot*, 22–23.

11. John Middleton, *The World of the Swahili: An African Mercantile Civilization* (New Haven: Yale University Press 1992), 117.

12. Velten, *Desturi*, 306.

13. Burton, *Lake Regions*, 517. See also Charles New, *Life, Wanderings, and Labours in Eastern Africa: With an Account of the First Successful Ascent of the Equatorial Snow Mountain Kilima Njaro, and Remarks upon East African Slavery* (London: Hodder and Stoughton, 1873), 58.

14. Velten, *Desturi*, 307–8.

15. Compare, for instance, BAB, RKolA 7382/27: 69, "Berichte der einzelnen Verwaltungsstellen in Deutsch-Ostafrika über Sklaverei," Bezirksamt Lindi, Berichterstatter: Bezirksamtmann Zache, n.d. [1900]; BAB, RKolA 7382/27: 51–52, Bezirksamt Pangani, Berichterstatter: Bezirksamtmann Sigl, n.d. [1899]. See also Velten, *Desturi*, 309.

16. Kadhi A. O. Saadi, "Mafia—History and Tradition Collected by Kadhi Amur Omari Saadi," *Tanganyika Notes and Records* 12 (1941), 26.

17. Leue, "Sklaverei," 608. On this point, see also Laura Fair, "Dressing Up: Clothing, Class and Gender in Post-Abolition Zanzibar," *Journal of African History* 39, no. 1 (1998): 63–94.

18. Velten, *Desturi*, 310.

19. Older female slaves were called *wajakazi* (sing. *mjakazi*) in kiSwahili. See BAB, RKolA 7382/27: 69, "Berichte der einzelnen Verwaltungsstellen in Deutsch-Ostafrika über Sklaverei," Bezirksamt Lindi, Berichterstatter: Bezirksamtmann Zache, n.d. [1900]. For a detailed linguistic analysis of the term, see Katrin Bromber's contribution in this volume.

20. Leue, "Sklaverei," 607. See also Velten, *Desturi*, 51, 138. For a comparative perspective, see Margaret Strobel, "Slavery and Reproductive Labor in Mombasa," in *Women and* Slavery, ed. Robertson and Klein, 111–29.

21. Velten, *Desturi*, 207.

22. Ibid., 310.

23. BAB, RKolA 7382/27: 50, "Berichte der einzelnen Verwaltungsstellen in Deutsch-Ostafrika über Sklaverei," Bezirksamt Pangani, Berichterstatter: Bezirksamtmann Sigl, n.d. [1899].

24. Velten, *Desturi*, 394.

25. Ibid., 227; translation mine.

26. BAB, RKolA 1004/120: 2, "Bericht des Bezirksamts Kilwa," 10 September 1897.

27. Compare BAB, RKolA 7382/27: 42–93, "Berichte der einzelnen Verwaltungsstellen in Deutsch-Ostafrika über Sklaverei," particularly BAB, RKolA 7382/27: 65, Bezirksamt Kilwa, Berichterstatter: Bezirksamtmann von Rode, n.d. [1899]; BAB, RKolA 7382/27: 69, Bezirksamt Lindi, Berichterstatter: Bezirksamtmann Zache, n.d. [1900]; BAB, RKolA 7382/27: 48–56, Bezirksamt Pangani, Berichterstatter: Bezirksamtmann Sigl, n.d. [1899].

28. BAB, RKolA 7382/27: 63, "Berichte der einzelnen Verwaltungsstellen in Deutsch-Ostafrika über Sklaverei," Bezirksamt Rufiyi, Berichterstatter: Bezirksamtssekretär Spieth, n.d. [1899].

29. This description is based on RHO Afr Micr 472 R.8/MF 19, Mafia District Book, "Domestic Slavery in German East Africa," by N. King, Mafia, April 1915: 11.

30. BAB, RKolA 7382/27: 42–93, "Berichte der einzelnen Verwaltungsstellen in Deutsch-Ostafrika über Sklaverei," esp. BAB, RKolA 7382/27: 65, Bezirksamt Kilwa, Berichterstatter: Bezirksamtmann von Rode, n.d. [1899]. See also New, *Life, Wanderings, and Labours*, 62.

31. Leue, "Sklaverei," 607.

32. BAB, RKolA 7382/27: 43, "Berichte der einzelnen Verwaltungsstellen in Deutsch-Ostafrika über Sklaverei," Bezirksamt Tanga, Berichterstatter: Bezirksamtssekretär Blank, n.d. [1899].

33. Paul Reichard, *Deutsch-Ostafrika: Das Land und seine Bewohner, seine politische und wirtschaftliche Entwicklung* (Leipzig: O. Spamer, 1892), 475.

34. For more details, see Pouwels, *Horn and Crescent*, 193.

35. Reichard, *Deutsch-Ostafrika*, 475.

36. Glassman, *Feasts and Riot*, 4.

37. BAB, RKolA 1004/97: 1, "Bericht des Bezirksamts Bagamoyo," 14 September 1897. See also Mervyn W. H. Beech, "Slavery on the Coast of Africa," *Journal of the African Society* 15 (1916): 148; Glassman, *Feasts and Riot*, 61. In kiSwahili such slaves were sometimes also called *hamali* (pl. *wahamali*).

38. BAB, RKolA 7382/27: 52, "Berichte der einzelnen Verwaltungsstellen in Deutsch-Ostafrika über Sklaverei," Bezirksamt Pangani, Berichterstatter: Bezirksamtmann Sigl, n.d. [1899]. See also BAB, RKolA 1004/97: 1, "Bericht des Bezirksamts Bagamoyo," 14 September 1897; Velten, Desturi, 310–11.

39. Thus, for instance, the famous Mabruki, who accompanied Burton on his travels in East Africa, was a slave from the coast. See Burton, Lake Regions, 104. For itinerant slave artisans, see ibid., 229.

40. Ibid., 327, 517.

41. Velten, Desturi, 218.

42. BAB, RKolA 7382/27: 63, "Berichte der einzelnen Verwaltungsstellen in Deutsch-Ostafrika über Sklaverei," Bezirksamt Rufiyi, Berichterstatter: Bezirksamtssekretär Spieth, n.d. [1899]. See also Reichard, Deutsch-Ostafrika, 477; Velten, Desturi, 311. For an account of a "free" man who sold himself into slavery and then bought slaves from the proceeds, see David Livingstone, David Livingstone and the Rovuma, ed. G. Shepperson (1862; Edinburgh: Edinburgh University Press, 1965), 49.

43. This paragraph has been greatly inspired by Wendy James, The Ceremonial Animal: A New Portrait of Anthropology (Oxford: University Press, 2003), 44–45.

44. Prices are given in Maria Theresa thalers (dollars), a common international currency of the era.

45. Burton, Lake Regions, 520. Multiple currencies circulated in East Africa at the time, including the internationally used Maria Theresa silver thaler (dollar) and the British Indian rupee. According to Abdul Sheriff, one MT$ was worth from Rs 2.10 to Rs 2.23 at the time. See Abdul Sheriff, Slaves, Spices and Ivory in Zanzibar (London: James Currey, 1987), xix.

46. BAB, RKolA 7410–7412, "Sammlung der zur Mitteilung an das Spezialbüro bestimmten Nachweisungen," October 1892–November 1901. See also TNA G38/7, "Verzeichnis der Sklavenkäufe und Verkäufe, 1911–1914," n.d. [April 1914].

47. For the evidence regarding slavery in the interior, see Jan-Georg Deutsch, "Notes on the Rise of Slavery and Social Change in Unyamwezi, c. 1860–1900," in Slavery in the Great Lakes Region of Africa, ed. Henri Médard and Shane Doyle (Oxford: James Currey, forthcoming 2007).

48. The sources do not explicitly state that the highest redemption prices were paid for masuria, but this seems likely, given their high price of about 150 to 200 rupees.

49. Velten, Desturi, 229.

50. Wright, Strategies, 21–45.

51. See Leue, "Sklaverei," 608. On this issue, see also Fair, "Dressing Up," 63–94.

3

Women in Households on the Fringes of

Christianity and Commerce

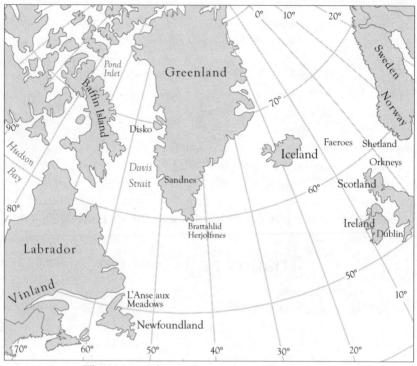

The Norse Atlantic, ca. tenth–twelfth centuries

6

THRALLS AND QUEENS

Female Slavery in the Medieval Norse Atlantic

KIRSTEN A. SEAVER

Although the North Atlantic settlements of the Norse, in Iceland and Greenland, were distant from continental African and Eurasian countries and their large populations, in the Far North slavery in general and female slavery in particular shared many characteristics with the major slaveholding societies elsewhere that have been the focus of much serious research. Northern investigators also have at least one problem in common with their colleagues elsewhere, that of defining and isolating female slavery in the context of a society where even nominally free women lacked personal freedom, as we understand that privilege today.

There were nevertheless unique aspects to those two small medieval North Atlantic Norse societies, where human bondage for largely practical reasons ended sooner than in the mother country of Norway, and where studying the social and economic conditions of women at that time must to a large degree rely on anecdotal material. Although archaeologists find evidence of female presence even at early settlement sites, women's work leaves few traces beyond those associated with keeping families fed and clothed, and neither social status nor human suffering leaves telltale remnants in the ground, except when a human skeleton shows deliberately inflicted physical damage, the use of restraints, or other obvious signs of abject powerlessness.

WHICH MEDIEVAL NORSE?

While the terms Norse and Viking are often lumped together as carelessly as the Nordic countries themselves, the present discussion will concern

Norse societies with their roots mainly in Norwegian culture and will only in part involve a group of people who, because of their violent livelihood, came to be known as Vikings.

Caution is also in order before we apply to medieval Iceland and Norse Greenland sources said to concern Norway and—by sometimes unjustifiable extension—Sweden and Denmark. Due in no small measure to the different geographical and topographical circumstances that dictated each country's domestic economy and relationship with adjoining regions, the histories and cultures of Norway, Sweden, and Denmark from early on developed along separate lines. Similar distinctions apply to Iceland and Norse Greenland and make the two countries different not only from Norway but also from each other. While medieval Nordic societies certainly maintained a web of contact through an essentially common language, similar legal systems, and trade, those who left Norway to make their homes in the British Isles in the late eighth century and subsequently went on to the Faeroes, Iceland, and Greenland invariably thought of themselves as denizens of their new homes, and the Norwegians shared this view, as we see in *Egil's Saga*, for example, where first-generation Icelanders visiting Norway are twice referred to as foreigners.[1]

Arab accounts about eastern (primarily Swedish) Norse raiders and traders in Russia are not reliable sources of information about prevailing customs among the western Norse, however deliciously lurid those tales may be.[2] Indeed, Ibn Fadlan's reported account of nubile women slaves sweetening a Norse chieftain's journey into the afterlife has little connection with the skeleton of an aged female slave who accompanied a privileged Norwegian woman buried in the elegant Oseberg ship sometime in the second half of the ninth century in southern Norway.[3]

Church archives and other continental repositories also require circumspection with regard to the Far North in general and the North Atlantic Norse settlements in particular, for throughout the Middle Ages—even after the introduction of institutionalized Christianity—Iceland and Norse Greenland remained alien to most continental Europeans.[4] Fortunately, the Icelanders and the Norwegians have preserved documents, annals, and sagas (oral tales eventually committed to parchment) that provide some idea of medieval life and attitudes in their common culture.[5] Material that specifically reflects events and conditions in Norse Greenland is woefully sparse, however. It is based mostly on Icelandic material that is unreliable as evidence for events that antedate the written accounts by a couple of centuries and that was written not just from a male point of view but also from one that regarded the past as a heroic time.[6]

Thus, while the Icelandic sagas do provide tantalizing glimpses of daily life in a medieval Norse farming society, to a substantial degree they commemorate male undertakings in which brawn frequently wins over brain, and the part played by women in these controversies surfaces only occasionally. As far as the saga writers were concerned, even free women and their work were unimportant, and slaves of either sex earned a place in this literature only when they participated in memorable events that also involved freemen and women.

The sagas nevertheless suggest that without the work of both male and female slaves, the two fledgling North Atlantic societies would have been far less successful than they in fact were. We may probably also take it for granted that without female slaves, the early populations of Iceland and Greenland would have grown considerably more slowly than they did, and we may be confident that these women's lives were at least as harsh as those of their sisters in bondage elsewhere. The pattern of their daily lives had been determined by the chieftains who spearheaded the colonization of both countries—farmers who carried with them their western Norwegian tradition of pastoralist farming augmented by hunting, fishing, and trade—and the use of force was a given component in that pattern.

NORSE PARTICIPATION IN HUMAN BONDAGE

Acknowledging the ubiquitousness of casual violence in medieval societies (as well as in many modern ones) is important to the study of both slavery and the vulnerability of women, including in the Far North. Although it is difficult to imagine physical bondage detached from violence, violence can exist without the institution of slavery.

Early medieval Europeans knew violence and slavery, separately and linked, as part of their daily lives both before and after Viking raids contributed significantly to the number of slaves in the market place.[7] The Viking Age lasted from the late eighth century until about 1050 to 1100 and constitutes only a segment of the Middle Ages, especially as the term applies to the Nordic countries, where medieval conditions lasted technologically, culturally, and economically until at least 1500.

Regardless of the social status of women in the western Norse orbit, they took up weapons as a last resort and were mostly passive in times of war or during other physical hostilities, in which their males engaged with some regularity, and in which they themselves frequently suffered loss of life or limb in skirmishes not of their own making. They are not known to have participated actively in Viking raids. A Norse wife might well accompany her husband on a voyage to visit relatives or to trade, but she would come along with her children and household only when the intention of a journey to a new place was to settle there. In the case of both Iceland and Greenland the settlers came to empty lands and had no need to fear the violence that might arise from competition with an indigenous population.

Viking marauders in square-rigged sailing ships descended on the English monastery at Lindisfarne in 793 CE and soon after struck other hapless locations in the British Isles and Ireland as well as on the Continent. At least two centuries earlier, however, Norwegians and Danes in large ocean-going *rowing* vessels had made trading voyages to the Continent and, quite likely, also to the British Isles, indulging their owners' tastes for exotic goods that probably included women.[8] The story of what happened later, during Viking raids far from home, is much the same whether one reads contemporary Irish and French accounts, the *Anglo-Saxon Chronicle* (begun at the end of the ninth century), or the Icelandic *Book of Settlements* (composed between 1122 and 1132). The Vikings clearly filled their ships with as many portable valuables as they could gather, including people. Given their rough livelihood and their eye for any opportunity to acquire wealth, it is hardly surprising that their raids both at home and abroad involved the abduction of men and women who could be held for ransom, sold to a third party, or simply taken along for personal use when the captor returned home.

Viking raids are unlikely to have initiated the institution of slavery in the North, however; the Eddic poem *Rigsthula*, composed sometime between the eleventh and thirteenth centuries,[9] suggests a society already comfortable with placing slaves at the bottom of the social scale. According to this poem, the god Rigr visited three couples, unceremoniously bedded each wife by turn, and sired three sons—a slave named Thrall, a freeman, and an earl. Thrall, dark of skin and hair, wrinkled and gnarled, found a wife as ugly as himself, and they produced a large brood of ugly sons and daughters doomed to slavery. Their daughters' names— Drudge, Daggle-Tail, Slattern, Serving-Maid, Cinder-Wench, Stout-Leg, Shorty, Stumpy, Dumpy, Spindleshanks, and Sputterer—suggest the menial jobs these slave women were expected to do and the scorn with which they were to be regarded.[10]

Nobody knows how many regular slave markets there were all around Europe in the period between 800 and 1200, but we do know that the Vikings contributed considerably to the trade in people moving through them. As their raids on Irish and other sites in the British Isles intensified in the second half of the ninth century, so did the capture and sale of people of both sexes, some of whom subsequently ended in Iceland, where planned settlement had begun around 870 CE.[11] The slave trade was still brisk when Eirik the Red and his followers began the Norse settlement of Greenland at the end of the tenth century, and in the eleventh century "Dublin was probably the prime slave market of western Europe," supplying Anglo-Saxon as well as Norse customers in the British Isles and serving the older Scandinavian countries and Iceland as well. The Irish proved as adept as the Norse at capturing rival warlords' people in order to sell them as slaves, so when Norse power over Ireland waned, the country was reclaimed by squabbling Irish kings, who inherited the trading advantages established in such Viking cities as Dublin, Limerick, Waterford, and Cork, but especially in Dublin. The Irish slave trade nevertheless appears to have petered out in the early twelfth century along with the Viking Age itself.[12]

By that time, both Iceland and Greenland had proved themselves viable as Norse communities, dominated by chieftains and untrammeled by kings. Both these North Atlantic outposts functioned socially, legally, and economically in ways that were adapted to the rugged physical characteristics of their new countries and that owed much to the work of free and unfree women—work that is largely unsung in the surviving literary sources. Only by reading between the lines does it become obvious that wool cloth—a product of female skills and ceaseless labor—on which both Icelanders and Greenlanders relied for their domestic needs as well as for export, represented a major contribution to the economy of both countries.

SETTLING ICELAND AND GREENLAND

Iceland, a volcanic island in the middle of the North Atlantic, had no indigenous population when the Norse arrived there in the ninth century, although a few Irish hermit monks used the remote island as a summer retreat.[13] The initial Norse colonizing phase was already over by about 930 CE, by which time the population had formed a hierarchical society run by chieftains and other free, landowning farmers without a formal executive head. According to the Íslendingabók, it was at around 930 that a man named Ulfljót brought a degree of order by going to Norway, memorizing the western Norwegian law governing the Gulathing (Gula assembly), and bringing it thus back to Iceland.[14] Ulfljót's version has not survived, and so we do not know what, if any, adaptations to specific Icelandic legal needs may have occurred at that time. However, it is surely safe to say that neither differences nor similarities concerning bondage would matter much in later laws that were enacted *after* slavery had ceased to be a reality.

The first Icelandic settlers made extensive landgrabs, some of which they distributed among relatives and others whose loyalty to a chieftain landowner was important in a society that regularly engaged in blood feuds, in which women often found themselves at the center of the dispute. Within a few generations, further subdivisions of land had resulted in a preponderance of medium-size farms and smallholdings, but there were still no towns or villages. From the start, homesteads had been scattered, separate, and largely self-sustaining units, some within easy reach of their neighbors and others so isolated that even a "free" woman, confined as she was to domestic duties, is likely to have found her existence testing, while a female domestic slave would have had the additional burden of being unable to seek outside help against abuse that was unacceptable even by that time's harsh standards.

Work on the farms in these high latitudes was hard for women and men alike, and all but the smallest holdings required more help than a nuclear family could muster. Because Iceland in its pristine state was covered with birch forests and willow scrub, extensive land clearance was necessary during the initial settlement phase. The owners of the large, early land takes brought along a good number of male slaves, whom they had varying success in controlling, judging from a grueling story of early enterprise that also reveals a lot about the imported female slaves.

Hjörleif, the foster brother of Iceland's famous early settler Ingolf Arnason, had reportedly brought along to Iceland ten Irish slaves acquired during one of his Viking raids, but only one ox; therefore he made the Irishmen pull the plow at his new settlement. Not surprisingly, they decided to escape. They killed Hjörleif's ox and blamed the deed on a bear, and when Hjörleif sent out a party to search for the bear, the escaped slaves murdered both their master and his free servants before seizing "the women" and other portable goods from his farm and fleeing aboard his ship's boat. When Ingolf and his slaves caught up with the party, they killed all the males *but brought the women back with them*.[15]

The fact that the male Irish slaves had linked up with these females strongly suggests that the latter also were slaves, whose owners considered them too valuable to waste in a land so distant from the European slave markets and so sparsely populated. The Old Norse word the saga used to describe these women, *kona,* can mean woman, either a wife or other female bought for sexual services. Female slaves always had value for potential procreation, and volunteers among free women partners of Norse would-be settlers for early emigration to Iceland are likely to have been in short supply. It is interesting in this connection that a recent study of mitochondrial DNA in the modern Icelandic population found that a substantial proportion of this maternal genetic material pointed not just to Norway but also to parts of the British Isles where the Norse had settled and harried both before and after the Icelandic settlement began. Although a Celtic element seemed to form an important part of the gene pool investigated, the authors of this study caution that it is too soon to say with any certainty where the females in the early settlement came from originally,[16] but given a number of indications that many early settlers in Iceland had spent a generation or two in Ireland, Scotland, or the Scottish Isles, Icelanders with a Celtic genetic inheritance would not be unexpected.[17]

It is also reasonable to suggest that not every sexual union represented a love match or involved a woman who had been free to choose going on a voyage whose destination was not necessarily attractive. Regardless of the women settlers' points of origin, those from a non-Norse background who were bundled into open ships to make their way into the northwestern Atlantic evidently wasted no time in adapting to Norse customs, societal norms, and language, given that modern Icelandic remains close to Old Norse (the language also used in Norse Greenland while the colony existed) and that only the high-latitude resource exploitation learned by countless generations of northwestern Norwegians would have enabled them to survive in their new country.

It has been estimated that some ten thousand people were already living in Iceland by the early tenth century, their number swelling by 1100 to around fifty thousand.[18] The island is habitable only along the coasts, and therefore many Icelanders are likely to have been short of land at the end of the tenth century, when they left their country in order to farm, fish, and hunt in Greenland, a vast country of impressive natural resources and located so close to North America that the two areas are regarded as both a geological and essentially economic unit.

Like the Icelanders, the Norse Greenland settlers (consisting mainly of Icelanders and Norwegians) created a society catering to, and run by, free, landowning males—a society in which neither free women nor female slaves had more protection than their male relatives or owners were able and willing to give them. As in Iceland, a system of independent, scattered farms made for an absence of villages. The Greenlanders also resembled the Icelanders with regard to subsequent subdivision of land. For example, archaeological excavations have demonstrated that Eirik the Red's large chieftain seat at Brattahlid (Steep Slope) was eventually divided into at least three farm complexes.[19]

Slaves would have been integral parts of the fledgling Greenland society. It is clear that Eirik had kept slaves while still living in Iceland, because *Eirik the Red's Saga* recounts the troubles that followed when his slaves had caused a landslide to fall on a neighboring farm.[20] Female slaves were also a part of the Icelandic scene, and it has therefore often been suggested that because Eirik's irascible daughter Freydis was born to a woman other than his wife Thjodhild[21] and the sagas never mention the woman's name, she was probably of low status, possibly a household slave. In any case, Eirik acknowledged Freydis as his daughter, and subsequently she was clearly considered a useful addition to a family in a new land where women would be badly needed for procreation as well as for both outdoor and indoor labor.

SLAVE, SERVANT, WIFE, OR QUEEN?

In a number of ways, the Norse Greenlanders would have had more in common with the Icelanders than with the Norwegians, but their two island societies nevertheless developed in dissimilar ways, especially due to the differing economic potentials of their distinct physical and geographical settings. Iceland was subject to earthquakes and volcanic eruptions, while Greenland necessitated even longer voyages to and from the rest of Atlantic Europe, with all that distance entailed for trade as well as for cultural and other developments. Traders nevertheless risked long ocean voyages to both islands to obtain eiderdown, walrus ivory, sulfur, wool cloth, hides, furs, blubber, fish, and butter, which they bartered for grain, honey, and other rare commodities, and—at least for a while— human beings.

The Old Norse word *thraell* still survives in English *thrall*, and for as long as slavery was a fact of life in both Norway and its Atlantic satellites, those condemned to this designation appear to have had a similar legal status within the western Norse orbit. The term signified both slave and servant—usually, but not exclusively, of the male gender. Thirteenth-century saga writers used *thraell* to describe any condition in which a person could be seen as deprived of personal liberty in some way.[22] As noted earlier in connection with the rebellion of Hjörleif's slaves, the word *kona* (woman) also lacks a precise modern equivalent. A woman who was an outright slave was more likely to be called an *ambatt*, which similarly carried several shades of meaning from complete bondage and varying degrees of servant status to the connotation of mistress, in the sense of a woman whom a man beds at will without benefit of marriage.[23]

The historian Judith Jesch surmises that "the story of the Irish princess Melkorka in *Laxdæla saga*, although a romantic fiction, is what may very well have happened to many young women of all nationalities captured by Vikings (or indeed by other slave traders active at that time)." She also argues persuasively that for the earlier period that included the Viking Age, it can often be difficult to know when a woman was considered a wife and when she was simply a temporary female companion, free or slave.[24] The line between a bride price and a slave's purchase price could be very fine indeed.

A woman who was powerless despite being "free" might see suicide as her only way out, as did an Icelandic woman named Sigrid, who hanged herself after her husband had traded wives with another man.[25] Even a Norse woman who by every legal definition was a free person was sexually unfree, because in medieval Norse societies men decided the question of whom she married, or otherwise served sexually. She had no choice, whether she was ravished or bargained away in an arranged marriage; only widows with property of their own stood a reasonable chance of doing their own bargaining. If a strong-minded, independent woman made those decisions for herself, she was certainly remembered for it!

The man or men in a woman's life also decided where she was to live, and men decided what constituted matrimonial legitimacy as well as the legal status of any child born out of wedlock—an especially important issue if one or both parents had slave status. Innumerable instances of Norse children fathered by a single male but born to any number of casual liaisons, both at home and abroad, suggest the importance of male prerogative in these matters. A father who considered the child promising could claim it as his own and give it rights equal to those of other children of his born in wedlock, but if the father was not willing or able to do so, the mother alone became responsible for her child's future. In this situation as in so many others, regardless of the arrangements imposed upon her, a woman with male relatives was immeasurably better off than a woman who had none at all, the most extreme example being a slave woman far from home.[26]

A free woman with no property and no male relatives to protect her had no bargaining power and was only marginally better off than a slave woman torn from a distant home. Without a dowry, such a woman had little hope of marrying a man in better circumstances than her own, and without male relatives she could offer no useful alliances in the armed skirmishes through which Norse men frequently resolved their differences. Furthermore, if a woman's male relatives were physically powerless to protect her, neither their social standing nor her own could prevent her from being captured by others. In practice, destitution thus merged with enslavement. Well-born woman were also, even particularly, vulnerable to enslavement if there was a chance to exact a nice ransom. The social cachet of keeping a well-born woman for personal use was evidently considerable, as was the case with a petty king named Hjör in Norway, said to have taken the daughter of a king in Biarmia (the Norse name for the region adjacent to the White Sea) as part of his booty when he harried there. Taken far away, back to Rogaland in southern coastal Norway, she enjoyed the status of petty queen, with at least one slave woman of her own to serve her.[27]

Usually, however, a queen of any sort, if captured and sold into slavery rather than retained, was no better off than a dairymaid in the same situation, as illustrated in the *Saga of Olaf Tryggvason* by the poignant story of Queen Astrid Eirik's-daughter, whose son Olaf ruled Norway from 995 to 999 or 1000 CE. While Olaf was still a little boy, he and Queen Astrid had to flee abroad for their lives, and in the process they encountered Estonian pirates, who looted their goods and killed those whom they did not share out among themselves as slaves. Young Olaf was sold and resold several times before he was located by relatives, bought free of captivity, and taken back home. He was already king of Norway when an old Norwegian family friend in an Estonian slave market recognized a pale and poorly dressed Queen Astrid about to be resold. She promised to marry this friend if he would ransom her and take her back to Norway, and there they were wed with the consent of her male relations.[28]

Astrid had little choice in the matter, whereas her new husband had much to gain by a union with the Norwegian king's mother. Nor did she have a say in her daughter's marriage to the powerful chieftain Erling Skjalgsson (d. 1028), which took place after King Olaf is said to have picked all the feathers off his sister's hunting hawk and sent the bird to her as a warning of what might happen to her if she did not submit to his will. All told, King Olaf—although converted in England to Christianity—exhibited toward the women closest to him few of the Christian virtues supposedly involved in conversion.

Peter Foote and David Wilson suggest that the introduction of Christianity, combined with the need for close social cooperation in the nascent Icelandic society, may have been conducive to less exclusionary conditions for slaves there than in Norway.[29] Common sense and historical evidence suggest that early small Icelandic and Norse Greenlandic households would have involved closer relations among masters, slaves, and other servants than in the mother country—greater interdependence would have ensured survival—but it is risky to assume that Christianity as such inculcated concern for either the human rights of slaves or for decisions profoundly affecting any woman's future.

There is nothing to make us believe that Christianity with one stroke had made either the Norwegians or the Icelanders and Norse Greenlanders sensitive to human charity or obedient to the Christian message of universal love. Indeed, there are plenty of examples to the contrary, one being the continuation of blood feuds. Other old customs also persisted, such as arranged marriages and women's exclusion from public matters, whether they had been born free or bought free. In fact, it is painfully evident that Christian principles by themselves had little to do with ending the practice of slavery in the Far North, which continued well beyond the introduction of Christianity. Powerful men had their own way, as before, even when they formally acquiesced to some of the dictates of Church authorities, and men of low birth saw little change in their social position even if they were hired as priests.

Several of the earliest Norse settlers in Iceland were Christians, including slaves brought along from Ireland, where Christianity had long been well established. Aud the Deepminded, the widow of King Olaf the White of Dublin, was reportedly a devout Christian when she emigrated to Iceland with twenty freemen, slaves, freed slaves, and a handful of marriageable granddaughters. Although Aud moved her entire household with her, her granddaughters are the only other females mentioned by name, and then only in connection with the men to whom they were married off. Revered in early Icelandic history, Aud was clearly a remarkable woman, but nothing in her story as we know it hints at a specifically Christian concern with female consent in marriage nor at any kind of empathy with her granddaughters as she briskly arranged their futures, handing off two of the young women during her progress north—one in the Orkneys and one in the Faeroes. Once arrived in Iceland, Aud is said to have given land to those men under her who had either been born free or to whom she granted their freedom. Nowhere does it say that she freed any of her women slaves.[30]

With a few notable exceptions, the most that women slaves could expect if they were lucky enough to be freed would be more of what they had been doing all along, from mucking out cow stalls to helping a mistress on and off with her clothes. Many of their tasks in "freedom," however onerous, must nevertheless have been preferable to the experience of a bondage that had begun with capture and sale, exacerbated by being torn from familiar surroundings.

A WOMAN'S "HOME" MIGHT BE FAR AWAY

Extreme cultural and social isolation threatened all captives removed from their homeland, and it would obviously have been the lot of all women called upon to be among the very first settlers in a distant new land. It was this circumstance more than any other that made the situation of female slaves in Iceland and Norse Greenland different from the experience of their sisters in the older Nordic countries. In neither island settlement would the established law codes concerning slaves have overridden situational conventions, and they are no more likely to have applied during an early-eleventh-century attempt at colonization of the American mainland that originated in Greenland. This enterprise involved the region that Eirik the Red's son Leif had dubbed Vínland (Wine Land), the southernmost of three North American areas given Norse names.[31] Vínland is definable only as the general St. Lawrence estuary, including a part of Nova Scotia and part or parts of Newfoundland.

Of the five women said to have accompanied the expedition leader Thorfinn Karlsefni[32] and his sixty men on that westward voyage, the only one mentioned by name in the *Saga of the Greenlanders* is Karlsefni's wife, Gudrid Thorbjörn's-daughter.[33] The *Saga of Eirik the Red* notes both Freydis Eirik's-daughter and Gudrid, making it clear that separate voyages were involved. Neither saga provides details about the four other women with Gudrid, which suggests that their social status was low. Given the risk-filled nature of that American enterprise, it is likely that they were either slaves or else women little better than slaves, brought along for sexual and household services.

The remains of a small, round hut excavated on the site of the Norse settlement at L'Anse aux Meadows in northern Newfoundland have been interpreted as quarters for the slaves who had been brought along to do the heaviest manual work.[34] If so, they would surely have been male slaves; women slaves would likely have stayed in one or another of the larger dwellings. In addition to food preparation and keeping order indoors, the women would have been responsible for keeping the men's clothes in good repair and for weaving more cloth. Any idle moment would have been spent in spinning yarn, a task we know was performed by at least one Norse woman thrust into the American wilderness at that time, because a characteristic spinning whorl found in a house ruin at L'Anse aux Meadows was the first definitive evidence that it constituted an ancient Norse site.[35]

Karlsefni's wife, Gudrid, evidently a free woman born in Iceland, had been brought to Greenland as a young adult. The other women taken along to the L'Anse aux Meadows site were probably not Greenland born either, because the Norse Greenland colony was still in its infancy during the short period of the embryonic American settlement's construction and use. Regardless of where those five women had been born and raised, however, and no matter what their social status, in that American enterprise they were all de facto captives because they could not change their situation unless the men decided that it was time to set sail and leave. For as long as they stayed (Karlsefni's expedition is said to have lasted almost three years), they had no recourse either to the security of a normal community or to any social contacts besides the expedition's men.

In those European outposts of Vínland, Greenland, and Iceland, the free and the unfree alike relied for their survival on together wresting a living from land and sea, which in Greenland included hunting walrus far north in the Davis Strait and in Baffin Bay. It has generally been taken for granted that such ventures involved men only, but that assumption was recently questioned by the Canadian archaeologist Patricia Sutherland. While analyzing Norse-related material from a medieval Dorset site in northern Baffin Island, she found a three-meter strand of expertly spun yarn containing fur from arctic hare and with close technical similarities to yarn discovered during a Norse Greenland excavation in which she had participated. Other items from the same Baffin Island site have been radiocarbon-dated to the late thirteenth or early fourteenth century.[36] Unless Greenland had retained bondage for longer than was the case in Iceland, this late dating suggests that the Norse woman who had sat spinning at a Canadian High Arctic camp site had been technically free, but her likely circumstances may make one wonder what kind of freedom she had in fact enjoyed. The skill she would have needed most for her personal survival would in any case not have been spinning but rather the ability to adjust her expectations to the vulnerability that the affairs of men had imposed on her.

A WOMAN'S EXPECTATIONS

Among the medieval Norse, the rights of men and the duties of women were so deeply ingrained that the modern Icelandic historian Gunnar

Karlsson finds little change in this area between pre-Christian and post-Christian practices.[37] Jenny Jochens also sees continuity in pre- and postheathen practices within a social and legal system shared by other early Germanic societies, in which there was a "prevalence of concubinage, extramarital liaisons, and arranged marriages, and divorces" with which the Church had not yet come to grips in the thirteenth century.[38]

Among Norse landowning families, marriage remained for several centuries essentially a business transaction negotiated by men, in which the willingness of the bride-to-be might or might not be a factor. To a slave woman at any time, the nicety of marital consent would have mattered little, for she had no consent to give and no dowry over which to negotiate; she was simply property and could be bought, sold, and bedded at her owner's will. She could also form a sexual partnership with another slave, but the security of this arrangement—indeed her physical safety—would have been uncertain at best. Although no woman, regardless of her status, was proof against rape or abduction, there was no legal punishment for raping one's own slave, and the rape of another man's female slave would at most have constituted misuse of another man's property. Raping or abducting a freeman's daughter, sister, or wife was quite another matter, even supposing the woman had been willing.

Egil's Saga provides an illustration of such a complicated event in the story of the Norwegian Björn Brynjólfsson. Björn fancied a beautiful girl with the beguiling name of Thora of the Embroidered Hand, but her powerful chieftain father objected to the match. Björn then abducted the girl, to the horror of his relatives. The pair married in the Shetlands and proceeded to Iceland, where, long after Thora's death, Björn's actions continued to involve prominent Icelanders in his tangles with powerful families back in Norway.[39] Regardless of Thora's status as a free and well-born woman, her hand had not been hers to give or for Björn to accept, which was why her male relations wanted their revenge.

At the other social extreme, there is a famous saga story of how a slave woman and her son were accepted into the highest level of early Icelandic society. The tale comes from the *Laxdæla saga* (Saga of the People of Laxárdal) and involves Thorgerd, granddaughter of the good Christian Aud the Deepminded. Thorgerd's son Hoskuld achieved early fame in both Iceland and Norway. He secured for himself the daughter of a wealthy Icelandic farmer, Jorunn, but several children later he decided to spend some time in Norway again, and there he bought a woman, thought to be a mute, from a slave trader. He took her to bed that same evening, then dressed her in good clothes, and eventually brought her back to Iceland, where he told his wife, Jorunn, that the slave woman was to live with them and to be treated with respect. The woman's name, Melkorka, was unknown to him, however, until he overheard her speaking to their two-year-old son, Olaf, and revealing not only her name but also the fact that she was no mute.

After Jorunn had hit Melkorka with a pair of socks and the slave woman had retaliated with a blow to Jorunn's nose, Hoskuld decided to set up his mistress and little Olaf on a separate farm, where the boy became such a fine and showy figure that Hoskuld eventually suggested that Melkorka should be maintained by her son, not by himself. In addition, Melkorka suffered repeated humiliations, which included Olaf's still being referred to as the son of a slave woman. Angrily, she ordered her son to consent to her marrying a freeman who had long wanted her as his wife, because the union would make it impossible for anyone to call her a slave. By the time Hoskuld learned about that marriage, Olaf was already sailing abroad with a fair wind, both literally and figuratively. When he returned to Iceland, a wealthy man, he again became Hoskuld's pride and joy and eventually built Hjardarholt, the most magnificent home ever seen in medieval Iceland.[40]

Demonstrably, in that society there were several ways in which to merge the freeborn and the slave born, involving conditions that may well have contributed to an earlier end to slavery in Iceland and Norse Greenland than in Norway itself. One might usefully compare those young societies with the early American West, where, regardless of social status at birth, a man (and occasionally a woman) could make his way with the right combination of luck, skill, and personal effort. However, one may not assume that in any of those Norse societies, the conditions under which female slaves were set free were similar to those involved in freeing enslaved males. For example, while freeing a male slave involved a considerable amount of ceremony on the part of both owner and slave,[41] no such ceremonies are known for Norse woman slaves. Their obscurity may well be linked with the fact that they would have brought very little improvement in their social status. Among the other privileges gained by freed male slaves was participation in the annual assembly, but even freeborn women had no role to play in that event except as onlookers.

SLAVERY ENDS

Compared with the large farms belonging to powerful Norwegian landowners, the properties available to their social equals in Iceland and

Norse Greenland were notable both for their smaller sizes and for other physical and economic limitations. These differences created disparities in general levels of wealth that inevitably affected the lives of both free and unfree women and probably contributed to an earlier end to slavery in the two outpost countries than in Norway.

Gunnar Karlsson notes that slavery was simply abandoned in Iceland in the eleventh or early twelfth century; it is not known that any law was ever passed against the institution as such.[42] Other scholars, too, have observed that slavery in Iceland was at its end by the twelfth century and ceased in Norway as well later in the twelfth century.[43] However, while it is certainly true that slavery, including debt slavery, ended somewhat later in Norway than in Iceland (and, very likely, in Greenland), it was not until sometime in the first half of the twelfth century, when slavery was no longer practiced in Iceland, that we see the emergence of the assemblage of miscellaneous laws there with the title of *Grágás* (Greylag).[44] Put differently, the effective end to formal slavery in Iceland essentially coincided with the development of a more comprehensive and uniform legal environment.

Modest economic opportunities appear to have been chiefly responsible for the de facto end of slavery in Iceland. Gunnar Karlsson notes, for example, that on small farms in a sparsely populated country where supervision was difficult, slavery never made much sense. (Several sagas suggest that slaves were sometimes given a great deal of responsibility and acted as supervisors of others.) Supervision would not have been much of a problem in the case of female slaves, whose work would rarely have taken them far from the farm, except when working at the mountain farms used for summer grazing, or when gathering fuel for heat and cooking. Karlsson also argues that slavery ceased to pay when the population grew and scarcities of land suitable for farming meant that few freemen were able to obtain farms of their own, thus increasing the free, but dependent, workforce.[45] This second argument makes considerable sense, given the general economic developments in Iceland and Greenland.

This reasoning, that hired help became increasingly available as land ownership became less accessible, was first published in 1983 by the historian Anna Agnarsdóttir and her economist husband Ragnar Arnason.[46] They had been looking for the reason(s) why slavery in Iceland had stopped before the end of the twelfth century and took their point of departure in the apparent coincidence of the cessation of slavery and other developments in Icelandic society during its first three centuries of existence.

The two authors note that some scholars have argued that the early-eleventh-century ban on infant exposure was specifically aimed at the exposure of slave children (despite slight evidence that slave children were exposed). They themselves do not believe that this ban caused the end of slavery some hundred years later, however, because Norway and Denmark had a similar ban on infant exposure, and in both countries slavery continued for longer than in Iceland. They observe, furthermore, that if keeping slaves had still been an economically viable practice after infant exposure had become illegal, the Icelanders would certainly have found it worth their while to subject the children of slaves to inherited slavery, especially when the end to Viking raids had evidently dried up outside supplies, eventually causing the Irish slave trade to peter out in the early twelfth century.

Anna Agnarsdóttir and Ragnar Arnason believe that those who wanted to limit the number of slaves they owned had options other than infant exposure, such as manumission (which the Norse had practiced even before the Icelandic settlement began), killing any who proved too unruly or too numerous, or selling them abroad in one of the other Nordic countries where slavery had continued. The two scholars also question the argument that Iceland's natural conditions discouraged keeping such large flocks of cattle that slaves were necessary for the daily chores, and that slavery therefore had never been particularly useful in Iceland. On the contrary, they note, the earlier period had actually seen a number of large farms with numerous livestock. Summing up, they observe that in the old Icelandic commonwealth, slavery had probably been useful at various times and places but not at others, and that it is very unlikely that the first settlers would have brought along such large numbers of slaves of both sexes if they had had no real use for them.

As the Icelandic population increased and no more habitable land was available for the taking, the socioeconomic picture in Iceland changed from one in which slavery had a function to one in which landowners began to rely on hired help, which became available when people had no chance of obtaining a holding of their own. Anna Agnarsdóttir and Ragnar Arnason thus see a situation in which farmers no longer found it economically advantageous to rely on slaves who worked only during the short growing season in those far northern climes but needed to be fed the year round, and who might reward their owners with mutiny or murder. It made increasing sense to hire people for seasonal work, whether it involved fishing or haying.

In Norse Greenland as well, where farmers used the same methods as the medieval Icelanders, the population is likely to have peaked by the end of the twelfth century, after the best farmsteads had long since been taken. Even more distant from the slave markets in Europe than their immediate neighbors to the east, the Norse Greenlanders, like the Icelanders, would have had to reckon with dwindling supplies of new slaves of either sex, except that by that time it is unlikely to have mattered. If they still wanted slaves, they could have relied on hereditary slavery, but in an economy that depended so heavily on marine resources for food at home and trade abroad, a crew of freemen aboard a small boat would have been far safer than a group of angry thralls looking for an opportunity to escape their bondage.

For women who had graduated from legal slavery to the virtual slavery of their gender, subject to a never-ending cycle of looking after people and animals seven days a week, the difference between bondage and legal freedom may scarcely have been perceptible. While one would naturally like to know whether the Norse Greenland woman who sat in northern Baffin Island and twisted hare fur into flawless yarn was a slave or a free woman, it seems more important to remember that she and countless other women in the Far North lived lives so unimaginably hard that only the strongest survived into old age.

NOTES

1. Egil's Saga, in The Complete Sagas of the Icelanders, gen. ed. Vidar Hreinsson, 5 vols. (Reykjavik: Leifur Eiriksson, 1997), 1:33–177, esp. 33, 106, 120, 135. Egil's Saga, whose action begins in the second half of the ninth century, is believed to have been composed in the second quarter of the thirteenth century by the famous Icelandic historian Snorri Sturluson.

2. Judith Jesch warns against indiscriminate use of these and other sources both with regard to easy assumptions about human sacrifice in general and the sacrifice of women in particular, for example, as burial companions. Jesch, Women in the Viking Age (Woodbridge, UK: Boydell, 1991), 24–27, 88.

3. Gutorm Gjessing, Vikingskipsfunnene (Universitetets Oldsaksamlings Håndbøker) (Oslo: J. Petlitz Boktrykkeri, 1950), 10, 12.

4. See, for example, the receipt that the Roman curia issued to the Norwegian Bishop Alf of Stavanger. That city was believed to be in Ireland—evidently another insignificant Atlantic country as far as the curia's clerk was concerned. Letter dated July 24, 1464, Diplomatarium norvegicum 17:1085.

5. For a printed collection of Icelandic documents, consult Diplomatarium islandicum, 16 vols. (Copenhagen, 1857–1959). For a printed edition of the medieval annals, see Gustav Storm, comp. and ed., Islandske annaler indtil 1578 (1988; Oslo: Norsk Historisk Kjeldeskrifts-Institutt, 1977); Annálar 1400–1800, 5 vols. (Copenhagen: Hid Íslenzka Bókmenntafélag, 1922–61). For a good annotated translation of the Icelandic sagas, see Hreinsson, Complete Sagas.

6. Historians concerned with medieval Iceland and Norse Greenland also owe a heavy debt to researchers in tangential fields such as archaeology, philology, and linguistics.

7. See, for example, Kirsten A. Seaver, *The Frozen Echo: Greenland and the Exploration of North America ca. A.D. 1000–1500* (Stanford: Stanford University Press, 1996), ch. 7, esp. 179–80; Peter G. Foote and David M. Wilson, *The Viking Achievement* (London: Sidgwick and Jackson; New York: St. Martin's, 1970), 67.

8. Bruce E. Gelsinger, *Icelandic Enterprise: Commerce and Economy in the Middle Ages* (Columbia: University of South Carolina Press, 1981), 124–25; *Nytt fra Norge* (Oslo), 44, no. 3 (13–19 January 1998): 14.

9. *The Lay of Rigr,* composed sometime between the eleventh and thirteenth centuries. Thomas D. Hill, "Rigsthula," in *Medieval Scandinavia: An Encyclopedia,* ed. Phillip Pulsiano and Kirsten Wolf (New York: Garland, 1993), 535–36; Birgit Sawyer and Peter Sawyer, *Medieval Scandinavia: From Conversion to Reformation circa 800–1500* (Minneapolis: University of Minnesota Press, 1993), 142–43. The authors do not consider the poem itself either pre-Christian or a realistic description of social structure, but rather as reflecting the problems of plain Norse farmers in the thirteenth century, when they found themselves increasingly pressured by chieftains and kings and may well have felt the need to distinguish themselves from the slave class—the lowest of the low.

10. Henry Hollander's translation of the *Rígsthula,* http://depts.washington.edu/scand/rigsthula.html. Peter G. Foote and David M. Wilson translate these names as She-lump, Clump, Thicklegs, Beaked-nose, Noisy, Slave-maid, Torrent-talker, Tatter-coat, and Crane-shank; Foote and Wilson, *Viking Achievement,* 76.

11. Peter Sawyer, ed., *The Oxford Illustrated History of the Vikings* (New York: Oxford University Press, 1997), 87–96.

12. Poul Holm, "Ireland, Norse in," in Pulsiano and Wolf, *Medieval Scandinavia,* quote, p. 324; Sawyer, 101–3. Although Dublin was briefly controlled by the Norse king of Man and the Hebrides from 1078 to 1094, the town had by this time become as influenced by Anglo-Saxon culture as formerly Norse-dominated towns in England, most notably York.

13. Hermann Pálsson and Paul Edwards, eds. and trans., *Landnámabók* (Book of Settlements) (Winnipeg: University of Manitoba Press, 1972), 3–4, ch. 1. The *Book of Settlements* was originally composed by Ari Thórgilsson the Learned. The first extant version was written by Sturla Thórdarson (d. 1284).

14. *Íslendingabók* (Book of the Icelanders), in *Islendinga sögur,* ed. Gudni Jónsson, 13 vols. (Reykjavik, 1968), 1:1–20, esp. ch. 2.

15. Ibid., chs. 6–8.

16. For the latest mitochondrial DNA studies intended to unravel the genetic heritage of modern Icelanders, see Agnar Helgason, Sigrun Sigurdardottir, Jeffrey R. Gulcher, Ryk Ward, and Kari Stefansson, "mtDNA and the Origin of the Icelanders: Deciphering Signals of Recent Population History," *American Journal of Human Genetics* 66 (2000): 999–1016.

17. The basic text here is the *Book of Settlements.* See Pálsson and Edwards, *Landnámabók.*

18. Gunnar Karlsson, *History of Iceland* (Minneapolis: University of Minnesota Press, 2000), 15.

19. See, for example, Daniel Bruun, "Arkaeologiske Undersøgelser i Julianehaab Distrikt," *Meddelelser om Grönland* 16 (Copenhagen, 1917); Poul Nörlund and Mårten Stenberger, "Brattahlid," *Meddelelser om Grönland* 88, no. 1 (Copenhagen, 1934); Knud Krogh, *Viking Greenland* (Copenhagen: National Museum, 1967). See also Seaver, *Frozen Echo*, ch. 1, esp. p. 20.

20. *Eirik the Red's Saga*, tr. Keneva Kunz, in Hreinsson, *Complete Sagas*, 1:2–3.

21. Robert Kellogg, introduction to Hreinsson, *Complete Sagas*, 1:xli.

22. See, for example, *Egil's Saga*, in Hreinsson, *Complete Sagas*, 1:35. It is a stock notion in the early Icelandic literature that the Norse chieftains who emigrated to Iceland wanted to escape the hardfisted rule of Norwegian kings, beginning with that of King Harold the Fairhaired, and this resulted sometimes in statements about so-and-so who did not want to become "the king's slave."

23. See, for example, Leiv Heggstad, Finn Hödnebö, and Erik Simensen, *Norrön ordbok* (Oslo: Det Norske Samlaget, 1975), 28.

24. Jesch, *Women*, 88, 97.

25. Pálsson and Edwards, *Landnámabók*, ch. 41.

26. For a useful summary of women's position in early Icelandic society, see Karlsson, *History of Iceland*, 54–55.

27. Pálsson and Edwards, *Landnámabók*, ch. 112.

28. *Olav Tryggvason's saga*, tr. Anne Holtsmark and Didrik Arup Seip, in Snorri Sturluson, *Norges kongesagaer*, ed. Finn Hödnebö and Hallvard Magerøy (Oslo: Gyldendal Norsk Forlag, 1979), chs. 1–8, 52 (pp. 129–33, 171).

29. Foote and Wilson, *Viking Achievement*, 70. Jenny Jochens also thinks that Christianity made a difference by introducing the concept of female consent in marriage. Jochens, *Women in Old Norse Society* (Ithaca: Cornell University Press, 1995), 5–16.

30. Pálsson and Edwards, *Landnámabók*, chs. 95–108. Note that Aud was called Unn in the *Laxdæla Saga*.

31. The region north of Vínland was Markland (Forest Land) and north of that again, Helluland (Slab Land).

32. In Old Norse *Karlsefni* means "the stuff a man is made of."

33. *Grænlendinga saga* (Saga of the Greenlanders), ch. 7, in *The Vinland Sagas: The Norse Discovery of America*, trans. and ed. Magnús Magnússon and Hermann Pálsson (Baltimore: Penguin Books, 1967).

34. Birgitta Linderoth Wallace, "Norse Expansion into North America," rev. version, www.heureka.fi/en/x/nx/wallace.html.

35. For a comprehensive account of the earliest excavations at L'Anse aux Meadows, see Anne Stine Ingstad, *The Discovery of a Norse Settlement in America* (Oslo: Universitetsforlaget, 1977), vol. 1.

36. News release, Canadian Museum of Civilization, Hull, Quebec, 1 December 1999; Patricia Sutherland, pers. comm. See also Patricia D. Sutherland, "The Norse and Native Norse Americans," in *Vikings: The North Atlantic Saga*, ed. William W. Fitzhugh and Elizabeth I. Ward (Washington: Smithsonian Institution Press, 2000),

238–47, esp. 241; Patricia Sutherland, "Strands of Culture Contact: Dorset-Norse Interactions in the Eastern Canadian Arctic," in *Identities and Cultural Contacts in the Arctic,* ed. M. Appelt, J. Berglund, and H. C. Gulløv (Copenhagen: National Museum, 2000), 159–69. I am grateful to Sutherland for the opportunity to examine these artifacts at the Museum of Civilization in October 2001.

37. Karlsson, *History of Iceland,* 53.

38. Jochens, *Women* , 5–16 (quote 6).

39. *Egil's Saga,* in Hreinsson, *Complete Sagas,* 1:33–177.

40. *The Saga of the People of Laxárdal,* tr. Keneva Kunz, in Hreinsson, *Complete Sagas,* 5:1–120, esp. chs. 7–9, 11–13, 16, 20–24.

41. Foote and Wilson, *Viking Achievement,* 72–74.

42. Karlsson, *History of Iceland,* 52.

43. See, for example, Ruth Mazo Karras, "Slavery," in Pulsiano and Wolf, *Medieval Scandinavia,* 598–99.

44. For an overview, see Hans Fix, "Laws (Iceland)," in Pulsiano and Wolf, *Medieval Scandinavia,* 384–85.

45. Karlsson, *History of Iceland,* 53.

46. Anna Agnarsdóttir and Ragnar Arnason, "Thrælahald a thjodveldisöld," *Saga* 21 (1983): 5–26.

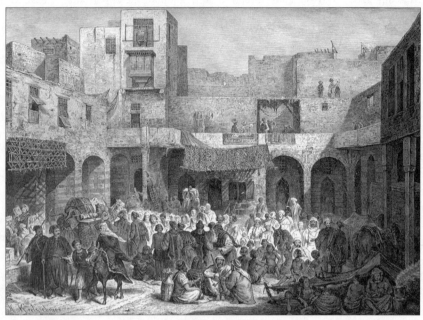

Slave Market. Engraving by H. Kretzschmer, from Georg Ebers,
Egypt: Descriptive, Historical, and Picturesque, vol. 2, translated from
the German by Clara Bell (London: Cassell, 1885), facing p. 37.

7

AFRICAN SLAVE WOMEN IN EGYPT, CA. 1820 TO THE PLAGUE OF 1834–35

GEORGE MICHAEL LA RUE

The years from 1820 to 1835 in Egypt saw the invasion of the Sudan, the creation of a new army of African slaves, the establishment of a western-ized national health system, the importation of a new generation of en-slaved Africans, the arrival of European medical personnel and Saint-Simoniens, the outbreak of plague, and the Ottoman pasha Muhammad 'Ali's well-known attempts to modernize Egypt's army and economy. This conjuncture of events brought the new African slaves and European and mixed-race observers together in Egypt's modernizing medical, economic, and social environment. The African slave women were not living in frozen, ahistoric Qur'anic times; they had real lives, knew real suffering, and took part in these well-documented historical events.

Obvious as this affirmation of the sub-Saharan women in Lower Egypt may seem, earlier scholars held only two limited views of female slavery in Muslim countries. The first portrayed the idealized benevolent treat-ment of female slaves based on specific passages from a thousand-year-old Qur'an, while the second presented eroticized Victorian-era images of slave women living luxuriously in harems, painted in words or oils by Eu-ropeans fantasizing about forbidden pleasures of the Orient. The major block to the historicized approach developed here was Orientalism, the long-dominant Western view of the Muslim world. Western Orientalists' views reflected those of their informants among the 'ulama (Muslim scholars), who portrayed the treatment of female slaves in Muslim lands in unchanging conformity with the eternal prescriptions of Islam. After learning these formal rules for the proper treatment of women slaves, the Orientalists assumed there was no more on the subject to learn.

In the 1970s Edward Said and others sharply critiqued this older Ori-entalist approach, arguing that modern Western dominance had dis-torted Western knowledge of the Muslim East to give rise to deliberate and powerful caricatures of the Muslim world. Of these, perhaps the most persistent had been the sensual images of elite slave women of the harem, depicted without personal pasts, without biographies. The Orientalists had noted the presence of other female slaves—often Africans—who performed mundane tasks in elite households in major Muslim cities. Believing slavery to be unaffected by economic change, they made little effort to collect demographic information on slaves in Egypt, or to track fluctuations in the trans-Saharan slave trade. *Orientalism*, Said's major critique, however, was also silent on African slaves (male or female), perhaps because his binary world view of the dominant West and the subjected East left no room to comment on Egypt's imperial relationship with the Sudan or to acknowledge the presence of the Africans enslaved in "Oriental" societies.[1] Orientalists and anti-Orientalists alike had assumed away the narrative history of slavery in nineteenth-century Egypt!

The UNESCO Slave Route Project (begun in 1994 and still ongoing) suggests that studies of slavery in North Africa and the Middle East should begin in Africa, with the history and cultures of those enslaved, examine the processes of their enslavement, then follow the slaves from their points of capture to slave markets in North Africa and the Middle East, and on to their final destinations in urban centers, military barracks, commercial towns, or agricultural centers. Finally, investigators should follow the communities they formed, their processes of creating new cultures from older African and Muslim forms, and their individual and community experiences down to the present. Using this UNESCO approach to recover the lives of African slave women in Egypt encourages the use of new historical sources and aims to create a coherent narrative of their experiences. Using it to trace the fates of the generation of African slaves who reached Egypt between 1820 and 1834 tracks those who died in the Sudan resisting enslavement, others who succumbed in transit in the slave *qafilas* crossing the Sahara, in boats along the Nile, in the holding camps in Upper Egypt, the survivors sold in slave markets in Lower Egypt, or those who eventually served their Egyptian owners.

Their varying fates were determined in part by their genders. Between 1821 and 1825, perhaps eighty thousand slaves were sent north from the Sudan, including male and female adults and children. Those of the adult males are roughly known: many were sent to Egypt and placed in the *nizam al-jadid*—Muhammad 'Ali's newly formed army regiments, trained by European military officers, and armed with the latest European weapons. Many of these male slave recruits died of disease, but others served in Egyptian armies in Greece, the Hejaz, and the Sudan.

The generation of Sudanese women enslaved between 1820 and 1834 has not been so well studied. They are simply mentioned as arriving in

Egypt as they reached the slave markets. So large an influx of female slaves was undoubtedly hard to absorb. Scattered evidence suggests that some of them were sent on to markets elsewhere in the Ottoman world,[2] but most probably remained in Egypt. The very size of this influx of these African slave women raises questions about their presence. How did they live and what did they do? If many were of child-bearing age, what happened to their children?

Answers to these questions can be found by considering the historical context in which these enslaved African women lived and following them from their moments of enslavement through their lives in Egypt. They sought first to survive the hardships of enslavement and the trans-Saharan Middle Passage and then to secure places for themselves in Egyptian society. There they formed ties to powerful individuals, fostered social networks with other slaves, and acculturated to Egyptian life by learning Arabic, observing Muslim practices, and applying or adopting skills from laundering to cooking, childcare, and midwifery.

Even post-Orientalist economic and social historians have struggled to find sufficient evidence to write a general history of African slavery in Egypt, including consideration of the African women enslaved there.[3] Fortunately, however, after 1840, abolitionist pressures in Britain and France led European diplomats in Egypt to begin recording information on the slavery and slave trading everywhere around them.[4] From 1798, Europeans, Egyptians (and other North Africans), and sub-Saharan Africans (free and enslaved) in Egypt exchanged information not only between East and West but also between the lands north and south of the Sahara.[5]

European medical personnel in Egypt provided some of the most interesting information about African slave women, while also setting slavery in broader medical, social and even familial contexts. Rather than creating simply a new caricature of African slaves as patients, their reports show the complex interactions of slave women, medical observers, and others in the microcosm of the household of a French doctor, Dussap, set against the plague epidemic of 1834–35 and its devastating impact on this generation of African slaves.

MUHAMMAD 'ALI'S INVASION OF THE SUDAN AND THE ACQUISITION OF AFRICAN FEMALE SLAVES

Of all Sudanese captured by Egyptian forces between 1820 and 1825, perhaps a quarter were males fit for military service. What happened to the others? The very old and the very young were often killed at the point of capture or died along the desert roads to Egypt. Women were put to work immediately by their captors—preparing food, grinding grain, carrying water, cooking, doing soldiers' laundry, and serving as concubines. Young women and boys often served Egyptian officials or were sold in Egyptian slave markets to staff the households of middle- and upper-class Egyptians, and also Europeans. Others were sold farther into the Ottoman world, ending up in Istanbul or other Ottoman cities.

The invasion of the Sudan and the capture of African populations in the sultanate of Sinnar, in Kordofan (then a province of the Dar Fur sultanate) and in the Nuba hills of Kordofan are often described in general histories of the Sudan.[6] Muhammad 'Ali, ruler of Egypt, sought wealth in sub-Saharan Africa, and the enslavement of African populations was one of his key motives.[7]

Muhammad 'Ali requested that African males be sent first, to fill the ranks of his army and provide additional field labor. But he also specifically directed his generals to enslave women in the Sudan and send them north to Egypt: "When you have captured negroes, you will separate the women and the children and keep them with you. You will send us the men who are fit for conscription. When we will have 10,000 males, you will then send the women you have kept."[8]

Of the first captives sent north in August 1821, males suitable for the army were a distinct minority: "The first consignment of these unfortunate beings totaling 1900 men, women and children arrived in Isna north of Aswan in August 1821. Those who were suitable were selected for military service; the others were to be sold in slave markets in Cairo."[9] Another source perhaps describing the same mixed group of about two thousand slaves noted that they left Kordofan in May 1821. About six hundred reached Aswan: "To see them, one would have said that they were ghosts. Mothers and girls were exhausted and fell to the sand, and finished their suffering by leaving this life."[10]

Following the invasion, Egyptian troops often raided villages in Sinnar and Kordofan: "On the pretext of furnishing soldiers to Egypt, entire families were removed and taken to Aswan where despite cries and tears, the men were torn violently from their dearest loves to be thrown into an army barracks. Women of all ages, and girls were taken to Cairo to be sold there at low prices, because the large supply had lessened their value."[11] The men stopped in Upper Egypt, while women and children continued to Cairo for sale.

Europeans witnessed the movement of captured Sudanese women to Egypt and repeated the explanations provided at the time. For example, in early 1822 the Baroness Minutoli, accompanying her husband on his scientific journey to Egypt, wrote that during her cruise on the Nile they

> met several boats filled with Negro slaves of both sexes, coming from Darfour and Sennaar, and laden besides with elephant's teeth, ostrich feathers, gold dust, parrots, etc. The people who are engaged in this traffic are called *gelaps* [*jallaba*]; they generally carry off children by force or by stratagem, and even frequently purchase them of the parents themselves. Not being accustomed to this sight, we felt at the view of these poor wretches, deprived of their liberty and forced from their native land, a sentiment of pity which would not have been so lively if we had known the state of destitution and misery which they experience in their own country.[12]

The invasion threw the commercial slave trade into disarray. Merchants at times purchased slaves from soldiers and officers in the Sudan, and at times were deliberately blocked from engaging in trade. The Egyptian army's early attempts to march large slave caravans to Egypt were unsuccessful. Many of the enslaved—especially those who were shackled, wounded, hungry, thirsty, old, young, or burdened with small children—died between their homes and the sub-Saharan collecting points. Laggards were abandoned or killed. The desert crossing was equally bad, and soon Muhammad 'Ali sought to ensure that more slaves survived the trans-Saharan Middle Passage.[13] New wells were dug, food was provided along the way, and boats were collected or built to bring more slaves alive to Egypt.[14]

Eduard Ruppell, a German naturalist and explorer, described the heavy mortality of the enslaved Sudanese before reaching Egypt: "after the Daftardar bey's 1822 campaign in the southern Nuba mountains, nearly 40,000 slaves were captured. However, through bad treatment, disease and desert travel barely 5,000 made it to Egypt. Of those, a proportion was female."[15] Thus, only one out of eight slaves captured by Egyptian forces reached Egypt. The medical sources considered here indicate arrival in Egypt did not end the captives' health concerns.

The exact number of African slaves in Egypt between 1820 and 1835 is not known at present, nor is the precise number of Sudanese women slaves arriving there between 1820 and 1825. There were many captives: beyond Ruppel's estimate of forty thousand from the Nuba hills in 1822 alone, the Egyptian finance minister, Daftardar Muhammad Bey (son-in law of Muhammad 'Ali and commander of the Egyptian expedition in Sudan), estimated 75 percent mortality to meet Muhammad 'Ali's demand for ten thousand men, so he rounded up fifty thousand blacks. A few months later ten to twelve thousand blacks reached Asyut in Upper Egypt. Another report cites thirty thousand slaves captured in Kordofan and taken to Manfalut in Upper Egypt.[16] Slave raids continued throughout the period, and at least half the slaves sent across the desert were female.

THE HEALTH OF NEWLY IMPORTED SLAVES IN THE EARLY 1820S

Dr. Dussap came to Egypt as a nurse with the French Expedition in 1798 and stayed behind when the French army left. Without further formal education, he became known as a doctor.[17] While visiting the Cairo slave market shortly before 1820, he was quite taken by a Sudanese slave woman, Halima, and purchased her. They soon had two children.[18] Following the invasion of the Sudan, Muhammad 'Ali appointed Dussap his chief army medical officer and charged him with dealing with the new male slave recruits from the Sudan, in poor health and dying rapidly, to Upper Egypt.[19] Halima accompanied Dussap there, working alongside him. He had little success, and the French surgeon Antoine Barthélémy Clot replaced him in 1825.[20]

The Sudanese slave women in these early years could not have been healthy. They were captured in the same slave raids as the men, traveled in the same caravans, and initially stayed in the same camps in Upper Egypt. The men were dying at a rapid pace, and European doctors treated them for a variety of ailments. Guinea worm afflicted everyone involved in the military campaigns in Sudan from 1820 to 1824—Turkish soldiers, European doctors, and Sudanese males brought back to Egypt. Though Sudanese slave women surely had no special immunity, no record of guinea worm among them has been found.[21] Sudanese slave soldiers were also victims of the 1824 epidemic of plague, even as they went to Ottoman wars in Greece. Though the sources are again silent on the ailments and treatment of Sudanese slave women in this period, in contrast to later periods, must also have suffered from plague.

AFRICAN SLAVE WOMEN IN LOWER URBAN EGYPT IN THE 1830S

Though the African slave women in Egypt were likely among the victims of the 1824 plague epidemic, slave raids in the Sudan steadily supplied replacements to Egyptian slave markets. Importation of enslaved Greek women during the Greek war (1821–28) may have provided supplementary supplies of women slaves, especially in the harems of government officials. In July 1833 Baron Charles-Edmond de Boislecomte, in Egypt on a diplomatic mission for the French government, reported twenty thousand blacks, out of an estimated three million Egyptian residents: "One scarcely sees black [males] in Egypt except in harems in the service of the rich, [but] black women are still numerous enough for the service of private houses, the markets of Cairo still abound with them, whereas one hardly finds black males other than children and rarely, only a few whites."[22]

By late 1831 the army medical officer Clot realized that local custom made it nearly impossible for male doctors to treat or instruct Egyptian women.[23] Childbirth was the leading cause of death for Egyptian women who gave birth either without trained assistants or with *dayas* (lay midwives), who varied in skill and experience. Initially, Clot could not train any Egyptian women as midwives, but finally he realized he could train female slaves to be professional midwives and instructors in his School of Midwifery. With Muhammad 'Ali's permission, Clot bought ten Abyssinian and Sudanese women in the slave market in 1831 and arranged for their supervision by two of Muhammad 'Ali's eunuchs.[24] They were taught Arabic for two years and trained in midwifery by faculty at the school of medicine. Their rigorous six-year curriculum included instruction in the theory and practice of obstetrics; pre- and postnatal hygiene and the care of newborns; the treatment of simple wounds and inflammations; cauterization and the techniques of vaccination; scarification, cupping, and the application of leeches; and identification and preparation of the most common medicines.[25] Two professional French midwives provided practical training in a local hospital. Ten more slaves, ten orphan girls, and four more eunuchs later joined the group.[26]

Modern studies of Clot's midwifery school have not focused on the race of the early students and its implications.[27] Visitors were impressed by the "knowledge they had acquired, and by the incredible intelligence of the students."[28] As Clot put it, "Their aptitude is astonishing especially when one compares what is happening before our eyes with the ravings [*deblatérations*] of some pessimists who have wished to deny any intelligence in the Negro race."[29] Precarious enrollments for more than two decades qualify the optimism of Clot's own narrative.[30] Nonetheless, not only the Abyssinians excelled but "also negresses from Sinnar and Merowé."[31]

CHEZ DUSSAP

Dussap might have faded from view after his dismissal from Muhammad 'Ali's service in 1824 but for the arrival of the French Saint-Simoniens in the 1830s. Several were doctors, and like Clot before them, they sought "Doctor" Dussap's advice. Saint-Simoniens Thomas Urbain and Suzanne Voilquin, who arrived in Cairo in 1833 and 1834 respectively, each stayed for a time chez Dussap. These Saint-Simonien guests provide details of the lives of the African women who served in Dussap's household.

Thomas Urbain was the son of a French father and a *mestive libre* (free woman of mixed race) from Cayenne, Guyana. By law in Guyana, his parents were not allowed to marry, making him illegitimate. He had grown up in Cayenne, been sent to France for further education, and there sought to resolve his personal identity crisis by joining the Saint-Simonien community near Paris.[32] Urbain shared their growing interest in bridging the gap between East and West. The Saint-Simonien leader, Père Enfantin, chose Urbain to join a delegation they formed to seek "the Mother" in the Orient. The group left France in 1831, passing through Istanbul and several points in the Levant, and reached Egypt in 1833. On the voyage from France, they studied the Qur'an and encountered tales from the East depicting a young guest in an older man's household who became the lover of his host's wife, as well as his favorite slave.[33]

Urbain, then about twenty-two, stayed chez Dussap in Cairo from mid-February 1834. His earlier experiences seem to have prepared him to associate black women with beauty and sensuality. He had empathy for and was involved with several black slave women in Egypt. One modern biographer suggests that Urbain found "the Mother" he personally sought in Halima, Dussap's still-young slave wife. Halima impressed Urbain as being "of a very distinguished intelligence. . . . This woman was able in a few years to learn for herself the language and manners of Europe." She was "respected by European women. . . . She was also sought by black women who loved her as their mother and also chose her to mediate in their quarrels." Halima received French lessons for teaching him Arabic. She had been baptized into Christianity, although she was "still attached to Muslim mores." Her exact origin along the upper Nile is unclear: she is labeled either Abyssinian or Sudanese. Urbain's liaison with her began in April 1834 and continued until his transfer to Damietta shortly before Halima's death from plague in August of that year.[34]

However, the positions of such women were precarious, as is made clear in a letter from Père Enfantin. Enfantin reported that Halima's son by Dussap, 'Arif, "has his harem, he has his Abyssinian woman and takes her with a happy heart."[35] The young Abyssinian slave was in a dangerous position: If she resisted, she faced 'Arif's anger. If she submitted, she faced pregnancy and betrayal by others in the household. Dussap's household, typical or not of its Islamic counterparts, illustrated the range of opportunities and pitfalls for African slave women in Egypt.

AFRICAN FEMALE SLAVES AND THE PLAGUE

The plague reportedly arrived by boat from Jerusalem and claimed its first victims, two monks in the Greek convent in Alexandria in July 1834. On 5 August 1834 "a certain Capt. Dimitri, commanding the Turkish brig Leonidas" died of a confirmed case of plague. Investigators discovered "the captain had visited some girls [black women] opposite the European hospital at the village of Fouah."[36]

By 1834, Dr. Clot had become the head of Egypt's medical service and took the controversial position that plague was not contagious. This and the epidemic's severity prompted great debates between contagionist and anticontagionist medical factions in Egypt and Europe. The resulting medical literature often described specific African slave women among the early plague victims, giving details of their lives and social contexts.

In Alexandria, Louis-Rémy Aubert-Roche, a French Saint-Simonien doctor working in Egypt, described one of several black residential areas. The Arab houses did not fill all the space between the wall delimiting the city on the land side and the sea. Here and there were: "mud huts [huttes en terre] which made up a neighborhood, but to which the special name of 'villages' is given. Thus, the one of the Negroes, near the European hospital, that of Ras-el-Tin, near the palace of the Pasha, at the point known as Figtree Point, etc. All are part of the 'villages.'"[37] John Bowring, in Egypt on a fact-finding mission in 1837 for the British foreign secretary, Lord Palmerston, narrated the events: "On the 13th of August, in the said village, and another in its vicinity, both inhabited by Negroes, various deaths took place in succession in the course of a few days. The plague was found to exist, and on accurately examining the origin, it was clearly ascertained that two black washerwomen inhabiting one of the villages had been at work in the Greek convent for the first time, when the effects of the monks who had died of the plague were collected together."[38] Bowring indicates forty-eight deaths in a village of blacks in August 1834.

These villages were evacuated and some inhabitants moved to an open space, the local bocce court. Both black villages were thoroughly fumigated with burnt lime. Two Negro women died in the Kalafati household (which was under quarantine) on 23 and 24 October, and then two more in the black villages.[39] The fumigation was effective until 11 November. From 20 November 1834, many more people died.[40] In the sizeable black community in Alexandria, some black women worked as washerwomen, others as prostitutes. Even those in live-in domestic service were in contact with the "black villages."

Basing his report on eyewitness accounts, Clot found that susceptibility was affected by race, general physical condition, gender (women were more susceptible), age (the young more vulnerable), profession, and residence: "Those people who in following their profession are exposed to hard physical work to excesses of fatigue, to the harshness of the seasons, to sharp changes of temperature, are more apt than others to contract the plague. Manual laborers, bakers, blacksmiths, cooks fall in this category. . . . The unfortunate who live in filthy and poorly ventilated quarters, just as those who suffer from all sorts of privations, have furnished numerous victims to the plague."[41] Most African female slaves fit into one or more of those categories. Race, rather than directly increasing vulnerability to the plague, may have been a marker for the crowded and infested conditions in which the slave women of the city lived. However Grassi, an Italian doctor living in Alexandria, noted his belief that race affected the plague's spread: "among the Negroes I have frequently had occasion to observe a type of plague which by reason of the rapidity of its progress, could receive the name 'apoplectic.'"[42] Several examples of this pneumonic form of plague can be seen among African female slaves in Cairo.

Although many people traveled from Alexandria to Cairo, the contemporary contagionists pointed to a single individual as the plague carrier: M. Giglio, a Maltese merchant who made that trip in early 1835. Dr. Grassi, the leading contagionist, noted the sequential deaths in the Giglio household, and the plague's spread to neighboring families. He called this death the "beginning of the plague of 1835" in Cairo.[43] Aubert-Roche, an anticontagionist, who witnessed some of Cairo's early cases provided additional details but disputed Grassi's conclusions.

Descriptions of Giglio's case provide glimpses of the lives of African slave women in Cairo and the social networks they formed. After the Giglio house was put under quarantine, other family members died or managed to transfer their quarantine to Cairo's outskirts.[44] Only two people remained in the house: on 3 February, the Abyssinian slave woman died of plague, and the old Arab serving-woman discovered a fatal bubo. In that section of Cairo, houses were built side by side with flat roofs used as terraces. After Giglio died, the adjacent house inhabited by the Marco Iliadi family was also put under quarantine. But the plague killed a black slave woman, a child, and Marco himself in the adjacent house. For the contagionists, the black slave women clearly spread the disease as they interacted over the adjoining roof terraces.

When the plague reached Cairo, the Saint-Simonien doctor, Four-cade, was visiting the Ezbekiah hospital and about to leave for Alexandria. He asked to stay and to be assigned to verifying plague cases. The next day, to avoid the complications of quarantine, a family in the Jewish quarter, a large area in the western half of old Cairo with narrow lanes and an accumulation of rubbish, threw their ailing Abyssinian slave woman out into the street.[45] Dr. Fourcade examined her and confirmed her condition on the third day of the disease.[46] A hospital entry records that "Bokhite, négresse, 20 ans" was admitted on 17 February and died 19 February 1835. An autopsy was performed. Four days later Fourcade him-self contracted the disease and died.[47] Bokhite had frequently visited the black slave woman in the Marco Iliadi house before it was quarantined.

The symptoms of plague's pneumonic form were so dramatic that some victims were initially thought to be intoxicated, delaying their treatment. On 10 February 1835 a black slave woman belonging to M. Lussato fell in public at 2:00 P.M., vomiting reddish matter and babbling, and was thought to be drunk.[48] Aubert-Roche states that she was "found in the Frank quarter lying in the middle of the street, and I [the doctor] had her immediately removed and transported to the hospital, where a few minutes later she died, having all the symptoms of the plague."[49] She had been in contact with seven persons, including the young child she usually tended. Like Bokhite, Lussato's slave woman had been left unat-tended for three days—apparently no one valued these women enough to perceive their suffering.

Saint-Simonienne Suzanne Voilquin joined Dussap's daughter, Hanim, in training to treat Muslim women in Cairo. In mid-February 1835, Dr. Dussap informed Voilquin that the plague had spread beyond the Jewish quarter.[50] He predicted that the epidemic would be severe and general that year and invited her to move in with his family late in the month. As an experienced doctor long resident in Egypt and widower of an African slave woman, Dussap was in a unique position to report on its effects among those who had arrived as slaves. He had a reputation for treating the poor. He and Hanim introduced Voilquin to the lives of African women there.[51] During the epidemic he frequently brought plague patients home, and Voilquin observed as many as five at a time in the house. Once he brought home two black female patients: one died of plague, and Dussap supervised as Voilquin delivered the other's infant. Seven days later, she attended a Muslim blessing ceremony in the baby's honor.[52] On 24 March, Voilquin helped the doctor as a young Greek woman with the plague delivered a stillborn child. She had been abandoned by her spouse with only an old black servant to attend her.[53] These experiences brought Voilquin into close contact with Cairo's African slaves and the texture of their lives during the epidemic.

From 26 March through 3 April, Voilquin herself had plague symptoms. Dussap treated her, and sought to amuse her. Once, he brought two black slave women to her room to dance for her:

> In Mabrouka's case, a Congo slave, with thick protruding lips, a receding forehead, the ugliest type among the black races, I saw her feet turn while sliding slowly to facilitate the movement of the upper body which undulated, snakelike right to the belt and bending until one feared that it would break in two. In order to speak sensibly of this voluptuous perfection, the black women [of her country] must exercise themselves in such gymnastics from childhood. In the dance of the Abyssinian woman, it was the opposite: only the lower part of the body moved, forward and back from the haunches. These disordered movements, which I found singularly lascivious, belong truly to the black peoples of Africa.[54]

The term Congo was not an ethnic descriptor but rather indicated only Mabrouka's dark skin color. She was probably Nuba from Kordofan, an area frequently raided for slaves.

After a few feverish days, Voilquin recovered. Earlier that year she had learned of Urbain's liaison with Hanim. They had declared their love on the tomb of her mother, Halima, during Urbain's visit to Cairo in January 1835.[55] Urbain felt that Dussap's African slave wife had favored "this tender affection for her daughter, whom he had started to love as her daughter, then as a sister, then as his lover, and finally as a dear spouse."[56] Hanim saw things differently.[57] She knew of her mother's liaison with Urbain, and now her brother 'Arif threatened to tell their father unless she ended the relationship.[58] Resorting to a ruse, Hanim shared a ritual meal of bread and salt with Urbain, which made them adoptive siblings and precluded their marriage.[59] Soon the epidemic broke up the household.

On 10 April, Hanim had an uncharacteristic display of temper, followed by severe headaches. Perhaps she felt uncomfortable with her dead mother's lover, or feared her father's reaction, and became careless in her handling of her plague patients. Dussap despaired when the classic bubo appeared under her right arm. By 14 April, Hanim, daughter of an African slave woman, had died.[60] Dussap refused to leave the city to escape the epidemic but sent his son Arif to Upper Egypt to wait out the plague season. One Abyssinian slave in the household, Keledaski, died the same day, followed a week later by Tronga, Hanim's favorite among the slaves of the household.[61] One of them had been Arif's lover. After 25 April, the epidemic claimed Dussap himself; Bahri, the black slave *bawwab* (porter) and his wife; and the slave woman Mabrouka, the household cook. Of the entire household, only Voilquin, the absent Arif, and its two black male slaves survived.

The plague had killed all the African slave women of Halima's generation and those of her daughter's age in Dussap's household, where the medical treatment of the time was readily available. Other medical evidence shows that many less fortunate slave women in Cairo died alone, pushed out of their quarters in private homes into the streets, where a few of them attracted the attention of European doctors. Their stories only emerge in the debate over plague's contagiousness or through the testimony of compassionate observers.

Other evidence from the Muslim court archives in Cairo confirms the devastating effect of the epidemic on Cairo's female slave population. On 8 November 1835 judgment was rendered in a dispute over an expensive female slave, probably a light-skinned Ethiopian woman, between a merchant in the slave market and one of his customers. They disputed whether she had been pregnant at the time of sale, and her death on 6 April 1835 (at the height of the epidemic) complicated the case. In court, the slave merchant stated, "During the time of the plague, no one buys slaves."[62] Most of the slaves on display in the slave market were women. Of 500 slaves in the Cairo slave market, 482 died of the plague in 1835.[63]

Though the precise number of blacks who died in the epidemic may never be known, official reports counted nearly seven thousand black bodies taken out of Cairo for burial, and contemporary estimates place the number of black deaths at twice as many. Given the repeated reports that most blacks in Cairo were slave women, one can assume that most of these deaths were of African women.[64]

REMARKABLE CHANGES

One can readily see causal connections between the estimated fifteen thousand deaths of African slaves, mostly women, in the plague epidemic of 1834–35,[65] the large slave raids conducted by Muhammad 'Ali's forces in 1837 and subsequent years, the high estimates of imports of African slaves by Bowring in 1838 and Richard Madden in 1840, and the abolitionist pressures placed on Muhammad 'Ali. The deaths of African slaves (particularly women) in the epidemic and the broader loss of Egyptian lives led to a labor shortage. The resulting large raids in the Sudan and increased importation of slaves caught the attention of alarmed European observers.[66] Bowring, Madden, and Victor Schoelcher, all representatives of the larger abolitionist movement in Europe, led a new campaign to end slavery in, and the slave trade to, Egypt.

The epidemic of 1834–35 killed most of the surviving African slave women who had reached Egypt between 1820 and 1834. The slave deaths in the Dussap household are probably illustrative. The mature adult slaves and the young adults had grown up in Egypt, acculturated to Egyptian society, acquired facility in Arabic, learned about Islam, and most important, knew how to survive in Cairo. Slave survivors of the plague were faced with "renegotiating" their servitude with new masters if their former owners had died.

The new slaves after 1835 had to begin again. There was a fresh wave of violence to capture them. The trans-Saharan crossing with its attendant horrors again became a fresh memory.[67] Bowring spoke to a female slave from Dar Fur who recounted the desert crossing: "We had not food enough to eat, and sometimes we had no drink at all, and our thirst was terrible; when we stopped, almost dying for want of water, they killed a camel, and gave us blood to drink. But the camels themselves could not get on, and then they were killed, and we had their flesh for meat and their blood for water."[68] Even Edward Lane, the renowned Arabic scholar who lived in Egypt from 1825 to 1828 and again from 1833 to 1835, saw the suffering of the new slave women and implied that most Abyssinian and black female slaves were raped by *jallaba* (trans-Saharan merchants) en route to Egypt.[69] Nor did their suffering stop in Egypt: "Even when they have reached and are settled in the Egyptian cities, their average term of existence is deplorably short—not so much from ill-usage, for, on the whole, they are treated with tolerable kindness by the Mahometans—but from the change of climate, altered modes of life, seclusion and pestilential visitations."[70]

Both Lane and Bowring displayed sympathy for the African slave women. After the epidemic of 1834–35, Bowring explained the scarcity of slave descendants: "The number of blacks appears to decrease, notwithstanding the perpetual immigration. The black women are indeed many of them mothers, but nearly half of their offspring die; the great proportion of their children are mulattoes. . . . When they marry, their descendants seldom live; in fact the laws of nature seem to repel the establishment of hereditary slavery; death comes to break the chains of inherited bondage; man holds his tyrant right over man but a few short years; the emancipation of the grave is always at hand."[71] Dr. Nicolas Perron, who had taught in the Egyptian Medical School and served through the plague epidemic, confirmed Bowring's viewpoint: "Women slaves in particular nearly all die at a young age. Negro and Abyssinian women rarely attain the age of forty. At twenty years old they have already become old, because they have often served as Muslim concubines since the age of eight or ten. And of all the children who are born of these concubines, how many remain? And of those who survive, how few escape scrofulous diseases!"[72]

These reports suggest several demographic patterns among African slave women in Egypt: many were raped at young ages; frequently they bore children by Egyptian masters rather than by African slave men; their children suffered high rates of infant mortality; the women themselves aged rapidly; and both mothers and children were swept away by epidemics.

Abolitionist observers in the late 1830s reported higher levels of slave imports than in any other period between 1800 and 1850. The new slaves were more visible than their predecessors. First, they arrived in new locations within Cairo and Alexandria. Given the high mortality rates during the epidemic of 1834–35, the slave market of Cairo and the black villages of Alexandria were viewed as potential health threats. The slave market (*wakalat al-jallaba*) in Cairo was relocated, and the slave "villages" in Alexandria were eliminated in a wave of urban renewal.[73] The new slaves were not only deprived of the experience of the earlier generation of slaves but also faced Egyptians who were unaccustomed to their presence in the new locations.

Second, as the slaving frontier in the Sudan and Chad moved southward, the new generation of slaves came from areas beyond the Muslim sultanates of Sinnar and Dar Fur in Sudan, or Wadai and Bagirmi in Chad.[74] The new slaves rarely found people of their own ethnic backgrounds established in Egypt, and they reinforced Egyptian negative racial stereotypes of African slaves as uncultured unbelievers who spoke little Arabic.

The Irish doctor and abolitionist Richard R. Madden, just back from playing a key role in the *Amistad* trial, took part in the initial meetings of the British and Foreign Anti-Slavery Society in London in 1840, and carried its abolitionist message to Muhammad 'Ali in Egypt. He reported that some ten to twelve thousand Sudanese were enslaved but that the adult males had been retained in the Sudan and that nearly five thousand women and girls (and some boys) were brought into Egypt in 1840 alone. He also visited the slave markets in Cairo and Alexandria.[75]

Madden compared the situation of female domestic slaves in Egypt to their counterparts in the Atlantic world:

> The poorer classes, moreover, in Mohammedan countries, who hold slaves not from motives of pride or pomp, but simply for the purpose of domestic service, are those amongst whom the condition of slaves is the worst. Their female slaves are generally condemned to a life of domestic drudgery, they are seldom allowed to go abroad, and still more seldom allowed to marry with people of their own race. On the death of their owners they are liable to be sold again, or for any signal misconduct or defect after they have been purchased, they may again be sent to the market place. They are likewise subject to the caprices of their owner's wives, and are frequently exposed to the resentment of their jealousies; and the use of the courbash [whip] is by no means uncommon in the harems of the people of the middle classes.[76]

His observations support other evidence of neglect and abuse presented here.

The high mortality of African female slaves in Alexandria and Cairo left its mark in the contemporary medical records. The medical literature is full of suffering and death and supports the alarmed concern of leading abolitionist writers. Like the sympathetic eyewitness accounts of Voilquin and Urbain, the medical realities were filtered out of the Orientalist canon. Restoring the medical context validates the concern of Bowring and Lane for the enslaved African women in Egypt, shines new light on the lives of individual women slaves, explains the timing of the increased slave imports after 1835 reported by abolitionists, and suggests that historians of slavery in nineteenth-century Egypt might well find further traces in the medical records.

Rather than simply seeing the exotic sensuality of the harem and unchanging and faceless slavery, historians can find an intricate history of enslaved women making places for themselves, even in the midst of abuse and death. Looking at the triangular relationships among Europeans, Egyptians, and black Africans, African slave women emerge as individuals struggling to live under difficult and changing circumstances. The period from the invasion of the Sudan in 1820 to the plague epidemic of 1834–35 was a critical conjuncture in Egypt's history. It should not be surprising that slavery and the slave trade changed, and that contemporary observers recorded those changes. But for many then and since, it was easier not to face up to the suffering of enslavement, the harshness of the slave trade, the pain and indignities of slavery, and the sorrows of the deaths enslaved sub-Saharan blacks far from home in modernizing Egypt.

NOTES

1. Edward Said, *Orientalism* (New York: Vintage, 1979). Two important works critical of Said's views are Billie Melman, *Women's Orients: English Women and the Middle East, 1713–1918* (Ann Arbor: University of Michigan Press, 1992); John MacKenzie, *Orientalism: History, Theory and the Arts* (Manchester: Manchester University Press, 1995).

2. For slaves from Dar Fur and Sinnar in Constantinople's slave market, see R. R. Madden, *Travels in Turkey, Egypt, Nubia and Palestine in 1824, 1825, 1826 and 1827*, 2 vols. (London: Henry Colburn, 1829), 1:6.

3. Gabriel Baer, "Slavery in Nineteenth Century Egypt," *Journal of African History* 8, no. 3 (1967): 417–41, and "Slavery and Its Abolition," in Baer, *Studies in the Social History of Modern Egypt* (Chicago: University of Chicago Press, 1969), 161–89. Also see Judith E. Tucker, *Women in Nineteenth-Century Egypt* (Cambridge: Cambridge University Press, 1985), 164–93; Terence Walz, *The Trade between Egypt and Bilad as-Sudan, 1700–1820* (Cairo: Institut Français d'Archéologie Orientale, 1978).

4. Ralph A. Austen, "The Trans-Saharan Slave Trade: A Tentative Census," in *The Uncommon Market: Essays in the Economic History of the Atlantic Slave Trade*, ed. H. A. Gemery and J. S. Hogendorn (New York: Academic, 1979), 23–76; Austen, "The Mediterranean Islamic Slave Trade Out of Africa: A Tentative Census," in *The Human Commodity: Perspectives on the Trans-Saharan Slave Trade*, ed. Elizabeth Savage (London: Frank Cass, 1992), 215–48. For the basis of population estimates from 1798 to 1850, see Edmé François Jomard, *Description de l'Égypte*. On slave exports to the Ottoman Empire after 1840, see Ehud R. Toledano, *The Ottoman Slave Trade and its Suppression, 1840–1890* (Princeton: Princeton University Press, 1982).

5. George Michael La Rue, "The Export Trade of Dar Fur, ca. 1785–1875," in *Figuring African Trade*, ed. G. Liesegang, H. Pasch, and A. Jones, Kölner Beiträge zur

Afrikanistik, no. 11 (Berlin: D. Reimer, 1986), 636–68; La Rue, "The Hakura System: Land and Social Stratification in the Social and Economic History of the Sultanate of Dar Fur (Sudan), ca. 1785–1875" (PhD diss., Boston University, 1989). See also Muhammad ibn Umar al-Tunisi, *Voyage au Darfour*, trans. Dr. Perron (Paris: Benjamin Duprat, 1845); al-Tunisi, *Voyage au Ouaday* (Paris: B. Duprat, 1851); Dennis D. Cordell, *Dar al-Kuti and the Last Years of the Trans-Saharan Slave Trade* (Madison: University of Wisconsin Press, 1977); Cordell, "Eastern Libya, Wadai and the Sanusiya: A Tariqa and a Trade Route," *Journal of African History* 18, no. 1 (1977): 21–36; Fulgence Fresnel, "Extrait d'une notice sur les caravanes de Waday, par M. Fresnel, consul de France à Djeddah," *Bulletin de la Société de Géographie*, 3d series, 12 (1848); Fresnel, "Mémoire sur le Waday," *Bulletin de la Société de Géographie* 14 (1850): 153–92.

6. Janet Ewald, *Soldiers, Traders, and Slaves: State Formation and Economic Transformation in the Greater Nile Valley, 1700–1885* (Madison: University of Wisconsin Press, 1990); Richard Hill, *Egypt in the Sudan, 1820–1881* (London: Oxford University Press, 1959); Richard Gray, *A History of the Southern Sudan, 1839–1889* (London: Oxford University Press, 1961); P. M. Holt, *A Modern History of the Sudan* (New York: Grove, 1961); John O. Udal, *The Nile in Darkness: Conquest and Exploration, 1504–1862* (Wilby, Norwich: Michael Russell, 1998), 194–256.

7. See Baer, "Slavery and Abolition," 164; La Rue, "Export Trade," 642; Ewald, *Soldiers*, 53; Gerard Prunier, "Military Slavery in the Sudan During the Turkiyya, 1820–1885," in Savage, *Human Commodity*, 129–31; Prunier, "La traite soudanaise (1820–1885): Structure et périodisation," in *De la traite à l'esclavage*, ed. Serge Daget (Nantes: Centre de Recherche sur l'Histoire du Monde Atlantique, 1988), 521–26; Khalid Fahmy, *All the Pasha's Men: Mehmed Ali, His Army, and the Making of Modern Egypt* (Cambridge: Cambridge University Press, 1997), 40, 86–87.

8. Prunier, "Military Slavery," 129, citing a letter from Muhammad ʿAli to Ibrahim, 18 December 1821.

9. Fahmy, *All the Pasha's Men*, 88.

10. Victor Schoelcher, *L'Égypte en 1845* (Paris: Pagnerre, 1846), 111.

11. Ibid.

12. Baroness of Minutoli, *Recollections of Egypt* (Philadelphia: Carey, Lea and Carey, 1827), 111.

13. Prunier, "Military Slavery," 130.

14. See ibid., 130; Udal, *Nile of Darkness*, 242, 240; Fahmy, *All the Pasha's Men*, 8.

15. Prunier, "Military Slavery," 130.

16. Georges Douin, *La Mission du baron de Boislecomte: L'Égypte et la Syrie en 1833* (Cairo: Société Royale de Géographie d'Égypte, 1927), 149; Boislecomte to the Minister, Alexandria, 3 July 1833; R. R. Madden, *Egypt and Mohammed Ali: Illustrative of the Condition of His Slaves and Subjects* 2d ed. (London: Hamilton, Adams and Co. 1841), 67.

17. Edmond Cadalvène and J. de Breuvery, eds., *L'Égypte et la Turquie de 1829 à 1836*, 2 vols. (Paris: A. Bertrand, 1836) 1:443–48.

18. Jacques Tagher, "Le Docteur Dussap, un Français 'original' d'Égypte," *Cahiers d'histoire égyptienne* 4, no. 4 (1851): 342–46.

19. Antoine Barthélémy Clot, *Aperçu sur le ver Dragonneau observé en Égypte* (Marseille: Feissat ainé et Demonchy, 1830), 19.

20. Tagher, "Docteur Dussap," 344.

21. Clot, *Ver Dragonneau*. See also Susan Watts, "An Ancient Scourge: The End of Dracunculiasis in Egypt," *Social Science and Medicine* 46, no. 7 (1998): 811–19.

22. Douin, *Mission*, 108; Boislecomte to the Minister, Alexandria, 1 July 1833.

23. Amira al-Azhary Sonbol, *The Creation of a Medical Profession in Egypt, 1800–1922* (Syracuse: Syracuse University Press, 1991), 45.

24. Antoine Barthélémy Clot, *Compte rendu des travaux de l'École de Médecine d'Abou Zabel (Égypte)* (Marseille: Feissat, 1832), 76.

25. Antoine Barthélémy Clot, *Aperçu général sur l'Égypte*, 2 vols. (Paris: Fortin, Masson et Cie., 1840), 2:396; Clot, *Compte rendu*, 31.

26. J. Heyworth-Dunne, *An Introduction to the History of Education in Modern Egypt*, 2d ed. (London: Frank Cass., 1968), 132.

27. Training these slave women to become midwives has been widely reported. See ibid., 427; John Bowring, *Report on Egypt and Candia,* Parliamentary Papers, Reports from Commissioners, 11 (1840): 138, 140; Baptistin Poujoulat, *Voyage dans l'Asie Mineure* 2 vols. (Paris: Ducollet, 1840), 2:517–20; Tucker, *Women*, 120; Sonbol, *Creation*, 46; Toledano, *Slavery and Abolition*, 78; LaVerne Kuhnke, *Lives at Risk: Public Health in Nineteenth-Century Egypt* (Berkeley: University of California Press, 1990), 186–87, 268; Mervat F. Hatem, "The Professionalization of Health and the Control of Women's Bodies as Modern Governmentalities in Nineteenth-Century Egypt," in *Women in the Ottoman Empire*, ed. M. C. Zilfi (Leiden: Brill, 1997), 66–80 ; Khalid Fahmy, "Women, Medicine, and Power in Nineteenth-Century Egypt," in *Remaking Women: Feminism and Modernity in the Middle East*, ed. Lila Abu-Lughod (Princeton: Princeton University Press, 1998), 47–48.

28. Serge Jagailloux, *La médicalisation de l'Égypte au XIXe siècle (1798–1918)* (Paris: Editions Recherche sur les Civilisations, 1986), 57.

29. Clot, *Aperçu général*, 2:393.

30. LaVerne Kuhnke, "The Doctoress on a Donkey: Women Health Officers in Nineteenth-Century Egypt," *Clio medica* 9 (1974): 193–205. See also Schoelcher, *Égypte en 1845*, 45.

31. Ibid., 394.

32. Ismayl Urbain, *Voyage d'Orient: Suivi de Poèmes de Ménilmontant et d'Égypte*, ed. Philippe Régnier (Paris: L'Harmattan, 1993), 246. See also Régnier, "Thomas-Ismayl Urbain, Métis, Saint-Simonienen et Musulman," in Jean Claude Vatin, *La Fuite en Égypte* (Cairo: CEDEJ, 1989), 302–4.

33. Régnier, "Thomas-Ismayl Urbain," 304–5. See also Urbain, *Voyage*, 134–40, 148–54, 162–67.

34. Régnier, "Thomas-Ismayl Urbain," 305–7; Urbain, *Voyage*, 52, 77, 79, 107, 113, 169.

35. *Oeuvres de Saint-Simon et d'Enfantin* 25 vols. (Paris: E. Dentu, 1872), 9: 198–99; Enfantin to Lambert in Alexandria, 17 June 1834, letter 178.

36. Bowring, *Report*, 104.

37. Louis Rémy Aubert-Roche, *De la peste; ou, Typhus d'Orient: Documents et observations receueillis pendants les années 1834–1838 en Égypte, en Arabie, sur la Mer Rouge, etc.* (Paris: Librairie des Sciences Médicales, 1840), 26n1.

38. Bowring, *Report*, 104.

39. Aubert-Roche, *De la peste*, 20–25.

40. Bowring, *Report*, 104.

41. Antoine Barthélémy Clot, *De la peste observée en Égypte: Recherches et considération sur cette maladie* (Paris: Fortin, Masson, 1840), 8.

42. Ibid., 11.

43. R. C. Prus, *Rapport a l'Académie de Médecine sur la peste et les quarantaines* (Paris: J.-B. Baillière, 1846), 305, 397.

44. A. F. Bulard de Méru, *De la peste orientale d'après les matériaux recueillis à Alexandrie, au Caire, à Smyrne et à Constantinople, pendant les années 1833, 1834, 1835, 1836, 1837 et 1838* (Paris: Locquin, 1839), 56.

45. Bulard, *Peste orientale*, 56, 322–33; Prus, *Rapport*, 584.

46. Bulard, *Peste orientale*, 323.

47. Ibid, 171; Prus, *Rapport*, 584 ; Suzanne Voilquin, *Souvenirs d'une fille du peuple, ou la Saint-Simonienne en Égypte* (Paris: Maspero, 1978), 271; Phillippe Régnier, *Les Saint-Simoniens en Égypte, 1833–1851* (Cairo: Amin Fakhry Abdelnour, 1989), 91, 104.

48. Clot, *Peste observée*, 324.

49. Aubert-Roche, *De la peste*, 324.

50. For Dussap's prediction, see Voilquin, *Souvenirs*, 271. On Cairo's Jewish quarter, see Sophia Lane Poole, *An Englishwoman in Egypt* (London: C. Knight and Co., 1842), 150; James Ewing Cooley, *The American in Egypt* (New York: D. Appleton and Co., 1842), 402–6.

51. Régnier, *Saint- Simoniens*, 87, 90, 133; Voilquin, *Souvenirs*, 274.

52. Voilquin, *Souvenirs*, 281–84.

53. Ibid., 285.

54. Ibid., 288–89.

55. Urbain, *Voyage*, 77–79.

56. Ibid., 75.

57. Régnier, "Thomas-Ismayl Urbain," 308.

58. Régnier, *Saint-Simoniens* , 133.

59. Ibid.; Urbain, *Voyage*, 78–79; Suzanne Voilquin, "Lettres sur l'Égypte, no. 11-suite et fin," *Le Siècle*, 30 August 1837.

60. Voilquin, *Souvenirs*, 289–94.

61. Ibid., 292–95.

62. Walz, *Trade*, 215–20.

63. Clot, *Peste observée*, 111–12n2.

64. Pierre N. Hamont, Review of *De la peste observée en Égypte* by M. Clot-Bey, *Annales d'hygiène publique et de médecine legal* 27 (January 1842): 457–58.

65. Félix Mengin, *Histoire sommaire de l'Égypte* (Paris: Didot, 1839), 472n1.

66. Madden's views were shaped by Bowring and the German naturalist Ignatius Pallme, whose report on slave hunts in Kordofan (Sudan) first appeared in

Madden, *Egypt and Mohammed Ali*, 154–76, and was subsequently published as *Travels in Kordofan* (London, 1841) and in the *Anti-Slavery Reporter*, 13 January 1841. Hamont observed slavery in Egypt and had contact with Boreani, a mining engineer who served the viceroy in the Sudan. Hamont, *L'Égypte sous Méhémet-Ali*, 2 vols. (Paris: Léautey et Lecointe, 1843), 2:530, 539–76; Schoelcher, *L'Égypte en 1845*, 1, 100, 111–12, 114. See also Jean Marie Carré, *Voyageurs et écrivains français en Égypte*, 2nd ed., 2 vols. (Cairo: Institut Francais d'Archéologie Orientale, 1956), 1:295.

67. See the Sudanese slaves described in P. E. H. Hair, "The Brothers Tutschek and Their Sudanese Informants," *Sudan Notes and Records* 50 (1969): 53–62. For the travel of Djalo, one of these slaves from Kordofan, through Cairo to Bavaria, see Ewald, *Soldiers*, 3, 164–67.

68. Bowring, *Report*, 84.

69. Edward William Lane, *The Manners and Customs of the Modern Egyptians*, 2 vols. (London: J. M. Dent; New York: Dutton, 1944), 1:257.

70. Bowring, *Report*, 92.

71. Ibid., 92.

72. Perron, introduction to al-Tunisi, *Voyage au Ouaday*, 35.

73. Robert Ilbert, *Alexandrie, 1830–1930: Histoire d'une communauté citadine*, 2 vols. (Cairo: Institut Français d'Archéologie Orientale, 1996), 1:194, 2:519.

74. See Ewald, *Soldiers*, 160–62; La Rue, "Export Trade," 646, 656; Cordell, *Dar al-Kuti*.

75. Madden, *Egypt and Mohammed Ali*, 115–16, 135.

76. Ibid., 118–19.

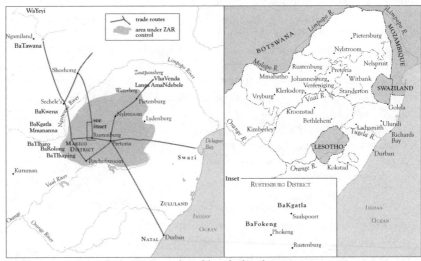

Left: Transvaal and borderlands, ca. 1865;
right: South Africa, twenty-first century

8

FEMALE *INBOEKELINGE* IN THE SOUTH AFRICAN REPUBLIC, 1850–80

FRED MORTON

Adela was her only name. In the 1860s she lived with her master, Van Zweel, in Pretoria, Boer settler capital of the new Zuid Afrikaansche Republiek (ZAR, South African Republic) of the Transvaal. There she remembered seeing other children brought into town in wagons and hawked about. Every white person in town seemed to have at least one or two black children. ZAR president M. W. Pretorius, after whose father Pretoria was named, had his order in for a "half dozen at a time."[1] Adela knew that she came from someplace in the Zoutpansberg, but exactly where in this mountain range populated by VhaVenda, Northern Sotho, and other language groups, she had forgotten. Her only memory of home was of the thatched rondavels on the day they were set on fire. She recalled scampering out into the open, seeing Boers on horseback riding about, shooting down men and women or herding them into a cattle kraal, where they were murdered. She and the other children were rounded up, lifted onto horses or driven ahead to the laager (fortified encampment), where they were parceled out. Van Zweel took her and rode back to Pretoria.[2]

Adela was among thousands of African children taken into slavery in the ZAR. And she was typical. She had been acquired by Boers taking part in commando raids along the border or in hunting and trading expeditions outside the ZAR. Almost all the slaves brought into the ZAR were children.[3] These youngsters were forced to walk or ride tens, sometimes hundreds, of kilometers over days, weeks, and occasionally even months before being handed over to individual Boer or English owners.

Those too small or too weak to trek by foot were carried in ox wagons or on horseback in sacks or baskets.

In one respect, however, Adela is unusual. Hers is one of the few surviving accounts of these raids and of the lives of the victims. Since the father of President Pretorius and his fellow Voortrekkers had signed the Sand River Convention in 1852, gaining diplomatic recognition by the British for their fledgling republics in the South African interior, slave raiding and trading had been illegal. Sellers and buyers tried therefore to keep these activities out of public view. When entering ZAR towns, particularly when high-ranking ZAR officials returned at the head of a commando, the captured youngsters were classified as "orphans." They were registered as "apprentices" (*inboekelinge*), allotted to masters, and commonly sold from one owner to another. Outsiders were kept away from them, and the inboekelinge were kept ignorant of their languages and origins. They grew up speaking Dutch and were given single names like January or April if they were boys, Sophia or Odela if they were girls. Only a few reached adulthood knowing who they were, much less telling the world about their pasts (perhaps Adela's name—"Noble One"—destined her story to be told).

But there is no doubt that Africans who had not been enslaved knew what might be in store for them. "We are Kaffirs [to you] which means we are dogs or monkeys to be shot down or otherwise ill-treated as you may find convenient," wrote Chief Khama III to ZAR commandant L. M. Du Plessis from the Ngwato capital of Shoshong. "[You are] wicked men . . . buying and selling black people for less money than they sell their horses and cows, and treat them worse than their dogs."[4] Thanks to the words left behind by Adela and others, enough information survives to reconstruct how slave trading was conducted in the old ZAR and to outline these children's experiences in the years following their enslavement. Regrettably, the record is fragmentary.

What is clear, however, is that their experiences reveal a form of slavery distinct from other systems in Africa and elsewhere. Bound mainly to isolated white (Boer) farm households geared to cattle and stock raising, hunting, and fruit farming, slave girls provided domestic service until their late teens, at which point they appear to have been married off to enslaved males and allowed to live with them and raise their own children, though the ex-inboekelinge family, including the children, remained in quasiservice to their masters. By the 1880s, as diamond and gold mining in the region spurred industrialization and urbanization, such farms declined, as did commando raids and the supply of and demand for apprenticed labor. Thereafter clusters of ex-inboekelinge, distinguished by their Dutch names and use of Dutch as a first language, settled on the fringes of towns.[5] To some degree, the ex-inboekelinge (often referred to by the Boers as *orlaams* or *oorlams kaffers*) resemble the so-called Cape Coloured and other Dutch-speaking non-European groups (Griqua, Kora, Bastaards) of the Cape, except that they had originated as Bantu-speaking black South Africans inside or along the borders of what became the ZAR and had entered service after the arrival of the Voortrekkers north of the Vaal River in the 1840s. In contrast to the slaves of the Cape Colony, the inboekelinge discussed here were an indigenous, captive element indistinguishable racially from the African population but stigmatized by their servitude and their loss of African cultural ways. Rarely were they able to reattach themselves to their original or related societies as adults. Grown women among them were not wanted as wives by men who had not themselves been uprooted by war or migration. However, they gained admission to African communities detached from indigenous African villages and wards, such as those on or connected to missions, and found spouses among the "new men" created by new economic forces.

SLAVE RAIDS AND SLAVE TRADING IN THE ZAR

Boer commandos, which with their African auxiliaries took the female captives described here, represent a variation of raiding systems practiced throughout the highveld and sandveld, in which slaves were obtained as part of the process of expansion through the acquisition of stock. Tswana-speaking people moving into the Kalahari in the eighteenth century took violent possession of the people they found there, along with their cattle and sheep, forcing the original occupants to be herders and hunting laborers in the case of men, and domestic slaves and concubines in the case of women.[6] In the early nineteenth century, during the raiding of the so-called Mfecane/Difaqane widespread through southeastern Africa, Sotho- and Nguni-speaking followers of rising leaders often expanded through cattle raids and absorbed people they conquered into the new societies they were forming through attachment to their own ward or lineage groups or through conscription into regimental systems with low status, if not as slaves. Their raids for cattle nevertheless could be brutal, particularly against adult men. Women and children were more likely to survive and be taken captive.[7]

The Dutch-speaking Boer migrants into the interior were not unlike these other African cattle-rustling enterprises. Apart from their European language and socioreligious culture, and inclination to live in scattered homesteads rather than in concentrated settlements, Boer families shared with their African counterparts an attachment to strong leaders and kin-based social groups and the ability to graft outsiders onto their labor, military, and social arrangements.[8] As expanding pastoralists dependent on wagons, oxen, horses, guns, and other imports, Boers sought grazing territory connected to long-distance trade routes and envied the substantial herds of their indigenous African cattle-owning competitors. Theirs was a mirror reflection of mounted, armed parties of Griqua and Kora that also purloined large stocks of cattle and sheep from Tswana and Sotho peoples on the highveld plateau in the 1830s and 1840s.[9] Boer raids targeted adult males and often women for death and rounded up children for removal with rustled herds.

After capture, children became part of a system of exchange within the Boer-controlled territories, or republics. Children not kept by individual commando members were parceled out or sold off to male family heads and brought into ZAR towns for registration. As a result, slave routes corresponded to the main arteries connecting the ZAR towns with the borders of the territory, and the towns where slaves were exchanged corresponded to the locations where commandos assembled before setting out and where they returned before dispersing. Thus, Mooi River (Potchefstroom) and Pretoria were the most important commando assembly points in the 1850s and 1860s, and the most active slave-trading centers, receiving slaves captured from African communities bordering the ZAR to the west and north-northeast, respectively. Children seized from the Tswana chiefdoms on the fringe of the Kalahari were sold or exchanged in Potchefstroom. No main route connected Potchefstroom to these raiding zones, which were reached overland strictly by horseback. Magaliesberg (Rustenburg) served as a commando assembly point and trading center for children brought in from the north in the early 1850s, but Pretoria (founded in 1855) soon became the main trafficking point in this direction.[10]

By far the largest number of slaves was generated by commandos entering the mountainous northern borderlands and attacking Sotho-Tswana and Ndebele communities.[11] These commandos were often akin to military contingents, traveling with cannon, ox wagons, large numbers of armed African auxiliaries, and slaughter stock. Rather than launch quick raids on settlements, they preferred to besiege Africans in caves or on mountaintops and starve or parch them into submission. In addition to slave children, these large commandos returned with herds of cattle and flocks of sheep and goats.[12]

Some of the slaves in Boer hands were obtained by their African auxiliaries. The Swazi were helpful on the eastern borderlands, and the BaKgatla of Chief Kgamanyane joined future ZAR president Paul Kruger, Kgamanyane's neighbor, on a number of commandos. Kgamanyane, who with many of his followers resided on Kruger's farm, Saulspoort, boasted in the *leboko* (praise poem) he had composed of "seizing young children . . . even infants at the breast [and giving them] to the red men [*bahibidu*]."[13]

The rest of the slaves were purchased outside the ZAR by hunters and traders and brought into the Transvaal along established communication links. A popular route was the Road to the North, which connected the western border to the Tswana chiefdoms of the Kalahari as far as Ngamiland bordering (modern) Angola. In the 1840s and 1850s, Griqua and Boer ivory hunters visiting Ngamiland returned with a few young slaves and on some occasions with large "batches." They purchased them from Letsholathebe, king of the BaTawana, whose troops had raided them from Bushmen, BaYeyi, and Damara. In 1869 ZAR official and hunter Jan Viljoen trekked back from Ngamiland with seventy items of "black wool" in his party's ox-wagons.[14]

Another early trading post was Delagoa Bay (Maputo) on the Indian Ocean coast to the east, which the Boers and their Portuguese trading partners visited to purchase slaves for importation into the Transvaal via Ohrigstad and Lydenburg.[15] Slaves could also be purchased from the Swazi. On visits to Swaziland in the 1840s, hunters such as Paul Kruger returned with slaves and ivory.[16]

Upon their arrival in one or another of the ZAR towns, these young inboekelinge were registered and often exchanged in ones and twos with local town dwellers, surrounding farmers, and traders and wagon drivers visiting from as far away as Natal. In the 1850s and 1860s travelers in the interior commonly found that every white farm had at least several young African children as servants and workers.[17] Exchange values varied widely, from £3 to £30 depending on times, locations, and the perceived qualities of the slave. According to ex-slave Rachel, who lived in Pretoria with her master before being sold to an African wagon driver from Natal, children were sold in that town for "£3 to £8, according to size." Values of female slaves often translated into bovine worth, reflecting the close association of slavery with cattle herding. Rachel herself had been bought for "£6 and a cow in calf" and was resold twice each time for £6— the approximate value of a young ox. Ex-slave Odela, sold for £30 to a "Natal Kaffir wagon-driver," had first lived in Pretoria when prices ranged from £6 to £12, depending on age.[18] In Pretoria and Potchefstroom girls fetched the highest prices.

FEMALE INBOEKELINGE

In the 1840s and 1850s, Boer trekkers migrated into the Transvaal, bringing with them the institution of *inboekstelsel* (lit., registered apprenticeship, a euphemism for slavery) and the ideal of the large, single-family pastoral farm, for which slaves and servants were needed. By the mid-1860s,
roughly 10 percent of the ZAR population consisted of slaves acquired in
this fashion.[19] Though impossible to determine with certainty, the available evidence suggests that a significant proportion, though perhaps not
a majority, of the captured children were girls. Sold, exchanged, and
eventually put to work in individual homesteads, female inboekelinge
did the laundry, housecleaning, cooking, childcare, and knitting, among
other chores. Their role was to assist the large nuclear white farm family,
in which the husband, his unmarried sons, and male slave attendants
were away for extended periods tending stock (mainly cattle), hunting,
trading, or participating in commando raids. The largest slave owners,
who were also the well-to-do farmers and landowners, were apt to be absent even more frequently, as they made up the majority of elected or appointed officials.[20] Laws governing inboekstelsel required owners to release their apprentices in their early twenties, but enforcement was lax.

General references and brief biographical sketches of eight female
slaves show that most lived on isolated farms, where they lost any memory of their origins, parents, or kinfolk. Young and intentionally deraci-
nated, they were acculturated in a patriarchal, Dutch-speaking environment in which they remained dependent on their masters for all their
needs. Prominent slave owners exemplified a paternalism that was rooted
in Boer religious and racial assumptions, particularly in Dutch Reformed
Church (DRC) communities. Some leaders, the very men who led commando raids for slaves and cattle, had their young inboekelinge taught
Dutch and, in some cases, Christian catechism and even Bible literacy.

Among the better-documented cases of female slaves is that of Matlhodi Kekana (aka Paulina), as told by her descendants to her grandson,
Naboth Mokgatle.[21] In or around 1853, while young, Matlhodi was captured in the Pietersburg area of the northern Transvaal during a Boer
commando raid on the Langa AmaNdebele followers of Chief Mokopane.
She became the inboekeling of a prominent Boer, remembered by Mokgatle's family as KaMongoele. Mokgatle does not mention the Boer's
given name, but the evidence—his Tswana nickname, which played on
his intense religious piety (Kamangole, "on the knees"), the Christian
name he gave to Matlhodi, and the close ties he had with a prominent

BaFokeng chief near his farm—points to him as none other than Paul Kruger. In 1853, when Matlhodi was captured, Kruger was a Rustenburg *veldkornet* and one of the leaders of the raid on Mokopane.[22] Since becoming a young man, Kruger had combined hunting with slave trading and, as an assistant veldkornet in 1845, had been an active participant in commando raids for cattle and children.[23] In 1852 he was elected a full veldkornet and began to acquire farms through sharp dealing. He led many commando raids while his political star continued to rise. After Paulina was attached to his household, Kruger went on to become Rustenburg District commandant, ZAR commandant general, and eventually president of the ZAR.

Paulina's responsibilities as Kruger's slave included working in the house, where as a young woman she was trained as a cook for his large family and its many visitors. She gained a reputation for her "European-style" cooking, which together with her attractive features caught the attention of Kgosi (chief) Mokgatle, whose people lived on portions of Kruger's farms and who, according to the traditions collected by Naboth Mokgatle, visited Kruger often. Kgosi Mokgatle, on his way to becoming wealthy, wanted Paulina as one of his wives and as his cook. It is revealing of Kruger, known as much for his intense religious conservatism as for his avarice and ambition, that he demanded bridewealth in cattle from Mokgatle. A "number of cattle" then changed hands, at which point Paulina transferred her residence to Mokgatle's capital (Phokeng) and began her life as Mokgatle's wife. She bore him four children, of whom two survived.

Paulina's transfer from Kruger to Mokgatle reflects the purposes to which slave women were put by Transvaal's emerging Boer elite. Kruger and Mokgatle were allies in an arrangement that gave Kruger access to Mokgatle's male BaFokeng followers as military auxiliaries and to their wives and daughters as seasonal agricultural laborers on Kruger's farms.[24] For their service to Kruger's commandos, Mokgatle's men received cattle booty and possibly women ("cattle without horns") captured in raids. They were allowed also to keep guns for hunting game and were exempted from labor service to the Boers, while Mokgatle used the Kruger connection to concentrate his followers on Kruger's farms, keep their loyalty through tribute, and build up his personal wealth. Owning farms and encouraging chiefs to collect their followers thereon enabled men like Kruger to magnify their wealth and influence in the ZAR, just as Mokgatle and other chiefs were able to increase their followers and become rich.[25] Mokgatle achieved a much higher standard of living than most Boers in the Transvaal at the time. His rising material status and purchasing power enhanced his stature among white and black. He owned guns, carpentry and metal-working tools, ploughs, grindstones, wagons and wore European-style clothing. Standing near to his large dwelling was a wagon house and an enormous stone cattle kraal. The white doctor from Rustenburg paid him house calls, often staying overnight in the guestroom featherbed, and a white tutor was employed to instruct his children in English. By the early 1860s, Mokgatle and his town had become a tourist attraction, where white visitors to Rustenburg were run out for the spectacle. Paulina, groomed by Kruger to cook and serve food fit for Transvaal's new royalty, was acquired by Mokgatle to live near his main house and cater to him and his white visitors: "One large house belonging to one of the principal wives of the Chief had a number of compartments beautifully moulded and polished, with great taste, and furnished among other utensils with Basins, Cups, and Saucers, Pots and Pans, and even Foot pans, bought at Rustenburg. There was also a Box of Tools, which were turned to good account, for they sat us down upon chairs made after European models . . . and Tables the same."[26]

In the ZAR, Paulina represented the slave/servant/wife as emblematic of her owner's or husband's ruling status. As a domesticated version of a European servant, she was expected to understand and adhere to the preferences of the prevailing culture, mirror its appearance and language, submit to its authority, and aspire to its approval. She had entered the category of oorlamse ("civilized" kaffir) and, as a black female, Paulina enabled leading Boers like Kruger to convince themselves that the ZAR at heart was committed to elevating its black population and that they were fulfilling their civic and religious duties by educating inboekelinge in the Dutch language and Bible knowledge. The ZAR leadership, which had been lambasted in the English press in South Africa for conducting slave raids, used oorlamse like Paulina and westernizing chiefs like Mokgatle to counter the popular notion that ZAR Boers were themselves half-civilized bumpkins running a predatory operation.

Paulina's usefulness, in turn, depended on her acquisition of the skills needed by a prosperous white family aspiring to modernize—Dutch language, domestic refinement, familiarity with cooking, cleaning, laundry, sewing, and a host of related knowledge. Kruger's farms, and others in Rustenburg District, were introducing irrigation to support fruit orchards and tobacco and cotton fields, while breeding trek oxen, tanning hides, and acquiring ivory for export to the Cape. Young inboekelinge, rewarded for their attentiveness, and isolated from their original homes and the Africans living in surrounding chiefs' towns, were trained as sawyers, tanners, lime burners, masons, thatchers, ploughmen, wagon drivers, and marksmen.

Paulina's sexuality was inconsequential for promoting this material culture, though her attractiveness as a young woman threatened her value to the Kruger homestead. Mixed offspring are known to have been born in this area.[27] Yet the scandal arising would have been devastating for any Boer male member of the DRC-connected elite. As will be discussed below, white men who impregnated or were known to have sexual relations with, or to have physically abused black females in their care were publicly denounced. It is therefore logical that Kruger would have accepted Mokgatle's offer to take Paulina off his hands before she entered or was forced into a liaison, while she had value to Mokgatle as a virgin, so that Kruger could demand cattle in return. His inboekelinge was, after all, a form of property investment.

She was also given to outbursts. Her grandson relates the family tradition that, after being acquired by Mokgatle as his wife, Matlhodi (Paulina) was apt, when in a cross mood, to swear in her original Northern Sotho (SeTswana), a language she had somehow kept alive over the years while growing up and learning in a Dutch-speaking world. She also understood at this time that her father was Kekana, a chief among the Langa Ama-Ndebele of Mokopane. This anecdote is full of possible meanings. Matlhodi was said to have been captured when only two or three years old. If she knew Northern Sotho when captured, she must have been at least six or seven at the time, or, if she was as young as the story goes, then she would have been permitted to learn, perhaps even been coached in, Northern Sotho after joining Kruger's household, and told of her background. The latter is not improbable, because other youngsters from her area likely grew up in and around Kruger's home. Paulina's master, too, was fluent in SeTswana.[28] It is altogether reasonable to assume that Kruger's ability to communicate with this young child in her mother tongue served to expand and sustain her ability in her own language. His command of her language would have made her more suppliant to his will, though retaining her past could not have made it easy for Paulina to be reconciled with her present circumstances. And her departure from his household might be attributable to Kruger's awareness and disquiet that Paulina was more apt as a mature woman to express dissatisfaction with her servile life. Anticipating her resistance, or rebelliousness, he converted her into cattle.

Once married, though to a chief, and though claiming to be a chief's daughter herself, Matlhodi's slave past relegated her to an uncertain status among Mokgatle's wives and followers. Mokgatle kept her close to his own house, a sign of high rank in his eyes. Mokgatle placed her in the compound (*lapa*) of his recently deceased first wife, Nkhubu, and Matlhodi became caretaker of Nkhubu's children, her cattle and her lands.[29] However, according to the story told to Naboth Mokgatle, Matlhodi was regarded by the BaFokeng as a lowly person. In attempts at repelling their insults, she swore in Northern Sotho and asserted she was the daughter of a Langa chief, but she was not believed. Only after her children were born was her background discovered, her royal provenance acknowledged by the BaFokeng, and her status formalized through a second marriage rite, this time between the Kekana family and Mokgatle. Her rehabilitation notwithstanding, the Langa-Fokeng connection practically speaking was at best tenuous and, in the long term, a liability for her children. Her sons pursued no contact with their mother's homeland, and neither the BaFokeng nor the Boer government considered either of her sons or her foster sons, the children of Mokgatle's first wife Nkhubu, as eligible to succeed Mokgatle.[30] Matlhodi, who never visited her original homeland, lived permanently in Phokeng, dying there, completely blind, at an old age.

The relatively privileged life of Matlhodi (aka Paulina) may be compared with that of female inboekelinge who were owned by persons of less wealth and political stature than Paul Kruger. Certain characteristics apply generally. Like Paulina, other young girls were captured amid violent, often traumatic circumstances, grew up in Dutch-speaking environments far from their original homes, did domestic work, and remained isolated from other Africans until their maturity. As young women they sought ways to leave their white masters, often through liaisons with African men, free and otherwise. They were married off for cattle or money and were unable to return to their homeland. Some escaped, thanks to the new trade routes traveled by a new figure in the South African highveld, the African wagon driver. The truncated accounts of females that follow, derived mainly from F. W. Chesson, represent inboekelinge who made it out of slavery; they come with a caveat—they are of limited use for generalizing about the thousands of girls and women unable to extricate themselves from bondage in the ZAR.[31]

Odela was "very little" when she was taken by Boers in the Zoutpansberg in northern Transvaal. Yet she remembered in some detail the horror surrounding her capture. The commando came before daybreak, shot old people at random, and herded "big people . . . into stone kraals" (presumably where they were shot—a common phenomenon on such raids).

She must have been taken to Lydenburg, *ingeboekt* (registered as an inboekeling), and sold off, because she remembers that while growing up she "often saw commandos go out and the people return with children." She had seen ZAR commandant general Stephanus Schoeman and president Marthinus W. Pretorius among them. Children were sold in town for between £6 and £12. From another woman from Zoutpansberg, living then in Pretoria, she heard that children were being brought there for sale as well.

Another girl, Adela, whose experience of capture while very young introduced this article, stayed in Pretoria until she was fourteen with her master, Van Zweel, at which point he sold her for £30 to a "Natal Kaffir wagon-driver" in the employ of an English trading firm. She relocated with him to Natal and lived with him for a number of years. African wagon drivers were among the few who had money in their pockets, the means to travel, and knowledge of the region. The circumstances of their employment suggest they were part of an outcast element, if not themselves ex-inboekelinge, then without suitable connections to an African chief's community to marry in the usual way. Adela was typical among inboekelinge and oorlamse in gaining acceptance among other dislocated Africans, especially on mission stations.

Another extricated through marriage to a wagon driver was Rachel, who, like Paulina, had been enslaved during a Boer raid on her people, the Langa AmaNdebele. After the men of her community were driven off or killed, the Boers rounded up women and children, shooting the former. Small children were placed on horses, the older ones forced to run ahead to the laager. Rachel was allotted to one of the commando members, with whom she lived for several years. She was then sold to a Pretoria man for £6 and a cow in calf. When grown, she was sold for £6 to a Natal wagon driver, who beat her until she ran away and returned to her Boer ex-master. She was again sold for £6 to yet another wagon driver, who remained in Pretoria with her for two years. When he left with her for Natal, her master confiscated all her property. She never saw her registration papers or those of any of the other inboekelinge, and like them she was whipped if she raised the question. Once in Natal, she remained with her husband.

Not all women needed marriage to escape. Some ran away on their own. An example is Leah of Mzilikazi's AmaNdebele. Leah was captured as a child together with her young sister by the Boers and their African allies in one of the raids and battles in 1837, when Mzilikazi was still in the western Transvaal. She and other young captives were taken to the laager from which the raid had been launched. She remembers that a "great number of cattle . . . and a very great number of children, great and small," were parceled out among commando members, and she was separated from her sister. For the next six years she lived with her master, whom she does not name, and received food and clothing in return for domestic service. Leah makes no mention as to where she lived, but members of the commando that captured her and the other children included people who settled in the future Orange Free State and parts of the ZAR. Leah accompanied her owner to Natal, where he had "produce" to sell. Just before he returned upcountry, she ran away. She joined the Wesleyan mission society, married, had children, and earned money by "taking in washing," presumably from white residents. Another example is Sylvia, who had been brought together with her siblings and mother from the Cape by her master, William Neethling, into the Transvaal, where she did domestic and heavy field work. When put to service as an ox-wagon leader on a trip back to the Cape, she absconded and was never seen again.[32]

Another escapee was Sophia of Natal, who was captured during a war between the Boers and the AmaZulu. She was among children and women rounded up from hiding places "in the kloofs" following the defeat of their menfolk. The children were taken away on horseback and their mothers ordered back on threat of being shot. Sophia's mother "followed for some distance but at last I lost sight of her." After living with the Boers in the Transvaal many years and despairing of being released from her apprenticeship or receiving any wages, she heard of the English in Natal from "Natal Kaffir waggon-drivers and leaders" and decided to escape and seek refuge with them. One night she ran to the house of an Englishman who had a "Dutch" (Boer) wife "who knew me." The wife hid Sophia until her husband took her in his wagon to Natal, where she stayed, joining the Wesleyans.

As these accounts demonstrate, young women were not likely to be released from their apprenticeship or to extricate themselves unless they were living in a town with main-road connections to the coast or near a major trade route, and were assisted by African men using these avenues. Though the incentive to escape was common, being purchased as a wife was the most likely way out of slavery. Observed Rachel, who had been a slave in Pretoria, "I do not know of any one having got their liberty except by marriage to men not resident there."[33] For those who remained close to where they had been apprenticed, options to inboekstelsel were restricted to those created by their masters. Release from apprenticeship was governed by law—at twenty-one years of age for men, twenty-five for women—though enforcement varied widely and depended often on the wishes of the master. Only two cases have surfaced in which mistreatment of women became grounds for punishment of their owners and the extrication of their inboekelinge. Such abuse was observed in towns, however, where few inboekelinge lived and whose treatment was more difficult to conceal from nonowners than was the case in the countryside. The first pertained to the torture of two eight-year-old girls by one Fitzgerald, a British resident of Rustenburg, and the second to the harsh physical abuse of a "servant girl . . . brought from Zoutpansberg [northern Transvaal] some years ago" at the hands of her owner, P. A. van Yperen, magistrate of Utrecht. Both sparked outcries from the white townspeople and resulted in court cases against the perpetrators, as well as their ostracism. Fitzgerald was divested of his inboekelinge, but Yperen retained his servant. Utrecht's townspeople, however, helped her escape to Natal and join her lover, a Zulu migrant worker she had met in Utrecht.[34]

It is doubtful that most inboekelinge either had access to a court that would support their release from the terms or conditions of apprenticeship or the wherewithal to relocate elsewhere. Even if released from service, ex-inboekelinge were not necessarily willing or able to move away from their masters' reach or deny them their labor. The few rural ex-inboekelinge about whom evidence is available tended to marry while remaining on or near their respective masters' farms and gave up any notion of returning to their people, even when presented with the opportunity. Apparently, growing from childhood to young adulthood in a Dutch-speaking environment had divested them of such ambitions. A case in point is Rachel of Kliprivier, Natal (not to be confused with Rachel of Pretoria), who since she was a child of five or six had lived in the service of Kliprivier farmer Gert Greyling. In the mid-1860s, during a northern Transvaal raid led by acting ZAR president Stephanus Schoeman on the BaBirwa of Makgatho, she had been captured along with her mother, three of her siblings, and many other women and children. Her mother escaped and her siblings were distributed to other owners. Her father (Morake) survived the raid, later met up with his wife, and the two resettled with Klaas Makapan's people at Makapanspoort, near Pretoria. Soon after the British annexed the Transvaal (1877–81), Morake began looking for his children and traced three of his four to Heidelberg District, where he asked Heidelberg magistrate Carl Ueckermann to release them into his custody. By this time, his daughter who knew of herself only as Rachel (her SiBirwa name does not appear in the record) was twenty or twenty-one and had been allowed to leave Gert Greyling ("with a good heifer and three ewes and goats") to marry April, an inboekeling of Nicholas Kamper. When given the option of returning with her father to live with him and her mother, she refused: "I have no wish to leave either my husband or this district to go with my father, whom I do not recollect or care for now." She stated that she and April intended instead to return to Greyling's farm at the end of the next harvest.[35] The few cases known of ex-inboekelinge wanting to return to their origins suggest that the success rate was low at best.[36]

In this regard, the ex-inboekelinge associated with DRC missionary Henri Gonin provide the most detailed examples. Of the tens of ex-inboekelinge he encountered, he mentions only one who attempted a reconnection. The others settled with one another as families near to where they had been apprenticed. All could identify the people from whom they had been captured. In 1888, Gonin appealed on behalf of twenty families of what he called Orlaamse, located on Welgeval and the adjacent farm Schaapkraal. At the time they were threatened with removal by an impending *plakkers wet* (squatters' law).

> They live on those places, the heads of those people come from different tribes and were taken away as children during the war[s], they served the Boers for ten to twenty years and some of them are fifty years of age, if not sixty. They are civilized and have built themselves fairly good houses. Some of them were members of my mission community. . . . Often the elders send their children to work for their former *baasen* [masters] they almost always acted according to the laws of the country, they pay their taxes, go on commando if asked to do so, they work hard, they take care when sickness is around, they cannot go back to a kaffir location because they have nothing to do with their former kaffir *kapteins,* Mankopane, Mapela, Ramapulane, Malitsi, Zebedela, etc. They don't have any kaffir habits any more, they are farmers like the white people.[37]

Accepting one's identity as an ex-slave formed the basis of their clustering in small oorlamse communities in the ZAR. Some took root on the fringes of urbanizing Transvaal, but more typical were individual couples like Rachel and April, and small clusters of ex-inboekelinge living on farms owned by their masters or by missionaries. In these cases, the fortunes of women were tied to the prospects open to their spouses or created by missionaries for women.

FEMALE EX-INBOEKELINGE ON MISSIONS

In the late 1850s, ZAR officials began to allow select missionaries to work among Africans. In 1856 the old ZAR nemesis in neighboring Bechuanaland, Chief Sechele, asked President Pretorius to send him a "teacher and bricklayer" as a "symbol of peace." At the urging of Marico District official Jan Viljoen, Pretorius invited the Hermannsburg Mission Society (HMS), then operating in Natal, to extend its mission field to the ZAR. In 1857 Heinrich Schröder started an HMS mission at Sechele's, while other HMS stations were soon established in the Transvaal. The Berlin Mission Society and the DRC then followed.[38] The missionaries were reluctantly welcomed by the chiefs residing near Boer farmers, whose suspicions of missionaries ran deep. But white newcomers in collars commonly got the support of Boer officials, who, like Paul Kruger, earned considerable sums by selling them some of his farms. Although research into the question is undeveloped, evidence from DRC sources indicates that most of the early African mission residents were inboekelinge and ex-inboekelinge from surrounding Boer farms. Gonin, who in 1864 established his first mission on his newly purchased farm Welgeval, was assisted by September (who read Dutch "rather well") and his brother January (baptized Petrus), already alluded to, their sister (not mentioned by name), and their wives. Welgeval grew as a residence for them and other families, and they helped Gonin establish a school. September (baptized Abraham) and his wife Abrahama (aka Matabela) raised their four children—Fatima, Johana, Isaak, and Simon—on the mission. Welgeval was visited regularly by persons with names such as Niklaas, April, and Jakob, indicating they, too, were oorlamse.[39] A photograph of early Christians at the HMS mission station at Bethanie (on the farm Losperfontein 119) suggests strongly that they, too, were of inboekelinge origin. Their uniformly Western dress, adopted only by a certain few of the chiefly families in the nineteenth century, stands in sharp contrast to the traditional dress worn by most African women and men of the time.[40]

Gonin, who revealed very little about African converts and mission dwellers in his correspondence, leaves enough clues to show that ex-inboekelinge played a prominent role in developing the Christian community that grew up around his mission headquarters, which shifted from Welgeval to Saulspoort, capital of chief Kgamanyane of the numerous BaKgatla, in 1866. Gonin moved to Saulspoort to gain access to a large indigenous African settlement, because inboekelinge alone were coming to him at Welgeval. Nevertheless the early converts who formed the nucleus of his following and produced the first Dutch Reformed Church catechists and teachers at Saulspoort are identified by Gonin only as persons originating from outside the area (mostly from the northern Transvaal). All the catechists were men, but wives and especially daughters became the bearers of the Western, literate culture permeating African societies in the area. Whereas in the case of Paulina, whose skills in cooking and knowledge of Dutch endeared her to a westernizing but non-Christian chief, the next generation of African leaders adopted increasingly a Western, Christianized appearance and promoted literacy in African languages and English among royal families. Like Paulina, who came ready-made to fulfill the role of cook and mother, the wives of the modernizing, monogamous royals were supposed to mirror the achievements of their husbands and raise the new elite's children. Thus the educated daughters of oorlamse could vault in status from that of lowly outsider to that of the highest royal rank.

Cases in point are the daughters of Stephanus Moloto, ex-inboekeling and early visitor at Welgeval, who settled at Schaapkraal, where he raised a family. Already literate and Christian before he met Gonin, he married Hannah Malau, an inboekeling from Makooskraal, and they raised three daughters—Martha, Rebecca, and Johanna—each of whom became important mission workers for Gonin. Martha and Rebecca married catechists. Martha became a prominent figure in the district. After her husband died sometime in the 1890s, she continued working for the mission, joining Johanna at Holfontein. Then, in 1904, she married the widower BaKgatla chief of Saulspoort, Ramono Kgamanyane Pilane, and bore two future chiefs.[41] Martha's marriage into the royal Pilane line signifies the process by which African chiefs were adopting European dress and material culture and accepting Christianity as southern Africa was colonized by Great Britain. In spite of her origins as inboekeling, a status that had obstructed Paulina's future and those of her children, Martha's career as a Christian teacher and mission worker elevated her prospects and assured the futures of her children. After British rule was established throughout South Africa with the defeat of the Boers in 1902, the fact that Martha was in a Christian marriage guaranteed, too, that British authorities would entitle her and her sons alone to inherit her husband's estate, regardless of customary laws.

Ramono and other leaders had sought educated daughters of literate Christians since the 1880s. Ramono's first marriage was to the daughter of a London Missionary Society (LMS) catechist of obscure, probably inboekeling, origin, by the name of Matsau. After a falling out with the

LMS, Matsau attached himself to Bechuanaland Kgatla chief Linchwe, Ramono's elder brother. Matsau's daughters were soon married respectively by Ramono and his half-brother Segale, both of whom then were emerging as leading royal Christians among the Kgatla.[42]

Changes within Kgatla and other African societies, which created opportunities for ex-slaves to advance materially and socially, were related to the close of the settler frontier, the onset of mining capital, and the spread of British control over southern Africa. Between the discoveries of diamonds (1867) and gold (1884), slave raiding virtually ceased, and the pastoral economies that had characterized Boer and African societies on the highveld were steadily replaced by the demands for labor and supplies in the urbanizing mining centers, many of which were located in the ZAR. Turning away from pursuits based on herding and hunting, these Boers oriented themselves to controlling smaller territories, negotiating governing rights with Great Britain, and taxing the male and female labor within. After the Anglo-Boer War (1899–1902), delivering male labor into the mining centers was organized through the collaboration of the British colonial and Bechuanaland Protectorate governments in the region and with their internal administrations, including chiefs.

But these societies, accustomed to capturing and holding slaves in the premining past, maintained certain roles in spite of their reorientation toward the mining centers and establishment of British liberal labor policies. As was common elsewhere in Africa, ex-slaves continued to be slaves in the eyes of their former masters, though capture, sale, and exchange of new slaves virtually ceased. Some Boer farms in the Transvaal continued to attach unpaid agricultural and domestic workers to their homesteads, and the Kgatla elite among the Tswana, who married literate ex-slave women to enable westernization of its next generation, at the very time continued to hold Kgalagadi herders in permanent servitude on their cattle posts. These herders were descendants of slaves owned by Sechele's Kwena and captured by the Kgatla along with Kwena cattle, in the 1870s.[43] As these examples demonstrate, female ex-slaves had widely mixed experiences in the aftermath of inboekstelsel. Some, like Martha Ramono, joined the highest levels of African society of the day, whereas women living in orlaamse wards on the edges of Transvaal towns continued their past roles, fending for domestic work among white households.

Because slavery in its fullest form was relatively short-lived in the Transvaal and has left behind mere traces of evidence, important questions regarding female slavery in the Transvaal remain unanswerable. It is clear that girls were valued primarily as domestic servants, and that growing up in close proximity to Boer families likely resulted in their learning Dutch along with adoption of Boer manners. Helping kaffer children to become "civilized" was justification for their enslavement and testimony to the worthiness of the master in the eyes of the Boer community. In a land where the majority of the population was African and unconquered, Boer farmers needed constant reinforcement of their notions of racial and cultural superiority, and it is no surprise that often they regarded inboekelinge and oorlamse with affection and retained them into their old age as appendages to their families. Needed as submissive allies in the war against "savagery," they were valued for their imitation of Boer values and given protection as long as they remained distinct from the African communities around them.

In the white patriarchal society of the Transvaal, which strongly defended female domesticity, the service of girl slaves was restricted as a rule to the home. The story of Sylvia, who was forced to work in the fields, suggests that female slaves of poorer white immigrants, who were more apt to be short of farm labor, were less apt to remain in the domestic sphere and also less likely to be acculturated to the Boer lifestyle. Her bold escape indicates that her master also had fewer means than wealthy Boers to bind their inboekelinge to his service. The psychological development of female domestic slaves in homes such as those that could produce a Paulina must have inculcated among oorlamse a self-image of "high" culture that created distinctions from Africans around them. But, in practical, daily terms, female inboekelinge had to be reminded, too, that they had no place within the Boer family or the larger community other than as servants. We have at present no way of knowing, moreover, to what extent their role was defined by Boer women or men.

The sexual exploitation of female domestic slaves and its attendant profound influence on spousal and familial relationships, which characterized plantation slave societies, appears not to have become significant among the Boer farming community. This suggests that as a rule Boer women exerted controlling influence in their homes and over the domestic servants owned by the patriarch. Privacy, too, was relatively limited in these homes. Living arrangements, even among the better-off, were characteristically plain and close—grandiosity was not in fashion among the Boers, whose manner of acquiring wealth was too uncertain and subject to reversals to risk putting it into houses and social entertaining other than on a modest scale. It seems that the lack of privacy discouraged intimacy, though not large families. We are concerned here with a community led by men who eschewed alcohol, earned their followings within religious sects of the DRC, built personal networks through marriage alliances, and amassed wealth by virtue of holding office. Scandal easily could ruin the ambitious.

It would be tempting to conclude that female domestic slaves, particularly those belonging to the better-off families, shared in their masters' rise in status and increased their security thereby, while accepting the superiority of the Dutch language and the Boer way of life. But to do so would run counter to the stories of Odela, Rachel, and the few others of the thousands in bondage who found ways to escape inboekstelsel. Strikingly absent from their brief accounts are yearnings to reconnect with their original families or accusations of physical or sexual abuse at the hands of their owners, leaving the reader to guess their motives for escape apart from the desire for personal freedom or the opportunity to marry and raise children. Not that such motives are insufficient in themselves, but the fact is that they are not clearly stated by ex-inboekelinge.

The skills acquired among the Boers while enduring years of hardship could serve as a ticket out of servitude and a means of gaining entry into an African society or a Christianized mission community. The answers, therefore, are less likely to be found in the countryside, where most inboekelinge lived and remained, but rather in the records of literate, mission communities that attracted ex-inboekelinge. If enough of their biographies can be added to the slim pickings offered here, a fuller picture is sure to emerge.

NOTES

1. Eric Anderson Walker, A History of Southern Africa (London: Longman, 1962), 283n.

2. F. W. Chesson, The Dutch Republics of South Africa: Three Letters to R. N. Fowler, Esq. M.P., and Charles Buxton, Esq., M.P. (London: William Twecdie, 1871), 20.

3. Fred Morton, "Slavery in South Africa," in Slavery in South Africa: Captive Labor on the Dutch Frontier, ed. Elizabeth A. Eldredge and Fred Morton (Boulder: Westview, 1994), 251–69.

4. Khama to Du Plessis, 11 March 1877, Dorsland Trek Documents, A779, vol. 2, 23, 26, South African National Archives, Pretoria.

5. Peter Delius and Stanley Trapido, "Inboekselings and Oorlams: The Creation and Transformation of a Servile Class," in Town and Countryside in the Transvaal: Capitalist Penetration and Populist Response, ed. Belinda Bozzoli (Johannesburg: Ravan Press, 1983), 53–81.

6. Barry Morton, "Servitude, Slave Trading, and Slavery in the Kalahari," in Eldredge and Morton, Slavery in South Africa, 215–50.

7. R. Kent Rasmussen, *Migrant Kingdom: Mzilikazi's Ndebele in South Africa* (London: Rex Collings, 1978); Edwin W. Smith, "Sebetwane and the Makololo," *Bantu Studies* 15, no. 2 (1956): 49–74.

8. Norman Etherington, *The Great Treks: The Transformation of South Africa, 1815–1854* (London: Longman, 2001).

9. Rasmussen, *Migrant Kingdom*, esp. 73–81; Martin Legassick, "The Griqua, the Sotho-Tswana, and the Missionaries, 1780–1840: The Politics of the Frontier Zone" (PhD diss., University of California, Los Angeles, 1969).

10. Chesson, *Dutch Republic*, 19–20.

11. Jan C. A. Boeyens, "'Black Ivory': The Indenture System and Slavery in Zoutpansberg, 1848–1869," in Eldredge and Morton, *Slavery in South Africa*, 187–214.

12. Dederik Justin Erasmus, "Re-thinking the Great Trek: A Study of the Nature and Development of the Boer Community in the Ohrigstad/Lydenburg Area, 1845–1877" (MA thesis, Rhodes University, 1995), 58–76.

13. Isaac Schapera, *Praise Poems of Tswana Chiefs* (Oxford: Oxford University Press, 1965), 66, 68.

14. B. Morton, "Servitude, Slave Trading," 222–32.

15. Erasmus, "Rethinking the Great Trek," 73–74.

16. Philip Bonner, *Kings, Commoners and Concessionaires: The Evolution and Dissolution of the Nineteenth-Century Swazi State* (Cambridge: Cambridge University Press, 1983), 80–81; Peter Delius, *The Land Belongs to Us: The Pedi Polity, the Boers and the British in the Nineteenth-Century Transvaal* (Berkeley: University of California Press, 1984), 98, 101–3, 139.

17. John Sanderson, "Memorandum of a Trading Trip into the Orange River (Sovereignty) Free State, and the Country of the Transvaal Boers, 1851–52," *Journal of the Royal Geographical Society* 30 (1860): 242; Alfred Aylward, *The Transvaal of To-Day: War, Witchcraft, Sport, and Spoils in South Africa* (Edinburgh: William Blackwood and Sons, 1881), 150.

18. Chesson, *Dutch Republics*, 19, 21; Hendrik W. Struben, *Recollections of Adventures; Pioneering and Development in South Africa, 1850–1911*, ed. Edith Struben (Cape Town: T. M. Miller, 1920), 86. Currency values were not standardized in the ZAR at this time, but £6 or £7 would have been the approximate value of a young ox in the Pretoria District. See testimony of Mathibe Kgosi, 27 September 1871, in *"To Make Them Serve": The 1871 Transvaal Commission on African Labour*, ed. Johan S. Bergh and Fred Morton (Pretoria: Protea Book House, 2003), 107.

19. Fred Morton, "Captive Labor in the Western Transvaal after the Sand River Convention," in Eldredge and Morton, *Slavery in South Africa*, 173.

20. Stanley Trapido, "Reflections on Land, Office and Wealth in the South African Republic, 1850–1900," in *Economy and Society in Pre-industrial South Africa*, ed. Shula Marks and Anthony Atmore (London: Longman, 1980), 350–68.

21. Naboth Mokgatle, *The Autobiography of an Unknown South African* (Berkeley: University of California Press, 1971), 37–51.

22. Paul Kruger, *The Memoirs of Paul Kruger, Four Times President of the South African Republic, Told by Himself* (London: Unwin, 1902), 42–47; Schapera, *Praise Poems*, 65–69.

23. David Livingstone, *David Livingstone: Family Letters, 1841–1856*, ed. Isaac Schapera, 2 vols. (London: Chatto and Windus, 1959), 2:57–58; Thomas Baines, *Journal of Residence in Africa, 1842–1853*, ed. R. F. Kennedy, 2 vols. (Cape Town: Van Riebeeck Society, 1964), 2:113–14, 123, 131, 170n36, 171–72; Bonner, *Kings, Commoners*, 80–81; Johan S. Bergh, *Geskiedenis atlas van Suid-Afrika: Die vier noordelike provinsies* (Pretoria: J. L. van Schaik, 1999), 156.

24. Belinda Bozzoli with the assistance of Mmantho Nkotsoe, *Women of Phokeng: Consciousness, Life Strategy, and Migrancy in South Africa, 1900–1983* (Portsmouth, NH: Heinemann, 1991), 39–40.

25. F. Morton, "Captive Labor," 167–85.

26. *Natal Mercury*, 11 December 1866.

27. Botlhale Tema's great-grandfather Polomane was of "half and half" origins, a tall, light-skinned, wavy-haired man whose African mother named him Polomane "after his father," a remark pregnant with significance for a blessed event that took place in Paul Kruger's neighborhood. Tema, *People of Welgeval* (Cape Town: Zebra Press, 2005). The mother likely was from one of the villages in the area and raised her son away from a white farm. Tema's account does not explain how Polomane himself became a servant of a white farmer named Joubert.

28. Kruger, *Memoirs*, 47.

29. Regarding Nkhubu (MmaDikeledi) as Mokgatle's first wife, see Paul-Lenert Breutz, *The Tribes of Rustenburg and Pilansberg Districts* (Pretoria: Department of Native Affairs, Ethnological Publications, no. 28, 1953), 64–65. For another interpretation, based on more recent oral accounts, see R. D. Coertze, *Bafokeng Family Law and Law of Succession* (Pretoria: SABRA, 1987), 46–48; Mokgatle, *Autobiography*, 40–42.

30. For the succession, see Breutz, *Rustenburg and Pilansberg*, 65–66.

31. For the accounts of Odela, Adela, Rachel of Langa AmaNdebele, Leah, and Sophia, see Chesson, *Dutch Republics of South Africa*, 18–23.

32. Delius and Trapido, "Inboekselings and Oorlams," 71.

33. Chesson, *Dutch Republics*, 20.

34. *Natal Mercury*, 14 March 1867, 6 October, 14 November 1868, 24 June 1869; *Transvaal Argus*, 21 February, 14 March, 16 May 1867. I am grateful to Barry Morton for these newspaper sources.

35. Rachel's statement, 6 September 1880, SN 4, N244/80, National Archives of South Africa, Pretoria. For a description of the raids on BaBirwa and other Zoutpansberg communities in the 1860s, see Boeyens, "'Black Ivory,'" 196–202.

36. See for example two ex-inboekelinge, both named August, enclosures 2 and 3, both dated 18 May 1874, in no. 24, Colonial Office Confidential Prints, CO 879/7/61, 153, 155. I am grateful to Barry Morton for these sources.

37. Gonin to P. J. Joubert (Superintendent of Natives), 27 April 1888, 15/7/2(C), Dutch Reformed Church Archives (hereafter DRC), Cape Town, tr. Wom van den Akker. The chiefs listed were located in the northern ZAR districts of Waterberg and Zoutpansberg. For an extended account of the Welgeval and Schaapkraal families, see Tema, *People of Welgeval*.

38. *Hermannsburger Missionsblatt*, April 1866; J. Du Plessis, *A History of Christian Missions in South Africa* (London: Longmans, Green, 1911), 284–85; Andrea Mignon,

The 19th Century Lutheran Mission in Botswana (Gaborone: Botswana Society and National Archives and Records Service, 1996), 4–9; Bernard Mbenga and Fred Morton, "The Missionary as Land Broker: Henri Gonin, Saulspoort 269 and the Bakgatla of Rustenburg District, 1862–1922," *South African Historical Journal* 36 (1997): 145–67.

39. Gonin to DRC, 15 July 1864, 30 December 1865, 15/7/2(E), as well as other Gonin correspondence in 17/5/2 (A), DRC Archives.

40. Mignon, *Lutheran Mission in Botswana*, 26.

41. Tidimane Pilane and Noel Pilane. The details of Martha's life have been re-constructed from Gonin's correspondence, Ramono's 1918 will and testimony (NA 61/55, NTS 333, South African Archives), and interviews with the late E. S. Moloto (Gaborone, 22 February 1982), Tidimane Pilane (Saulspoort, 4 January 1982), Rev. J. Ramodisa Phiri and England Mpudule Tshomankane (Saulspoort, 6 January 1982). See also Fred Morton, "Cattleholders, Evangelists and Socioeconomic Transformation among the BaKgatla of Rustenburg District, 1863–1898," *South African Historical Journal* 38 (1998): 79–98.

42. F. Morton, "Cattleholders, Evangelists," 91–92, 95.

43. For Kgalagadi testimony, see Linchwe Estate files, s. 343/19–27, Botswana National Archives, Gaborone. For similar twentieth-century examples, see B. Morton "Servitude, Slave Trading."

4

Women in Imperial African Worlds

9

WOMEN, GENDER HISTORY, AND SLAVERY IN NINETEENTH-CENTURY ETHIOPIA

TIMOTHY FERNYHOUGH (†)

Although the scholarly literature on Ethiopia has grown substantially in recent years, two significant historiographical lacunae remain. The first is the absence of substantive work on women and gender; the second is the institution of slavery and its lifeblood, the slave trade. This chapter proposes to begin filling these lacunae by examining the role of women and slavery in nineteenth-century Ethiopia in terms of power and gender relations and showing how the experiences of slave women were shaped also by such other forces as ethnicity, culture, religion, community, and family.

There is no single comprehensive work on women in Ethiopia.[1] A growing body of scholarship has explored the sociolegal condition of Ethiopian women, their role in education and training, and gender issues in health care, the media, and rural development.[2] However, there are few notable historical studies of women or gender issues. Richard Pankhurst looked at the role of women from the medieval period to the mid-nineteenth century,[3] while Bairu Tafla has done the same for the early twentieth century.[4] Chris Prouty examined the lives of leading women during Ethiopia's "time of troubles," the Zamana Masafent (era of the princes), as well as the career of Empress Taytu Betul, the country's de facto ruler between 1908 and 1910.[5] Donald Crummey has explored the extent to which elite women exercised formal rights to land.[6] Unfortunately, these studies have tended to focus on women whose lives were hardly representative of those

---

Owing to the sudden death of Timothy Fernyhough, this paper has been edited by Richard B. Allen, who assumes responsibility for any errors.

of most women in Ethiopia, particularly female slaves, who belonged to the country's laboring classes. We know, by way of comparison, more about slavery and slave trading in Ethiopia.[7]

THE IMAGE OF THE FEMALE SLAVE

The term for slave—*barya*—in Amharic and Tegrenya (the two major languages in modern Ethiopia) carries mostly negative connotations that reflect the historic power relations between the powerful core of Christian Ethiopia and the relatively dispersed ethnic groups on its peripheries. Historically, this term derived from the long-standing interaction between Abyssinians and the lowland Barya and Kunama of northwest Ethiopia and Eritrea, who were raided so heavily for captives that their very name came to mean slave.[8] *Barya* came to refer to an inherently inferior and servile person different in language, religion, ethnicity, and appearance from highland Ethiopians who spoke Amharic or Tegrenya, were Christian, and were of relatively light ("red," or *qay*) skin color. *Shanqella*, commonly used to describe "blacks" or the Nilo-Saharan peoples of Ethiopia's western frontiers, was an equally loaded word. Vulnerable to repeated raids from the Abyssinian highlands, peoples described as shanqella were regarded basically as reservoir populations of potential slaves. *Shanqella* had the strong "secondary meaning" of slave and, like *barya*, became a common appellation for slave.[9]

Skin color and racial features set baryas and shanqellas apart from the peoples of highland Ethiopia. Arrogant and denigrating attitudes toward the *tsalim barya* (dark slave) and shanqellas tell us much about the asymmetrical power relations between the historic Abyssinian state and its peripheries.[10] However, such linguistic analyses have not examined how gender articulated with language and ethnicity to create the image of the female slave. Ethiopian society was patriarchal. Women were viewed as inferior and subordinate and often as impure and licentious.[11] These negative views were not confined to historic Abyssinia. Many Ethiopian peoples denigrated women and their femininity, frequently portraying them as lazy, unstable, unreliable, shrewish, treacherous, and even as hyenas.[12] All women were widely expected to be reserved, modest, and submissive.

Scholars need to be careful, however, in assessing these pejorative views of women. First, they were not held by all the peoples of Ethiopia. The non-Muslim Oromo, for example, have a "relatively benign view of women" and may have a somewhat different view of female sexuality than prevails elsewhere in Ethiopia.[13] A recent survey of eleven major national groups suggests that the Oromo lie at one end of a spectrum by according women high social status, while the Afar and Anuak accord them low status, with the Amhara falling somewhere in between.[14] Second, views of women's role and status vary between the sexes. The same survey suggests that men and women differ markedly in their assessments of their roles as family breadwinners, a conclusion that would seem reasonable to project into the past.[15] Third, commonly held views that depreciate women's position and status may obscure their political significance in the past, their substantial legal rights, and their role in making important household and other domestic decisions.[16] Even where men were politically, ideologically, and legally dominant, women questioned and challenged male authority and occasionally even enjoyed preeminence and political influence.

These negative attitudes toward women were often amplified when applied to female slaves. The characterization of women as lazy, untrustworthy, and immoral was also held to be typical of slave behavior.[17] The attribution of an often-fearsome sexual allure and appetite to women reinforced the commonly held image of the female slave's "immense sexual prowess,"[18] an image that persisted in spite of the fact that masters controlled their sexual and reproductive capacities. In Gurage, Kaffa, and Konso, for example, women were regarded as "inherently immoral," dangerous because of their "avid sexual desires," and fearsome because they might sap men of their vitality through sexual activity.[19] Such a reputation for female sexual prowess may help to explain why these three regions were such important sources of Ethiopian slaves in the nineteenth century.

The metaphorical relationship between sex and ethnicity was not always replicated on the ground. Despite the low regard in which shanqellas were generally held, unions between Christian Ethiopians and shanqellas occurred frequently. Nevertheless, in the Christian heartland shanqellas "were not thought to be proper marriage partners for Abyssinians."[20] Moreover, as Pankhurst has observed, the taint of slave descent was a matter of great consequence that extended to the seventh generation of an Abyssinian-shanqella union.[21]

Sex and ethnicity combined to determine the demand for and the prices of slaves. The demand for attractive women and girls was greater than for any other group except eunuchs. Ethnicity and place of origin helped to define which female slaves were deemed to be attractive and useful and which were not. "Red" slaves from the Oromo and Omotic regions and from lacustrine groups like the Gurage and Konso were more highly valued than pastoral shanqellas from the Sudanic frontiers. Arab merchants at Ethiopia's ports and frontiers also prized slaves from the

Oromo or "Galla" kingdoms of the southwest and the "red Ethiopians" from Gurage.[22]

THE CONDITION OF FEMALE SLAVES

Male dominance in highland Abyssinia and the Omotic and Oromo states of southwestern Ethiopia is demonstrated most clearly by the potential for male, but not female, slaves to rise to high office and status. Walter Plowden observed that Empress Manan Liban, her son, *Ras* Ali Alulu of Bagemder (de facto ruler of Ethiopia, 1834–54), and Ali Alulu's rival, *Dajazmach* Webe Hayla Maryam, all staffed their administrations with trusted eunuchs.[23] Men of slave origin also rose to political prominence on the southern edges of the Christian highlands. *Abogaz* Bazabeh, for example, was appointed one of Emperor Tewodros's governors of Shawa and later served the future emperor Menilek II as a district governor in Tegulet. *Azaj* Walda Tsadeq, a Gurage war captive, likewise became one of Menilek's most valued advisors, with responsibility for much of Shawa's civil and commercial administration, and then served as governor of Ankobar and Ifat.[24]

Though only a few male slaves ever gained such rank and office, no female slave ever rose so high politically. At best, female slaves might enjoy influence with their masters or the confidence of queens and noblewomen. At the Shawan royal court during the 1840s, favored female slaves were "decked out like the first ladies of the land" in a manner "calculated to strike respect into the heart of the most indifferent beholder." The presence of their attendant eunuch was, however, a reminder that these enslaved women could not "roam at pleasure."[25]

Such restrictions on women are not surprising. Nineteenth-century Ethiopian societies rested on gendered conceptions of political authority, occupational boundaries, and social status. Elite women occasionally enjoyed rank, privilege, and even real power, but the discourse and dynamic of power relations guaranteed that women were largely excluded from political life. In such contexts, male slaves might rise to high political office, but female slaves stood little chance of doing so. In states that needed capable administrators, talented male slaves could gain rank, office, power, and freedom. In societies that valued military skills, male slaves also had opportunities to rise as warriors and military leaders. Historically, most Ethiopian rulers and nobles employed slaves as soldiers and guards,[26] and loyal slaves who distinguished themselves on the battlefield could even become provincial governors.[27]

Such avenues of political and social mobility were not open to female slaves, who were commonly consigned to performing the myriad menial tasks needed to maintain elite households. They were also objects of sexual gratification for their masters, who might exploit their reproductive capacities to father children. Through unions with male slaves, enslaved women could also be used to breed a new generation of servile laborers. The king of Kaffa, for one, confined slave couples to the royal compound and assigned lands for them to work when they produced children. Female slaves who failed to produce offspring within a year risked being sold.[28]

Female slaves were conspicuous social and economic entities in nineteenth-century Ethiopia, a fact reflected by the volume of the slave trade in northern Ethiopia and the Gulf of Aden. At least two-thirds of the slaves caught up in these trades were female, some of whom were children.[29] Female slaves regularly outnumbered their male counterparts in palace and household settings. The majority of slaves at Sahla Sellase's court in Shawa during the 1840s, for example, were young girls or women who worked in the royal palaces at Ankobar, Angolala, Dabra Berhan, and Kunde. European sources suggest that there were over a thousand female slaves at Ankobar; of these, three hundred women and girls ground flour, two hundred served as cooks, and several hundred prepared hydromel and beer for the royal household. As many as six hundred female spinners were found at Dabra Berhan, some two hundred of whom produced the fine thread used for clothing worn by the royal household. The remainder of these spinners created the coarser yarn that ultimately clothed the royal bodyguard. The first group of female slaves, guarded by several eunuchs and held in seclusion, was also depicted as royal concubines.[30] Female slaves similarly predominated at the courts of the Gibé-Gojab states. In Limmu-Enarya, the royal *masseras* held thousands of slaves, mostly female.[31]

Absolute numbers of female slaves are difficult to determine. The total number of slaves in early twentieth-century Ethiopia is estimated at between two and four million in a total population (in 1900) of about eleven million—that is, up to a third.[32] Estimates of the slave population's size during the nineteenth century are largely conjectural. The proportion of slaves in the Gibé-Dedesa and Omotic states was clearly higher than in northern Ethiopia and Shawa. Contemporary European estimates for the southwestern states of Gera, Janjero, Jimma, Kaffa, Kucha, and Walamo suggest that slaves constituted perhaps one-third to two-thirds of the total population.[33]

The few specific figures at our disposal are tantalizing. According to Cecchi, the three thousand slaves at the royal massera of Challa, in Gera, made up one-fifth of this Oromo kingdom's total population of fifteen to sixteen thousand in 1880.[34] Applying the standard ratio of one male to every two female slaves suggests that Gera contained no fewer than two thousand female slaves—approximately 13 percent of the kingdom's total population. A contemporary estimate posited eighty thousand slaves in Kaffa in 1897, a figure that points to a female slave population of not less than fifty-three thousand, or slightly more than 21 percent of a total population of two hundred fifty thousand.[35] The same male-to-female ratio, when applied to the country as a whole, suggests the presence of no fewer than two million female slaves in early-twentieth-century imperial Ethiopia who constituted just over 18 percent of the empire's population.

The primary function of slaves was service, and their lives were correspondingly menial and monotonous. Long lines of slaves, both male and female, leading oxen and sheep and bearing wine, milk, teff, peppers, and honey were a familiar sight at the court of Emperor Yohannes (r. 1872–89). Similar slave trains served food and beverages at the royal table.[36] At the Shawan royal court, most male slaves labored as craftsmen, porters, and woodcutters; their female counterparts served in the palace harem as spinners and weavers, in the royal bakeries and breweries, and as cooks, cup and plate bearers, water carriers, and cowherds.[37] The majority of the three thousand slaves residing at the court of Gera likewise performed duties within the royal household.[38] At the much larger court of Jimma at Jiren, royal wives also maintained their own large slave retinues.[39]

Prominent nobles and officials replicated imperial household retinues on a smaller scale. In northern Ethiopia these included Dajazmach Walda Sellase, ruler of Tegre (ca. 1800–16), Ras Berru of Tegre (ca. 1873), and Dajazmach Tasamma Engeda, one of Emperor Yohannes's troop commanders in the mid-1880s. All three, like most other leading nobles, possessed hundreds of slaves who visibly demonstrated their masters' power and wealth. In these northern provinces all but the poorest households used servile labor. As always, domestic tasks were "usually performed by slave women."[40]

Further south, in Shawa, royal governors likewise "possessed many slaves," but here too, as W. C. Harris observed, "every house . . . possesses slaves of both sexes, in proportion to the wealth of the proprietor."[41] Charles Johnston encountered domestic slaves, mostly girls, in a number of homes.[42] In Limmu-Enarya and Jimma, slaves attended regional governors in large numbers. Indeed, throughout the southwestern states the noble and the wealthy coveted slaves.[43] In Gudru, the rich employed slaves for their daily needs and rarely traveled without a slave entourage. Besides being indispensable as house guards, porters, and servants, slaves were a symbol of wealth in Gera, where an eldest son received his father's bondsmen as part of his inheritance and a wealthy woman's dowry usually included slaves.[44]

Not all slaves worked in households or served in their masters' retinues. The existence of a relatively large slave sector in southwest Ethiopia may reflect an expanded role for servile labor in the Oromo and Omotic kingdoms. As I have argued elsewhere, the extensive use of slaves in agricultural and industrial production distinguishes slavery in southern Ethiopia from that in the northern part of the country in the nineteenth century.[45] While male slaves were used as field hands in Christian Abyssinia, there are no references in Shawa, for instance, to the large-scale use of slaves in agriculture. Slaves in the Oromo and Omotic polities of the southwest, on the other hand, were heavily engaged in agricultural production.[46] In Kaffa, male and female slaves worked royal and noble estates, while favored subjects were often given slaves for agricultural labor.[47] In the Gibé states, slaves of both sexes worked royal and noble estates.[48] In Limmu-Enarya they tended and harvested the king's "woods of coffee"; in Jimma they worked on coffee plantations and produced food for the court at Jiren.[49]

Slaves of both sexes also contributed substantially to craft industries in the Omotic and Gibé states. In Kaffa and Kullo, female slaves wove textiles, while male slaves engaged in metalwork.[50] The royal masseras at Jiren in Jimma and at Garruqe in Limmu-Enarya were industrial centers, and here too women slaves worked as spinners. At Jiren, King Abba Jifar II set aside quarters for them, while royal weavers and tailors, invariably men, turned their spun cotton into clothes for the court, for export, or for diplomatic gifts.[51]

Wherever they worked, slaves across Ethiopia enjoyed a limited measure of legal protection. In northern Ethiopia and Shawa, the medieval law code, the Fetha Nagast, dictated that masters who mistreated their slaves might lose their property, be imprisoned or, in the case of the premeditated murder of a slave, face the death penalty. A badly beaten slave, for example, might recover his or her freedom.[52] The Fetha Nagast also notionally forbade marriage or sexual relations between a free man or woman and a slave, prohibited concubinage, and offered the same protection against rape to both free women and female slaves.[53] The extent to which these injunctions were enforced remains unknown, but by the nineteenth century they were largely honored in the breach. In the Gibé-Dedesa states, as elsewhere in Ethiopia, male and female slaves had neither legal identity nor any claim to property nor rights of redress against brutality. Excessive cruelty was, however, much at odds with custom. In Gudru it was considered unacceptable for a master to disfigure or murder a slave in domestic service. In Gera slaves of both sexes could appeal openly against injustice or poor treatment and guilty slaveholders could be punished. Nevertheless, the reality of power relations in Gudru meant that a slaveholder was a "complete master of his slaves" and could mutilate and kill them with relative impunity. When a free man killed a slave in Gera and Limmu, the compensation due the slave's owner was merely another slave or five head of cattle.[54]

The penalties inflicted on male and female slaves for their crimes reflect a rare instance of gender neutrality in their lives. These penalties ranged from corporal punishment or imprisonment in chains in Shawa to incarceration, blinding, and even brutal execution in the Gibé states.[55] In Gera, Cecchi observed the awful fate of a woman slave held responsible for the illness of one of the king's sons. Publicly beaten, severely mutilated, and chained in the heat of the day, she soon resembled "a frightening mummy."[56] Runaway slaves also faced harsh penalties. In Jimma, fugitive slaves were beaten and held in chains; in Limmu-Enarya, as in Jimma, they ended up at the state prison where their imprisonment in stocks meant that they "were as good as dead."[57]

Overt cruelty toward valuable and familiar household slaves was rare. Europeans recorded that slaves in Bagemder during Tewodros's reign were treated "very kindly" as members of their masters' families. In Shawa, where most of them lived with their masters, slaves were usually treated with "lenience" and "even indulgence."[58] In Gudru and the Gibé kingdoms, slaves often had their own houses, land, and property. Legally, such property reverted to their masters at death but, in practice, it often passed to their children.[59] In both Shawa and the Gibé-Gojab states slaves could also enjoy benevolent treatment. Johnston recorded that domestic slaves in Shawa were "invariably" regarded as family and often treated as "near relations" and even as "foster children." At one family supper, he observed how the hostess ended the meal by personally distributing choice morsels of food to each guest in turn, giving her slave girl "attendant and companion," who had dined with the assembled family, a larger portion than anyone else.[60] Cardinal Massaia was taken by how two slave converts, a young man and woman, were "loved as brother and sister" by their master and mistress. All four had grown up together, and the former now looked to the latter to act as their godparents.[61] In Jimma a quarter of a century later, Jules Borelli acknowledged that cruelty was rare among the many slaves who lived with their owners' families.[62]

Kindly treatment could never disguise the fact that most slaves, not least of all women in domestic service, had little prospect of freedom while they were still young enough to enjoy it. Chances of manumission were limited and, coming late in a slave's life, especially if he or she were freed without material resources, could be a mixed blessing. In the Gibé states, where slaves might occasionally buy their liberty or be adopted into their masters' families, the spread of Islam increased the number of manumitted slaves, most of whom were in their mid-thirties to mid-fifties.[63] In Christian Ethiopia, the Fetha Nagast defined the grounds for manumission. Ege has stressed that young, healthy slaves were rarely freed in Shawa and that most manumittees were elderly.

Concern for their investment underpinned the kind treatment afforded slaves by some slave merchants and traders. Slaves in transit often faced considerable hardships. If at times they were well fed, rested, and unfettered, at other times they had to endure forced marches through harsh terrain in often-hostile climates and under threat of attack by bandits.[64] The caravan road to Khartoum, for instance, was long reputed for its high slave mortality.[65] Two-thirds—and perhaps three-quarters—of the transit slave trade and the bulk of slave exports consisted of women and young girls, not all of whom survived en route to market.[66] Many teenage girls (*wasef*) and boys were deeply distressed by their often abrupt and violent separation from their families.[67] Conditions at major slave markets were often little better. At Saqa in Limmu-Enarya young girls were held hungry and weak in dirty huts; at Basso and Ifag both elderly slaves and young women lay for days bound in filth and squalor.[68] At Qallabat slave merchants resolutely refused to acknowledge sickness among underfed captives kept in "stifling" booths, fearing that to do so would reduce prices.[69]

As noted earlier, sex and ethnicity were important factors determining the demand for slaves. After eunuchs, light-skinned "Galla" or "Gurage" young wasef made the most valuable slaves, followed by teenage boys. Demand for these teenagers determined the proportions of slaves obtained through raids, tribute, and kidnapping. *Negus* Sahla Sellase's brutal expeditions into the Fenfeni valley and the contiguous plains south of Entoto (the area of modern Addis Ababa) in the 1840s yielded thousands of young women and girls, while the men were "indiscriminately slain."[70] The pattern of Shawan and imperial expansion southward between the 1870s and 1890s was much the same. As Menilek's forces and those of his leading chiefs razed whole districts, soldiers often slaughtered the male defenders and hunted and enslaved their women and children.[71] Thousands of these unfortunates passed through Shawan slave markets at Andodi, Rogge, and Abdel Rassul en route to the coast during the 1870s and 1880s.[72] Menilek's successor, *Lej* Iyasu, also seized thousands of slaves, mostly young women and children, in expeditions into Kaffa, Gemira, and Anuak country.[73] Shawa was not the only nineteenth-century state to acquire slaves in military expeditions, although it was the most successful.

Young women and girls figured prominently in four other modes of slave acquisition: tribute, kidnapping, deception, and "voluntary" enslavement. In the first instance, they were a primary component of the tribute that Ethiopian rulers paid to one another, and that merchants paid to propitiate kings and provincial or district governors. Thus the kings of Konta and Kullo recognized Kaffa's hegemony by paying tribute in male and female slaves, while the king of Gera extracted slaves from Muslim caravans traveling north from Kaffa.[74] On the border of Gudru and Gojjam, slave traders eased their passage into northern Ethiopia in the 1850s by delighting the district governor with tribute of young girls.[75]

Young women were also the targets of much of the kidnapping that occurred in nineteenth-century Eritrea and northern Ethiopia.[76] In southern Ethiopia the demand for young boys and girls fueled a vigorous market for Gurage children stolen from their parents at night.[77] Bandits seized and enslaved the unwary in Arsi during the 1870s, often on open roads, and ambushes of young girls were common elsewhere in southern Ethiopia.[78]

Slave merchants also deceived young men and women, sometimes with false offers of employment or trips to holy places. In the 1830s a fraudulent priest enticed a whole group of pilgrims from Gojjam and Bagemder onto a ship bound not for Jerusalem and the Holy Land, but for Jidda and slavery in Arabia.[79] A decade later the case of a Christian girl from Tegre who was suddenly sold by her patron—a Muslim merchant—to a slave trader who shipped her swiftly to Jidda became a cause célèbre.[80] Whole families from southern Ethiopia were lured into slavery by false promises and deceit.[81]

Perhaps the most tragic of all were those forced by famine, pestilence, and taxation to sell themselves into slavery. Thousands of Shawans threw themselves on the mercy of Negus Sahla Sellase in the wake of famine and epidemic cholera during the early 1830s. There is no evidence that any of these "famine slaves" were ever sold, unlike the Tegrean victims of the Great Famine of 1890–91, many of whom sold their children and, at times, themselves to Muslim merchants.[82] In southern Ethiopia the Gibé kings exercised their right to enslave and sell the children of parents too impoverished to pay their taxes; rulers of Kucha allowed merchants to buy the poverty stricken.[83] In Kaffa a father was legally entitled to sell his wife and children into slavery when times were hard. Even an unborn child could be sold in Kaffa, in which case the mother was obliged to provide her milk to the newborn for two years before the child passed to the buyer.[84] Women and children were sold by their relatives in Gurage and Janjero during hard times—and possibly when things were not so hard. The Danakil also reputedly sold "their own daughters."[85]

The continuing demand for women, especially young women and girls, is attested to in other ways. Gender was an important factor in determining slave prices.[86] Between 1830 and 1850, for example, male slaves at Abdel Rassul, in Shawa, cost from nine to sixteen Maria Theresa dollars; female slaves, on the other hand, cost MT$12–25, while a beautiful teenage girl cost MT$25–30, and even as much as MT$50–80.[87] At the Gojjamé market of Basso during this same period, a boy cost MT$4–8, a man MT$10, and a young or adult woman MT$4–12 depending on her age, but a beautiful teenage girl fetched MT$16.[88] These price differentials were maintained, and often increased, beyond Ethiopia's borders. At Shendi, north of Khartoum, males sold for MT$20–80, compared to MT$160–300 for females. Male and female slaves sold respectively for MT$25–100 and MT$60–150 in the Hejaz and Yemen, where an attractive teenage girl might ultimately cost as much as MT$240; in the Persian Gulf, male and female slaves respectively cost MT$200–600 and MT$300–1,000.[89] Merchants in Ethiopia probably realized about 20 percent profit on the majority of slaves they sold, a rate that rose to 30 to 40 percent for teenage girls and eunuchs.[90] Profit margins for slave merchants who ventured south of Basso to Saqa and Asandabo (Gudru) or who shipped slaves across the Red Sea may have been greater.

Women remained in high demand because they were perceived to be well suited to domestic service, easy to train, and least likely to resist. Teenage girls held even higher value because of their potential roles as wives or concubines. Yet gender was not the only variable that governed slave prices. Ethnicity, health, and physique were also important. At Basso in the early 1840s, a shanqella field hand might cost MT$4–6, whereas an Oromo man suitable for domestic service might cost MT$10.[91] At Massawa, a male Oromo fetched MT$35–50 and a female Oromo

MT$50–60; a male or female shanqella, on the other hand, brought only MT$25.[92] A slave's age also mattered. An elderly woman sold at Qabena in the late 1870s for MT$4–5 compared to a young woman who cost MT$10–15 and a teenage girl who fetched MT$30–35. A similar pattern characterized the price of male slaves: MT$7–8 for an elderly man, MT$12–15 for a young man, and MT$10–16 for a teenage boy who was perceived most amenable to training.[93]

The distance between slave markets and sources of supply similarly influenced prices. Slaves who cost 20–30 *amole* (salt bars), or approximately MT$4–5, in the Oromo and Omotic states cost four times as much in coastal entrepôts such as Massawa, and could sometimes bring as much as ten times their original purchase price.[94] Female slaves cost ten to fifteen times more on the Red Sea coast than at sources of supply; a teenage girl could bring possibly even more. These prices changed dramatically between the periods 1830–50 and 1870–90, partly due to increasing demand both inside and outside Ethiopia, but primarily because of inflation. By the mid-1870s the Maria Theresa dollar had lost half its value against the amole, the currency with which most slaves were first purchased in southern Ethiopia.[95] As a result, slave prices in the Gibé states, at Basso, and in Shawa rose significantly by 1870–90. Slaves who cost no more than MT$5 in Limmu-Enarya and Jimma before 1850, for example, now cost MT$15–25, and a teenage girl as much as MT$30.[96] In Basso, the boy who sold for MT$4–8 in the 1840s cost MT$20 by the late 1870s; the woman who cost MT$4–12 now brought MT$40–60, while an attractive wasef, who once cost MT$16, commanded as much as MT$100.[97]

A better sense of domestic production of slaves in Ethiopia can be obtained by applying the one-to-two male to female ratio to previous estimates of total exports.[98] Hence, of the 15,000 slaves produced annually in southern Ethiopia between 1830 and 1850, perhaps 5,000 were male and 10,000 were female. Men may have accounted for 4,600 of the 14,000 slaves who passed through Hermata, Basso, and Abdel Rassul each year, the balance of whom were women. Annual exports from Massawa and Qallabat may have amounted to about 1,100 men and at least 2,200 women, while possibly 1,400 male and over 2,800 female slaves left Tajurah, Zeyla, and Berbera each year. Projections based on these data suggest that 1,800 newly harvested male slaves and 3,600 newly obtained female slaves remained in Ethiopia each year between 1830 and 1850.

Female slaves were clearly valued and in great demand as trade commodities in nineteenth-century Ethiopia. Enslaved women were significant socially and economically as domestic servants, agricultural laborers, and craft workers. Assessing the overall importance of their activities is, however, a problematic undertaking. In contrast to some male slaves, female slaves had little opportunity to gain or exercise political power. The administrative and military avenues through which male slaves might make their mark were simply not open to women. Females who exerted political influence did so through the agency of men whose confidence and trust they had earned.

Economically, all slaves—including women and girls—helped with the chores that kept households running and, particularly in southern Ethiopia, contributed in substantive ways to industrial and agricultural output. Slaves also provided cheap portage for many of the products exported to northern Ethiopia and the Red Sea ports. Commodities themselves, slaves also carried the gold, ivory, coffee, hides, musk, and spices that enriched the Oromo and Omotic states of southwest Ethiopia during the nineteenth century.[99] Assessing the significance of their contribution to the Ethiopian economy is, however, very difficult. Profit margins suggest that most slave traders had limited opportunities to accumulate capital unless they dealt in large numbers of eunuchs and wasef, or had the resources to extend and vertically integrate their operations close to sources of supply and demand. With the possible exception of Kaffa, neither the sale of slaves nor taxes on slaves in transit were vital to nineteenth-century Ethiopian state economies. Annual transit taxes on slaves in Shawa, for example, netted no more than five percent of total government revenues from tribute and trade during the 1840s.[100] Beyond concluding that they were undoubtedly significant, the value of slaves' contributions to nineteenth-century Ethiopia's economy is difficult to ascertain since it is impossible at present to disaggregate slave output from economic output generally.

The contradictions between the perceptions of nineteenth-century Ethiopians and the analytical observations of modern historians make assessing the social impact of slavery and gender relations within slavery equally difficult. To slave owners, servile labor made an essential contribution to social and economic life. From their perspective, there can be little doubt that the labor that female slaves performed—fetching water, gathering firewood, washing clothes, milling grain, baking bread, cooking foods, and preparing beverages—held Ethiopian households together. Female slaves also allowed the royal and noble elite to maintain their harems, although concubines' sexual services could also overlap with other household or industrial duties.

For many, if not most, women slaves, other aspects of their experience surely stood out in their minds. These included the violence of their passage into captivity and servitude, their heartrending separation from family and community, hardships en route to slave markets in Ethiopia and beyond, their demeaning status at the very bottom of society, the humiliation and drudgery of much of their daily labor, and their physical and sexual vulnerability. Their value as bonded laborers, kindly treatment by merchants and masters, and legal and customary protections undoubtedly served to mitigate some of the hardships they faced, but, for most female slaves, their subordination was an enduring fact of life.

Modern historians would find it very hard to argue that female slaves were not important in nineteenth-century Ethiopian society and economy, or that the "arduous and exacting chores" that Almaz Eshete regards as elemental to the experience of most free women in Ethiopia were not magnified for slave women and girls. However, to suggest, as Pankhurst has done, that women played a "major" role in Ethiopia's economic, social, and cultural life is arguable. To infer that they did so as "servants and slaves" is more than tenuous. It is not enough, as Almaz has argued, simply to record the physical presence of women in Ethiopian history or report their activities. Women, not least female slaves, performed all manner of tasks that permitted nineteenth-century Ethiopian societies to function. There is no evidence, however, that women were endowed with a "strong identity."[101] In a land dominated politically, ideologically, and culturally by men, there were few concessions to women, and hardly any to female slaves. Their gender and servile status dictated that female slaves controlled neither their destinies nor their daily lives. They were important only for their monetary value, for their labor, and as sexual objects. Sadly, one is forced to concur with the Oromo slave girl Edmond Combes and Maurice Tamisier encountered in a caravan in Hamasen in the mid-1830s. Shown a Maria Theresa dollar, the girl captured pithily the value that most nineteenth-century Ethiopians set on their slaves. Still a child herself, but wiser than her years, she threw the coin into the air, crying, "Et voilà donc ce qui sert à acheter les enfants et les hommes!"[102]

NOTES

Abbreviations

FO—Foreign Office records, Public Record Office, Kew
IOL/BSP/LG—India Office Library, Bombay Secret Proceedings, Lantern Gallery

1. Timothy Fernyhough and Anna Fernyhough, "Women, Gender History, and Imperial Ethiopia," in *Women and the Colonial Gaze*, ed. Tamara Hunt and Micheline Lessard (New York: New York University Press, 2002), 188–201.

2. Recent works include Hirut Tefere and Lakew Woldetekle, "Study of the Situation of Women in Ethiopia," Institute of Development Research, Research Report 23, Addis Ababa, 1986; Hanna Kebede, "Gender Relations in Mobilizing Human Resources," in *Ethiopia: Options for Rural Development*, ed. Siegfried Pausewang et al. (London: Zed Books, 1990), 59–68; Tsehai Berhane-Selassie, *Gender Issues in Ethiopia* (Addis Ababa: Institute of Ethiopian Studies, Addis Ababa University, 1991); M. P. Porter, "Law in Conflict: The Status of Women in the Constitution and Laws of Ethiopia," in *Ethiopia in Broader Perspective*, ed. Katsuyoshi Fukui, Eisei Kurimoto, and Masayoshi Shigeta, 3 vols. (Kyoto: Shokado, 1997), 3:585–99.

3. Richard Pankhurst, "The Role of Women in Ethiopian Economic, Social and Cultural Life: From the Middle Ages to the Times of Tewodros," in *Proceedings of the First National Conference of Ethiopian Studies*, ed. Richard Pankhurst, Ahmed Zekaria, and Taddesse Beyene (Addis Ababa: Institute of Ethiopian Studies, Addis Ababa University, 1990), 345–63; Richard Pankhurst, "The History of Prostitution in Ethiopia," *Journal of Ethiopian Studies* 12, no. 2 (1974): 159–78; Richard Pankhurst, "Dynastic Inter-Marriage in Medieval and Post-Medieval Ethiopia," in Fukui, Kurimoto, and Shigeta, *Ethiopia in Broader Perspective*, 1:206–20.

4. Bairu Tafla, "Marriage as a Political Device: An Appraisal of a Socio-Political Aspect of the Menilek Period, 1889–1916," *Journal of Ethiopian Studies* 10, no. 1 (1972): 13–21.

5. C. Prouty, "Eight Ethiopian Women of the Zemene Mesafint, 1769–1855," *Northeast African Studies* 1, no. 2 (1979): 63–85; Prouty, *Empress Taytu and Menilek II: Ethiopia, 1883–1910* (Trenton, NJ: Red Sea, 1986).

6. Donald Crummey, "Women and Landed Property in Gondarine Ethiopia," *International Journal of African Historical Studies* 14, no. 3 (1981): 444–65; Donald Crummey, "Women, Property and Litigation among the Bagemder Amhara, 1750s to 1850s," in *African Women and the Law: Historical Perspectives*, ed. Margaret Jean Hay and Marcia Wright (Boston: African Studies Center, Boston University, 1982); Donald Crummey, "Family and Property among the Amhara Nobility," *Journal of African History* 24, no. 2 (1983): 207–20.

7. Cf. Richard Pankhurst, *Economic History of Ethiopia, 1800–1935* (Addis Ababa: Haile Selassie I University Press, 1968), 74–134; Mordechai Abir, *Ethiopia: The Era of the Princes* (London: Longmans, 1968), esp. 53–70; J. Edwards, "Slavery, the Slave Trade and Economic Reorganization of Ethiopia, 1916–1935," *African Economic History* 11, no. 1 (1982): 3–14; James McCann, "'Children of the House': Slavery and Its Suppression in Lasta, Northern Ethiopia, 1916–1935," in *The End of Slavery in Africa*, ed. Suzanne Miers and Richard Roberts (Madison: University of Wisconsin Press, 1988), 335, 338–40; Charles W. McClellan, *State Transformation and National Integration: Gedeo and the Ethiopian Empire, 1895–1935* (East Lansing: Michigan State University Press, 1988), esp. 117–18; Tekalign Wolde Maryam, "The Slave Trade in the Economy of Jimma," in *Proceedings of the Eighth International Conference of Ethiopian Studies*, ed. Taddese Beyene (Addis Ababa: Institute of

Ethiopian Studies, 1989), 2:309–14; Guluma Gumeda, "Subsistence, Slavery and Violence in the Lower Omo Valley, ca. 1898–1940's," *Northeast African Studies* 12, no. 1 (1990): 5–19; Suzanne Miers, "Britain and the Suppression of Slavery in Ethiopia," *Slavery and Abolition* 18, no. 3 (1997): 256–88; Abdussamad Ahmad, "Trading in Slaves in Bela-Shangul and Gumuz, Ethiopia: Border Enclaves in History, 1897–1938," *Journal of African History* 40, no. 4 (1999): 433–46.

8. Richard Pankhurst, "The History of the Bareya, Sanqella and Other Ethiopian Slaves from the Borderlands of the Sudan," *Sudan Notes and Records* 63 (1977). See also Donald Levine, *Greater Ethiopia: The Evolution of a Multiethnic Society* (Chicago: University of Chicago Press, 1974), 56.

9. Donald Donham, "Old Abyssinia and the New Ethiopian Empire: Themes in Social History," in *The Southern Marches of Imperial Ethiopia: Essays in History and Social Anthropology,* ed. Donald Donham and Wendy James (Cambridge: Cambridge University Press, 1986), 12–13; Teshale Tibebu, *The Making of Modern Ethiopia* (Lawrenceville, NJ: Red Sea, 1995), 60.

10. P. T. W. Baxter, "The Creation and Constitution of Oromo Nationality," in *Ethnicity and Conflict in the Horn of Africa,* ed. Katsuyoshi Fukui and John Markakis (London: James Currey, 1994), 173.

11. Kebede, "Gender Relations," 59; Almaz Eshete, "Issues of Gender and Sexuality in the Context of Cross-Cultural Dynamics of Ethiopia—Challenging Traditional Pervasives," in Fukui, Kurimoto, and Shigeta, *Ethiopia in Broader Perspective,* 1:570–72; Helen Pankhurst, *Gender, Development and Identity: An Ethiopian Study* (London: Zed Books, 1992), 129–32.

12. Donald Levine, *Wax and Gold: Tradition and Innovation in Ethiopian Culture* (Chicago: University of Chicago Press, 1965), 79; Levine, *Greater Ethiopia,* 54–55.

13. Levine, *Greater Ethiopia,* 54.

14. Hirut Tefere, "Gender and Cross Cultural Dynamics in Ethiopia with Particular Reference to Property Rights, and the Role and Status of Women," in Fukui, Kurimoto, and Shigeta, *Ethiopia in Broader Perspective,* 3:541–68, esp. 555–56.

15. Ibid., 568.

16. Allan Hoben, *Land Tenure among the Amhara of Ethiopia: The Dynamics of Cognatic Descent* (Chicago: University of Chicago Press, 1973), 1–28; Dan Franz Bauer, *Household and Society in Ethiopia: An Economic and Social Analysis of Tigray Social Principles and Household Organization* (East Lansing: Michigan State University Press, 1977), 240–42; James McCann, *From Poverty to Famine in Northeast Ethiopia: A Rural History, 1900–1935* (Philadelphia: University of Pennsylvania Press, 1987), 51–52; James McCann, *People of the Plow: An Agricultural History of Ethiopia, 1800–1990* (Madison: University of Wisconsin Press, 1995), 73–74; H. Pankhurst, *Gender, Development,* 102–18; Yared Amare, "Women's Access to Resources in Amhara Households in Wogda, Northern Shewa," in Fukui, Kurimoto, and Shigeta, *Ethiopia in Broader Perspective,* 3:752–53.

17. Levine, *Greater Ethiopia,* 54; Teshale, *Making of Modern Ethiopia,* 58.

18. Teshale, *Making of Modern Ethiopia,* 58.

19. Levine, *Greater Ethiopia,* 54–55.

20. Donham, "Old Abyssinia," 12.

21. R. Pankhurst, "History of the Bareya," 42; Donham, "Old Abyssinia," 12; Teshale, *Making of Modern Ethiopia*, 59.

22. W. C. Harris, *The Highlands of Æthiopia*, 2nd ed., 3 vols. (London: Longman, Brown, Green, and Longmans, 1844), 1:234; J. L. Krapf, *Travels, Researches and Missionary Labours during an Eighteen Years' Residence in Eastern Africa* (London: Trübner and Co., 1860), 74–75; P. Mérab, *Impressions d'Éthiopie: L'Abyssinie sous Ménélik II*, 3 vols. (Paris: H. Libert, 1921–29), 1:367; Teshale, *Making of Modern Ethiopia*, 197.

23. Walter C. Plowden, *Travels in Abyssinia and the Galla Country: With an Account of a Mission to Ras Ali in 1848*, ed. Trevor Plowden (London: Longmans, Green, and Co., 1868), 44–48, 56, 380.

24. R. H. Kofi Darkwah, *Shewa, Menilek, and the Ethiopian Empire, 1813–1889* (London: Heinemann, 1975), 49–55,133–36, 174–75; Bairu Tafla, "Two Ethiopian Biographies: Wahni Azaj Walda Sadeq Abba Menzir, 1838–1909; Fitawrari Habte Giyorgis Abba Mechal, 1853–1926," *Journal of Ethiopian Studies* 6, no. 1 (1968).

25. Harris, *Highlands*, 2:60.

26. Richard Pankhurst, *A Social History of Ethiopia: The Northern and Central Highlands from Early Medieval Times to the Rise of Emperor Téwodros II* (Addis Ababa: Institute of Ethiopian Studies, Addis Ababa University, 1990), 111–12; Richard Pankhurst, "History of the Bareya," 22–23; Plowden, *Travels*, 56–57, 70; Harris, *Highlands*, 2:58, 178; Charles Johnston, *Travels in Southern Abyssinia: Through the Country of Adal to the Kingdom of Shoa*, 2 vols. (London: J. Madden and Co., 1844), 2:75–77; Krapf, *Travels*, 35–36; Antonio Cecchi, *Da Zeila alle frontiere del Caffa*, 3 vols. (Rome: E. Loescher, 1886), 2:152–53, 292, 437; L. Traversi, "Escursione nel Gimma," *Bollettino della Societa Geografica Italiana* 13 (1888): 914–15; Enrico Cerulli, *Etiopia occidentale* (Rome: Sindacato Italiano Arti Grafiche, 1932–33), 109–10; P. Soleillet, *Voyages en Éthiopie* (January 1882–October 1884) (Rouen: E. Cagniard, 1886), 192.

27. Jules Borelli, *Éthiopie méridionale: Journal de mon voyage aux pays Amhara, Oromo et Sidama, septembre 1885 à novembre 1888* (Paris: Librairies-imprimeries réunies, 1890), 323, 392.

28. G. Massaia, *I miei trentacinque anni di missione nell' Alta Etiopia*, trans. A. Lavery, 12 vols. (Milan, 1885–95; Addis Ababa: Institute of Ethiopian Studies, Addis Ababa University, 1975), 5:15–16, 54.

29. Girls aged six to thirteen made up 90 percent of a typical slave caravan leaving Shawa in April 1843. IOL/BSP/LG, 204, 1146, Harris, 14 April 1843, para. 2. See also Abir, *Ethiopia*, 58.

30. C. W. Isenberg and J. L. Krapf, *Journals of the Rev. Messrs. Isenberg and Krapf . . . in the Kingdom of Shoa* (London: Seeley, 1843), 120; Johnston, *Travels*, 2:74, 79–80; IOL/BSP/LG 196, 3491, Harris, Slave Report, 20 July 1842, para. 34; Harris, *Highlands*, 3:306.

31. M. Abir, "The Emergence and Consolidation of the Monarchies of Enarea and Jimma in the First Half of the Nineteenth Century," *Journal of African History* 6, no. 2 (1965): 214.

32. R. Pankhurst, *Economic History*, 76.

33. Cecchi, *Da Zeila*, 2:289; Borelli, *Éthiopie méridionale*, 339–40; Traversi, "Excursione," 902; Soleillet, *Voyages*, 169; Massaia, *Trentacinque anni*, 5:55–57; M. de Salviac, *Les Galla: Un peuple antique au pays de Ménélik* (Paris: H. Oudin, 1901), 314. See also Ernesta Cerulli, "People of South-West Ethiopia," in *Ethnographic Survey of Africa: North-Eastern Africa*, part 3, ed. D. Forde (London: International African Institute, 1956), 107; Eike Haberland, *Untersuchungen zum Äthiopischen Königtum* (Wiesbaden: F. Steiner, 1965), 266.

34. McCann, *People of the Plow*, 153, 164.

35. R. Pankhurst, *Economic History*, 75; A. Hodson, *Where Lion Reign: An Account of Lion Hunting and Exploration in S.W. Abyssinia* (London: Skeffington and Son, 1929), 25.

36. E. A. De Cosson, *The Cradle of the Blue Nile: A Visit to the Court of King John of Ethiopia*, 2 vols. (London: J. Murray, 1877), 2:7; W. Winstanley, *A Visit to Abyssinia: An Account of Travel in Modern Ethiopia*, 2 vols. (London: Hurst and Blackett, 1881), 2:196.

37. Johnston, *Travels*, 2:77–79.

38. Cecchi, *Da Zeila*, 2:292.

39. Herbert S. Lewis, *A Galla Monarch: Jimma Abba Jifar, Ethiopia, 1830–1932* (Madison: University of Wisconsin Press, 1965), 71.

40. Winstanley, *Visit*, 1:269, 2:77, 83.

41. Darkwah, *Shewa*, 167; Harris, Slave Report, paras. 31, 36; Harris, *Highlands*, 3:309. See also S. Ege, "Chiefs and Peasants in the Socio-Political Structure of Shawa about 1840" (MPhil thesis, University of Bergen, 1978), 57–58.

42. Johnston, *Travels*, 2:166, 200, 241.

43. Cecchi, *Da Zeila*, 2:292. See also Abir, *Ethiopia*, 83; Lewis, *Galla Monarchy*, 66.

44. Massaia, *Trentacinque anni*, 4:20, 222–24. See also Cecchi, *Da Zeila*, 2:292.

45. Timothy Fernyhough, "Slavery and the Slave Trade in Southern Ethiopia: An Historical Overview, ca. 1800–1935," in *New Trends in Ethiopian Studies*, vol. 1, Humanities and Human Resources, ed. H. Marcus (Lawrenceville NJ: Red Sea, 1994), 681–8; Fernyhough, "Slavery and the Slave Trade in Southern Ethiopia in the Nineteenth Century," *Slavery and Abolition* 9, no. 3 (1988): 105–6.

46. McCann, *People of the Plow*, 161–62.

47. Cecchi, *Da Zeila*, 2:492; Massaia, *Trentacinque anni*, 5:56. See also W. J. Lange, *History of the Southern Gonga* (Wiesbaden: Steiner, 1982), 268–69; A. Orent, "Refocusing on the History of Kaffa prior to 1897: A Discussion of Political Process," *African Historical Studies* 3, no. 2 (1970): 283.

48. Mohammed Hassen, *The Oromo of Ethiopia: A History, 1570–1860* (Cambridge: Cambridge University Press, 1990), 129.

49. Ibid., 122–24; Lewis, *Galla Monarchy*, 66–67; Tekalign, "Slave Trade," 15–17.

50. Cecchi, *Da Zeila*, 2:462.

51. Lewis, *Galla Monarchy*, 98; Hassen, *Oromo*, 170.

52. Harris, Slave Report, para. 30; Ege, "Chiefs and Peasants," 57. See also R. Pankhurst, *Economic History*, 77, 80. By the nineteenth century much of the Fetha Nagast was obsolete.

53. R. Pankhurst, *Economic History*, 82.

54. Massaia, *Trentacinque anni*, 3:209; Cecchi, *Da Zeila*, 2:273, 292.

55. Harris, Slave Report, para. 29; Cecchi, *Da Zeila*, 2:274.

56. Cecchi, *Da Zeila*, 2:275–76.

57. Lewis, *Galla Monarchy*, 113; Cecchi, *Da Zeila*, 2:162–63; Hassen, *Oromo*, 169–70.

58. T. Waldmeier, *The Autobiography of Theophilus Waldmeier, Missionary* (London: S. W. Partridge, 1886), 37; Harris, Slave Report, paras. 36–38; Harris, *Highlands*, 3:310.

59. Harris, Slave Report, para. 32; Plowden, *Travels*, 308; Lewis, *Galla Monarchy*, 67. See also Hassen, *Oromo*, 125.

60. Johnston, *Travels*, 2:166, 176, 241.

61. Massaia, *Trentacinque anni*, 4:14.

62. Borelli, *Éthiopie méridionale*, 289.

63. Hassen, *Oromo*, 128.

64. C. T. Beke, "Abyssinia—Being a Continuation of Routes in that Country," *Journal of the Royal Geographical Society* 14 (1844): 20; Harris, Slave Report, paras. 21, 24; IOL/BSP/LG 204, 1146, Harris, 14 April 1848, para. 4; Harris, *Highlands*, 1:223–24, 234–35, 3:307; R. Pankhurst, *Economic History*, 90–92; Abir, *Ethiopia*, 58–60; IOL/BSP/LG 185, 1440, Barker; J. M. Bernatz, *Scenes in Ethiopia* (London: Bradbury and Evans, 1852), plates 8, 9.

65. E. Combes and M. Tamisier, *Voyage en Abyssinie dans les pays des Gallas de Choa et d'Ifat, 1835–1837*, 4 vols. (Paris: L. Desessart, 1838), 4:95–96.

66. IOL/BSP/LG 192, Kemball to Robertson, 8 July 1842, para. 2; IOL/BSP, Range Series, 387, vol. 10, 660, Wilson, 28 January 1831, para. 9.

67. R. Pankhurst, *Social History*, 246.

68. Cecchi, *Da Zeila*, 2:195; P. Mateucci, *In Abissinia* (Milan, 1880), 274–76; Massaia, *Trentacinque anni*, 2:126–27, 176–77.

69. Cosson, *Cradle of the Blue Nile*, 2:169–70.

70. Harris, *Highlands*, 2:192–95, 202–3, 3:374–75.

71. Timothy Fernyhough, "Serfs, Slaves, and Shefta: Modes of Production in Southern Ethiopia from the late Nineteenth Century to 1941" (PhD diss., University of Illinois, Urbana-Champaign, 1986), 183–91.

72. Cecchi, *Da Zeila*, 2:538–39; Soleillet, *Voyages*, 311 13; Harold G. Marcus, *The Life and Times of Menelik II, Ethiopia, 1844–1913* (Oxford: Clarendon, 1975; Lawrenceville, NJ: Red Sea, 1995), 73.

73. FO 403/430, 52, Thesiger to Grey, Addis Ababa, 29 August 1912; Hodson, *Where Lion Reign*, 26; Mérab, *Impressions*, vol. 2, 260–61; Gabra Sellase [Guèbrè Sellassié], *Chronique du règne de Ménélik II, roi des rois d'Éthiopie* (Paris: Librairie Orientale et Américaine, 1930, 1932), 2:625; W. J. Lange, "Gimira (Remnants of a Vanishing Culture)" (PhD thesis, Johann Wolfgang Goethe-Universität zu Frankfurt am Main, 1975), 171.

74. Cecchi, *Da Zeila*, 2:292, 517.

75. Massaia, *Trentacinque anni*, 2:176–77.

76. James Bruce, *Travels to Discover the Source of the Nile*, 5 vols. (Edinburgh: J. Ruthven, for G. G. J. and J. Robinson, London, 1790), 3:91; Plowden, *Travels*, 369; S. Gobat, *Journal of a Three Years' Residence in Abyssinia* (1834, 1851; repr., New York: Negro Universities Press, 1969), 39. See also Mansfield Parkyns, *Life in Abyssinia: Being Notes collected during a Three Years' Residence and Travels in that Country* (London: J. Murray, 1868), 364; Beke, "Abyssinia," 8–9. For kidnapping in Hamasen, see Plowden, *Travels*, 24; Nathaniel Pearce, *Life and Adventures of Nathaniel Pearce*, 2 vols. (London: Henry Colburn and Richard Bentley, 1831), 2:52–53, 150.

77. Harris, *Highlands*, 3:319–20; Isenberg and Krapf, *Journals*, 179–80.

78. Soleillet, *Voyages*, 159–60; Borelli, *Éthiopie méridionale*, 331–32; Krapf, *Travels*, 46; Combes and Tamisier, *Voyage*, 4:97–98.

79. Massaia, *Trentacinque anni*, 1:173.

80. Parkyns, *Life in Abyssinia*, 364–36.

81. Massaia, *Trentacinque anni*, 4:80–83.

82. Johnston, *Travels*, 2:158–61; Harris, *Highlands*, 3:296–98; P. Picard, *Les missions catholiques* 23 (1891): 230, 24 (1892): 438.

83. Combes and Tamisier, *Voyage*, 4:98; Harris, *Highlands*, 3:71.

84. Massaia, *Trentacinque anni*, 5:56.

85. Harris, *Highlands*, 3:318–20; Krapf, *Travels*, 46, 69; Johnston, *Travels*, 2:446.

86. R. Pankhurst, *Economic History*, 84–87; Abir, *Ethiopia*, 57, 59; Fernyhough, "Slavery in the Nineteenth Century," 104–5, 113–14, 119–22; A. Moore-Harell, "Economic and Political Aspects of the Slave Trade in Ethiopia and the Sudan in the Second Half of the Nineteenth Century," *International Journal of African Historical Studies* 32, nos. 2–3 (1999): 415–16.

87. Harris, *Highlands*, 3:303–8; Bernatz, *Scenes*, plates 3, 24; Krapf, *Travels*, 50–53, 74; Harris, Slave Report, paras. 21, 25; IOL/BSP/LG 189, 2060G, Report on Trade, para., 42. See also R. Pankhurst, *Economic History*, 85.

88. C. T. Beke, "A Memoir on the Market of Baso," in *Letters on the Commerce and Politics of Abessinia and other Parts of Eastern Africa* (London: private, 1852), 22.

89. Moore-Harell, "Aspects of the Slave Trade," 415; H. Salt, *A Voyage to Abyssinia and Travels* . . . (London: F. C. and J. Rivington, 1814), 311; Combes and Tamisier, *Voyage*, 4:93; Bernatz, *Scenes*, plate 3; Krapf, *Travels*, 74; IOL/BSP/LG 192, 2762, Kemball to Robertson, 8 July 1842, para. 2.

90. Fernyhough, "Slavery in the Nineteenth Century," 113.

91. Beke, "Market at Baso," 22.

92. Abdussamad Ahmad, "Trading in Slaves in Bela-Shangul and Gumuz, Ethiopia: Border Enclaves in History, 1897–1938," *Journal of African History* 40 (1999): 98.

93. Cecchi, *Da Zeila*, 1:490, 2:60.

94. Harris, *Highlands*, 3:76; Beke, "Abyssinia," 86–87; Bernatz, *Scenes*, plate 24; Isenberg and Krapf, *Journals*, 217, 257.

95. Fernyhough, "Slavery in the Nineteenth Century," 123; Moore-Harell, "Aspects of the Slave Trade," 414.

96. Cecchi, *Da Zeila*, 2:194–95; Borelli, *Éthiopie méridionale*, 289.

97. Mateucci, *Abissinia*, 274–79.

98. Fernyhough, "Slavery in the Nineteenth Century," 109–11.

99. Combes and Tamisier, *Voyage*, 4:92; Soleillet, *Voyages*, 167; Cecchi, *Da Zeila*, 2:517–18, Salviac, *Galla*, 256.

100. Fernyhough, "Slavery and the Slave Trade, 1800–1935," 686; Fernyhough, "Slavery in the Nineteenth Century," 14.

101. Almaz, "Issues of Gender," 570.

102. "This is what serves to buy children and men." Combes and Tamisier, *Voyage*, 4:192.

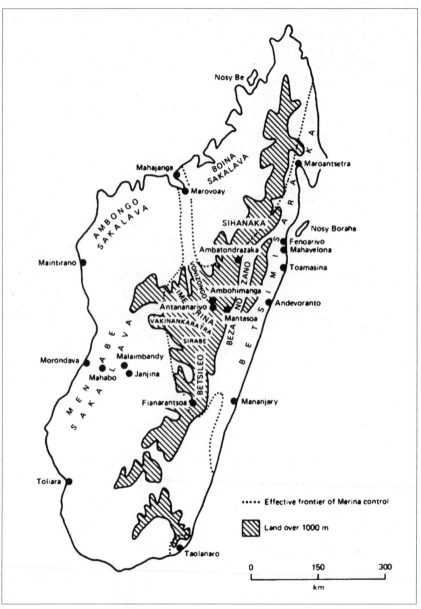

The Merina empire, Madagascar, ca. 1830. Reprinted from Gwyn Campbell, "Slavery and Fanompoana: The Structure of Forced Labour in Imerina (Madagascar), 1790–1861," *Journal of African History* 29, no. 3 (1988): 464, with the permission of Cambridge University Press.

10

FEMALE BONDAGE IN
IMPERIAL MADAGASCAR, 1820–95

GWYN CAMPBELL

THE FEMALE ROLE IN THE TRADITIONAL ECONOMY

In Imperial Madagascar (ca. 1795–1895), as in most of the preindustrial world, labor was the critical factor of production. Skilled male labor was relatively scarce and valuable. Most men were unskilled, valued primarily for their concentrated bursts of strength. By contrast, women could sustain physical activity at lower concentrations of energy over longer periods and were more easily constrained than men. Control over women was thus vital in preindustrial societies, particularly in regions such as Africa where high land-labor ratios tended to lead to diffused settlements of low population densities.

Women played vital roles in the traditional Malagasy economy, which was characterized by a marked sexual division of labor. They were active in riziculture, which dominated the eastern littoral and central highlands, while in the mainly pastoral regions of the south and west they were largely responsible for growing other staple crops: maize, millet, haricot beans, coconut palms, manioc, and saonjo (an edible arum).[1] Again, women were chiefly responsible for the manufacture of cloth, mats, baskets, and pottery.[2] Women also participated in local, long-distance, and foreign trade. Most Western merchants required agents familiar with Malagasy dialects and customs, and women provided many of these services, as well as acting as local sexual companions. Smaller traders unable to afford experienced Creole or European agents took advantage of the custom of Malagasy parents offering their daughters to foreigners to fulfill their sexual and other needs.[3] The girl gained a higher standard of living, enhanced status, and, with greater commercial and linguistic expertise, the prospect of regular "employment" with a wealthy merchant.[4] Such contractual relationships were also commonly sought by indigenous long-distance traders who, however, "married" both adult and infant females along their trading routes, for the familial bonds of trust and mutual assistance that such alliances engendered were as important, if not more so, than their spouses' personal commercial skills.[5] From the 1860s women also served in cheap wayside "restaurants" that developed to cater for itinerant traders and porters.[6]

Slavery was a traditional institution in most Malagasy societies, slave women being in demand for productive (agriculture and crafts) purposes, as household servants, for sexual services, and, in elite families, as status symbols. Until the rapid development of slave imports from the adjacent Mozambican mainland in the nineteenth century, the vast majority of such slaves were the products of local warfare or raids carried out by one Malagasy ethnic community against another. The Sakalava of the western side of the island, for most of the seventeenth and eighteenth centuries the most feared slave raiders, were replaced from the end of the eighteenth century by the Merina of the high central plateau, who, after achieving political unity under Andrianampoinimerina in about 1795, engaged in a series of wars of imperial expansion in which they enslaved thousands of highlanders (mostly Betsileo) and lowlanders (notably agriculturalists from the southeast of the island, but also significant numbers of Bara and Sakalava pastoralists from the south and west). Initially these armies enslaved both male and female captives, retaining some in Imerina and selling others to foreign merchants for shipment to the Mascarene Islands to the east, where a burgeoning French sugar plantation sector had established a huge demand for servile labor, mostly male. By the 1810s domestic slavery had become so widespread in the highlands that it freed many slave-owning Merina from productive activity. This process accelerated following the 1820 Merina ban on slave exports, after which domestic slave markets were so glutted with men that, fearing a revolt, the court instructed that in the future all males captured in military campaigns be executed.[7]

THE GROWTH OF BONDED FEMALE LABOR IN IMPERIAL MADAGASCAR, 1820–95

Following the ban on slave exports in 1820, and the adoption from the mid 1820s of autarkic policies based on labor-intensive agricultural and industrial production, Merina state and elite demand for the servile labor of both sexes increased dramatically. That demand was met through a large increase in the enslavement of non-Merina Malagasy and dramatically increased slave imports from mainland Africa, as well as through a reconstituted and enormously expanded system of *fanompoana* (unremunerated forced labor; in effect, state corvée). Both slavery and fanompoana involved harsh and exploitative labor and both engaged large numbers of females.

ENSLAVEMENT

In the nineteenth century the total Malagasy population probably fluctuated between 2 and 3 million, while that of Imerina grew from approximately 100,000 to 500,000 in the 1820s, at which general level it remained until the late 1870s, when it increased again to about 800,000. The population of Antananarivo, the Merina capital, rose from about 17,000 in 1820 to 50,000 in 1860, and in the subsequent decade reached 100,000, a level around which it hovered despite sharp short-term fluctuations. Imerina received approximately 120,000 non-Merina captives enslaved in military expeditions from 1816 to 1863, after which imperial slave raiding virtually ceased. Slave imports into Madagascar from East Africa from 1821 to 1895 are estimated at about 400,000.[8] As relatively small numbers of Merina migrated permanently to nonplateau regions, it is likely that in total Imerina gained about 250,000 forced immigrants up to 1850, notably between 1823 and 1837, and about 112,500 between 1850 and 1895.

Most of the enslaved were female.[9] For example, it was commented of the return in 1830 of an expedition against the Bara, "The army came home from the South last week and brought a great deal of *baba* [*babo*, booty or captives] with them. It was [sic] affecting scene to see about 800 persons (chiefly women with little ones) ascending up to Town [Antananarivo] tied one to another, and carrying a very heavy loads [sic] on their heads, their child on their back and many of them leading one or two children in their hands."[10]

Again, in 1832, the Merina army slaughtered 8,000 men and enslaved 20,000 women and children in Ikongo, on the southeastern edge of the plateau. In 1832 they pushed further south, again enslaving mainly females, and in 1836 they enslaved a further 9,000 Betsileo women and children.[11] From 1832 to 1838 some 50,000 women and children were enslaved in the southeast of the island.[12] Most were retained by the Merina elite in central Imerina, notably Antananarivo, where together with African slaves they formed two-thirds of the population.[13]

Females also constituted the majority of imported Africans retained as slaves in Madagascar. Most originated from the Shire region of Malawi.[14] As the 1820 slave export ban entailed a progressive impoverishment for ordinary Merina, many were obliged to sell or pawn the slaves they had acquired: by 1869 at least one third of "free" Merina owned no slaves. Most were held by the Merina state and elite.[15] In Imerina the average price of a slave doubled, from around $30 in 1860 to $62 in the early 1870s, and by mid-century a skilled or beautiful female slave could command a price of up to $100.[16]

Imerina elite families employed female slaves chiefly in riziculture, water carrying, spinning, weaving, and washing clothes, as household servants and concubines.[17] Some were also incorporated into the state's attempt to forge an industrial revolution and in construction: in the 1860s building boom the court elite drafted female slaves to transport earth in baskets, while one hundred royal slaves carried water, used to prepare mortar, from a pond near the top of the ridge on which Antananarivo was situated. Of the latter, William Ellis commented, "About once every hour, for two or three days, I saw them pass in unbroken [sic] single line, each woman with a jar of water on her head."[18]

As elsewhere, excepting the United States and possibly West Africa,[19] the slave population in Madagascar experienced a high mortality rate and low birthrates and thus failed to reproduce itself, despite comprising mainly women. First, African slaves imported with them deadly diseases, as was the case with the 1888 smallpox outbreak in Maintirano.[20] In addition, slaves were the greatest victims of the tangena, a poison ordeal used until 1861 as a chief judicial means of determining guilt, notably in cases of suspected witchcraft and sorcery. Christopher Wrigley considers witch manias to be a reflection of the rage of a male-dominated power structure against women and procreation, and therefore a device to limit population growth,[21] although in Madagascar the persecution mania was applied to males (sorcerers) as well as to females (witches).[22] In his turn, Patrick Manning considers the resurgence of witchcraft accusations and executions to be an "example of both the declining value of humans and the psychic pressures on societies facing conquest."[23] Many tangena victims were accused of undermining Merina sovereignty and promoting European interests in Madagascar,[24] but this was not true of slaves, its major victims. Should misfortune befall a master, there was cause for suspicion. Thus, when Andriantsovatra, Ranavalona I's niece, died of whooping cough, large numbers of her slaves—including many women—were accused of witchcraft and, on being administered the tangena, died. In 1854 it was estimated that slaves who had served Ranavalona I since the commencement of her reign in 1828 had endured at least seven such ordeals.[25] Given the high proportion of women among slaves in Imerina, the tangena must have affected chiefly females.

David Griffiths claimed an average fatality rate of 33 to 50 percent from *tangena*[26] which, it is estimated, killed an annual average of one thousand people in the early 1820s, rising to three thousand deaths each year between 1828 and 1861. However, fatalities from the ordeal in individual cases and years could be much greater; in 1838 it killed an estimated 20 percent of Imerina's population (possibly one hundred thousand people) and 85 percent of the 163 Tantsaha subjected to the ordeal in one case in 1853. If three-quarters of the victims were slaves, tangena ordeals would have each year killed between about 1 and 4.5 percent of Imerina's slave population—again, mostly females. Although officially abolished in 1863, the tangena ordeal continued to be practiced secretly in some Merina regions and openly elsewhere in the island.[27]

In addition, female slaves experienced low rates of reproduction. First, they were sexually isolated, due to a sharp sexual division of slave labor and, contrary to most of tropical Africa, rigid caste prohibitions against sexual relations between slaves and "free" subjects. Thus in December 1855 Ranavalona I had a slave girl stoned to death for sleeping with a "Mozambique" slave.[28] Some free Merina males and females took slaves in "concubinage," but the incentive for the woman to procreate in such liaisons was limited, as resultant offspring were ascribed slave status, while after death a women slave's property passed to the owner, not to any children she might have.[29] Also, sexual unions between slaves could not gain the legitimacy of a marriage contract and were thus inherently unstable, a popular saying concerning slaves being, "It's not their concern to get married for they could be separated the very same day" (*Hivady tsy toinana, ary hisaraka anio hiany*).[30] Such vulnerabilities inevitably limited slave reproduction, slaves sometimes preferring to invest in slaves of their own rather than in children.[31] Indeed, it is probable that female slaves in Madagascar, as on neighboring Mauritius, induced abortions and practiced infanticide.[32]

In all, contrary to Maurice Bloch's claim that slave numbers increased steadily from the 1820s to reach 50 percent of the population by the late nineteenth century, the increase leveled off from the mid-1830s. By then probably about one-third of Imerina's population, rising to two-thirds in

Antananarivo, were slaves. Of the half million slaves liberated in 1896, 43.6 percent lived in Imerina, where they formed 20 to 26 percent of the population, half the unsubstantiated figure claimed by Bloch.[33]

Moreover, the enslavement of women was not a one-way flow of non-Merina into Imerina. Merina military campaigns slackened from 1838 and virtually ceased from 1852, as Merina military power waned. Military weakness permitted Sakalava, Bara, and increasingly also fugitive bands of highland refugees from Merina rule to raid the plateau for captives, chiefly females aged fourteen to thirty.[34] These raids reflected the greater ease of kidnapping women and children—as men tended both to resist capture and, once enslaved, to seek to escape—and demand for females in markets throughout the western Indian Ocean. The loss of the female captives exported would have reduced the birthrate in the remaining population, thus heightening labor shortages and the demand for further slave imports, and also further impoverishing the traditional agricultural sector.[35]

Until 1861, Sakalava bands regularly penetrated central Imerina, venturing as far as the periphery of Antananarivo, capturing mainly women and children and driving off cattle. If threatened by Merina soldiers, they killed their captives and fled. Such raids diminished during the 1860s but resumed from the 1870s, notably under the Menabe king Itoera, who boasted an army of ten thousand men equipped with foreign arms. Similarly, bands of runaway slaves and army deserters in the northeastern forests raided eastern Vonizongo and Imerina, again killing males and enslaving women and children.[36] The Bemihimpa, a large brigand community comprising Sakalava and refugee highlanders, also regularly raided the plateau for women, children, and cattle.[37] The Sakalava sold many plateau captives to foreign merchants on the coast. Whereas most male slaves exported from Madagascar originated from west-coast societies or Mozambique and passed via west-coast entrepôts to the French Mascarenes plantation islands, most female slaves exported were of highland origin. Demand for female slaves was greatest in the Muslim Comoros, though some were probably exported to the Swahili coast and to the Red Sea and Persian Gulf. For West Africa, Joseph E. Inikori estimates a 33:67 male-to-female ratio in the slaves exported to Muslim countries and 60:40 to the New World.[38] This same contrast may have been mirrored in the distinct Malagasy trades to Muslim and French markets. However, the Sakalava also retained a proportion of enslaved plateau females as agricultural workers, domestic servants, and concubines: a slave woman could be worked for the prime years of her life and subsequently still, due to price differentials, fetch a high price from the French or Merina.[39]

FANOMPOANA

While slave labor was significant to the imperial Merina economy, fanompoana was of greater importance to the state and Merina elite. Initially associated with honorable, male ritual prestations to the sovereign, fanompoana was progressively expanded to include labor for public works by free subjects organized into geographically fixed groupings termed *foko*. Internally, caste ascriptions, focusing on the cult of the ancestors, ensured a high degree of endogamy. Externally the foko structure was forcibly maintained by the top Andriana caste, which thus ensured royal control over scarce manpower resources essential to labor-intensive riziculture.[40] While fanompoana was not slavery, it became characterized in the nineteenth century by such extreme forms of servile labor that it could be termed "virtual slavery."[41]

Fanompoana was intensified in the mid-1820s following the adoption of autarky by the Merina state, which aspired to promote industrial self-sufficiency, notably in textiles and armaments. Thereafter the Merina court aimed to conquer the entire island militarily and generate economic growth through exploitation of its resources. As attempts to stimulate "legitimate" exports failed, and foreign investment remained negligible, the court reoriented its bid for military and economic power toward forced labor. Henceforth, fanompoana was applied universally.[42] In the early 1820s, Radama I formed fanompoana units of from ten to one thousand individuals on a territorial caste basis. He also adapted European institutions, notably the school and army, to recruit and organize fanompoana labor. Until the expulsion of the London Missionary Society (LMS) in 1835–36, its schools became contributors to fanompoana training, used to give Merina youth basic literacy.[43] As the missionaries later remarked: "The number of scholars is fixed by the Government and is an affair over which we have no control. The Government also regulates the Stations, the towns, the villages, the proportions to be presented by the different classes of people, the proportion of Males and females [generally in the ratio 2:1] &c. The Government also provides the School Rooms and makes the very duties of the Teacher a Government service."[44]

Fanompoana initially affected mostly males, drawn into the army and factories, but increasingly it also involved females. Import substitution was first achieved in luxury cloth; in 1824, a factory was established where forty to fifty females from the missionary sewing groups produced European-style overcoats of twilled calico and bordered woolen cloth as well as gowns, trousers, shirts, and kerchiefs, all of which sold well in the mission shop that operated in Antananarivo from 1825 to 1829. These women possibly formed the core of a later group of seamstresses, one of a number of skilled fanompoana units described as "a sort of Government slaves" confined to their villages and occupations for life.[45] In arms production, women were drafted into porterage of raw materials. From the 1830s the daily collection and carriage of urine (for ammonia) for the Ilafy powder works fell to the villagers of Namehana, near Antananarivo, while a female fanompoana unit from Antananarivo collected and carried offal (again probably for ammonia) to the Analakely gunpowder factory. In addition, "free" women often accompanied and cooked for their unsalaried menfolk drafted into construction work, which also involved female fanompoana.[46]

By 1855, fanompoana had drafted and relocated most of the entire "free" Merina population, including women. As a result large tracts of Imerina became depopulated, except for slaves, most of them owned by members of the Merina court. Fanompoana relaxed in the 1860s, when Imerina, which opened up after 1861 to foreign trade and investment, experienced a decade of relative prosperity. However, in the 1870s economic growth slowed and the crown reasserted control over the island's labor resources, much to the chagrin of foreigners, some of whom could access labor only through liaisons with local women in whose names they purchased slave labor.[47]

To streamline labor conscription the imperial court resurrected the idea, employed from 1820 to 1836, of using missionary structures to recruit fanompoana. In 1869 the crown created a state church that, from the outbreak of the first Franco-Merina War in 1883, used mission churches and schools specifically to recruit fanompoana, with missionary and other state church agents playing increasingly significant administrative roles both in drawing up fanompoana quotas and in overseeing fanompoana units.[48]

The impact of this state-church fanompoana was probably far greater on females than males, due to the tendency of younger adult males to be drafted into the imperial army or to flee conscription.[49] From 1869 Protestant missionaries, henceforth de facto state officials, summoned fanompoana labor, notably to erect churches and chapels to cope with the largely compulsory mass conversion to the state church.[50] Circumspect in their use of forced labor in Antananarivo and its immediate

vicinity because of the growing publicity that Imerina received in abolitionist Christian circles in Europe, missionaries used fanompoana labor
chiefly in the remoter towns and chief villages in the Merina countryside
and the imperial provinces, where the building of church property became referred to ironically as *ny fanompoany an'Andtr* (fanompoana for
God).[51] Moreover, after 1862 the LMS was joined in Madagascar by a
number of other nonconformist and by Roman Catholic missionary
agencies. From 1869 to 1870, the number of LMS congregations in Imerina increased from 148 to 621, and their schools from 28 to 359, while
between 1870 and 1880, seven hundred LMS state churches were erected.
The 1879 Reform and the 1881 Code enforcing school attendance further spurred mission construction, as thereafter schools were built separate from chapels, and denominational rivalry grew fierce. By 1880 the
LMS claimed 1,024 chapels and 862 schools; by 1881, in which year it
was reported that the LMS and Roman Catholics were erecting rival
chapels in every village in the Ambohimandroso district of Imerina, the
Jesuits boasted 228 mission stations, 144 chapels, and 170 schools.[52] Most
communities were pressured into constructing and maintaining at least
two rival Christian denominational establishments. Although men were
responsible for the transport of building materials, particularly timber,
women and children assisted them in porterage and were heavily involved in other aspects of church construction:

> In building a church in Madagascar, the people not only give a
> donation of money, but they also do much of the work . . . with
> their own hands . . . the ground is levelled, and the foundation
> prepared, by the congregation, who make an appointment for a
> certain morning, when the men, women, and children come in a
> body with spades and baskets and do the necessary work. An esti
> mate is also often made of the number of bricks which will be re·
> quired, and then a division is arranged . . . according to social po
> sition occupied, or the supposed ability to furnish the number. . . .
> In the case of the tiles with which our church at Fianarantsoa is
> covered, the men, women, and children voluntarily carried the
> 24,000 tiles from the place where they were made and burnt to
> the building, a distance of more than a mile, and involving hun
> dreds of journeys to and fro, and up and down a rather steep hill.[53]

A similarly demanding aspect of the intense missionary rivalry was the
purchase of European clothes, which the poor could ill afford, and the

observation of Christian *fady* (taboos): in preparation for a nonworking Sabbath, women were obliged to spend most of Saturday washing clothes, bathing the family, and dressing hair.[54]

However, the impact of state-church fanompoana on women was probably most severe late in the nineteenth century as, in the wake of the 1883–85 war, the economic straits of the regime grew more desperate. Females were, for example, widely used in crown goldfields, where labor conditions were generally harsher than most other forms of fanompoana. As most workings were alluvial, gold fanompoana was generally drawn on a seasonal basis from mission chapels and schools. From at least 1887 in Mananadona region (North Betsileo), a four-hundred-strong gold fanompoana draft was imposed on Norwegian Missionary Society (NMS) churches: men excavated river beds and women removed and washed the soil for its gold content. In addition, children of both sexes were drafted for the first time.[55]

Fanompoana had a major demographic impact. Whereas before the 1820s it is probable that the birthrate in the free population of Madagascar equaled if not surpassed the average of forty-eight per thousand postulated for precolonial sub-Saharan Africa generally,[56] fertility rates were profoundly diminished from the mid-1820s by the autarkic policies of the state, especially fanompoana. First, fanompoana was unremunerated. Thus, in contrast to the proto-industrialization era in Europe, where the advent of wage labor might have lowered the average age of marriage and thus enhanced natality, in Madagascar it decreased income opportunities for young adults—which probably resulted in a rise in the average age of marriage and consequently decreased the number of children that women bore. The only significant body of wage earners were slave porters, who were men predominantly young and unattached.[57] Gavin Kitching argues that in Africa, in contrast to Europe, responsibility for child rearing rested with the extended rather than with the nuclear family, so that parental income may not have influenced family size to a degree parallel to Europe,[58] but in Imperial Madagascar such was the scale of fanompoana that the ability of the extended family to sustain its own members, notably the very young and old, was steadily undermined.[59]

Second, fanompoana involved long periods of harsh physical labor and inadequate rations, which in women delayed puberty and altered ovulatory cycles, which in turn depressed fertility and increased the incidence of miscarriages.[60] From the 1820s, as ownership of slaves narrowed to elite circles and ordinary Merina farmers were conscripted for military and other fanompoana, plateau women were obliged to fulfill agricultural tasks normally executed by males, supplemented by enslaved females in the brief period of relative prosperity during the 1860s and 1870s. However, from the early 1880s nonelite slave ownership again dropped, while the exploitation of female labor for fanompoana increased steadily, peaking after the 1883–85 Franco-Merina War, notably in the goldfields.[61] Third, the frequency of conception was reduced as fanompoana often separated husband and wife for long periods and, in the case of wives of absent soldiers, draconian punishments effectively restricted adultery.[62]

State labor policies also indirectly assisted the spread of venereal diseases, which further lowered fertility and contributed to miscarriages. In 1865 an estimated 10 percent of clinic patients in Antananarivo had syphilis, and a decade later 70 percent of LMS dispensary patients in Imerina, 20 percent in Betsileo, and most in Menabe reportedly suffered from syphilis-related complaints.[63] The early French colonial administration considered venereal diseases to be responsible for the large number of stillbirths in Madagascar.[64] However, it is impossible in early medical reports to distinguish between cases of venereal disease and farasisa—the Malagasy term for all chronic diseases with cutaneous symptoms.[65] Nevertheless the venereal variety probably spread rapidly in the late nineteenth century, due chiefly to the increased tempo of fanompoana from the late 1870s, which, as in the rubber system in the Congo, seriously disrupted social life, causing the disintegration of families, undermining monogamy, and promoting promiscuity and prostitution, as desperate women infected with venereal diseases circulated widely in both a geographical and a social sense.[66] By the late nineteenth century such was the barrenness of plateau women that many made votive offerings to phallic-shaped standing stones in an attempt to regain their fertility;[67] numerous taboos also emerged in nonplateau regions to restore their ability to conceive and to enhance the chances of a successful birth.[68]

Early French colonial surveys between 1899 and 1905 indicate that Imerina, despite having the best medical and administrative services in the island, had the lowest rates of fertility and the highest rates of infant mortality.[69] The resulting drop in reproduction skewed the demographic age profile for the area toward an older population. In 1853, for example, Ellis estimated that the average number of children per household was 3.5 on the east coast, compared to 2.5 in Imerina,[70] figures lower than the average estimated for sub-Saharan Africa in general (4.9 and 5.25 children per household during precolonial and recent times, respectively). In early colonial Madagascar 24.0 percent of the coastal population and 37.1 percent of the plateau population were less than sixteen years old—

compared to an African average closer to 55 percent. In overall terms, low rates of fertility, birth, and infant survival meant that the reproduction rate on the plateau was just sufficient to enable the region to maintain or possibly permit a slight natural increase in population.[71] This indubitably increased the demand in Imerina for slaves.

Fanompoana also raised the general rate of mortality. Whereas in 1826, at the start of autarky, a British visitor claimed that most Merina survived past their eightieth year,[72] the bulk of evidence points to a low life expectancy from birth in nineteenth-century Madagascar, and a correspondingly high death rate.[73] First, as in continental East Africa, the incidence of disease in Madagascar soared from the mid-nineteenth century. This morbidity was due partly to increased communications, facilitating the international exchange of viruses, and partly to climatic changes, notably from 1884 to 1894, when precipitation dramatically increased.[74] However, the high incidence of disease in Madagascar was also directly influenced by its harsh labor regime. This influence was evident with malaria, the major killer disease in the traditionally malaria-free highlands, where the population possessed neither acquired resistance nor genetic defense against malaria. Thus increasing numbers of highlanders who, due to Merina expansionism, traveled to coastal regions from 1817 proved almost as vulnerable as Europeans to the disease. An estimated 25 to 50 percent of Merina soldiers (all fanompoana-ed) in lowland provinces—and the wives or slave concubines who accompanied them—died each year, mostly of malaria.[75] Also, from around mid-century, malarial cases increased markedly on the plateau due to the mass circulation of forced-labor units that included women—officially or unofficially—between the plateau and malarial lowland areas and to the progressive abandonment from the 1870s, due to fanompoana drafts or flight from fanompoana, of large stretches of the irrigated riziculture network that subsequently became malarial breeding grounds.[76] The incidence of malaria and similar unspecified diseases increased sharply from 1884 to 1894 during a decade of unusually wet weather—often associated with malarial infection, which in 1895 caused mortality reported at near 25 percent.[77] Indeed, by 1905 the only highland region free from malaria was Antsirabe.[78] Malaria had less devastating effects on lowland peoples and on slaves from Africa, many of whom carried the sickle cell, although a pregnant woman's acquired resistance to malaria decreases with the length of her pregnancy, heightening the risk of anemia, which was a frequent cause of neonatal death.

The incidence of all diseases increased dramatically with stress, malnourishment, and extreme fatigue, all common under fanompoana, which upset the internal physiological balance and permitted low-grade infections to become fatal. Morbidity was further accentuated by the rapid rise in alcohol consumption from the 1870s.[79] Unlike the fishing, pastoral, and swidden (slash-and-burn) economies of lowland regions, the highly sophisticated and labor-intensive system of hydraulic riziculture on the plateau required production units of a certain minimum size to ensure its viability. Mortality from diseases, although granaries might help withstand short term dearth, rendered that system increasingly untenable from the late 1870s through being deprived of sufficient labor.[80] As noted, especially significant on the plateau was the large scale drafting of women, the backbone of the agricultural labor force, into state goldfields from the early 1880s.

Warfare further increased mortality. Traditional warfare in Madagascar had been of little direct demographic importance, as it affected only biologically expendable males, and it normally took the form of a ritual game that cost few lives of either sex. However, from 1820 the Merina state adopted European military techniques and weapons, and their program of imperial expansion increased fatalities. From 1816 to 1853 possibly sixty thousand non-Merina (approx. sixteen hundred per annum) were killed by Merina troops, whose own casualties were lower because of their immense military and numerical superiority. While most of the dead were adult males, as a prime objective of Merina campaigns was the enslavement of women, indirect "military" mortality due to famine resulting from the enemies' scorched-earth tactics was high for those women who escaped enslavement.[81]

FEMALE AGENCY

The reaction of bonded labor to extreme exploitation was often to flee or revolt. However, the roles performed by females within Imperial Madagascar's two highly exploitive systems, slavery and fanompoana, varied considerably, as did their reactions to their exploitation. In contrast to many other systems of servile labor, "free" females drafted into fanompoana performed predominantly hard labor, in construction and gold mining, whereas female slaves were primarily valued for their domestic house skills, sexual services, and agricultural work. This contrast meant that female slaves, far more than "free" females subject to fanompoana, were employed in households where they enjoyed a greater variety of positions that presented them with a potentially wider range of strategies for survival.

As noted, some female slaves practiced abortion and infanticide, in part to deprive their master of the opportunity to exploit their offspring, and also in part, possibly, to reduce their own child-rearing responsibilities. Similarly, dread of fanompoana for any future children probably led significant numbers of "free" women of nonelite status to practice abortion and infanticide. James Sibree estimated that infanticide caused the deaths of 25 percent of Malagasy babies in the mid-nineteenth century, and Raymond Decary projected a colonial-era estimate of 14.3 percent,[82] figures that fall within the 15-to-50-percent infanticide rate calculated for aborigines in Pleistocene Australia, although there is no comparable indication that in Madagascar more female babies than males were exposed.[83]

Most female slaves also strove to improve their status. Of particular importance in a culture dominated by reverence for ancestors, from which non-Malagasy slaves, as foreigners, were excluded, was to attain a spiritual standing recognized by the slave-owning society. Such recognition was often expressed in food rituals, dress, religion, and magic. From the late 1820s a number of female slaves achieved some such standing through membership of the Christian Church, tolerated until 1833, and clandestine thereafter until the early 1860s, when Christianity was again officially accepted. Of particular importance in the early church was the *taratasy*—the ability to read and write, focused on the Christian scriptures—which were widely considered to be a sacerdotal form of power, and the genuine sense of equality that slave women attained in the ranks of proselytes.[84] Others, particularly young female slaves, earned recognition among free Malagasy as ancestral mediums.[85] This was the case of the young slave girls possessed by the spirit of the recently deceased queen Ranavalona I, who in 1863 traveled from Betsileo to the imperial capital of Antananarivo to demand that the Western-influenced Radama II return to ancestral ways.[86]

Female slaves working within the households of ordinary slave owners often gained considerable opportunities also to enhance their conditions of work and living. They frequently performed services, many of an intimate nature, that over time incorporated them as important, if inferior, members of that household. Their ancillary standing is reflected in the terminology applied to slaves, who were often referred to generically as *ankizy* (children) and given affectionate personal names.

Such bonds of intimacy were reinforced as the century progressed and fanompoana became generalized and increasingly severe, drawing upon ordinary "free" men, women, and, from the mid-1880s, children. In such circumstances many families depended on the slave to cultivate and maintain the household. Also, as ordinary cultivators became steadily more impoverished under the imperial Merina regime, different house-holders often combined their resources to purchase a slave to cultivate for the collective. Joint ownership in turn generally presented the slave woman with greater opportunities to extract concessions by playing one "master" off against the other(s), notably in the form of clothes, provisions, and leisure. Some slaves also managed to accumulate money, sometimes enough to purchase their freedom or another slave. In reality, some slaves with the resources to purchase their own liberty refused to do so lest they be drafted into fanompoana.[87]

There is little evidence in Imperial Madagascar of female slaves rebelling or fleeing, although, as in Mauritius, the predominantly male maroon, or brigand, bands abducted women for sexual services, companionship, and domestic labor. In 1853, for example, three thousand Ikongo warriors attacked Fianarantsoa, the Merina headquarters in Betsileo, and seized many women and children as slaves.[88] However, the harsh realities of maroon life acted as disincentives to female slaves voluntarily joining most maroon communities. Overwhelmingly composed of young adult males, maroon bands sought sanctuary in remote and generally inhospitable areas. They were obliged to raid settled communities in order to survive and were constantly on alert to fend off harassment by the authorities. Few established a viable independent existence. Moreover, slave owners possibly exercised greater surveillance over female slaves. It was, for example, particularly difficult for women to flee or revolt from within households. Also, women tended to move more slowly than a young male fugitive and were thus recaptured more easily.

Those with commitments to children and other enslaved kin or friends seldom considered flight or revolt an option. Indeed, the aim of most female slaves was to secure a niche within the dominant society for themselves and for their children, to improve that position over time, and, if granted nonslave status, to assume a new ethnicity. Individual slaves therefore sought to forge linkages not with other slaves but with slaveholders, who alone could ameliorate their working and living conditions and elevate their status and that of their offspring. Central to this strategy of assimilation was the acculturation of slaves. Slave owners placed a premium on acquiring children and young adults as slaves who could more easily learn the language or dialect and accept the religious ideology of slaveholders—which in turn justified enslaving them. Acculturation was essential for the slave concerned, but it also enabled female slaves to transmit local belief and value systems to their children. Indeed, the evidence is that even following French colonial emancipation of slaves in 1896 most female slaves remained attached in unofficial bondage to the household of their former slave owners. Moreover, their children, initially brought up with the children of the "master" and "mistress," were separated at school age and subsequently retained in the fields or in other menial tasks.[89]

Similarly, nonslave women, more deeply attached to children and household than their menfolk, were more reluctant than males to flee fanompoana. Considerable numbers expressed their dissent from state-church pressures through clandestine maintenance of practices associated with the ancestors, or through breakaway Christian sects, often with millenarian messages, a number of which appeared in the late nineteenth century, notably in Betsileo. In the goldfields, some defied the state monopoly on the gold they produced and engaged in smuggling it. Also a few fled state fanompoana and joined refugee communities, notably Ikongo, which by 1863 boasted a population of thirty thousand people. Its women helped repulse Merina attacks by rolling large boulders and logs of wood upon assailants attempting to scale the rock fortress where they made their stand.[90] However, these communities were subject to constant harassment by Merina authorities with only a handful, such as Ikongo, establishing a precarious but viable long-term existence.

NOTES

Abbreviations

AHD African Historical Demography, 2 vols. (Edinburgh: Centre of African Studies, University of Edinburgh, 1978, 1981)

AMA Académie Malgache, Antananarivo

SOAS/LMS MIL Archives of the London Missionary Society, School of Oriental and African Studies, London, Madagascar Incoming Letters

1. R. P. Callet, *Histoire des rois: Tantaran' ny Andriana*, trans. G. S. Chapus and E. Ratsimba, 4 vols. (Tananarive: Librarie de Madagascar, 1974), 4:276–77; James Hastie, "Diary" (1824–25), Colonial Office series, Public Record Office, 167/78.

2. Nicolas Mayeur, "Voyage au pays d'ancove, autrement dit des hovas ou Amboilamba dans l'intérieur des terres, Isle de Madagascar," 165–66, British Library Add. 18128; Hastie, "Diary" (1817), 167, Colonial Office series, Public Record Office, 167/34; S. P. Oliver, *Madagascar: An Historical and Descriptive Account of the Island and its Former Dependencies*, 2 vols. (London: Macmillan, 1886), 1:492–3, 2:11 12; R. Baron, "Notes on the Economic Plants of Madagascar," *Antananarivo Annual and Madagascar Magazine* 22 (1898): 218–23; Alfred Grandidier and Guil-

laume Grandidier, *Histoire physique, naturelle et politique de Madagascar* (Paris: Imprimerie Nationale, 1928), 4:167–68.

3. Hastie, "Diary" (1817), 185.

4. Hastie, "Diary" (1820), 482.

5. Dumaine, "Voyage au pays d'ancaye, autrement dit des Bezounzouns, Isle de Madagascar" (1790), 274, British Library Add. 18128.

6. S. P. Colin et Suau, "Album Malgache," *Les missions catholiques* (1896), 11; Grandidier, *Histoire physique*, 4:354.

7. Gwyn Campbell, "Slavery and Fanompoana: The Structure of Forced Labour in Imerina (Madagascar), 1790–1861," *Journal of African History* 29, no. 2 (1988): 463–86; William Ellis, *History of Madagascar*, 2 vols. (London: Fisher, 1838), 1:194.

8. Gwyn Campbell, introduction to *Abolition and Its Aftermath in Indian Ocean Africa and Asia*, ed. Gwyn Campbell (London: Routledge, 2005).

9. Gwyn Campbell, "The State and Pre-colonial Demographic History: The Case of Nineteenth-Century Madagascar," *Journal of African History* 32, no. 3 (1991): 415–45.

10. Johns to Freeman, Antananarivo, 14 October 1830, SOAS/LMS MIL, B3 F5.

11. A. Boudou, "Journal de route d'une expédition de Rainimaharo en 1838," *Bulletin de l'Académie Malgache* 15 (1932): 89–90.

12. Freeman to Philip, Antananarivo, 26 August 1832, SOAS/LMS MIL, B4 F4 JB.

13. Gwyn Campbell, "Labour and the Transport Problem in Imperial Madagascar, 1810–1895," *Journal of African History* 21 (1980): 341–56; Campbell, "Slavery and Fanompoana."

14. Gwyn Campbell, "Madagascar and Mozambique in the Slave Trade of the Western Indian Ocean, 1800–1861," in *The Economics of the Indian Ocean Slave Trade in the Nineteenth Century*, ed. William Gervase Clarence-Smith (London: Frank Cass, 1989), 166–93; Gwyn Campbell, "The East African Slave Trade, 1861–1895: The 'Southern' Complex," *International Journal of African Historical Studies* 22, no. 1 (1989): 1–27.

15. Campbell, "Labour and Transport"; Campbell, "Slavery and Fanompoana."

16. Gwyn Campbell, "Madagascar and the Slave Trade," *Journal of African History* 22, no. 2 (1981): 203–27. These were Malagasy dollars called *ariary*.

17. Ellis, *History of Madagascar*, 1:194; Campbell, "Slavery and Fanompoana."

18. William Ellis, *Madagascar Revisited* (London: John Murray, 1867), 476; see also 475.

19. Patrick Manning, "Contours of Slavery and Social Change in Africa," *American Historical Review* 88, no. 4 (1983): 853–54; Martin A. Klein, "The Demography of Slavery in Western Soudan: The Late Nineteenth Century," in *African Population and Capitalism*, ed. Dennis D. Cordell and Joel W. Gregory (Madison: University of Wisconsin Press, 1994), 56–57.

20. Knott to Aitken, Mojanga, 21 March 1888, in *Anti-Slavery Reporter* (November–December 1888), 217.

21. Christopher Wrigley, "Population and History: Some Innumerate Reflexions," *AHD*, 2:24.

22. Campbell, "Demographic History."

23. Manning, "Contours of Slavery," 856.

24. Gwyn Campbell, "The Role of the London Missionary Society in the Rise of the Merina Empire, 1810–1861" (PhD diss., University of Wales, 1985), 344–64.

25. David Griffiths, *Hanes Madagascar* (Machynlleth, UK: Richard Jones, 1843), 24–25; Ellis, *History of Madagascar*, 1:114; James Sibree, *Madagascar and Its People: Notes of a Four Years' Residence* (London: Religious Tract Society, 1870), 384.

26. Griffiths, *Hanes Madagascar*, 24–25.

27. Campbell, "Demographic History."

28. Finaz, "Tananarive, capitale de Madagascar: Séjour d'un missionnaire catholique en 1855, 56 et 57," sect. 2, Diaires, no. 20, 110, Archives historiques de la Vice-Province Société de Jésus de Madagascar, Antananarivo.

29. H. M. Dubois, *Monographie des Betsileo (Madagascar)* (Paris: Institut d'Ethnologie, 1938), 585, 718.

30. Campbell, "Slavery and Fanompoana"; see also Klein, "Demography of Slavery," 56–57.

31. Klein, "Demography of Slavery," 59–60.

32. Megan Vaughan, *Creating the Creole Island: Slavery in Eighteenth-Century Mauritius* (Durham, NC: Duke University Press, 2005), 139.

33. Campbell, "Demographic History," 442–43; Maurice Bloch, "Modes of Production and Slavery in Madagascar," in *Asian and African Sytems of Slavery*, ed. James L. Watson (Berkeley and Los Angeles: University of California Press, 1980), 110.

34. Gwyn Campbell, "The History of Nineteenth Century Madagascar: 'Le royaume' or 'l'empire'?" *Omaly sy anio* 33–36 (1994): 331–79.

35. Campbell, "Demographic History"; Yvan-Georges Paillard, "Les recherches démographiques sur Madagascar au début de l'époque coloniale et les documents de l'AMI," *Cahiers d'études africaines* 27 (1987): 33.

36. Gwyn Campbell, "The Menalamba Revolt and Brigandry in Imperial Madagascar, 1820–1897," *International Journal of African Historical Studies* 24, no. 2 (1991): 259–91.

37. Grandidier, *Histoire physique*, 4:253, 255, 259–61; Adolphe Razafintsalama, "Quelques concepts anthropologiques de base en vue du recueil des traditions orales," *Colloque d'histoire, Université de Madagascar* (Toliara, 1979), 12.

38. J. E. Inikori, introduction to *Forced Migration: The Impact of the Export Slave Trade on African Societies*, ed. J. E. Inikori (London: Hutchinson, 1981), 13–60.

39. Campbell, "Madagascar and Mozambique"; Campbell, "East African Slave Trade"; Campbell, "Missionaries, Fanompoana and the Menalamba Revolt in Late Nineteenth Century Madagascar," *Journal of Southern African Studies* 15, no. 1 (1988): 54–73.

40. Campbell, "Slavery and Fanompoana."

41. See Suzanne Miers, "Slavery and the Slave Trade in Saudi Arabia and the Arab States on the Persian Gulf, 1921–1963," in Campbell, *Abolition and Its Aftermath*, 120–36.

42. Gwyn Campbell, "The Adoption of Autarky in Imperial Madagascar, 1820–1835," *Journal of African History* 28, no. 3 (1987): 395–411.

43. Campbell, "Slavery and Fanompoana."

44. "Report of the Madagascar Mission," for the half year ending 30 April 1834, SOAS/LMS MIL, B5 F1 JC.

45. Oliver, *Madagascar*, 2:89, 192–93; Grandidier, *Histoire physique*, 1:370; Campbell, "London Missionary Society," 247–49.

46. J. J. Freeman and D. Johns, *A Narrative of the Persecution of the Christians in Madagascar* (London: John Snow, 1840), 45; Raombana, "Annales" (1853), 357, AMA; Raombana, B2, livre 13, 29, AMA; J. Chauvin, "Jean Laborde, 1805–1878," *Mémoires de l'Académie Malgache* 29 (Tananarive: Académie Malgache, 1939), 8. For production of ammonia from animal offal by dry distilling see E. G. Al-Jahiz (ca. 776–869), *Kitab al-hayawan* (Book on Animals), noted in "Sciences," page 6, http://www.drruqaia.com/en/courses/islam_sciences.pdf (accessed 4 February 2007).

47. Campbell, "Slavery and Fanompoana."

48. Campbell, "Missionaries, Fanompoana."

49. Campbell, "Menalamba Revolt and Brigandry."

50. Sibree, *Madagascar and Its People*, 530.

51. J. C. Thorne, "Elementary Education in Madagascar," *Antananarivo Annual and Madagascar Magazine* 9 (1885): 43.

52. Campbell, "Missionaries, Fanompoana."

53. Joseph Pearse, "LMS Churches and Congregations and Christian Life," *Antananarivo Annual and Madagascar Magazine* 19 (1895): 318–19.

54. Ibid.," 319.

55. Gwyn Campbell, "Gold Mining and the French Takeover of Madagascar, 1883–1914," *African Economic History* 17 (1988): 99–126.

56. Jones and Griffiths to Burder, Antananarivo, 4 August 1825, SOAS/LMS MIL, B2 F2 JB; "School Report" (1825), SOAS/LMS MIL, B2 F3 JG; John Iliffe, "The Origins of African Population Growth," *Journal of African History* 30, no. 1 (1989): 168; David Voas, "Subfertility and Disruption in the Congo Basin," *AHD*, 2:785–86; D. Ian Pool, "A Framework for the Analysis of West African Historical Demography," *AHD*, 1:49.

57. Campbell, "Labour and the Transport Problem"; Campbell, "Slavery and Fanompoana"; Gavin Kitching, "Proto-Industrialisation and Demographic Change: A Thesis and Some Possible African Implications," *Journal of African History* 24, no. 2 (1983): 221–40.

58. Kitching, "Proto-Industrialisation," 234.

59. Campbell, "Slavery and Fanompoana."

60. G. T. Nurse, J. S. Weiner, and T. Jenkins, *The Peoples of Southern Africa and Their Affinities* (Oxford: Oxford University Press, 1985), 253–54.

61. Campbell, "Slavery and Fanompoana"; Campbell, "Gold Mining"; Campbell, "Missionaries, Fanompoana."

62. Gwyn Campbell, *An Economic History of Imperial Madagascar, 1750–1895* (Cambridge: Cambridge University Press, 2005), 142.

63. George A. Shaw, "The Betsileo: Country and People," *Antananarivo Annual and Madagascar Magazine* 3 (1877): 79; Grandidier, *Histoire physique*, 1:330; Joseph Sewell, *The Sakalava: Being Notes of a Journey made from Antananarivo to some Towns*

on the Border of the Sakalava Territory, in June and July, 1875 (Antananarivo: Friends' Foreign Mission Association, 1875), 12, 17.

64. Paillard, "Recherches démographiques," 23.

65. Ibid., 37.

66. Voas, "Subfertility and Disruption," 786–96; see also Nancy Rose Hunt, "'La bébé en brousse': European Women, African Birth Spacing and Colonial Intervention in Breast Feeding in the Belgium Congo," *International Journal of African Historical Studies* 21 (1988): 403–4.

67. Shaw, "Betsileo," 4; James Sibree, *Fifty Years in Madagascar* (London: Allen and Unwin, 1924), 41.

68. See Jorgen Ruud, *Taboo: A Study of Malagasy Customs and Beliefs* (Oslo: Oslo University Press, 1960), 244–45.

69. Jean Valette, "Notes sur la géographie médicale de l'Imerina à la fin de la monarchie (1889–1893)," *Bulletin de Madagascar* 246 (1966): 1143–45; Paillard, "Recherches démographiques," 25.

70. Grandidier, *Histoire physique*, 1:337.

71. Campbell, "Demographic History."

72. Locke Lewis, "An Account of the Ovahs, a Race of People Residing in the Interior of Madagascar, with a Sketch of their Country, Appearance, Dress, Language, &c," *Journal of the Royal Geographical Society* 5 (1835): 236.

73. J. C. Caldwell, "Major Questions in African Demographic History," *AHD*, 2:11; Wrigley, "Population and History."

74. Campbell, *Economic History*, 149.

75. Campbell, "Slavery and Fanompoana."

76. Francis Cornwallis Maude, *Five Years in Madagascar* (London: Chapman and Hall, 1895), 103; Campbell, "Missionaries, Fanompoana."

77. Campbell, "Demographic History."

78. Campbell, "Gold Mining"; Campbell, "Missionaries, Fanompoana."

79. London Missionary Society, *Ten Years' Review (1880–90)* (Antananarivo: LMS, 1890), 114.

80. Campbell, "Missionaries, Fanompoana"; Campbell, "Gold Mining"; Dubois, *Monographie des Betsileo*.

81. Campbell, "Adoption of Autarky"; Campbell, "Demographic History."

82. Sibree, *Fifty Years in Madagascar*, 253; Raymond Decary, "La population de Madagascar," *Bulletin de l'Académie Malgache* 28 (1947–48), 30; Decary, "Le voyage d'un chirurgien philosophe à Madagascar," *Bulletin de l'Académie Malgache* 36 (1958): 326.

83. Thurstan Shaw, "Towards a Prehistoric Demography of Africa," *AHD*, 2:586.

84. Campbell, "Adoption of Autarky"; William Ellis, *The Martyr Church* (London, 1870).

85. Gwyn Campbell, "Abolition and Its Aftermath in Madagascar, 1877–1949," in Campbell, *Abolition and Its Aftermath*; Campbell, "Crisis of Faith and Colonial Conquest: The Impact of Famine and Disease in Late Nineteenth-Century Madagascar," *Cahiers d'études africaines* 32, no. 3 (1992): 409–53.

86. Ellis, *Madagascar Revisited*.

87. Campbell, "Slavery and Fanompoana"; see also Klein, "Demography of Slavery," 56–57.

88. Raombana, "Manuscrit," 14, 17–18, AMA.

89. Sandra Evers, "Solidarity and Antagonism in Migrant Societies on the Southern Highlands," in *Fanandevozana, ou, esclavage: Colloque international sur l'esclavage à Madagascar*, ed. François Rajaoson (Antananarivo, 1996); John Campbell, pers. comm., Arivonimamo, 1978.

90. W. Rooke, "A Boat-Voyage along the Coast-Lakes of East Madagascar" (11 December 1865), *Journal of the Royal Geographical Society* 36 (1866): 62.

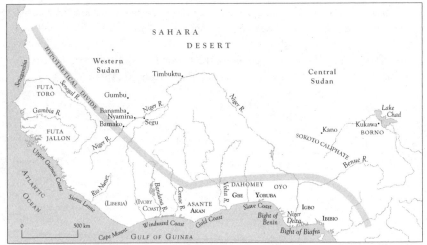

Hypothetical Sahara/Atlantic Divide, early nineteenth century

11

INTERNAL MARKETS OR
AN ATLANTIC-SAHARA DIVIDE?

How Women Fit into the Slave Trade of West Africa

PAUL E. LOVEJOY

The Atlantic and Sahara slave trades are often portrayed as serving two distinct forms of slavery, the first reflecting the preference for males over females for use as labor, especially in the fields, and the second representing the Muslim preference for women to fill harems, and correspondingly their relatively insignificant economic roles.[1] It is commonly accepted that only one-third of the enslaved Africans who crossed the Atlantic were females, whereas the gender ratio of the trans-Saharan trade favored females. The contrast in these images suggests an Atlantic-Sahara divide that separated two trades. However, these generalizations disguise discrepancies and historical change that can be traced to the political geography of Africa and specifically to restrictions on the slave trade that seem to have been enforced in Muslim areas of West Africa. The proportions of males and females in the Atlantic trade varied with the coastal region of origin and changed over time. Similarly, the Islamic lands sustained a demand for slaves that lasted into the twentieth century, but over time, and depending on place, the relative importance of the gender of slaves varied, depending on whether they were wanted for harems, for the

The research for this study has been supported by the Social Sciences and Humanities Research Council of Canada and the Canada Research Chair in African Diaspora History. I thank Suzanne Miers and Joseph C. Miller for their comments, and Gwyn Campbell for organizing the conference "Women and Slavery" (Université d'Avignon, 16–18 October 2002), at which this paper was first presented.

military, for domestic service, or for some other reason.[2] These variations and complexities raise issues about how slavery is studied and why and how gender mattered.

This chapter reconsiders the relative importance of females in the transatlantic and trans-Saharan trade in slaves in the eighteenth and nineteenth centuries. As Claire Robertson and Martin Klein have argued, a majority of slaves in western Africa were females.[3] This preference for females affected the demographic structure of the transatlantic slave trade, with the result that fewer females were sent to the Americas than were retained within Africa.[4] As is argued here, this preference for females within Africa was particularly pronounced in Muslim areas in the interior of West Africa, from where relatively few females, whether adults or children, were sent to the coast. The pattern seems clear: there were relatively few female slaves taken to the coast from the western Sudan, even from areas that were referred to as Bambara, a designation that was usually meant to apply to non-Muslims in the Mande areas of the western Sudan.[5] Similarly, I have previously drawn attention to the overwhelming predominance of young adult males in the movement of enslaved Africans from the central Sudan to Bahia in the early nineteenth century.[6] This regional specificity of the gender of those sold is one of the most striking characteristics of the slave trade of West Africa, which was reflected in the prices paid for males and females in the interior and at the coast.

The gendered division of the slave trade in the interior of West Africa affected the enforced flow of enslaved Africans across the Atlantic. Preferences for slaves among Muslims in particular explain why males usually cost more on the coast than females, while in the interior, particularly in Muslim areas, females generally cost as much as a third more than males. In short the internal market in Muslim areas, not some divide between Atlantic and Sahara, was a significant factor, and perhaps even the dominant factor, in the determination of prices. The practice of ransoming enslaved Muslims also affected prices, in part, at least, accounting for the differential in the cost of males and females in the interior. The practice of ransoming further establishes that conditions within West Africa were important in determining price. Females were in greater demand, but prices for all slaves in the interior were sufficiently low that if market demand alone had determined the flow of slaves, many more slaves would have been sent to the coast than actually were. The fact that Europeans were willing to pay more for males than for females—and considerably more than the price for either males or females in the interior—attracted some trade from the interior, but Muslim merchants nevertheless supplied a small proportion of the transatlantic trade, which therefore was supplied heavily from areas with little or no Muslim influence, especially the Bight of Biafra and West-Central Africa. The intention here is to examine the political and ideological factors that underpinned the price differential between the interior and the coast and the apparent unwillingness of Muslim merchants to sell slaves into the transatlantic trade.

THE SCALE OF THE SLAVE TRADE

While the exact proportions of the export and internal trade in slaves cannot be known, the scale of slaving in the interior rose substantially in the seventeenth and eighteenth centuries. Patrick Manning's efforts to estimate the size of the enslaved population, including those who died before reaching their destinations or who succumbed soon thereafter, have reinforced my own conclusions that between 1600 and 1800 the demographic impact of slavery was enormous.[7] The census for the Atlantic trade, which derives from quantifiable data, combined with assumptions from demographic theory, establish that the West African population did not grow in this period and may well have actually declined. Furthermore, the ratio of slave to free appears to have shifted toward a larger servile population that rivaled in size the slave societies in other times and other places. Moreover, both the scale of the trans-Saharan trade and the size of individual caravans in the interior of West Africa suggest that Muslim merchants had the ability to move many more slaves from the interior to the coast for export than they did, if there had been reason to do so and no conflicting reasons not to.[8]

Let us consider the idea that there was a divide between the Sahara and Atlantic, and because of that divide the population that may have entered the Atlantic trade was significantly different from that which went into and across the Sahara. Historically, the region to the west and north of the Niger delta had a long interaction with the Muslim world of the western and central Sudan, including exposure to itinerant Muslim merchants and craftsmen, as well as enslaved Muslims who had been taken in war or purchased. Hence the regions of the Atlantic often identified as the Bight of Benin (or "Slave Coast"), the Gold Coast, the Windward Coast, Sierra Leone, Upper Guinea, and Senegambia were areas that were in close proximity and ongoing interaction with Muslims and regions that were predominantly Muslim in population. This

Table 11.1. Origins of enslaved Africans destined for the Americas

	SENEGAMBIA AND OFFSHORE ATLANTIC	SIERRA LEONE	WINDWARD COAST	GOLD COAST	BIGHT OF BENIN	BIGHT OF BIAFRA	WEST-CENTRAL AFRICA AND ST. HELENA	SOUTHEAST AFRICA AND INDIAN OCEAN ISLANDS	TOTALS
1501–50	27,882	0	0	0	0	21,321	14,252	0	63,456
1551–1600	59,538	1,922	2,150	0	187	19,413	221,678	0	304,888
1601–50	114,164	810	0	2,821	9,013	43,810	541,251	1,115	712,984
1651–1700	85,354	5,513	305	107,397	299,372	160,372	527,497	25,332	1,211,142
1701–50	150,619	18,730	27,308	409,418	737,570	275,237	850,554	16,309	2,485,746
1751–1800	210,283	170,725	177,362	553,236	547,969	635,456	1,495,615	63,235	3,853,881
1801–50	98,651	168,669	43,389	87,506	370,804	555,350	1,762,603	402,918	3,489,889
1851–67	4,476	27,515	619	771	30,637	41,016	63,811	47,791	216,635
Totals	750,967	393,884	251,132	1,161,149	1,995,553	1,751,977	5,477,262	556,698	12,338,622
Muslim factor	100%	80–100%	10%	10%	10–60%	0%	0%	n.a.	

Source: These estimates are derived from the expanded, online Trans-Atlantic Slave Trade Database (alpha version) being developed at Emory University. It should be noted that these figures are preliminary. I wish to thank David Eltis for permission to cite these figures for purposes of estimating the Muslim factor in the transatlantic slave trade.

Muslim factor distinguishes a dual orientation that is different from the Atlantic orientation of the Bight of Biafra and areas of West-Central Africa further south.

Enslaved Muslims and non-Muslims who were from Muslim areas came only from the region west of the Niger delta. According to my calculations, this area supplied approximately 37 percent (4,550,000 people) of the enslaved Africans sent to the Americas in the eighteenth and nineteenth centuries (table 11.1). Not all these people were Muslims or came from areas under Islamic influence. Many of those who were identified as Akan, Gbe, or Yoruba were not Muslims, and they undoubtedly constituted the overwhelming majority of enslaved Africans leaving West Africa, to the west of the Niger delta, via the Atlantic. Hence the possible number of Muslims had to have been considerably less than 37 percent, and as is demonstrated in table 11.2, could not have been more than 10–12 percent of the total number of enslaved Africans sent to the Americas.[9]

The exported population that could have been Muslim, had lived under Muslim influence, or had been enslaved by Muslims is deliberately overstated in table 11.2 in order to test my hypothesis that internal demand was strong. All those from Senegambia are included in these categories. For Upper Guinea, it could be argued that only a portion of those sold into the Atlantic trade should be included as coming from Muslim areas, but I am including all persons from this region, recognizing that this assumption exaggerates the proportion of Muslims or those enslaved

Table 11.2. Origins of enslaved Africans — estimated Muslim factor				
REGION	1651–1700	1701–50	1751–1800	1801–67
Senegambia	85,354	150,619	210,283	103,127
Sierra Leone	5,513	18,730	170,725	196,184
Gold Coast	10,740[a]	40,942[a]	55,324[a]	8,828[a]
(all slaves)	(107,397)	(409,418)	(553,236)	(88,277)
Bight of Benin	29,932[a]	73,757[a]	109,593[b]	240,864[c]
(all slaves)	(299,372)	(737,570)	(547,969)	(401,441)
Total (Muslim factor)	131,539	284,048	545,925	549,003

[a] 10 percent
[b] 20 percent
[c] 60 percent

by Muslims. Nonetheless, the impact of the Futa Jallon jihad on the region suggests that the majority should be included, at least. The proportions of people from Muslim and non-Muslim areas who passed through the Bight of Benin and the Gold Coast are arbitrary estimates. Previously, I estimated the number of individuals from the far interior of the Bight of Benin who went to Bahia, and I am allowing that most of those enslaved in the Yoruba wars of the nineteenth century were directly or indirectly related to the jihad in the central Sudan that resulted in the consolidation of the Sokoto Caliphate and the disintegration of Oyo.[10] I am allowing that 25 percent of those leaving from the Bight of Benin either came from the central Sudan or were a product of the nineteenth-century wars. I am allowing a smaller proportion for the Gold Coast (10 percent), since most of the enslaved who left the Gold Coast castles were Akan or otherwise came from relatively close to the coast. Nonetheless, some of the enslaved came from the north. These estimates of the proportion of individuals reaching the Atlantic who were Muslims, enslaved by Muslims, or enslaved as a result of wars related to the jihad movement could not have been large—no more than 15 percent of all enslaved Africans destined for the Americas in the eighteenth and nineteenth centuries, and probably less.[11]

The relatively small proportion of people coming from Muslim Africa and adjoining areas is striking, even if allowance is made for the British blockade of West Africa after 1810, which shifted the Atlantic trade as a whole south of the equator. Southeast Africa was also tied to Muslim networks, which reached into the far interior by the late nineteenth century, after the ending of the transatlantic trade. For my purposes here, the Muslim influence in southeastern Africa is not considered, although the connection between West Africa and southeast Africa should not be dismissed: Heinrich Barth collected an itinerary in the Sokoto Caliphate in the early 1850s from a merchant in Kano who had traveled in the interior of Mozambique, apparently in the 1840s, if not earlier.[12]

For purposes of estimating the relative proportions of the enslaved who came from "Muslim" and "non-Muslim" areas, it is necessary to examine the somewhat arbitrary distinctions in the voyage database developed by David Eltis and his associates between segments of the coast. Europeans saw the coast in navigational terms and according to their presence on different parts of the coast. They seldom saw any direct relationship to the interior regions, from which slaves reached the Atlantic coastal ports as recorded in the database.

To relate the voyage database to the Muslim interior of West Africa, the focus of my analysis here, one must begin by noting that the Senegambia of the database—a Muslim region bordering the Sahara—is defined as anywhere north of the Rio Nunez, while Sierra Leone comprises the entire region from the Rio Nunez to Cape Mount inclusive. The Windward Coast of the database includes an area from Cape Mount to the Assini River, while the Gold Coast is defined as the area from there to the Volta River. Hence the region that is sometimes referred to as the Upper Guinea Coast corresponds to the categories Senegambia and Sierra Leone in the database, with an apparently arbitrary boundary that is suspiciously anachronistic in its coincidence with the boundary between the modern countries of Guinea and Guinea-Bissau. The boundary between Sierra Leone and the Windward Coast is similarly arbitrary in being identical with the modern border between Sierra Leone and Liberia, while that between the Windward Coast and the Gold Coast is the same as the border between modern Ghana and Ivory Coast.

Looking again at the regional divisions of the database from the perspective of the interior of West Africa, it is clear that the term Windward Coast had no African reality and, as a category, blurs important distinctions about the origins of the people from the interior. In fact much of the trade that is designated in the database as coming from the Windward Coast originated on either the far eastern portion of the coast or the far western. Its eastern portion drew on the Akan interior, making it part of the area associated with the Gold Coast and the rise of Asante as the dominant state in the interior. I would therefore allocate this portion of the slave trade more properly to the Gold Coast. Similarly the areas in the far western portion of the so-called Windward Coast in fact came from the same interior as for "Sierra Leone" and should be included in that region, whether it is called Sierra Leone or Upper Guinea. Much of the coast of Liberia and Ivory Coast was not important in the Atlantic slave trade and had few or no connections with the distant Muslim interior.[13]

Thus the areas of Senegambia and Sierra Leone of the database were heavily Muslim or were in close contact with the Islamic interior, and virtually everyone from these regions was Muslim or had had some contact with Muslims. The proportions of enslaved individuals from the Gold Coast and the Bight of Benin who were Muslims or who had had some contact with Muslims were certainly less but still significant. It is possible to argue that the actual numbers of enslaved Muslims is nonetheless underrepresented in the database because there is a large category of enslaved individuals whose coastal origins are unknown and who are listed in the database in an "unspecified" category. In any event, even if adjustments are made for these ambiguous components of the database, it is still highly unlikely that more than about 15 percent of those leaving Africa were Muslims or had any contact with Islam, and the proportion could well have been as low as 6 to 10 percent before the consolidation of the jihad states and the spread of Islam.

Of the people who can be thought to have originated in the interior region that was exposed to some hypothetical Sahara-Atlantic divide, I am focusing on females because decisions on where enslaved females were sold were determined in the interior, and largely by Muslim merchants. Hence the divide was not between Sahara and Atlantic but rather between regions in which Muslim merchants were active and where they were not. Such intervention in the market for slaves, whether internal or external, was one of the factors affecting the proportion of females in the populations deported from different regions (see table 11.3).

The proportion of females in the Atlantic trade from presumably Muslim areas of Senegambia and Sierra Leone was generally less than the percentage of females in the Atlantic trade as a whole, with the exception of the quarter century 1801–25, when relatively few slaves were exported in any case. From these estimates, it is possible to suggest that relatively few females were sent to the Americas from the interior of West Africa. Instead, females came from near the coast, whether in the rice-growing areas of the Upper Guinea Coast, the Akan of the Gold Coast, Gbe and Yoruba from the Bight of Benin, or Igbo and Ibibio in the Bight of Biafra. Absolute numbers of females from Senegambia and Sierra Leone were relatively low, except in the years of jihad in the second half of the eighteenth century and first quarter of the nineteenth century.

The relative unimportance of females from the western Sudan is apparent in calculating the proportion of females from Senegambia and Sierra Leone in the total female population sent to the Americas. The proportion of females from these regions was as low as 4–5 percent of the total number of females deported to the Americas and peaked at just over 13 percent in the years of jihad in Futa Jallon and Futa Toro. Despite this exception, very few females actually came from the western Sudan, far fewer proportionately than for the trade as a whole. Moreover, the proportion of children in the deported population from Senegambia and Sierra Leone was consistently less than for the trade as whole. There were

Table 11.3. Females in the transatlantic slave trade by region, 1651–1867 (percent)

REGION	1651–75	1676–1700	1701–25	1726–50	1751–75	1776–1800	1801–25	1826–50	1851–67
Senegambia	—	27.0	31.0	21.3	37.8	31.6	46.8	32.6	—
Sierra Leone	—	23.2	31.9	—	41.4	34.8	32.0	28.1	—
Windward Coast	—	—	—	39.7	38.4	33.0	26.3	25.7	—
Gold Coast	42.7	46.8	32.9	32.2	37.9	34.2	28.1	28.7	—
Bight of Benin	41.3	41.0	36.0	40.8	46.2	34.3	24.3	34.9	27.7
Bight of Biafra	50.3	41.1	48.3	24.6	39.9	42.6	35.0	34.3	—
West-Central	—	40.1	26.2	32.8	32.5	35.2	29.1	26.8	24.7
Southeast Africa	—	—	—	47.3	—	28.5	30.5	19.4	13.2
Origin unknown	38.5	40.6	34.5	33.6	43.4	30.1	31.3	24.8	27.3
Mean	45.0	41.3	33.9	33.8	38.5	45.1	31.2	31.7	24.5

Source: David Eltis, Stephen Behrendt, David Richardson, and Herbert Klein, The Atlantic Slave Trade: A Database on CD-Rom (Cambridge: Cambridge University Press, 1999).

simply fewer females, whether adults or children, traded from Muslim areas than from elsewhere.

The portion of slave exports from the Gold Coast and the Bight of Benin that came from the Muslim interior is difficult to guess, although the Muslim factor was significant in the Bight of Benin in the last decades of the eighteenth century and especially in the nineteenth century. I have previously calculated that females constituted no more than 5 percent of the enslaved Africans entering the Atlantic trade from the interior of the Bight of Benin.[14] The unknown factor in all these calculations is the large number of enslaved Africans whose regional origins have not been determined and are included in the database in the "unspecified" category.

At the end of the eighteenth and beginning of the nineteenth centuries, the trans-Saharan slave trade from the central and western Sudan was also considerable, although the proportion of males and females who were traded varied over time, by the routes they followed and according to the political and economic needs of the competing markets (table 11.4).[15] According to Ralph Austen, almost 1.5 million people were sent across the Sahara as slaves in the eighteenth and nineteenth centuries from the central and western Sudan; this figure does not include the undoubtedly significant number of slaves who were retained within the Sa-

Table 11.4. Estimated volume of the trans-Saharan slave trade

	18TH CENTURY	19TH CENTURY	TOTAL
Morocco	200,000	280,000	480,000
Algeria	70,000	31,000	101,000
Tunisia	80,000	45,000	125,000
Libya	270,000	263,700	533,700
Total	620,000	619,700	1,239,700

Source: Ralph Austen, "The Mediterranean Islamic Slave Trade out of Africa: A Tentative Census," in The Human Commodity: Perspectives on the Trans-Saharan Slave Trade, ed. Elizabeth Savage (London: Frank Cass, 1992), 214–48. The estimates for departures from sub-Saharan Africa should be adjusted for mortality in the Sahara crossing, according to Austen's calculations, as follows: 6 percent losses to Morocco (28,800), 10 percent to Algeria (10,100), 15 percent to Tunisia (18,750), and 20 percent to Libya (106,400), thereby raising the estimated number of enslaved people leaving West Africa to over 1,400,000.

hara.[16] His calculations are projections from estimates of the numbers of slaves arriving in Morocco, Algeria, Tunisia, and Libya.

For the eighteenth century, Austen estimates that 620,000 slaves arrived in North Africa and that an additional 530,000 arrived in the nineteenth century. He calculates that losses crossing the Sahara accounted for 6 percent of those arriving in Morocco, 10 percent for Algeria, 15 percent for Tunisia, and 20 percent for Libya, thereby raising the estimated number of people leaving the western and central Sudan to over 1.4 million for the eighteenth and nineteenth centuries. I have modified these figures for the central Sudan for the nineteenth century, suggesting that Austen underestimated the importance of the Sokoto Caliphate and Borno as sources of slaves.[17] Nonetheless, relying on his more conservative figures, it is still possible to suggest that the scale of the trans-Saharan trade from the western and central Sudan was greater than the size of the trade to the Atlantic coast for shipment to the Americas in the same period.[18] Presumably, at least some of these slaves could have been directed to the coast for shipment to the Americas, other factors being equal.

INTERNAL DEMAND FOR FEMALES

The incidence of slavery in the Muslim interior of West Africa was high, although the portions of the population in slavery are difficult to estimate before the end of the nineteenth century, well after the ending of the transatlantic trade in slaves. Nonetheless, the scale of slavery had to have been considerable, if reports from the Sokoto Caliphate on the movement of caravans and tribute payments in the form of slaves are included, or if the French reports on caravan movements in the western Sudan are to be trusted as an indication of probable levels of slaving.[19] As with the Saharan trade, the internal trade of West Africa appears to have been on a scale that could have made it possible to divert slaves to the Atlantic coast if merchants had found it desirable to do so.

The considerable slave population of West Africa appears to have increased in the eighteenth and nineteenth centuries. Estimates made at the end of the nineteenth century and in the first decade of the twentieth century (table 11.5) provide some idea of the scale of slavery there. The areas of the western Sudan that included Futa Jallon, Futa Toro, the Umarian state, and other areas of Muslim concentration had an estimated slave population in excess of 1.7 million in about 1900, while the

Table 11.5. Slave populations of the Western and Central Sudan, ca. 1900

REGION	EST. SLAVE POP.	% OF TOTAL POP.
Haut-Sénégal-Niger	822,000	21
Guinée	687,000	51
Sénégal	330,000	31
Sokoto Caliphate	1,000,000–2,500,000	25–50
Total	2,839,000–4,337,000	25–50

Sources: Martin A. Klein, *Slavery and Colonial Rule in French West Africa* (Cambridge: Cambridge University Press, 1998), 252–56; Paul E. Lovejoy and Jan Hogendorn, *Slow Death for Slavery: The Course of Abolition in Northern Nigeria, 1897–1936* (Cambridge: Cambridge University Press, 1993), 1, 305n.

Sokoto Caliphate, the largest state geographically and in population, had a slave population that was "many millions"—well in excess of one million and perhaps more than 2.5 million.[20] These large populations of slaves are a general indication of the enormous size of the market for slaves, which continued after the termination of transatlantic slave trading. I think it is reasonable to suggest that the scale of slavery in the middle of the nineteenth century was comparable to the Americas in its last years there. The Sokoto Caliphate probably had a slave population that matched that of Brazil, and may have been comparable to that of the United States in 1860. The Islamic areas of the western and central Sudan had slave populations that were roughly the same as the total number of slaves in the Americas at the end of the eighteenth century, and more than the total number of slaves in the Caribbean at any time.[21] Hence in terms of sheer numbers, the enslaved population of Islamic West Africa was of major proportions, and the market for slaves had to have been of such a scale to have influenced both the transatlantic trade and the trans-Saharan trade from western Africa.

Moreover, the proportion of females in the enslaved population appears to have been considerable, perhaps exceeding males, and indeed providing most of the states of West Africa with greater numbers of females than males in the general population and with the inevitable result that frontier areas around Muslim states correspondingly lost females. The best information on the gender ratio of the enslaved population comes from the end of the nineteenth century and the first decade of the twentieth century, again well after the ending of the transatlantic slave trade but still during a period when slaves were being sent north across the Sahara.

Demographic information collected by French colonial officials at the time suggests that about 60 percent of adult slaves were female. While the sources behind this estimate are of varying degrees of reliability, there is no reason to question the overall impression that adult females out-numbered adult males in the slave population.[22]

Approximately 1,436,000 enslaved people were sent across the Sahara in the eighteenth and nineteenth centuries, while it is unlikely that many more than 740,000 could have been sent into the Atlantic trade in the same period, according to my estimates of the number of males and females from the western and central Sudan who were sold into transatlantic slavery and across the Sahara. The transatlantic trade was thus only about half as large as exports across the Sahara from the interior of West Africa. Even if allowance is made for the fact that not all parts of the interior of West Africa were close enough to the coast to make trade profitable, and that some places were naturally closer to trans-Saharan and Saharan markets, the proportion of slaves coming from the interior destined for the transatlantic trade appears less than it might have been. Moreover, even if the number of females in the trans-Saharan trade has been exaggerated, the relative number of females in the two trades was re-markably different. In the trade from Muslim areas to the Atlantic, there were probably no more than 74,000 females, about than 10 percent of the estimated number of enslaved being deported via the Atlantic, while at least half the forced trans-Saharan migration (over 700,000) was fe-male, or almost ten times more than the number of females in the Atlan-tic trade.

ISLAMIC AND ECONOMIC CONSIDERATIONS

The striking discrepancy in the numbers of females who were sent to the Atlantic coast and those who were retained locally or sent into and across the Sahara suggests that there were constraints on the slave trade in the interior of West Africa that affected the market for males and fe-males. By limiting the number of slaves, particularly females, who were sold to the coast for the transatlantic slave trade, Muslim traders, and the religious leaders and scholars with whom they associated and with whom they were often related, appear to have acted on the basis of ethical con-siderations that affected the demographics of the trade. Such a possibility might give the impression that the transatlantic slave trade had limited economic impact on the interior of West Africa. David Eltis has claimed as much, especially in terms of production; however, his conclusion misses the political and religious context in which there appear to have been conscious attempts to outlaw the sale of slaves to Europeans.[23] Certainly in terms of impact, the export estimates presented here seem to bear out a conclusion that Muslim areas played a marginal role in the transatlantic trade in comparison with other areas of Africa. Nonetheless, it is another matter to conclude that the Atlantic trade had no significant impact on the interior.

Emmanuel Terray has also argued that the price differentials between the coast and the interior demonstrate that the transatlantic trade had little influence on the internal trade of West Africa: "The two markets were largely independent of each other. They are not supplied from the same sources nor were they supplied in the same way. The trading partners who frequented them were not the same either. In other words, the interior trade in slaves and the transatlantic trade formed two parallel networks separated by a barrier, which, in my opinion, was more or less impermeable."[24] While Terray recognizes the importance of local, internal demand in determining price, he fails to take into consideration the possibility that noneconomic factors also contributed to the apparent gap in the price structures of the coast and the interior. In addition to preferences for women, these also included Muslim cultural and religious opposition to selling slaves to Europeans, the practice of ransoming captive Muslims, and differing transportation costs between areas of origin within West Africa and the coast.

Although much of the slavery in the interior of West Africa has sometimes been referred to as *domestic*, this term obscures the actual prevalence of slavery by suggesting that its incidence was relatively low and confined to households. In fact this was not the case. If *domestic* is meant to refer to the domestic economy, as opposed to the export trade, it is apparent that slavery was very important within the Muslim regions of West Africa. Relatively speaking, very few slaves were exported, either across the Sahara or across the Atlantic. In this sense, the idea of an Atlantic-Sahara divide is misleading, because the distinction was between where Muslim merchants and states were dominant and where they were not. The extent to which Muslim merchants and governments engaged in the slave trade was not a product of European initiative, entrepreneurship, or economic stimulus but rather was owing to long-standing legal, moral, and social traditions. It is apparent that many Muslims, and specifically Muslim governments, tried consciously to stay out of the web of Atlantic slavery. That they were not always successful is perhaps not surprising. But the possibility that there was a deliberate policy to abstain has not hitherto been sufficiently appreciated.

The relative unimportance of Muslim areas and Muslim networks as suppliers of slaves for the transatlantic trade does not indicate a relatively minimal impact but rather an ideological and political commitment, based on religion, *not* to supply slaves to Christians or other infidels, while at the same time converting captives to Islam and thereby servic-ing a very large internal market that was large enough that it could have supplied the transatlantic market to a much greater extent than it did. No similar religious restrictions applied to the trans-Saharan trade, which served entirely Islamic markets. Therefore the movement of slaves across the Sahara increased in the nineteenth century for reasons that had little if anything to do with the decline in shipments to the Americas but in-stead resulted from demand in the Muslim world. In areas bordering the Senegal and the Gambia, the Sahara-Atlantic "divide" was at the coast, and there and elsewhere along the Upper Guinea Coast and in the Bight of Benin where Muslim merchants were involved, the tendency seems to have been avoidance of the sale of slaves to non-Muslims, except some-times for those accused of murder or political crimes, which were verdicts that had legal and historic precedents.[25]

It appears that Muslims generally avoided selling slaves, and particu-larly females, to the coast. This effort at prohibition was reflected in the price differentials for slaves by gender between Muslim and Atlantic markets. This explanation uncovers an imperfection in what Patrick Manning has insisted was a single "intercontinental market for slaves, beginning with the seventeenth-century increase in the volume and prices of slaves in the Occidental [transatlantic] trade, expanding across Africa and into the Orient [including North Africa] by the end of the eighteenth century, and then gradually undergoing restriction to Africa and portions of the Orient in the nineteenth century."[26]

However, Manning does not reconcile the apparent difference in price based on gender with the claim that there was an integrated "world market for servile labor." The question of the relative integration of prices in the interior with those at the coast has been addressed else-where, where it is suggested that interior prices were related to coastal prices and to prices in North Africa, with prices at export points on the Atlantic coast shadowing interior prices and those in North Africa over the long run, which does indeed suggest an integrated international market, as Manning has argued.[27] Nonetheless, prices for males in the interior were generally lower than those for females, while at the coast Europeans were usually willing to pay more for males than females. This price differential indicates that there was a stronger demand for females in the interior than at the coast, and that no matter how many people were enslaved, there was a relative surplus of males who could not be sold at prices comparable to females. The price for female slaves in the interior of West Africa was higher than the price for male slaves, in contrast to the situation on the Atlantic coast, where Europeans generally paid more for "prime" males but were also willing to pay the same for able-bodied women. In the interior the preference clearly was for young, attractive females.

While it may be desirable to develop a conception of a global labor market for slaves that incorporates large parts of Africa with the Americas, Muslim North Africa, the Middle East, and indeed the Indian Ocean basin, as Manning suggests, these areas should be seen as distinct, if interlocking, components of an international system of slavery. What distinguished slavery in Africa from the other parts of this international system was the integration of enslavement, the slave trade, and the productive exploitation of slaves—often associated with political states that had their own policies on social, religious, and ethical issues. Manning has constructed a demographic model that attempts to provide parameters within which this slave mode of production can be measured in terms of its demographic impact. By dividing a hypothetical West African population into groups raided for slaves, the people taken as slaves, others doing the raiding and trading, and those who died as a consequence of enslavement, Manning has been able to set demographic limits that can be used to examine the impact of slavery on West African populations.[28] The cultural and religious considerations examined here reinforce this methodological approach.

The practice of ransoming captives, which is overlooked in Manning's model, was an important factor in determining slave prices.[29] Freeborn Muslims, especially males, who were taken captive in war, through banditry or raids, were usually offered for ransom as an alternative to enslavement and sale. Such practices were common in the Muslim world surrounding the Mediterranean, where Christians were seized and held for ransom, as were Muslims by Christians. In West Africa, the ransom price was often twice the amount that could be realized through sale on the open market. Since males were more commonly ransomed than females, it is suggested here that the cost of ransoming affected the price of male slaves, so that the differential between the cost of males and females was actually less than it appears when slave prices alone are examined. This practice, which was common everywhere Muslims were to be found in West Africa, reinforces the argument that internal factors, not an Atlantic-Sahara divide, determined the price structure.

The cost of moving slaves to the coast or across the Sahara also influenced the price of slaves, although Austen and Dennis Cordell have concluded that relative transport costs between the interior and the coast were less important than previously thought: "the major cause of higher prices on the Atlantic was competitive bidding among a multiple of buyers, whose participation was a function of the lower entry costs—mainly in the form of lower [oceanic] transport costs—in this market." That is, European traders from various nations competed to drive up the prices paid for slaves destined for American markets, no matter what costs were incurred in moving slaves to the coast. Slave prices in the Sahara and interior markets rose more slowly because "Saharan commerce in captives . . . enjoyed the structural protection of an enclave North African market too small and too costly for Europeans to enter."[30] However, Austen and Cordell fail to mention the ideological and religious reasons that prevented Europeans from entering the slave trade of this "enclave market" on any scale.

An apparent Atlantic-Sahara divide that might have affected the price structure of the slave trade and could have determined the proportion of males and females in the export trade across the Sahara and the Atlantic proves to be deceptive. While the transatlantic trade tended to favor males by as much as two to one, across the Sahara the preference was for women, but this emphasis on the external demand overlooks the market within the societies and economies of West Africa, especially in Muslim areas. The demand for slaves in Muslim areas restricted the supply of enslaved individuals for the Atlantic trade, and this restraint was consistent with Muslim state policies that attempted to prevent the sale of slaves to Christian countries. The practice of ransoming freeborn Muslims and the prohibitions on the sale of Muslims to non-Muslims help to explain the high proportion of slaves retained internally and the relatively low levels of exports to the Atlantic coast. Hence the extent to which women were valued more than men reflected the importance of the internal West African market for slaves.

Because of the premium placed on females in the Muslim areas of West Africa, the pull of the transatlantic market was not sufficient to draw females, or even many males, from these regions to the ports of the Atlantic coast. The scale of the enslaved population and the capabilities of the slave-marketing networks meant that it was theoretically possible to have supplied the transatlantic trade much more than was actually the case. Moreover, the trans-Saharan trade could have shifted to cater for a transatlantic market, if Manning's assumed integrated single market for slaves had in fact been in full operation. However, political and religious constraints made females worth more in the interior than on the coast, where European slavers were active.

In terms of economic impact, both North African demand and expanding Saharan markets were relatively small by comparison with the transatlantic market for slaves, and therefore protected from European encroachment, as Austen and Cordell have suggested.[31] By contrast, the internal West African market for slaves in Muslim areas was large, so that cultural, political, and, above all, religious factors seem to explain the reluctance of merchants and officials in parts of West Africa to sell females to the Atlantic. The establishment of states through jihad in the eighteenth and nineteenth centuries and the expansion of commercial networks in the interior had the effect of restricting the sale of slaves to the coast for ideological and religious reasons. Rather than an economic division between Saharan and Atlantic markets, the dividing line, to the extent that one existed, was political and moral, separating Muslim West Africa from the Christian Atlantic. Economic demand alone does not explain the price structure for slaves or why larger numbers of females were retained within West Africa and sold across the Sahara than across the Atlantic.

NOTES

1. See, for example, Joseph Inikori, "Export versus Domestic Demand: The Determinants of Sex Ratios in the Transatlantic Slave Trade," *Research in Economic History* 14 (1992): 129, 152–53, 156–57. Also see David Eltis, *The Rise of African Slavery in the Americas* (Cambridge: Cambridge University Press, 2000), 107–8.

2. Ralph A. Austen and Dennis D. Cordell, "Trade, Transportation, and Expanding Economic Networks: Saharan Caravan Commerce in the Era of European Expansion, 1500–1900," in *Black Business and Economic Power,* ed. Alusine Jalloh and Toyin Falola (Rochester: University of Rochester Press, 2002), 80–113.

3. Claire C. Robertson and Martin A. Klein, "Women's Importance in African Slave Systems," in *Women and Slavery in Africa*, ed. Robertson and Klein (Madison: University of Wisconsin Press, 1983), 3, 5.

4. See, for example, the data presented in David Geggus, "Sex Ratio, Age, and Ethnicity in the Atlantic Slave Trade: Data from the French Shipping and Plantation Records," *Journal of African History* 30 (1989): 23–44.

5. For a discussion of Bambara and Mande or Mandinke, see Peter Caron, "'Of a Nation which Others do not Understand': Bambara Slaves and African Ethnicity in Colonial Louisiana, 1718–60," *Slavery and Abolition* 18 (1997): 98–121; Sylviane Anna Diouf, "Devils or Sorcerers, Muslims or Studs: Manding in the Americas," in *Trans-Atlantic Dimensions of Ethnicity in the African Diaspora*, ed. Paul E. Lovejoy and David V. Trotman (London: Continuum, 2003), 139–57.

6. Paul E. Lovejoy, "The Central Sudan and the Atlantic Slave Trade," in *Paths to the Past: African Historical Essays in Honor of Jan Vansina*, ed. Robert W. Harms, Joseph C. Miller, David C. Newbury, and Michelle D. Wagner (Atlanta: ASA Press, 1994), 345–70.

7. Patrick Manning, *Slavery and African Life: Occidental, Oriental and African Slave Trades* (New York: Cambridge University Press, 1990).

8. For elaboration, see my "Islam, Slavery, and Political Transformation in West Africa: Constraints on the Trans-Atlantic Slave Trade," *Outre-Mers: Revue d'histoire* 89 (2002): 247–82.

9. Enslaved Africans shipped from Mozambique and the region of modern Liberia and Ivory Coast account for the rest.

10. For an estimate of the number of enslaved Africans who were sent to the Americas, primarily to Bahia, from the Bight of Benin, see Lovejoy, "Central Sudan," 345–70. The Eltis voyage database has a built-in bias, in that the Bahian trade is not well represented, and hence the movement of Muslims or those enslaved as a result of jihad is partially obscured; see David Eltis et al., *The Trans-Atlantic Slave Trade: A Database on CD-Rom* (Cambridge: Cambridge University Press, 1999).

11. For these estimates, see Lovejoy, *Transformations in Slavery*, 51, 146, tables 3.4, 7.4.

12. See Heinrich Barth, *Travels and Discoveries in North and Central Africa* (New York: Harper and Row, 1857–59).

13. See Lovejoy, *Transformations in Slavery*. The question was initially pointed out by Philip Curtin and later addressed by Patrick Manning. Curtin, *The Atlantic Slave Trade: A Census* (Madison: University of Wisconsin Press, 1969); Manning, "The Slave Trade in the Bight of Benin, 1640–1890," in *The Uncommon Market: Essays in the Economic History of the Atlantic Slave Trade*, ed. Henry A. Gemery and Jan S. Hogendorn (New York: Academic, 1979), 107–41; see also Lovejoy, "The Volume of the Atlantic Slave Trade: A Synthesis," *Journal of African History* 22, no. 4 (1982): 473–501.

14. Lovejoy, "Central Sudan."

15. See, for example, the studies in Elizabeth Savage, ed., *The Human Commodity: Perspectives on the Trans-Saharan Slave Trade* (London: Frank Cass, 1992), which demonstrate that the composition of the trans-Saharan trade varied greatly. Also see Austen and Cordell, "Trade, Transportation," 91.

16. Ralph Austen, "The Mediterranean Islamic Slave Trade out of Africa: A Tentative Census," in Savage, *Human Commodity*, 214–48. Also see Austen and Cordell, "Trade, Transportation," 88–91.

17. Paul E. Lovejoy, "Commercial Sectors in the Economy of the Nineteenth-Century Central Sudan: The Trans-Saharan Trade and the Desert-Side Salt Trade," *African Economic History* 13 (1984): 85–116.

18. See, for example, E. Ann McDougall, "Salt, Saharans, and the Trans-Saharan Slave Trade: Nineteenth Century Developments," in Savage, *Human Commodity*, 76–80.

19. See David Tambo, "The Sokoto Caliphate Slave Trade in the Nineteenth Century," *International Journal of African Historical Studies* 9, no. 2 (1976): 187–217; Lovejoy, "Central Sudan," 345–70; Martin Klein, "The Slave Trade in the Western Sudan during the Nineteenth Century," in Savage, *Human Commodity*, 39–60; James L. A. Webb Jr., "The Horse and Slave Trade between the Western Sudan and Senegambia," *Journal of African History* 34, no. 2 (1993): 222–46.

20. For a discussion of the relative scale of slave populations, see Paul E. Lovejoy and Jan Hogendorn, *Slow Death for Slavery: The Course of Abolition in Northern Nigeria, 1897–1936* (Cambridge: Cambridge University Press, 1993). For the size of the slave population in the area that became Afrique Occidentale Française, see Martin Klein, *Slavery and Colonial Rule in French West Africa* (Cambridge: Cambridge University Press, 1998), 252–56. Klein bases his estimates largely on the reports of colonial officials, which are summarized in the reports of E. Poulet and E. Deherme, *Slavery and Its Abolition in French West Africa*, ed. A. S. Kanya-Forstner and Paul E. Lovejoy (Madison: African Studies Program, University of Wisconsin, 1994).

21. Herbert Klein, "African Women in the Atlantic Slave Trade," in Robertson and Klein, *Women and Slavery*, 29–38.

22. Martin Klein, "Women in Slavery in the Western Sudan," in Robertson and Klein, *Women and Slavery*, 69.

23. For the argument for the relative unimportance of the slave trade for African economic growth, see Eltis, *Rise of African Slavery*; David Eltis and Lawrence C. Jennings, "Trade between Western Africa and the Atlantic World in the Pre-Colonial Era," *American Historical Review* 93, no. 4 (1988): 936–59. This argument fails to address the autonomy of the Muslim interior.

24. Emmanuel Terray, "Reflexions sur la formation du prix des esclaves a l'intérieur de l'Afrique de l'Ouest précoloniale," *Journal des Africanistes* 52 (1982): 120.

25. See Paul E. Lovejoy, "The Clapperton-Bello Exchange: The Sokoto Jihad and the Trans-Atlantic Slave Trade, 1804–1837," in *The Desert Shore: Literatures of the Sahel*, ed. Christopher Wise (Boulder: Lynne Rienner, 2001), 201–28; Lovejoy, "The Context of Enslavement in West Africa: Ahmad Baba and the Ethics of Slavery," in

Slaves, Subjects, and Subversives: Blacks in Colonial Latin America, ed. Jane Landers and Barry Robinson (Albuquerque: University of New Mexico Press, 2006).

26. Patrick Manning, *Slavery and African Life: Occidental, Oriental, and African Slave Trades* (Cambridge: Cambridge University Press, 1990), 102–3.

27. Paul E. Lovejoy and David Richardson, "Competing Markets for Male and Female Slaves: Slave Prices in the Interior of West Africa, 1780–1850," *International Journal of African Historical Studies* 28, no. 2 (1995): 261–93. Also see Austen and Cordell, "Trade, Transportation," 88–99.

28. Manning, *Slavery and African Life.*

29. The issue is discussed further in Jennifer Loftkranz, "The Ransoming of Enslaved Muslims in the Western Sudan in the Nineteenth Century," paper presented at conference on Slavery, Islam and Diaspora, York University, Toronto, October 2003, forthcoming in *Slavery, Islam and Diaspora,* ed. Behnaz Asl Mirzai, Ismael Musah Montana, and Paul E. Lovejoy (Trenton, NJ: Africa World, 2007).

30. Austen and Cordell, "Trade, Transportation," 91.

31. Ibid., 82.

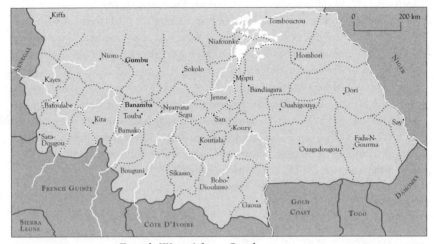

French West Africa, Soudan, ca. 1905

12

WOMEN, HOUSEHOLD INSTABILITY, AND THE END OF SLAVERY IN BANAMBA AND GUMBU, FRENCH SOUDAN, 1905–12

RICHARD ROBERTS

Banamba and Gumbu were important centers of slaveholding in the Western Sudan in the late nineteenth century. They were also sites of significant slave departures in the period after 1905. The slaves' exodus from Banamba preceded that of Gumbu by three years, and the patterns of slave departures and masters' responses show significant differences. In Banamba in 1905 masters resisted slave departures by force, but when the exodus resumed in 1906, they seemed to acquiesce in it. By the end of 1906 the slaves exodus from Banamba was over, although a trickle continued to leave the region.[1] In Gumbu slaves only began to leave in 1908. By then the French colonial position on slavery was clear: the French no longer supported masters' claims over their slaves. They no longer permitted the alienation of individual liberty through enslavement, and the newly created colonial native courts did not recognize the legal status of slave or master and thus the property rights of masters over their slaves.[2] The French therefore permitted slaves to leave their former masters as long as they paid their taxes.

The slave masters of Gumbu, however, were not willing to see their slaves simply pick up and go. Knowing that the French would not tolerate violence to keep their slaves in their fields, the owners used the new native courts to entangle their slaves in legal disputes to prevent their easy departure. This chapter uses court records from the Banamba and Gumbu provincial tribunals to examine the immediate postemancipation period.[3] The creation of the colonial legal system in French West Africa coincided with the end of slavery. The French established the native court system by decree in 1903, although the new courts were not instituted until 1905. In Banamba the native courts were not established until 1907. The slaves' exodus from Banamba began in 1905 and then spread outward in ever-widening circles over the next four or five years. Thus the Banamba court records do not coincide with the most dramatic moments in the slaves' exodus. By 1910 most of the slaves who wanted to leave had already made the move. The court records of Gumbu, however, capture a moment in the struggles between masters and slaves as they grappled with the end of slavery. Former masters as well as freedmen and women used these new courts to pursue their respective interests against one another. The records from Banamba and Gumbu also capture a sense of the social consequences of the end of slavery in the two regions.

Banamba and Gumbu were not identical. Gumbu was an administrative district (*cercle*); Banamba was a province of the larger Bamako District. Most of the slaves in Gumbu were concentrated in Gumbu town and twenty or so outlying villages. Located along the desert edge, Gumbu sat astride the northern limit of rain-fed agriculture. In the course of the nineteenth century, the economy had expanded around slave-based production of grain and cotton, much of which was destined to supply the ecologically specialized trade with the Maures of the neighboring desert.

The system of slavery that developed in Gumbu differed somewhat from that in the region of Banamba, which was located more fully in the savanna region, but also catered to the desert-side trade. Around Banamba and the seven other Maraka towns of Beledugu (*Marakaduguw wolonwula*), slaves tended to live together in outlying agricultural villages, which resembled plantations. Slave status among the Maraka of Banamba was hereditary, although the Maraka distinguished between newly purchased slaves and *woloso*—those "born in the house" of their master. In terms of labor relations, newly purchased slaves were more harshly treated than woloso. Although slavery was an ancient institution among the Maraka, the slave population of Banamba and Gumbu expanded dramatically after the mid-nineteenth century. Many were first-generation slaves, captured by the late-nineteenth-century state-builder Samory or by the warlords of Sikasso. By 1899 slave plantations surrounded Banamba for fifty kilometers in all directions, and slaves constituted the majority of the region's population.[4]

The slaves of Gumbu lived and worked differently from those in Banamba. According to Claude Meillassoux, they had distinctive "relations of production" depending on their social status. Newly acquired slaves had virtually no rights and worked for their masters in exchange for their subsistence. Once the slave was "seasoned" and did not show signs of flight, he or she entered a new status that influenced the work regime because these slaves now had "rights" to a certain portion of the day for themselves. They worked for their masters or mistresses six to fourteen hours per day, six days per week. The rest of the time, they worked on their own plots. Female slaves might leave the fields early, but since they were always members of households, they had household chores to accomplish in addition to their labor in the fields.

The final category of slaves was the *worosow* (suffix *-w* indicates plural) or "slaves born into the house" of the master. These slaves in the second and subsequent generations could, if their master approved, work entirely on their own fields in exchange for an annual rent customarily fixed at 150 *muule* (around 360 kilograms) of grain. Meillassoux calls this "rent slavery."[5] This relationship of an annual transfer of millet or sorghum featured significantly in the period after 1908, as the former masters of Gumbu sought to prevent their former slaves from leaving. Worosow probably lived in small hamlets dispersed throughout this ecologically sparse and fragile region. Masters and slaves developed mutually entangling webs of dependency, reinforced by loans of livestock and goods and by ritual practices. The end of slavery put to the test the depth and elasticity of these webs of dependency.

In this chapter I am particularly interested in examining how the postemancipation period in Banamba and Gumbu affected women and how women, slave and free alike, used the new French colonial courts to gain more control over their lives and sometimes their families. In French West Africa, a woman was always either a daughter, a wife, a widow, or a mother or a combination thereof. Marriage in most of the region's patrilineal, virilocal societies involved the transfer of rights to a woman's labor and reproductive power from her father's kin to those of her husband. Brides were rarely consulted on their wishes, and bridewealth solidified the transfer. Newly enslaved women were never "daughters" of their masters, but they could become wives and mothers. Like their free counterparts, slave women lived within domestic units headed by men, either their masters (or their mistress's husbands) or their husbands, who were sometimes also slaves. Where bridewealth had been transferred, the mother whether slave or free had no rights to her children if the marriage failed. Thus, when the end of slavery exacerbated household instability, women often had to choose between remaining in a potentially abusive environment or leaving their children behind.[6] Slave, free, and freed women shared in common varying degrees of gender-specific forms of social vulnerability, and their responses to periods of dramatic social change—such as the end of slavery—reveal different strategies relating to their statuses.[7]

Governor-general Ernest Roume established the system of native courts throughout French West Africa on 10 November 1903. The decree established three tiers of courts for African subjects that more or less resembled the three-tier court in the metropole. The first level court was the *tribunal de village*, which was designed as the forum for reconciling disputes at the village level. It was designed to be analogous to the French system of justices of the peace: local notables charged by the state with trying to reconcile disputes before they went to the more formal *tribunal de première instance*. According to the 1903 decree, the village tribunal was not obliged to keep written records, and I have not seen any archival traces of the deliberations of these tribunals.[8] Supervision of these tribunals fell to the French district officer. Few colonial officials had the time or the inclination to visit the village tribunals. However, the archival record contains enough bits and pieces of information to indicate that many litigants strategically bypassed these courts either because they were not interested in having the village chief adjudicate or because they did not wish to be reconciled.[9]

The native courts of the second tier were the *tribunaux de province*. These courts heard civil disputes and misdemeanor offenses. There was usually only one provincial tribunal in any one district, although larger districts such as Bamako had three. The chief judge was the *chef de province*, the French-appointed native ruler of the region, or another highly regarded notable, who was assisted by two other notables from the region. During the early stages of the court's operation, the French district administrator participated in or supervised closely the court's proceedings. The 1903 decree also required that registers of the court's activities be kept.[10] This job fell largely to the French administrator or his French assistant, since Africans literate in French were still relatively rare at this time. Separate registers were maintained for "civil and commercial" disputes and for what the French called *correctionnelle*, as distinct from *criminnelle*, cases. Criminal cases were heard at the district tribunal level. For this chapter, I have used only the civil and commercial registers of the provincial tribunals, which are for our purposes the entry-level court for civil disputes. The third level of native court was the *tribunal de* cercle, which was charged with hearing all the appeals from the lower courts and with jurisdiction over criminal matters. The district adminis-trator presided, assisted by two African notables.

The registers of disputes for the Gumbu and Banamba provincial tri-bunals do not provide a ready-made breakdown by types of cases. Al-though the records of each dispute tend to be sparse—usually no more than three or four lines—the registers contain five bodies of information. The first column indicated the date the dispute was brought before the tribunal. The second listed the names of the litigants, their domiciles, and sometimes their personal status. The personal status was a crucial piece of information, since it determined whether the disputants wished the complaint to be adjudicated according to customary or Muslim law. Only rarely, however, did the court record the type of custom employed in the case—Bambara, Malinke, Senufo, and so on. The third column contained a précis of the dispute, which provides the most interesting material for social historians. The fourth column indicated the decision taken by the tribunal, and the fifth column indicated whether the dis-putants wished to appeal the verdict to the district tribunals, the next stage in the hierarchy of courts.[11]

The introduction of colonial courts not only provides historians with source material to reconstruct lived history, but also provided new oppor-tunities for Africans to redefine their relationships to one another and therefore sharpened their struggles over the meanings of change. There are, however, many things that these records do not tell us, including whether the disputants had tried other venues before bringing their cases to the tribunal de province. Disputants may well have taken their griev-ances before family elders and village elders, as well as to Muslim judges, or qadis, especially where Muslims constituted a significant part of the population. These records provide only the sparsest of details. We do not get a sense of the deeper "history" of each grievance, or of the demeanor and interactions of the litigants and the assessors at the moment of the trial.[12] We cannot assume that the body of court records for the tribunal de province was equal to the total number of disputes in Gumbu and Banamba. Given the variety of alternative means to resolve disputes, the disputants who brought their cases before the tribunal de province did so because they may have anticipated a certain outcome, as Bernard Cohn and Robert Kidder have described for litigants in colonial India.[13]

The Gumbu court registers consist of 597 judgments rendered by the provincial tribunal between April 1905 and September 1912. Those from Banamba consist of 434 judgments rendered by the provincial tribunal from April 1907 to December 1912. Since Gumbu was the seat of the district headquarters, the district administrator oversaw the establishment of the provincial tribunal early in 1905. Banamba, on the other hand, merely had a customs station manned by a low-level clerk in 1905. The slaves' exodus in 1905 caught the French unprepared and focused their attention on Banamba in late 1905. They appointed a "resident," a French civilian employee, to Banamba in 1906. Unfortunately, we have virtually no surviving court registers for 1906.[14] It is important to remember that the Banamba provincial tribunal was not available to the masters in 1905, or most likely in 1906, so we do not know what kinds of civil disputes might have been brought between masters and slaves during the height of the exodus.

DISTRIBUTION OF THE CASES BY DISPUTE

Banamba province consisted of the agriculturally and commercially rich towns of Banamba and Touba (two of the seven Maraka towns of Beledugu). Gumbu was a district, but the densest area of settlement in this region of the Sahel was the town of Gumbu and its surrounding agricultural hamlets. The numbers of civil disputes brought to the Gumbu and Banamba provincial tribunals were roughly equivalent: on average seventy-two cases per year were heard by the Banamba provincial tribunal and eighty-five cases per year in Gumbu. The distribution of disputes by category indicates some significant differences between these two regions (figures 12.1, 12.2).

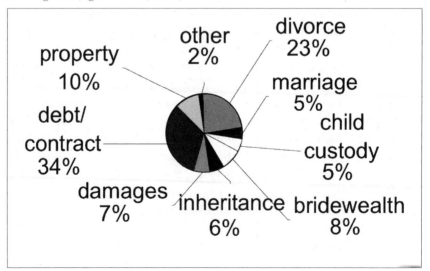

Figure 12.1. Distribution of disputes, Gumbu, 1905–12, n = 597. *Source:* ANM 2 M 122

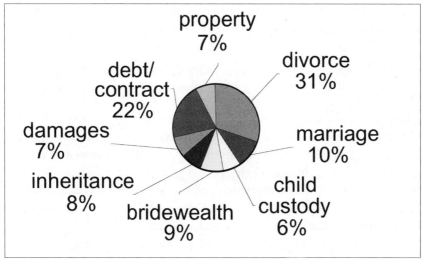

Figure 12.2. Distribution of cases, Banamba, 1907–12, n = 434. Source: ANM 2 M 54

Statistically the most significant categories of cases in both Gumbu and Banamba are debt and contract disputes (Gumbu, 34 percent; Banamba, 22 percent) and divorces (Gumbu, 23 percent; Banamba, 31 percent). But categories of disputes tend to cluster together. Debt/contract and property disputes are clearly tied together in Gumbu and were prominent during the height of the exodus in 1908. Together, debt/contract and property disputes constituted 44 percent of all the cases in Gumbu. Debt/contract and property cases in Banamba are not so clearly linked to the end of slavery in Banamba, although together they constituted 29 percent of all Banamba disputes. The relatively high incidence of these disputes in Banamba may reflect the greater importance of commerce in the Banamba region, which was a major commercial crossroads in the late nineteenth century and during the first five years of the new century.

Divorce, marriage, bridewealth, and child custody disputes are indicators of household instability. The incidence of bridewealth disputes, which stem from ruptures in the contract of marriage, was remarkably similar between these two regions (Gumbu, 8 percent; Banamba, 9 percent). The incidence of child custody disputes was also remarkably similar (Gumbu, 5 percent; Banamba, 6 percent). Divorce cases, most of which were brought by women seeking to end their marriage, constituted 31 percent of all disputes in Banamba and 23 percent in Gumbu. In contrast, marriage cases, in which husbands resorted to the courts to force their wives to return to their conjugal homes, constituted only 5 percent of the cases in Gumbu, but 10 percent in Banamba. Together, marriage and divorce cases constituted 41 percent of all cases in Banamba, but only 28 percent of the cases in Gumbu. In Banamba, then, there were 46 percent more marriage and divorce cases than in Gumbu.

DISPUTES OVER DEBT/CONTRACT AND PROPERTY:
SOCIAL CONFLICTS AT THE MOMENT OF DEPARTURE

The pattern of disputes over debts/contracts and property was very different in Gumbu and Banamba. The Gumbu courts were functioning during the height of the slaves' exodus in 1908, and the court records capture some of the immediate struggles between masters and slaves. This was not the case in Banamba, although Banamba debt cases witness a significant and anomalous spike that seems analogous to those of Gumbu. In Gumbu the spike in debt cases coincides with the exodus in July 1908; in Banamba the spike occurs in June 1909, fully two years after the height of the slaves' exodus.

Former masters in Gumbu seem to have quickly understood in 1908 that while the colonial state was no longer prepared to keep their slaves in the fields and working for them, they could use the newly established colonial courts to impose the logic of contract and property rights on their former slaves. In Gumbu District the master-slave relationship that was particularly susceptible to these new strategies by former masters was the rent slavery discussed above. In the absence of a strong state to coerce surplus production from slaves, masters spun webs of dependency around their slaves, keeping slaves from running away and tying them more fully to their masters. These webs often took the form of masters providing wives for their male slaves, permitting slaves to guard livestock in exchange for a share of the offspring, and sharing the harvest. Each

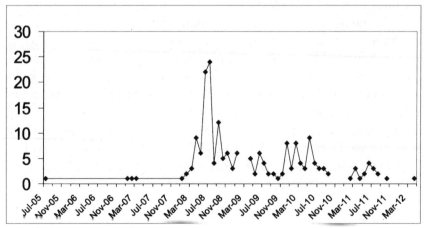

Figure 12.3. Incidence of debt disputes, Gumbu, 1905–12, n = 197. *Source:* ANM 2 M 122

year following the harvest, the slave presented his master with a set amount of grain.

I have elsewhere discussed the substance of the debt/contract and property disputes in Gumbu.[15] In essence, if a slave showed an inclination to leave Gumbu in 1908, his master brought suit against him to force him to honor his "contract" to deliver a share of the harvest or to recover property lent to his slave. In the rent model of slavery in Gumbu, wives were always dependents of their slave husbands or masters. Thus, I have no records of masters suing their female slaves over "contract" disputes.[16] The nature of the court registers and the verdicts rendered by the magistrates tended to exacerbate the "contractual" nature of the master-slave relationships. The judgments recorded at the provincial tribunal in Gumbu tell us very little about whether or not former masters tried to negotiate with their former slaves to find a mutually acceptable middle ground to resolve their disputes. The judgments awarded winners and punished losers of the disputes in no uncertain terms. In reaching their decisions, the magistrates probably reduced much more complex negotiations to a simple formula of unambiguous rights and obligations.

The situation in Gumbu in 1909 was very different. By then the numbers of cases brought before the provincial tribunal had diminished by two-thirds, although the volume of slave departures was higher in 1909 than in 1908. The district officer attributed this diminution of disputes to his perception that both the former masters and their former slaves "have come to understand our ideas [about justice] and no longer decry each other as enemies, as they did at the outset of the exodus of the slaves."[17] Instead of attributing the decline in disputes to the growing knowledge of French ideas of justice or to some greater sense of mutual respect, we could just as easily argue for a change in strategy by former slaves. After the first year of transition the freedmen understood their former masters' strategies to entangle them in legal disputes and preempted the disputes by settling them before their departures or by departing without announcing their intentions. The colonial state did not have the institutional capacity to pursue defendants in civil disputes who simply skipped town before their scheduled court appearances.

Although the spike in Banamba debt cases seems remarkably similar to the Gumbu spike, the context was different. The Gumbu debt spike coincided with the first wave of significant slave departures. The Banamba spike occurred three years after the last significant wave of slave departures. Nor can the Banamba cases be linked to specific social relationships, as can the Gumbu debts cases. Instead, the Banamba cases deal mostly with recovery of commercial debts. I cannot explain why there

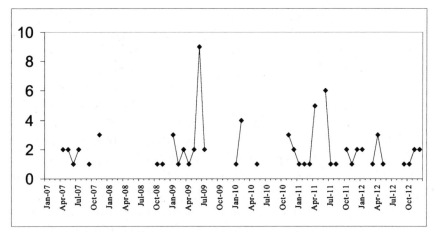

Figure 12.4. Incidence of debt cases, Banamba, 1907–12, n = 78. *Source:* ANM 2 M 54

was a surge in commercial disputes in June 1909, but there was a similar peak in May through July 1911. It could be that merchants were interested in recovering debts during the planting season in order to prepare for their dry-season commercial ventures. Two cases from the Banamba spike in June 1909 are worth developing because the judgments reflect the litigants' willingness to transform monetary debts into labor payments. These two cases may indicate a continuing labor shortage in Banamba following the slaves' departure.

Both cases were heard on 3 June 1909. In the first Diope Tereba brought Soumana Gakou to court to recover the sixty thousand cowries[18] the latter had not repaid. Gakou admitted his debt and offered to pay it off through his labor. Following a model remarkably similar to slavery, but with the addition of a monetary value attached to his daily labor, Gakou offered to work for Terebe until he paid off his debt if Terebe would house and feed him. Gakou assessed the value of his daily labor to be four hundred cowries. Thus, Gakou pledged himself to Tereba for 150 days. Tereba agreed to this deal.[19] The second labor-for-debt exchange came from the failure of the defendant, Moktar Doukouri, to adhere to the judgment against him in the provincial tribunal on 20 May 1909. On that date Doukouri agreed to repay Toumare Sampare F 15 within fifteen days. Doukouri paid only F 5 on his debt, and on the fifteenth day following the original judgment Sampare was back in court demanding the rest. Doukouri agreed, as did Gakou with his creditor, to work for Sampare for a daily wage that would be held by the plaintiff until the debt was fully acquitted, but while in service he would be housed and fed by the creditor. Both parties agreed to this.[20]

The exodus of the slaves left a serious labor shortage in both Banamba and Gumbu. Former masters tried to negotiate with their former slaves to stay on the farm and work for them. When negotiations failed, masters in Gumbu took their former slaves to court to keep them from leaving. But these were short-term solutions. Former masters turned to neighboring Bamana villages, where the young men's association (Bamana: *ton*) occasionally hired itself out, or they made cooperative labor arrangements with other former masters.[21] Most frequently, however, they turned to their own households—their wives, sons, and daughters—to help in the field. Marital instability was linked to this redefinition of household labor relations.

HOUSEHOLD INSTABILITY, WOMEN'S AGENCY, AND THE END OF SLAVERY

By 1908, as the slaves' exodus was becoming a flood, the Gumbu administrator noted that requests for divorce were "particularly abundant." The officer linked the high incidence of requests for divorce in Gumbu to the weak bonds of affection between African women, their husbands, their husband's kin, and their own children: "It is regrettable to acknowledge just how little a native woman is attached to her husband and her new family. Following the exodus of the slaves, many among these women do not hesitate to abandon their children to their husbands who wish to remain in his district so that they can return to their homelands."[22]

Although the cases the district officer was referring to were obviously cases of slave wives, the officer should have known that in patrilineal, patrilocal descent systems in which bridewealth has been paid, women, whether free or slave, had no legal claims on their children. Cases of divorce differ from those of contract/property and debt in that the majority of the plaintiffs were women. In Gumbu and throughout the French Soudan, women brought suits for divorce against their husbands because the new colonial legal system provided women with new opportunities to take control over at least a part of their lives. The new tribunals were also significant in that they often supported women's requests to terminate marriages in which their husbands had mistreated them or even in cases when women simply wanted to leave their husbands.[23] Fully 36 percent of all the cases heard by the provincial tribunal in Gumbu stemmed from marital disputes (divorces, marriage disputes, and bridewealth). Divorce alone constituted 23 percent of all the disputes heard at the Gumbu provincial tribunal. The Banamba data reveal even greater household instability. Divorce, marriage disputes, and bridewealth disputes constituted 40 percent of all disputes there.

Through the court data from Gumbu and Banamba we see how the slaves' exodus impacted households. The Banamba court data begin only in 1908, a year or two after the large-scale departures. Both sets of records reveal patterns of household instability during the years following the exodus. As I have argued elsewhere, the end of slavery offered slave men and women three broad choices and an almost infinite variation within them. Slaves could leave their masters and either return to their original homelands (if they remembered or imagined where they were) or set up new homes elsewhere, they could simply declare themselves free without having to leave, or they could renegotiate relations with their former masters. Some of these choices resulted in the separation of slave families if husbands and wives decided on different options, and some of these cases made their way into the courts. Few court records contain direct references to slaves, although sometimes the records will refer to the sanitized terms *servant* or *domestique* that the French began to use after 1905. Occasionally the telltale sign that a case involved former slaves is the absence of bridewealth transfers, the presence of merely a token transfer, or the indication that one of the parties wished to return to their "place of origin." Departure often meant leaving a spouse behind. Such was the case when Batouna Souka came to court seeking a divorce from her husband, Dji Diara. Diara told the court that he "wanted to leave Mamaribougou [a hamlet of Gumbu] to return to his land of origin." His wife did not want to follow him. She also told the court that no bridewealth had been paid. The court granted Souka a divorce.[24]

In the following child custody case heard in Banamba the dispute stemmed from the decision of former slave spouses to go their separate ways. This slave family first moved together from Gumbu, where they were slaves, to Banamba. Because it was an agriculturally rich region, Banamba attracted slaves leaving other parts of the Sahel.[25]

Married on the order of their master while they were his servants, Guedioumou Sissoko and Kadidja Souko had eight children. They left Gumbu in 1910 and found themselves in Banankoro in January 1911. At that time Souko learned that her father was living in N'Tobougou. Sissoko refused to accompany her and declared his intention to return to his village of origin. Souko returned to Banamba to claim her children and her property. Each claimed custody of the children. The children declared their wish to be with their mother.

In court, the parties agreed to part ways. In all likelihood no bridewealth had been transferred, since both spouses were slaves of the same
master, and thus, in the absence of bridewealth and the regularization of
the marriage, the children would belong to their mother. The court ordered that their communal property—consisting of one cow and 340
muules of millet—be divided into three parts. The cow was to be sold
and the proceeds as well as the millet were to be divided: two parts were
to go to Sissoko and one part to Souko.[26] This case is especially revealing
of the stages through which a slave family moved as they adapted to the
transition from slavery to freedom.

The Kadidja Souko case also indicates that freedmen and women
often chose not to remain together as family units but instead sought to
locate and live with their respective close agnatic kin. Souko preferred to
remain with her father rather than with her slave husband of many years.
And because no bridewealth had been transferred, she was able to claim
her children as well. In another case heard in Gumbu, the freed wife of a
slave wanted a divorce, not so that she could stay in the region but rather
in order to accompany her brother as he returned to Bouguni. In this case
the husband accepted his wife's request for a divorce but demanded the
return of the bridewealth he had transferred, 120 muules of millet. Such an
amount was clearly a low "slave" valuation, but it nonetheless reflected
considerable food value.[27]

The new courts empowered freedwomen who were not intimidated by
the (male) authority of the courts. Fatimata Ba used the courts to defend
her newfound independence. Ba, the widowed slave wife of Tiemoko
Guine, was in court in Banamba on 5 May 1907 to resist efforts by Guine's
brother, Fadougui Guine, to force her to accompany him to Sikasso, his
region of origin. Fatimata Ba had refused and moved instead to Nyamina,
where she married a man named Souare. Fadougui Guine had sent his
son, who had accompanied his father to Sikasso, to fetch Ba, whom he
claimed as his wife following the Malinke practice of levirate, in which
the deceased husband's kin (usually his eldest brother) inherited the
widow. The provincial tribunal ruled that Ba's marriage to Souare was in-
valid and that Ba must accompany Fadougui to Sikasso. In one of only
six cases that were appealed in Banamba, Fatimata Ba challenged the
provincial court's judgment at the district court, where the French administrator ruled that Ba's marriage to Tiemoko Guine was never regularized,
that therefore Fadougui Guine had no rights of levirate, and that Ba
was free to live with Souare.[28] While only one of a handful of appeals, the
Ba case demonstrates that freedwomen were knowledgeable about the

new court system, not intimidated by its authority, and prepared to exercise their rights to determine their own lives. More common in the court records are cases that reflect the adjustments that the formerly enslaved made at the end of their enslavement, in which one slave spouse left and the other remained. Binta Kamara sued for divorce in Banamba in 1909 because her husband had abandoned her two years earlier to return to his "land or origin" and she had not heard from him since.[29]

DIVORCE DISPUTES OVER TIME

Divorce cases in Gumbu reflect a very different trend from those observed in property/contract and debt disputes. Whereas most property/contract and debt disputes coincided with the first significant wave of slave departures from Gumbu in the spring of 1908, divorce disputes have two distinctive characteristics. First, they had a marked seasonality, rising sharply each year in April, May, and June and rising again, but less sharply, in November through January. They peaked each year for which we have data in April, which was when the heavy work of field preparation and planting was getting underway in the Sahel, where both these jurisdictions lay. The later, smaller rise coincided with the harvest, especially the cotton harvest. Second, the incidence of divorce increased each year up to April 1911, after which the number of divorce disputes decreased and then leveled out.

In Banamba the annual pattern of divorce disputes was similar to Gumbu, with seasonal spikes in April and May and then again during the harvest, November through January. The earlier spike in Banamba prob-

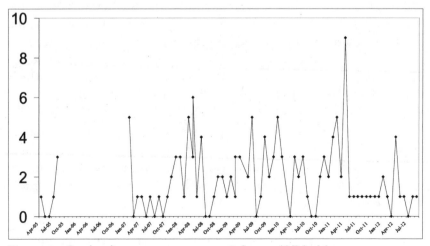

Figure 12.5. Gumbu, divorces, 1905–12, n = 138. *Source:* ANM 2 M 122

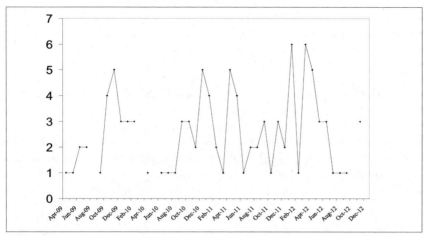

Figure 12.6. Banamba, divorces, 1907–12, n = 131. Source: ANM 2 M 54

ably reflects the beginning of the agricultural cycle with the addition of the May weeding. Weeding was one of the major labor bottlenecks in the agricultural cycle. Divorces in Banamba also show an increase over time, with the numbers of divorce disputes higher than in any prior year in 1912.

As indicated in the graphs on divorces, the monthly distribution of cases registered coincides remarkably with the seasonal peaks of slaves' departures and with the onset of heavy agricultural labor. Readers most familiar with the elaborate legal procedures of civil litigation in the United States and Western Europe should be aware that most disputes brought before the provincial courts in the early-twentieth-century French Soudan were heard and judged the same day they were presented to the court. The few exceptions to this pattern were decisions by the court either to collect additional information from individuals distant from the court or to examine a disputed field directly.[30] Reflecting patterns of adjustments to the departures of slaves from nearby Banamba and Bamako, former slave-owning heads of households turned increasingly to their own wives and children to make up the shortfall in agricultural labor. The wives of Gumbu and Banamba probably felt like the woman quoted in a 1907 report from Bamako: "my husband gives me nothing; my husband forces me to work. My husband does nothing himself and I, I work continuously."[31]

Both the seasonal increases and the increasing numbers of such disputes over the years seem to reflect the full effect of the loss of slave labor. Women were the usual plaintiffs in divorce disputes, but the incidence of divorce disputes suggests that conditions in marriages and households were becoming worse for wives. The increase in divorce cases also suggests that women—free and freed alike—were using the courts to end marriages that were not providing them with the kinds of security they wanted.[32]

HOUSEHOLD INSTABILITY AND THE AGRICULTURAL CYCLE IN THE AFTERMATH OF SLAVERY

Divorce disputes in Banamba and Gumbu also reflect the varying pressures of the agricultural cycle throughout the year. The departure of the slaves meant that masters had to rely on themselves and their households for most of their agricultural labor needs. In both Banamba and Gumbu preparation of the fields and the crucial first weeding (April, May, June) and harvest (November, December, January) were the labor bottlenecks. Not surprisingly, these were also the months with the highest proportion of divorce disputes. Since divorces were usually introduced by wives, their actions during these months indicate that they were reacting to increased pressures on their household and their lives.

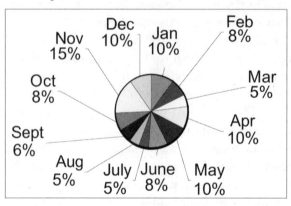

Figure 12.7. Banamba, divorces by month, 1907–12, n = 131. *Source:* ANM 2 M 54

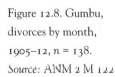

Figure 12.8. Gumbu, divorces by month, 1905–12, n = 138. *Source:* ANM 2 M 122

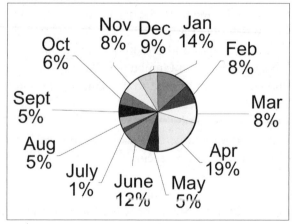

In contrast to divorce cases, marriage disputes were brought exclusively by husbands petitioning the courts to force their wives to return to the conjugal home. The Gumbu data on marriage disputes do not show seasonal patterns, but the Banamba data are very clear. In Banamba 45 percent of all the marriage disputes occurred during the two months of May and June—only one-sixth (17 percent) of the year, thus two and one-half times an averaged monthly rate. May and June were the peak weeding months, and this was the time that male household heads needed their wives' labor.

I am not sure how to explain the much higher incidence of marriage disputes in Banamba. Banamba had nearly 50 percent more marriage disputes than Gumbu even though Banamba had 27 percent fewer total cases. Yet both regions witnessed significant slave departures and similar consequent pressures on labor resources. Women in both Gumbu and Banamba were acting in their interests in pursuing divorces, since the data

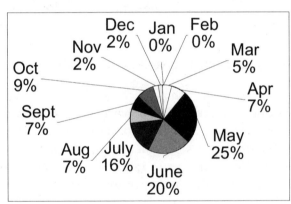

Figure 12.9. Banamba, marriage disputes by month, 1907–12, n = 44.
Source: ANM 2 M 54

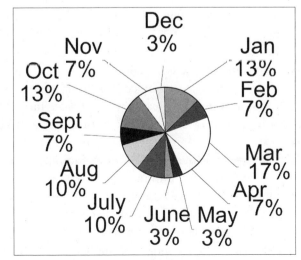

Figure 12.10. Gumbu, marriage disputes by month, 1905–12, n = 30.
Source: ANM 2 M 122

indicate nearly identical seasonal responses. In fact, women in Banamba pursued divorces more frequently than those in Gumbu (31 percent versus 23 percent).

Within the context of the precolonial Western Sudan, Banamba had a more developed urban, cosmopolitan culture than Gumbu, which was a rural backwater. The Maraka of Banamba had built not only a rich urban, commercial culture but also a highly developed Islamic one. As part of the Banamba urban, Muslim culture, Maraka invested some of their commercial profits from their slave plantations and their commercial ventures into freeing their wives from work. These urban, urbane, and newly secluded Banamba women may have felt the change in their status more acutely than their more rural Gumbu counterparts, many of whom may have continued to work in the fields even as rent slavery produced additional supplies of grain. Such dissatisfaction perhaps contributed to the higher rate of divorces initiated by women in Banamba, as their husbands sought to recruit them to fill the agricultural roles abandoned by their slaves.

THE CAUSES OF DIVORCE

Women seeking divorce in the courts of the French Soudan had to explain their reasons for seeking dissolution of their marriages. Among the most common reasons they gave were abandonment, mistreatment, the husband's failure to complete payments of bridewealth, illness of one spouse, and incompatibility (see tables 12.1, 12.2). In abandonment cases the husband absconded and neither left support nor provided news of his whereabouts. In mistreatment cases the husband remained in the household but the wife complained of the husband beating her or failing to provide adequate food or clothing.

In incompatibility cases either both spouses agreed mutually to a divorce or one spouse complained that she or he no longer wanted to remain in the marriage. The court records are not rich enough to interrogate the meanings of incompatibility more fully. To cite incompatibility usually meant an amicable separation, but amicable separations could also stem from changes in status and expectations of security within households and thus be tied to the end of slavery. Chronic illness (e.g., impotence, sterility, blindness, leprosy) could prevent one spouse from fulfilling the marriage contract either sexually or physically. Bridewealth was cited by wives as a cause for divorce when their husbands had not fulfilled their promises to transfer wealth, thus rendering the marriage contract incomplete. Such a charge had implications both for the respectability of

Table 12.1. Causes of divorce disputes, Gumbu, 1905–12

DATE	DIVORCE DISPUTES**	DIVORCES AS % OF ALL DISPUTES	ABANDONMENT AS % OF DIVORCES	MISTREATMENT AS % OF DIVORCES	INCOMPATIBILITY AS % OF DIVORCES	BRIDEWEALTH AS % OF DIVORCES	ILLNESS AS % OF DIVORCES	OTHER CAUSES AS % OF DIVORCES
1905	5	29%	40%	40%	0	0	0	20%
1906*	–	–	–	–	–	–	–	–
1907	15	37%	33%	20%	13%	7%	7%	20%
1908	23	14%	0	48%	26%	0	4%	22%
1909	34	30%	9%	65%	24%	0	3%	21%
1910	22	19%	14%	9%	18%	0	5%	55%
1911	28	35%	14%	25%	11%	4%	4%	43%
1912*	11	48%	45%	18%	0	0	0	36%
Total**	138	23%	16%	30%	17%	1%	3%	32%

Source: ANM 2 M 122
* 1906 data missing; 1912 data from January through September.
** Totals do not sum to 100 percent, owing to multiple issues in some disputes.

Table 12.2. Causes of divorce disputes, Banamba, 1907–12

DATE	DIVORCE DISPUTES**	DIVORCES AS % OF ALL DISPUTES	ABANDONMENT AS % OF DIVORCES	MISTREATMENT AS % OF DIVORCES	INCOMPATIBILITY AS % OF DIVORCES	BRIDEWEALTH AS % OF DIVORCES	ILLNESS AS % OF DIVORCES	OTHER CAUSES AS % OF DIVORCES
1907	19	25%	16%	5%	26%	0	5%	47%
1908*	6	40%	33%	16%	16%	0	16%	16%
1909	23	28%	35%	22%	22%	9%	0	13%
1910	23	38%	48%	26%	13%	4%	0	9%
1911	30	23%	30%	20%	20%	7%	3%	20%
1912	30	42%	33%	13%	20%	13%	10%	10%
Total	131	30%	33%	16%	20%	7%	5%	18%

Source: ANM 2 M 54
*1908 data only for fourth quarter
** Totals do not sum to 100 percent, owing to multiple issues in some disputes.

the spouses in the marriage and for custody of the children.[33] Other stated causes of divorce included the handful of cases in which husbands brought the suit, in which they usually cited their wives as being disobedient or disrespectful. This category also includes what are occasionally referred to in the court records as "numerous complaints" that are not specified.

I am particularly interested in the categories abandonment and mistreatment. As I have argued above, given the acute labor demands facing household heads with the end of slavery, they would most likely have turned to their households to make up for the labor needed after their slaves had left. I would have anticipated that women would have brought mistreatment cases as household heads used or forced their wives to work in the fields. We have already seen indications of this tendency in the seasonal concentration of marriage disputes in the months of hardest labor.

I would have anticipated that we might find abandonment cases lagging by several years as the spouses abandoned when one slave partner left (usually the wives) sought to have their marriages dissolved so that they might remarry. When we graph out abandonment and mistreatment as causes of divorce we see some differences between Banamba and Gumbu.

Allegations of mistreatment in Gumbu coincided with the slaves' exodus in 1908 and 1909. They declined sharply in 1910, spiked in 1911, and sank again in 1912. The Banamba records are different, since we do not have court data for the years of the exodus. The Banamba cases begin after most of the slaves had already left. What we see in the Banamba data is a gradual increase in mistreatment cases beginning in 1909, four or five years after the slaves left, continuing upward to 1911 and then declining. This pattern could indicate that household heads in Banamba continued to use their wives' labor and may have underfed them or otherwise failed as responsible husbands as they struggled to make ends meet.

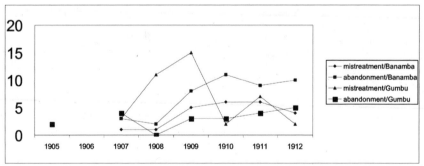

Figure 12.11. Abandonment and mistreatment as causes for divorce in Gumbu and Banamba, 1905–12. *Source:* ANM 2 M 54, 2 M 122

Abandonment cases in Banamba follow the same three-year lag. This delay may reflect the application of Muslim family law in the provincial courts, which were charged with applying the legal status of the litigants. It may also reflect a tendency for *shari'a* to "bleed" into African customs, particularly in regard to issues of the contractual nature of the male household head's responsibility to provide for his dependents. The Maliki school was widespread in French West Africa and it provided for divorce when a husband did not provide subsistence for his wife.[34] Abandonment is cited increasingly after 1909, reflecting the largest wave of the exodus that started in 1906, increased to 1910, and then leveled off. In Gumbu abandonment cases began in 1909, during the exodus itself, but also one year after the first wave of slaves left. Abandonment cases continued to increase until the end of my records, in 1912.

Not all abandonment cases stemmed from slave households, nor can all absconding husbands be linked directly to the end of slavery, although contemporary French observers of the slaves' exodus pointed first to the "destruction of the family" as a consequence of the end of slavery. The end of slavery initiated a huge population movement in a relatively short period, a movement that Klein estimates eventually amounted to one million slaves throughout French West Africa.[35] Picking up and leaving often meant leaving family behind. But former slaves were not the only group on the move during this period. Faced with the prospect of increased labor on the household farm, sons of former masters probably followed some of the same routes that former slaves had taken to areas in Senegal, Guinea, and the Ivory Coast offering new employment opportunities in mining, construction, and temporary agricultural work. In their study of the Soninke of Nioro District to the west of Gumbu, Eric Pollet and Grace Winter argue that the liberation of the slaves weakened the hierarchical principles of both the family and society.[36] Sons could leave because there were new opportunities outside the household economy and because, with the departure of the slaves, sons had little to anticipate in terms of inheritable property and much to fear from increased labor obligations.

The debate about whether the end of slavery was a smooth or contested transition continues to shape the historiography of slavery in Africa and has considerable implications for understanding the experience of women in the transition out of slavery. Slavery was a dynamic institution and slaves and masters both contributed to the practices of institutions in slaveholding societies. In the process, both slaves and masters spun webs of dependency around one other, which were especially important in societies where no strong states supported masters' rights over their slaves. The end of slavery put the depth and the elasticity of these webs of dependence to the test. This chapter contributes to understanding the immediate struggles between masters and slaves and among slaves as they grappled with the new options available to them in colonial courts of law following the end of slavery.

I have drawn on court registers of civil disputes in Banamba and Gumbu, two slaveholding regions that witnessed significant departures of slaves after 1905. These court registers provide precious data on the most common types of disputes—or at least those disputes that African litigants thought amenable to the adjudication of the new colonial courts. The new colonial native system was established by the French in 1903 but instituted only in 1905 in Gumbu and in 1907 in Banamba. The courts thus became one of many sites in which the residents of these regions played out the dramas of everyday life in the period coinciding with the end of slavery. The Gumbu court data may capture the actual moment of slaves' departures and masters' responses. The Banamba courts, which were established two years after the first wave of slave departures, may capture only aspects of the postemancipation adaptation in this former slaveholding society.

Some of the most interesting data to emerge from these court records reflect marital instability and the ways in which wives and husbands used the new colonial courts to pursue their own interests. The end of slavery produced significant new strains on African households, both slave and free. Slave families had to decide whether to stay with their former masters, whether to leave the region, and whether or not they wished to stay together. Individual cases of divorce offer evidence of the difficulties surrounding decisions to remain together as family units or to pursue separate paths, especially when bridewealth transfers meant that women had to leave children behind. Despite this risk, many women did seek divorce. In slave-owning households, the departure of slaves created new labor shortages. As households adjusted to the departure of their slaves, husbands often drew on household members to make up for the shortfall in labor, creating additional burdens on women.

The data on divorce and marriage disputes in Gumbu and Banamba showed that wives sued for divorce during periods of high demand for agricultural labor, suggesting that women were seeking to escape from households in which their sense of security and their understanding of their household roles were being eroded as their husbands forced them to work in the fields in order to compensate for the loss of slave labor. The data on marriage disputes for Banamba and Gumbu show that men often used the courts to force their wives to return home, especially during the peak weeding season in May and June.

In Gumbu, mistreatment of women seems to have been directly associated with the departure of the slaves in 1908 and 1909, and again when the full burden on them of the loss of slave labor was clear two or three years after the slaves' departures. Abandonment cases showed a two- or three-year lag from the height of the slaves' departures in both Banamba and Gumbu. As conditions in households worsened after slaves left, wives increasingly complained of mistreatment by their husbands.

The entry-level civil court data used in this chapter provide a valuable historical source for reconstruction of the everyday experiences of men and women, both freed and free, during the period of adaptation following the end of slavery in the French Soudan. These court data support the contention that women slaves (and free women as well) understood the opportunities available to them and prepared to act on this understanding to escape from marriages that they no longer wanted.

NOTES

1. Richard Roberts and Martin Klein, "The Banamba Slave Exodus of 1905 and the Decline of Slavery in the Western Sudan," *Journal of African History* 21, no. 3 (1980): 375–94.

2. For background, see Martin Klein, *Slavery and Colonial Rule in French West Africa* (Cambridge: Cambridge University Press, 1998).

3. This chapter draws on a portion of the data contained in the Malian Colonial Court Records Project at Stanford University. We have copies of all existing court registers for the French Soudan from 1905 to 1912. Thus far we have coded over thirty-six hundred cases. Plans are under way to publish the coded cases and the court registers on the Web in an effort to stimulate new research using court records. For a preliminary version, see http://shl.stanford.edu/Court/index.html.

4. Emile Baillaud, *Sur les routes du Soudan* (Toulouse: Privat, 1902), 295; Service géographique, Population du Soudan d'après renseignements reçus, 1 April 1899, Archives Nationales du Mali (hereafter ANM), 1 D 21; Rapport politique, Bamako, May 1907, ANM, 1 E 19; J. C. Brevié, "Etude sur l'esclavage, cercle de Bamako, 1904," Archives Nationales du Sénégal, AOF K 19.

5. See esp. Claude Meillassoux, "État et conditions des esclaves à Gumbu (Mali) au XIXe siècle," in *L'esclavage en Afrique précoloniale*, ed. Claude Meillassoux (Paris: Maspéro, 1975), 221–51; Meillassoux, *The Anthropology of Slavery: The Womb of Iron and Gold*, trans. Alide Dasnois (Chicago: University of Chicago Press, 1991); Klein, *Slavery*, 6–7, 13, 164–65, 170–72, 223.

6. For more detail, see Richard Roberts, *Litigants and Households: African Disputes and Colonial Courts in the French Soudan, 1895–1912* (Portsmouth, NH: Heinemann, 2005), ch. 6, "Bridewealth as Contract."

7. Martin Klein and Richard Roberts, "Gender and Emancipation in the French Soudan," in *Gender and Emancipation in Comparative Perspective*, ed. Diane Paton and Pam Scully (Durham, NC: Duke University Press, 2005), 162–80; Marcia Wright, *Strategies of Slaves and Women: Life-Stories from East/Central Africa* (New York: L. Barber Press, 1993). Emily Burrill, a PhD student from Stanford University, is investigating forms of gender-specific vulnerability in the postemancipation era in the southern French Soudan.

8. I have seen only a tiny handful of cases in which one of the litigants appealed the judgment of the village tribunal to the provincial tribunal. Most litigants at the provincial tribunal probably bypassed the lower court altogether.

9. See, for example, Rapport sur le fonctionnement des tribunaux indigènes, 3rd quarter 1906, Bouguni, ANM, 2 M 59; Rapport de M. l'Administrateur de cercle du Bamako sur le fonctionnement des tribunaux indigènes, 1st quarter 1909, Bamako, ANM, 2 M 54.

10. The requirement to keep records reflects efforts to regularize the colonial practices and to control for excesses. In the case of the courts, registers were required because of the professional magistrates of the Procureur Général's office in Dakar was charged with overseeing the functioning of the courts and the dispensation of punishments.

11. Because of the punitive fine on pursuing "frivolous" appeals, few judgments were actually appeals. Only 2 of the 597 judgments from Gumbu were appealed, and 6 of the 434 judgments in Banamba.

12. James Clifford, *The Predicament of Culture: Twentieth-Century Ethnography, Literature, and Art* (Cambridge MA: Harvard University Press, 1988).

13. Bernard Cohn, *An Anthropologist among the Historians and Other Essays* (Delhi: Oxford University Press, 1987); Robert Kidder, "Western Law in India: External Law and Local Response," in *Social System and Legal Process*, ed. Harry Johnson (San Francisco: Jossey-Bass, 1978), 155–80.

14. The 1906 court registers in the Malian archives are lacking for all the districts in the French Soudan. Because of the requirements of the 1903 decree establishing the native court system, the attorney general (*procureur général*) was to scrutinize these registers and see if they conformed to the regulations of the decree. Bits and pieces of the 1906 registers can be found in the Senegal National Archives, AOF M 120–121. I have found none for Banamba or Gumbu.

15. Richard Roberts, "The End of Slavery, Colonial Courts, and Social Conflict in Gumbu, 1908–11," *Canadian Journal of African Studies* 34, no. 3 (2000): 684–713.

16. Female plaintiffs do, however, appear in the court registers in disputes over contracts that they have entered into, especially regarding commercial transactions. See Richard Roberts, "Text and Testimony in the Tribunal de Première Instance, Dakar, during the Early Twentieth Century," *Journal of African History* 31, no. 3 (1999): 447–63.

17. Rapport sur la justice indigène, Gumbu, 3rd quarter 1909, ANM, 2 M 65.

18. The conversion of cowries to French francs varied considerably, but averaged around 500 to the franc. Gakou's debt was therefore about 120 francs.

19. *Diope Tereba v. Soumana Gakou*, 3 June 1909, tribunal de province, Banamba, ANM, 2 M 54. Four hundred cowries equaled around 90 centimes, which was just about the same as the daily rate in *Sampare v. Doukouri*, cited below.

20. *Toumare Sampare v. Moktar Doukouri*, 3 June 1909, tribunal de province, Banamba, ANM, 2 M 54.

21. Richard Roberts, *Warriors, Merchants and Slaves: The State and the Economy of the Middle Niger Valley, 1700–1914* (Stanford: Stanford University Press, 1987), 202–3.

22. Rapport sur le fonctionnement des tribunaux indigènes, Gumbu, 1st quarter 1908, ANM, 2 M 65.

23. Richard Roberts, "Representation, Structure, and Agency: Divorce in the French Soudan at the Beginning of the 20th Century," *Journal of African History* 40, no. 3 (1999): 389–410.

24. *Batouna Souka v. Dji Diara*, 17 June 1910, tribunal de province, Gumbu, ANM, 2 M 122.

25. I conducted some very rich interviews in Banamba with elderly descendants of slaves who had fled their masters. See especially interview with Mamuru Fomba, Ahmadu Traore, Modibo Yerengore, Alfa Traore, and Sulyman Samake, 21 July 1981, Sinzena.

26. *Guedioumou Sissoko v. Kadidja Souko*, 3 May 1912, tribunal de province, Banamba, ANM, 2 M 54.

27. *Kumba Sidibed v. Ouman Coulibaly*, 24 April 1911, tribunal de province, Gumbu, ANM, 2 M 122.

28. *Koba Toure v. Fatimata Ba*, 3 May 1907, tribunal de province, Banamba, ANM, 2 M 54.

29. *Binta Kamara v. Mamadou Taraore*, 18 November 1909, tribunal de province, Banamba, ANM, 2 M 54.

30. Roberts, *Litigants and Households*, 77–82.

31. Rapport politique, Bamako, May 1907, ANM, 1 E 19.

32. The increase in women's willingness to bring their household disputes to the newly created colonial courts certainly follows the initial success of pioneering women who tested the new courts' dispositions. The courts' disposition to listen to women and to agree to their wishes changed dramatically in Bamako around 1910. See Roberts, *Litigants and Households*, ch. 5.

33. Bridewealth disputes could take place before marriage occurred or after divorces. I code such cases as bridewealth disputes and not as divorce disputes, in which bridewealth is the cited cause.

34. Maliki family law approves divorce for women whose husbands have abandoned them, although the duration of abandonment varies considerably. See also Judith E. Tucker, *In the House of Law: Gender and Islamic Law in Ottoman Syria and Palestine* (Berkeley: University of California Press, 1998); Jamal J. Nair, *The Status of Women under Islamic Law and Modern Islamic Legislation* (London: Graham and Trotman, 1990).

35. Klein, *Slavery*, 197.

36. Eric Pollet and Grace Winter, *La société Soninke (Dyahunu, Mali)* (Brussels: Université libre de Bruxelles, 1972), 371, 394.

5

Women in Commercial Outposts

of Modern Europe

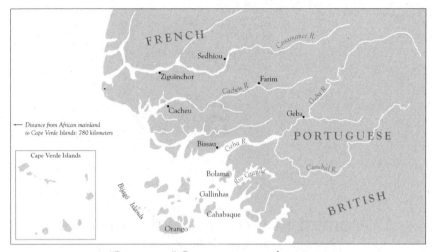

"Portuguese" Guinea, nineteenth century

13

FROM PARIAHS TO PATRIOTS

Women Slavers in Nineteenth-Century "Portuguese" Guinea

PHILIP J. HAVIK

From early contact in the fifteenth century along western African coasts, the Portuguese Crown claimed exclusive rights to strategic goods such as gold and slaves but farmed out concessions to explore other commercial opportunities on the Upper Guinea Coast to private traders. However, the private traders in the "Rivers of Guinea" showed little respect for royal privileges.[1] In the early stages, the hospitality of indigenous trading partners and the lack of fortified locations facilitated outsiders' settlement and de facto "free" trade. "New Christians" persecuted by the Portuguese Inquisition from the 1530s, forcibly exiled condemned criminals (*degredados*), and the rise of Creole trading strata in the Cape Verdean archipelago all contributed to the rapid growth of private commercial interests in the area. Legislation to curb their activities failed to achieve the desired effect, demonstrating the weakness of authorities on the mainland, particularly from the late fifteenth century, when rival European nations started to compete for the spoils of trade.

From the second half of the 1500s, these Afro-Atlantic trading communities, called Kriston in Guinean Creole, composed of baptized Africans, both free and servile, rapidly gained notoriety as go-betweens in local mainland and regional maritime trade networks. Working in domestic capacities, and also as sailors, pilots, interpreters, and petty traders, they lived along a large stretch of coast from the Senegal River in the north to Sierra Leone in the south. Both women and men made up their ranks, which grew as coastal trade increased demand for gold, slaves, hides, and beeswax, as well as such provisions as rice, fish, game, fruit, and vegetables. Although they lived in coastal trade settlements, they maintained ties with their communities of origin in the interior through trade, while also acting as wards for relatives coming down to the coast. From the middle of the seventeenth century, when the first human cargoes were shipped from the Guinea coast directly to the Americas, freeborn Kriston women from such coastal settlements as Cacheu, the so-called *tungumás*,[2] leave their mark in Inquisition files and official enquiries. Singled out for their trade acumen and kin links with ruling African strata, they were seen at once by Portuguese policymakers as threats to "royal" interests. Kriston women such as Crispina Peres and Bibiana Vaz de França emerged in the seventeenth century as powerful figures in their own rights, women of undeniable authority both in trade settlements and in the interior.[3] Official persecution of them served to highlight the significance of Kriston communities and, above all, the agency of women in the coastal networks.

Women traders were to figure, usually also disparagingly, in accounts of such eighteenth-century coastal trade settlements as Cacheu, Geba, Ziguinchor, Farim, and Bissau. The Kriol term generally referring to these African women of "noble extraction," *ñara*, derived from the respectful Portuguese term of address *senhora* (lady).[4] Incorporated into the mainland areas nominally administered by Portugal from the Cape Verde islands, these *prasas*[5] formed intricate networks linked by Kriston trading communities wherefrom the *signares*, *señoras*, and *senioras*, as other Europeans referred to them, conducted their businesses.[6] But at the same time, other Kriston women served as domestic slaves in traders' households, usually employed as washerwomen, cooks, bakers, cotton spinners, cloth dyers, and petty traders. The latter would be charged with visiting local and regional markets in order to barter home produce and artisanry for basic necessities such as rice, vegetables, fish, and meat. On account of their Christian and professional status, they were characterized as ladino slaves, regarded and treated as superior to the *boçais*, or uneducated captives. In short, women were in great demand in these settlements and formed the large majority of their inhabitants. Population censuses from the early 1700s showed free women owning most of the dwellings in them, keeping household slaves and running trade houses that bartered captives, ivory, hides, and beeswax. Female slaves also outnumbered their male counterparts, thus demonstrating their pivotal roles in the local labor force.

Throughout the eighteenth century the representatives of Portuguese state trading companies, such as the Companhia do Grão Pará e Maranhão, as well as private traders from northern Brazil and the Cape Verde Islands continued to rely on these women for extraction of slaves. These male outsiders established commercial and intimate relations with tungumás, whom they euphemistically called girlfriends or paramours.[7] The latter, colloquially referred to in documents as mãe (Kriol: mamé, mother; "big" woman), well-connected and familiar with local custom, carried on transactions in the interior, often far upstream.

When abolitionist pressures in the early 1800s from British and French quarters began to inhibit trafficking in slaves, the European, Cape Verdean, and Kriston trading communities began to seek alternatives. Again these big women acted as key agents. Obtaining land concessions from African rulers, they embarked on the cultivation of peanuts in the Guinea Bissau region, employing both slave and contract labor. Fed by a growing demand from European industry for vegetable oils, the cultivation of peanuts rapidly spread from the Gambia to other coastal areas, triggering large-scale labor migration in the interior. However, this transition toward so-called legitimate trade, which started in the 1830s, did not imply a definitive shift toward free labor; the move to islands off the coast or inhospitable creeks was also motivated by the need to "hide" ongoing trafficking in less conspicuous locations, far from British patrols. The kinship ties that these women maintained with coastal peoples were fundamental to the securing of access to these plots, or pontas. The fact that their kinfolk also served as suppliers of labor or as intermediaries in the slave trade was also a decisive factor. Rather than undermining these ties, the transition toward "legitimate" trade appeared to strengthen them, also by turning traditional chiefs into much-coveted partners.

The present essay takes a closer look at the impact these changes had on representations of ñaras in Portuguese and other published and archival sources. First, the rise of the ñaras as traders, brokers, and planters during the 1800s in coastal entrepôts is dealt with in biographical sketches of two powerful ñaras who left strong marks on nineteenth-century Guinea (Dona Rosa and Mãe Aurélia). Their careers, fortunes, relationships, and partnerships and the views of their contemporaries as well as posthumous perspectives are woven into these accounts. Special attention is given to the combination of slave trafficking and production of export crops that characterized this period of transition and to what extent these women profited from it. Social stratification involving slaves and gendered role patterns are placed within the shifting contexts of nineteenth-century Guinea and its Kriston communities. While the Portuguese portrayed ñaras as allies rather than enemies, these epithets did not benefit all women in trade settlements. It is argued that the flexibility of arrangements and the fluidity of concepts inherent in Kriston culture created a considerable margin for social mobility and for women's negotiation of their professional careers and personal prestige.

FEMALE AGENCY: RUNNING NETWORKS AND REINVENTING TROPES

For centuries before the 1820s, slave trafficking had demonstrated the importance of mediation for transactions along the Upper Guinea Coast. Brazilian, Cape Verdean, and Portuguese outsiders relied on local intermediaries. While they ordinarily sought the well-connected Kriston women as their partners, often with the connivance of local ruling lineages, metropolitan authorities frowned on them as impostors, spies, traitors, and heretics. Accused of intriguing on behalf of the presumed enemy (indigenous rulers), their presence was not only considered a threat to the Portuguese Crown's commercial and political interests but also—in spite of their designation as Kriston—seen as undermining the Christianization of the prasas.

Kinship links were central to Afro-Atlantic interaction. These relationships established channels of privileged access on both sides. Through them, the parties to exchanges along the coast tried to guarantee supplies of Atlantic goods such as iron bars, arms, gunpowder, alcoholic spirits, cloth, beads, and trinkets in return for slaves, beeswax, ivory, and hides. Despite the growing opposition from trader-officials who attempted to increase their own positions in these transactions, Kriston mediators retained their near monopoly of this relay trade well into the 1800s. These officials, appointed by Cape Verde or Lisbon to strategic posts as governors or military commanders in coastal towns such as Cacheu and Bissau (see map), were mostly unpaid and used their positions as cover for trafficking slaves, forging close relations with local suppliers in the interior for the purpose. They tended to use their sweeping but vaguely defined powers over putative Portuguese subjects in the region to acquire personal wealth rapidly during their brief tenures on the coast. Owing to the wide dispersal of the riverine entrepôts in the region, well-connected, reliable partners in these often remote locations were therefore essential. The Christianized ñaras related to native dignitaries were well placed to fulfill that role among ruling African lineages accustomed to, and accomplished in, working through close kin and through women in particular.

From the 1820s the coastal waters of Guiné were subject to regular patrols by English warships roaming there to enforce international treaties against the slave trade. The traffickers sought hideouts along the rivers, where they could assemble captives until suitable transatlantic transport arrived. While Portuguese ports such as Cacheu and Bissau were being carefully watched, trader-officials who had no real influence beyond the perimeter stockades of these settlements were forced to find new footholds in hitherto inaccessible and generally hostile territory. African women from founding lineages figured prominently in that quest.

At this juncture private trading interests and Portuguese political concerns merged: land was seen not only as a mercantile asset but also as a site for prospective settlement and expanded military control. Portuguese authorities, concerned also about growing territorial presence in the region of the French and British, requested the intervention of the then governor of Bissau, Joaquim António de Mattos, to settle the (uninhabited) island of Bolama, just south of Bissau. Thereupon the aforesaid governor indicated the name of his partner, Júlia da Silva Cardozo, also known as Mãe Júlia, as the best-placed intermediary for the purpose. Within a month, she negotiated a treaty for concession of usufruct rights with the ruling Bijagó matrilineage of a neighboring island, to whom she was related.[8] In the 1840s a wealthy Bissau-based official and trader negotiated a deal with a "reigning noblewoman" of Biafada origin, who ceded settlement rights for Portuguese traders to a location on the left bank of the Geba River. Accompanied by elders, the said *fidalga governante* (lady governor) received a "present" and a promise of an additional gift from the governor-general of Cape Verde.[9]

In the face of competition from other Europeans, Portuguese sources subsequently began to stress the importance of these "ñaras" as intermediaries and trade agents who strengthened—rather than, as formerly, weakened—national interests. They were also seen as pacifiers who could contain both African rulers in the interior and the conflict-ridden Kriston factions in the prasas. The sources began to refer to them respectfully as Donas, and even affectionately as mothers, evoking their "civilized" and "ladylike" status. The "bad reputation" of their seventeenth-century predecessors, subjects of persecution and invective, was replaced by a positive identity.[10] They were now portrayed in a manner more akin to the way French sources had initially expressed admiration in the seventeenth and eighteenth centuries for "big women" (i.e., the glamorous signares of St. Louis and Gorée, who enjoyed high repute among European visitors as skilled negotiators and charming *courtisanes*.)[11] However, as the newly "Portuguese" ñara rose to fame, French authorities in neighboring Senegal were actually reducing the influence of "Creole"

strata by abolishing slavery while curbing the autonomy and social mobility of signares who were ceding their privileged status as legitimate go-
betweens to male *habitants*.[12] The power base of the Portuguese ñaras lay
not only in the ownership of slaves, houses, and vessels in the prasas
but above all in their privileged kinship relations with ruling lineages
in the interior and their access to land beyond the reach of weak European authority.[13]

In the meantime they profited from the sex segregation of households
and family budgets common to African societies. While patriarchal custom
circumscribed their status in the interior, where control over strategic resources was reserved for husbands, brothers, uncles, or other male elders,
such limitations were much reduced or entirely absent in the bilateral
contexts of Afro-Atlantic trade settlements. Acting as de facto community authorities, the flourishing local *gan* (mercantile lineages) based in
coastal towns also seamlessly extended their influence into the public
realm and dominated local politics. The following sketches of the careers
of Dona Rosa and Mãe Aurélia illustrate the social and spatial mobility
of Kriston women from coastal trading settlements such as Bissau who
were able to thrive in the emerging era of rival European nations such as
Britain, France, and Portugal competing for secure footholds on African
soil. As these international rivalries set the stage for the scramble for
Africa, they were heralded as "national" heroines, defenders of Portugal's
vulnerable position vis-à-vis the rapid advance of French and British interests in the Senegambian region. However, as we will see below, upon
closer inspection these gendered tropes are ambivalent and asymmetrical
when analyzed in the context of Kriston communities and of the changes
that occurred the West African region in the course of the 1800s.

SLAVES AND RICE: DONA ROSA

The most powerful slave trader in the town of Cacheu during the first
half of the nineteenth century was undoubtedly Rosa Carvalho de Alvarenga. Dona Rosa, as she was called, was a member of a trading gan
that dominated the settlement of Ziguinchor from the mid-1700s. She
was born in Cacheu probably in the 1790s and died there in the late
1850s. During the last decades of the eighteenth and in the early nineteenth century, her father, Guinean-born Manuel de Carvalho Alvarenga, held the Portuguese-appointed post of military commander of
Ziguinchor, Cacheu, and Farim. Her brother, Francisco Carvalho de Alvarenga, a wealthy slave trader, was appointed commander of Ziguinchor

in the 1840s, stepping down in 1866, while her half sister or aunt, Josefa Carvalho de Alvarenga, born in the Cape Verde islands, was twice married to Cape Verdean officials with high-ranking posts in the Portuguese administration. Dona Rosa's husband, João Pereira Barreto, was the son of a priest originating from the Cape Verde islands and a Guinean slave. Working his way up through the ranks, he became commander of Cacheu in the early 1800s and set up a trading house in the town with the aid of the Alvarenga trading lineage. The alliance between the trading lineages resulted in the rapid growth of the resulting "family firm," turning it into the biggest trading house in the Casamance-Cacheu basin. Centering its trade on slaves and local produce such as ivory, beeswax, and hides, the enterprise flourished as a result of the partnership between Dona Rosa and her husband. After his death in 1829, it was continued by Dona Rosa and her son, Honório Pereira Barreto (born in 1813), who was to pursue a political career in the administration of "Portuguese" Guinea. Both mother and son died in the late 1850s, at a time when the slave trade had all but ended, while the cultivation of "cash" crops was already well on its way to becoming the main commodity export of the region.

Through her kinship ties, Dona Rosa had privileged access to *morgadios* (plantations) in the Cape Verde islands, since the Alvarengas were among the wealthiest residents in the archipelago. Large tracts of land in the islands were traditionally held by a small stratum of planter-traders (*morgados*), who imported slaves from the Guinea coast in exchange for cotton textiles, the so-called *bandas,* produced on the islands. Among these traders women figured prominently, especially on the leeward islands, such as Santiago and Fogo.[14] Some of the Alvarengas, well established on Santiago Island, also owned slaves in Dona Rosa's hometown of Cacheu on the mainland. Rosa's sister Josefina also owned morgados and slaves in the archipelago. In fact, in the 1820s she had bequeathed a part of her estate on Santiago to her brother-in-law. The Alvarengas were therefore particularly well placed to expand their business in the transatlantic slave market.

The papers of a ship apprehended in the Caribbean in the early 1830s show that of the 157 slaves on board, no fewer than a hundred were registered in the name of Dona Rosa's enterprise. These slaves had embarked in the vicinity of Cacheu under the cover of night, in order to delude coastal patrols. Her personal instructions to the captain of the vessel, which she owned, clearly indicated its route and the final destination of its cargo, the port of Matanzas on the north shore of Cuba, then one of the major remaining American destinations for slaves.[15] When a schooner was caught selling slaves in the late 1830s and three of them were identified as the property of her son Honório, the latter was excluded from political office for five years.[16] The commercial and political predominance of the Alvarenga trading house was also felt in the town of Ziguinchor, further north along the Casamance River, where Dona Rosa's brother, Francisco, had long occupied the post of military commander while himself also trafficking slaves. He too was seen as a stalwart of Portuguese interests, above all in connection with French influence in the Lower Casamance, which threatened the Alvarengas' Ziguinchor-Cacheu route.

The first signs in the early 1800s of the impending shift from relatively balanced and brokered trading connections toward direct Portuguese claims to territory passed by almost unnoticed when one of the Felupe (Sen/Fr: Diola, in the Casamance) headmen, himself a Christianized *kamarada*, or local intermediary for strangers, ceded usufruct rights to a strategically located stretch of land close to the mouth of the Cacheu River to the then commander of the garrison in the town of Cacheu, João Pereira Barreto, none other than Dona Rosa's husband. The contract conceded the right of the official to settle the area, to build forts, and to cultivate its soils. The location was called Ponta Alvarenga, after Barreto's wife.

Another land concession, this time along a network of waterways between the Cacheu and Casamance Rivers, would form a precedent in the region for successful export-oriented agriculture. Usufruct rights to the estate, Poilão de Leão, were ceded to Dona Rosa by ruling lineages of the Bañun resident in the area. Apparently worked by slave labor, it was said to be well cultivated in the late 1830s[17] and was described as a shining example of local entrepreneurship. It would form the hub of rice exports to the Cacheu settlement, as well as to Ziguinchor and Bathurst, and possibly to Cape Verde.

The region was already known for its African residents' rice paddies (*bolanhas*), and in the 1840s some illegal slavers kept *barracas* (barracoons) of slaves there and harvested rice to feed them.[18] Reports indicate that control over the route remained in the hands of "Blacks," who charged taxes (*daxa*; English cognate: dash) on all goods carried, while charging heavily for any supplies they provided.[19] The need to conceal the covert trafficking made the Poilão de Leão an ideal assembly point for captives awaiting export, while using their labor to reduce costs. Contemporary travel accounts leave no doubt as to Dona Rosa's supposed ownership of the ponta, as well as stating categorically that it was "the only agricultural unit that exists within the limits of Portuguese Guinea."[20] One may speculate as to the variety of crops grown and the composition of the labor force working Dona Rosa's ponta. We may assume that the variety of rice produced there was what was called white, or Gambian, rice (*Oryza sativa* L.), rather than the "red" rice (*Oryza glaberrima* Steud.) common to the region.[21] As far as can be determined, this was the first commercial exploration of this "Asian" variety in Portuguese Guinea.

Until then land in the hands of the Kriston inhabitants of the trading settlements had been generally limited to urban dwellings and the plots they stood on. On the question of women's rights to land for cultivation, littoral communities had a long tradition of shared access to arable land among women as well as men. Women in areas pertaining to Felupe/Diola, Bañun, Pepel, and Biafada communities traditionally worked personal garden plots around their houses as well as bartering surpluses they might produce from them at weekly regional markets. In and around the prasas, a commercial environment where inheritance and succession were generally bilateral and residence ambilocal, women could build personal estates, including plots and houses, and pass them on to heirs.

The alliance between Dona Rosa and João Barreto clearly exhibited the interweaving of social, economic, and political domains, so characteristic of the African cultures. It was continued by means of the partnership between Dona Rosa and her son, Honório Pereira Barreto. Guinea-born, and sent to Portugal for education—although his training was cut short when he was recalled to Cacheu following the death of his father—he rose rapidly in Portuguese Guinea's administration. Appointed governor of Cacheu in the 1830s, he later held the governorships of Bissau and of the Guinea district at various times until his death in the late 1850s. He left the running of the family trading house Dona Rosa Alvarenga e Filhos (and sons), to his mother, dealing by proxy through her and his relatives, and occasionally visiting Cacheu whenever his responsibilities for regional politics permitted. As a governor he would repeat his parents' well-worn formula of obtaining land concessions through his kinship and clientship networks to attempt to stem the tide of growing French military penetration into the Casamance-Cacheu region, which was seen as the Alvarenga-Barreto fiefdom.

The partnership between mother and son allowed their trading house to extend its influence further south to the town of Bissau, which in the nineteenth century had become the region's commercial center and administrative capital. In the mid-1840s they succeeded in obtaining the lucrative contract for management of Guinea's customs in the region.[22] Despite increasing restrictions on maritime slaving and close British surveillance, the house continued selling and transporting slaves well into the 1840s. The Sierra Leone international commission charged with overseeing complaints with regard to illegal exports of slaves from Portugal's West African territories found that large numbers of captives had been shipped from Cacheu in the 1820s,[23] which would have been impossible without the direct involvement of the Alvarenga family firm.

The first—and last—slave census in Portuguese-claimed territories conducted in the 1850s demonstrates the ongoing importance of slaves for the local economy and also Dona Rosa's preponderant position as owner.[24] The exercise, in good part one of futility but one imposed by abolitionist treaties and pressures by Britain on Portugal to register existing slaves, prohibit their further sale and transport, and free them, was carried out by her son Honório. The Alvarenga trading house acknowledged owning nearly a quarter (147) of the 648 slaves registered in Cacheu, while her son Honório had a further 61 in his personal possession, and her late daughter Barbara's estate counted 14 slaves. All in all, the Alvarenga gan owned a quarter (290) of all the slaves (1,085) acknowledged in Cacheu and Ziguinchor, more than half of them belonging to Dona Rosa herself.

Not only were these slaves used for domestic and agricultural purposes, they also provided armed protection for commercial operations and means to intervene in the unstable political situation in the region. The census identifies Dona Rosa's slaves individually by name and origin and specifies their skills—including pilots, rowers, smiths, stonemasons, carpenters, weavers, and cooks. The majority of captive personnel belonging to her trading house were women (77), many of them domestic servants, such as washerwomen, seamstresses, textile dyers, cooks, and bakers, their ages varying from one to sixty. Female slaves and employees also carried out important jobs as market traders, go-betweens, and healers. These female majorities follow the demographic pattern in all the coastal ports, where from the early eighteenth century less-detailed censuses of population by civil categories had shown distinct female majorities among Christianized captive and free African strata.[25]

Dona Rosa's career shows how powerful these well-connected women could become, as they invariably outlived their male partners and inherited the accumulated spoils of their joint trade while retaining the fruits of their own. Her connections combined kin links with a wealthy gan or trading family with connections among ruling African lineages in the Cacheu and Casamance regions. She constituted the linchpin of multiple Afro-Atlantic connections, concentrating power and authority in a single person. Such a configuration corresponds to what have been termed relations of *matronage*, wherein women form the center of overlapping social, political, and economic networks.[26]

SLAVES AND PEANUTS: MÃE AURÉLIA

Further South, in Bissau, another ñara also succeeded in crossing the boundaries between slaving and landed production of commodities. Descended from a ruling matrilineage on the Bijagó island of Orango (see map), Aurélia Correia, also known as Mãe Aurélia ("Mother" Aurélia), would become the most famous of all the women traders in nineteenth-century Portuguese Guinea.[27] Official sources present her as a queen, putting her in a class of her own, (posthumously) turning her into an icon of successful big women in the region, reinforced by local oral traditions that (still) celebrate her as Mamé Correia.

Born in all likelihood in the early 1800s out of a relationship between a Bijagó priestess and a Cape Verdean trader-official, Mãe Aurélia's eminence again confirms the extent to which Kriston women with privileged kinship ties were socially, economically, and politically upwardly mobile. Raised by her aunt, Júlia da Silva Cardoso, also of "noble" Bijagó descent, who kept a trading house in nearby Bissau, Mãe Aurélia quickly learned the tricks of the trade. Her presumed half sister, Mathilde Correia de Almeida, who also ran a business in Bissau, was her neighbor in the principal commercial quarter along the town's waterfront. Her (likely) father, José Correia da Veiga, was a high ranking Cape Verdean official in the Portuguese administration, who held important posts in several of the trade settlements in the region.

Mãe Aurélia's future husband and business partner, Caetano José Nozolini (1800–1850), who was appointed governor of Bissau in the early 1830s, must have appreciated his wife's father's local contacts and knowledge.[28] His successful trading career was indissolubly linked to that of his wife. The son of a Cape Verdean mother and an Italian father, Nozolini did not own an estate, or morgadio, on his native island of Fogo.[29] Pursuing a career on the mainland through military service, he went on to become governor of Bissau in the mid-1830s and used his office—as was common—as a convenient cover for slave trafficking. The trading house he set up in Bissau, which Mãe Aurélia directed, was to dominate transactions in the capital from the 1830s to the 1860s. Nozolini himself traveled frequently, mostly to the Cape Verde islands but also to other locations on the Guinea coast, and to Brazil, while leaving the day-to-day management of the enterprise to his wife.

Nozolini's and Mãe Aurélia's business thrived on the purchase of captives supplied by ruling Bijagó lineages, which for centuries had raided the coast and rivers of the Upper Guinea Coast. By the 1830s these transactions were arousing the suspicions of the British cruisers patrolling West African waters. Nozolini had been associated with slave trafficking from the 1820s by British diplomatic sources, who filed repeated complaints to the Portuguese government.[30] The British seizure of the schooner owned by Dona Rosa and her son in the late 1830s led to the discovery of a contract Nozolini signed in Praia, the capital of Cape Verde, concerning the transport of "a hundred and twenty assorted slaves, in good health and all young."[31] While the British condemned Nozolini as the leading Atlantic protagonist of a trade, the Portuguese celebrated Mãe Aurélia as their privileged African intermediary occupying a commanding position in Bissau-based commercial networks.

The strategy of the partnership became clear in the early 1830s when Mãe Aurélia settled on the island of Gallinhas, accompanied by her slaves from Bissau. She did so with the aid of her aunt, Mãe Júlia, who some years previously had negotiated usufruct rights with her Bijagó relatives and kept a plantation called Casadia there, together with her partner of Portuguese extraction and several times governor, Joaquim António de Mattos. A few years later, Mãe Aurélia moved to the settlement called Novo Mindelo on the neighboring island of Bolama, having again previously obtained consent from a Bijagó *oloño,* or head of the ruling matrilineage, through her aunt. The plots (pontas) were worked by slaves as well as by Kriston from Bissau and produced export crops such as rice, peanuts, cotton, and coffee. Not only did these islands offer novel opportunities for economic diversification, they also provided a convenient cover for trafficking in slaves. The relatively low costs of slave labor combined with expected high returns from the growing market for export crops, above all for peanuts, favored these remote locations, which were accessible only with the aid of local pilots.

From the 1820s, when the British introduced peanuts in the neighboring Gambia River basin as an export crop, cultivation of the legume spread rapidly through littoral areas further south.[32] This shift to peanuts greatly increased seasonal demand for labor, which could not be met exclusively by slaves. At the same time, local demand for food supplies rose

sharply following the establishment of such new coastal trade settlements as (British) Bathurst in the Gambia, and (French) Carabane and
Sédhiou in the Casamance region, as well as Gallinhas and Bolama
within the Portuguese sphere to the south.

Peanuts were usually cultivated in a three-year cycle, often in combination with a food crop such as rice. Crucially, access to labor and fertile
soils had to be secured by mediation with landowning communities,
which gave considerable leverage to women connected with these ruling
lineages such as Mãe Aurélia. Governors and officials, generally of Cape
Verdean origin, entered into partnerships with these ñaras. The limited
success of raids on the islands by British naval patrols demonstrated the
business acumen of the partnership, as well as Mãe Aurélia's personal
control over slaves and plots. Confiscating her schooner, *Aurélia Felix*, a
British officer then landed on the island of Bolama in 1838, taking on
board a number of slaves who were subsequently freed in Sierra Leone.
Requesting compensation for this seizure of her property, Mãe Aurélia argued that the loss of her slaves, of vessels, and of crops for lack of labor
had caused considerable damage to her interests.[33] She submitted similar
complaints following subsequent attacks on the settlement at Bolama
during the 1840s and early 1850s by patrols, all claiming damages on account of the "kidnapping" of her slaves and the loss of crops ripe for
harvesting. Following one such attack in the 1840s, the then governor of
Bathurst reported to London on "the total destruction of the slave factories at Gallinhas and Bulama" (by the captain of the British steam vessel
Pluto) and "his having redeemed from captivity seventy Africans whom
he found at the former island in deplorable conditions."[34]

According to an authoritative local source "the first peanut exports
took place in 1846 from Ponta Oeste (or Bolama of Dona Aurélia)."[35]
Mãe Aurélia had probably exported peanuts from her farm on Gallinhas
Island a few years earlier. A Portuguese report from 1847 stated that Mãe
Aurélia had been personally overseeing the harvesting of crops at the
time of a British raid.[36] Mãe Aurélia's "ponta" was worked by slave and
contract laborers who harvested significant amounts of peanuts and
maize, as well as indigo, beni seed, cassava, and rice.[37] At the end of the
1850s, the large plantation—Ponta Oeste or Ponta Aurélia as it is still
called—was still run by Mãe Aurélia. According to British sources, patrols "found a vast estate and extensive stores owned by a native woman
called Madame Oralia (Aurélia) and cultivated by about 300 slaves."[38]
The following year "Madame Aralia" was still referred to in British
sources as the "possessor of a very large farm on the South side of the

island."[39] She not only grew peanuts but also cotton, which she exported from her plantation on Gallinhas Island to Brazil.[40] At the time the British government, backed by the Manchester Cotton Association, which was "using every exertion to obtain supplies of cotton from Africa," had reported on "the cotton farm which Mr David Lawrence ('a coloured man and a British subject') has planted in compliance with the wish of the Br. government" in the area.[41]

Evidently, British interests in raw materials for commodity production, and thus seizures of lands, in the region were intensifying along with those of the Portuguese as so-called legitimate trade gradually overtook transatlantic slaving. The British accordingly took possession of the island in 1860, and Mãe Aurélia moved with her captive laborers back to Bissau, or rather to the Ilhéu do Rei, a few miles from the capital's harbor. From the late 1840s, when the Portuguese authorities had leased the island to the Nozolini trading house, the latter built a formidable complex there, including storehouses, a small railroad, a ship repair yard, several workshops, a sawmill, and a rice-husking machine, as well as a well-appointed residence. When a Portuguese governor visited the island in the 1850s, this considerable industrial complex was said to house over three hundred slaves, who cultivated peanuts and lived in a settlement nearby.[42] The fact that Mãe Aurélia's partner Nozolini withdrew his slaves from Bolama Island to the Ilhéu do Rei in 1849,[43] long before Aurélia herself did so, testifies to the continued protection from which she benefited in the Bijagó archipelago. The separate moves also demonstrate the gendered division of labor with regard to the partnership's resources, while at the same time illustrating the well-coordinated management of African and Atlantic spaces and interests.

The authorities made frequent requests to Mãe Aurélia to mediate conflicts between them and surrounding populations, which had paralyzing effects on trade. In fact, the former were often themselves to blame, given the temptation of governors—who doubled as traders—to break the Kriston's near monopoly of the riverine relay trade. When in the early 1840s the town of Bissau was in the throes of a revolt by its Kriston inhabitants, opposing their expulsion from the capital at the behest of Cape Verdean slave traders attempting to break the latter's monopoly of the riverine relay trade, they again called upon the mediating services of Mãe Aurélia. Portuguese authorities asked "the woman who administers the (trade) house of Major Nozolini, called Aurélia" to "restore order among the natives, as I have been told that she is respected by them, and that it is necessary on these occasions to employ the appropriate strategy in view of the customs of these peoples."[44] Her husband was among the said traders whose ill-considered intervention she was asked to put right. In the mid-1850s, when two British officers were killed by Bijagó raiders, the Foreign Office requested the intervention of the governor in Bissau, Dona Rosa's son. Mãe Aurélia quickly obtained the handover of the culprits through her son-in-law, then acting as official representative of the family firm. Thereupon, the Portuguese government expressed its appreciation of her "powerful cooperation" in an official letter.[45]

Mãe Aurélia's authority and prestige may also be inferred from the request put to her by the governor of Bissau to study the "implementation and harmonisation" of the manumission of slaves, a new Portuguese government initiative of the 1870s, intended primarily to ward off British and other pressures in the name of extending the antislavery policies that rationalized growing imperial ambitions. Attending a meeting of the Government Council with the representative of the Nozolini trading house, she was regarded as a "very competent person" and asked to give her "expert opinion" on the issue.[46] In addition, her contribution to a famine fund for the drought-stricken population on the Cape Verdean archipelago also put her in the league of prominent citizens of coastal towns.[47]

Before his death in 1850, Nozolini kept a residence on the riverfront in Bissau, close to his wife's own dwelling in the same privileged area. Although the trading house, rebaptized Nozolini Junior e Companhia, was inherited by their son, José Caetano, his mother continued to run it together with a legal representative appointed by the heirs. In the mid-1850s the then governor of Guinea, Dona Rosa's son, reaffirmed the authorities' growing reliance on the Nozolini trading house "without which Bissau was impossible to govern."[48] The 1856 slave census shows just how powerful the firm actually was. Nozolini Junior e Companhia owned a total of over four hundred slaves—one third of the joint total for the capital Bissau and the Ilhéu do Rei.[49] It also controlled the great majority of the 380 ladinu, or educated and trained slaves, enumerated in the census, including male rowers, pilots, iron smiths, and carpenters, and women as seamstresses, cooks, and bakers. From the census we also learn that Mãe Aurélia owned forty-two slaves, twenty-four of whom were female, their ages ranging from one to forty-one; some worked as seamstresses, textile dyers, and washerwomen. Some of the younger female slaves, who had been born in captivity, worked as apprentices with their mothers.[50]

Altogether, Mãe Aurélia and three of her legitimate daughters owned 163 slaves, many of whom were of Bijagó extraction, while others had been born on Bolama and Gallinhas Islands, as well as on pontas along the banks of the Rio Grande inlet. By that time however, the sex ratio of the slaves showed a surplus of males, on account of the shift toward the cultivation of export crops, in which mainly slave men were engaged. Just under half of all the owners of slaves listed in the census were women, but they retained less than a third of all registered slaves, although Mãe Aurélia and a few others were among the larger proprietors.[51]

From the 1860s, Mãe Aurélia also came to own a number of pontas on the right bank of the Rio Grande. These estates were obtained through concessions from ruling Bijagó matrilineages of the island of Kañabak, to whom the land in question pertained, consecrated in a treaty between the Dona Rosa's son and the oloño of the island. This arrangement provided her not only with secure access to land but also with protection from raids. However, it did not prevent attacks from Fulbe horsemen from the highlands to the east, who invaded the Rio Grande area in the mid-1870s. Mãe Aurélia, while harboring refugees from these assaults, was obliged to negotiate the payment of compensation to Fulbe warlords.[52] She probably died soon after, although the precise date has yet to be established. Her daughters, who married Portuguese officials and traders, also owned peanut pontas both in the Bijagó islands and on the coast. Like their mother, they also kept a number of river- and seagoing vessels for the transport of the commodities these lands produced, rather than for the transatlantic trade in slaves, which had almost petered out by the 1860s.

In the highly competitive environment of mid-nineteenth-century Bissau, when demand for oil-rich crops and agricultural labor began to predominate, Mãe Aurélia stands out as an icon of female agency. Acting sometimes in conjunction with, but also independently from, her male partner, she controlled large numbers of slaves and owned vessels and storehouses as well as land. Like Dona Rosa before her, Portuguese officials saw her as guarantor of peace and stability in a troubled region that they could not themselves control. Her forceful personality only added to the wealth and prestige she was credited with by officials, by the population of the Bissau prasa, and by her own relatives on the islands. While Dona Rosa had descended from an already established gan, Mãe Aurélia established her own trading lineage and pioneered the cultivation and export of a lucrative crop for the European market.

PIONEERS OF CHANGE?

By the 1820s it was clear that government attempts to purchase land and provide incentives for settlement in order to secure its territorial claims had failed.[53] Nevertheless, some local officials saw rice, maize, cotton, coffee, tobacco, and palm oil as viable alternatives,[54] proposing the settlement of impoverished migrant families from the Cape Verde islands to work plots that would produce these commodities. Others suggested that degredados, convicted criminals from the metropole, should be sent to cultivate the land.[55] However, none of these schemes proved realistic. Some officials thought that African "kings," if approached in a diplomatic manner, would be prepared to concede plots for cultivation to foreigners; however, any attempt to take land by force, they believed, would result in armed conflict that the government was not prepared to win. Littoral societies had consistently refused to allow settlement beyond the perimeter of the prasas, while they strategically controlled the supplies of potable water, food, and fuel to the towns. Whenever quarrels led to open conflict, the African ruling lineages in surrounding villages would cut off supplies, thereby holding the towns and their inhabitants to ransom.

Significantly, no one envisaged the use of local labor to cultivate crops, or advised against "the idea of civilising natives in order to make them work the land with agricultural tools (for export)."[56] But within fifteen years the same official, Mãe Aurélia's uncle, was to embrace the idea that Guiné could become a "new Brazil."[57] However, as long as local governors maintained that the key trading towns, such as Bissau, essentially depended on revenues from slave exports from Guinea to the Maranhão region in northern Brazil, these visions of the future appeared to be more akin to wishful thinking.[58]

The cases of the two "big women" detailed above show that their power and authority in an age of abolition was based on continuing the parallel businesses of slave tenure and trafficking, as well as production of crops. Large local firms, such as Dona Rosa's in Cacheu and Mãe Aurélia's in Bissau, combined slave with contract labor and trafficking in order to generate sufficient capital to invest in ships and shipyards, rice mills and storehouses. Their political and economic connections through male kin, partners, sons, and husbands who occupied key administrative posts gave them significant advantages in obtaining credits, above all from European trading houses. The authority these ñaras enjoyed with ruling African strata, including the strategically placed Pepel and Bijagó, also provided them with solid bargaining counters. Finally, their Kriston heritages gave them considerable leverage and prestige among these families so well entrenched in the trading settlements.

It also shows to what extent the partnerships between Kriston women traders and Cape Verdean officials filled the power vacuum during this period of rapid change and offered prospects for an economic upturn in the region. First rice and then peanuts, often cultivated in alternation, emerged as promising for the local trading community. It is therefore hardly surprising that official reports praised these women for contributing to the turnaround in Guinea's prospects. Dona Rosa, "this coloured lady, dominated the Guinean tribes; the indigenous chiefs were her vassals and therefore the natives in our dominions in Cacheu, Ziguinchor and Farim were blindly obedient to the authorities."[59] She was also depicted as "a very rich lady born here (in Cacheu) who exercises great influence over the Blacks";[60] in fact the local Kriston community were said to have "great respect . . . for the trading house of Dona Rosa de Carvalho Alvarenga."[61] Mãe Aurélia's prestige was thought to be similarly unassailable further south: "the trade of Bissau was in the hands of Mãe Aurélia who in her quality as 'queen' enjoyed special privileges among the heathen. And she performed relevant services to the country whilst maintaining the peace and quiet in the stronghold of Bissau."[62] In the adjacent Bijagó archipelago, on the island of Bolama, which then stood at the center of a dispute with Britain, sources underline the importance of the protection Aurélia Correia provided, by claiming she "never abandoned the island" and kept it and its inhabitants safe from "foreign occupation and Bijagó raids."[63] Governors posthumously described her as an "extraordinary personality who will become famous in the history of Portuguese Guinea for her valor and courage. By means of the genuinely Portuguese quality of her strong character, she was in a league of her own together with the leaders of her time."[64] Such comments demonstrate to what extent gendered role patterns and women's status were malleable in nineteenth-century Guinea, and to what extent they transgressed boundaries by combining economic with political leadership, whether the actors in question were slave traffickers or "legitimate" traders.

However, sources do reveal certain telltale signs of how the reputations of Dona Rosa and Mãe Aurélia were constructed. What is conveyed about their roots emphasizes their "noble" kin links rather than their possible "humble" origins. Whereas Dona Rosa's mother is never mentioned—she may well have been a ladinu Felupe or Bañun slave in her father's household—the precise identity of Mãe Aurélia's parents is still the subject of speculation. Some suggested that rather than being a Bijagó queen, she was actually a captured Pepel slave raised on the Bijago islands.[65] Interestingly, twentieth-century colonial historiography singled out Dona Rosa because of her "civilised" descent and her son's career, distinguishing her from the "Guinean Belles"[66] while largely ignoring Mãe Aurélia's feats.[67] The only (postcolonial) exception is Brooks, who acknowledges the latter's "historical significance" by portraying her as a powerful "Luso-African" entrepreneur and "one of the most influential persons" in the region at the time.

Ñaras' relations with their spouses and with their children were used to balance their commercial with their family roles as "mothers," as distinct from their public standing as mãe, a term that encompasses their big-woman status and even their role as lineage founders. Given that these big women were always on the move, their marriage bonds and domestic arrangements were evidently very flexible. Both mother, Dona Rosa, and son, Honório, lived in Cacheu; his monumental residence is described and pictured by his contemporaries. Dona Rosa was portrayed as a dedicated mother to her two legitimate children, Honório and her daughter Barbara; documents show that she formally took on the responsibility for their tutorship after her husband's death. Mãe Aurélia's residences in Bissau, and on Gallinhas, Bolama, and Ilhéu do Rei are all mentioned repeatedly in the sources and in one case even pictured. Her relations with the three daughters she had with Nozolini—with whom she participated in Bissau's gan society—seem to have been close, but less so with her son, a known troublemaker.[68]

In contrast, little is conveyed about their households and the way they were organized, thereby conveniently omitting the question of slave labor. One may well wonder under what conditions the gan labor force, composed of grumetes and grumetas, as well as ladinu and nonbaptized slaves worked in their houses, yards, towns, and pontas. Slave houses (funku) belonging to Dona Rosa are mentioned in some sources, as are those on Bolama Island pertaining to Mãe Aurélia. Dona Rosa's slave armies are referred to as quelling rebellions, and so was the sheer quasimilitary power Mãe Aurélia derived from the numerous slaves she commanded. While slave registers record the number of slaves they held and those that had professions, the large majority of their slaves remain no more than names and numbers. And contrary to Mãe Aurélia, Dona Rosa's household and company slaves are mixed together, while no data are forthcoming either on which slaves were put to work on their rice and peanut pontas. In addition, little is known about the destinies of these slaves during their masters' lifetimes and after their deaths. Incomplete registers show that while Dona Rosa freed a few slaves, others, besides those who died or fled, were pawned to settle debts, a common practice at the time. Documents refer to five slaves manumitted by Mãe Aurélia, including four Bijagó girls between nine and twenty years old, who although released under the 1856 law that freed the children of slave mothers, were obliged to work for their former master for ten years.

Essentially, tropes show the very selective emphasis on these women's pioneering activities in the realm of export crop production. The fact that they, just like their male partners, were also deeply involved in transatlantic slave trafficking is conveniently omitted in Portuguese sources. British reports leave no doubt as to Dona Rosa's—and her son's—roles in the trade. The apprehension of one of her schooners in the Caribbean with a slave cargo that included children in "a weakly and emaciated state, exhibiting incipient symptoms of scurvy and that from their present condition it may be fairly inferred they were in a starved and miserable state when embarked about seven or eight weeks ago" did not fit the image of the "noble woman" and "dedicated mother."[69] The conditions in which hundreds of slaves including infants were kept by Mãe Aurélia and her partner on Bolama island, chained, in barracoons, and who had been beaten into hiding in a nearby forest in order not be detected, blemished her image of a venerated queen and highly regarded ally. The fact that many of these slaves were working the land while others were awaiting transport was not exactly convenient for authorities who were held accountable for promoting "legitimate trade" and under attack for not complying with international treaties.[70] Seen in this light, the lack of concern about traders doubling as traffickers and planters was by no means surprising. In fact, the introduction of export crops by these slave traders therefore not only was a welcome cover for the banned trade in humans but also provided political legitimacy for the continued Portuguese presence there.

However, beyond the gendered tropes that were "officially" attributed to them, these ñaras themselves also proved to be able to redefine their identities. What distinguished them from contemporary African women in general were the attributes of personhood.[71] Rather than being treated and seen as property, they were themselves proprietors, owners of estates, of ships, of factories, and of slaves. For those who grew up in trade settlements or were adopted into them, Kriston communities offered opportunities to rise above and beyond servile anonymity. But unlike ñaras before them who had been stigmatized as smugglers and jezebels, those women were treated as individuals, successes in a commercialized world as entre-preneurs, partners and mothers, as citizens, and even as patriots. These women had European names and surnames, as well as individuated skills, intelligence, prestige, and power; at the same time, their regional agency as big women or ñaras defined their status in collective terms based on their kinship relations and privileged connections.

The ambiguities that characterize these women's lives were intrinsic to the kaleidoscopic Kriston communities in trade settlements under-going enormous changes. Instead of ambivalently classifying them as Luso-Africans or Eur-Africans, as some authors have done,[72] these women should be placed firmly within the political and economic context of Kriston communities and culture, which provided the foundations for their upward social mobility and ultimate personal power. Rather than operating through male-dominated networks, these ñaras succeeded in establishing their own trading lineages, or gan, in coastal settlements, guaranteeing them an unprecedented degree of autonomy vis-à-vis At-lantic and African interests. Boundaries were fluid, arrangements were flexible and tropes echoed this state of affairs. This same fluidity finds expression in the changes that took place during the nineteenth cen-tury, when these women, by skillfully exploring their relations of ma-tronage, were in a position to (re)negotiate their identities and project them onto the Afro-Atlantic screen, on footing equal to those of their male partners.

NOTES

Abbreviations

AHN Arquivo Histórico Nacional, Bissau
AHU Arquivo Histórico Ultramarino, Lisbon
PRO Public Record Office, National Archives, Kew, London

1. A. Teixeira da Mota, *Alguns aspectos da colonização e do comércio marítimo dos portugueses na África Ocidental nos séculos XV e XVI* (Lisbon: Centro de Estudos de Cartografia Antiga/Junta de Investigação Científica Ultramarina, 1976).

2. Or *tangomãos*, in many standard sources.

3. Philip J. Havik, *Silences and Soundbites: The Gendered Dynamics of Trade and Brokerage in the Guinea Bissau Region* (Münster: Lit Verlag; New Brunswick, NJ: Transaction, 2004); Philip J. Havik, "La sorcellerie, l'acculturation, et le genre: La persécution réligieuse de l'Inquisition portugaise contre les femmes africaines con-verties en Haut Guinée (XVIIe siècle)," *Revista lusofona de ciência das religiões* (Uni-versidade Lusófona) 3 (2004): 99–116.

4. And realized variously in the different European-language orthographies employed by visitors to the coast; an Italianate *signare*. Portuguese rendered the word as *nhara*.

5. Kriol (Guinea Creole) term derived from the Portuguese *praças* (as in *praça de guerra*, fortified town) currently meaning town center in Kriol. See Philip J. Havik, "Kriol without Creoles: Afro-Atlantic Connections in the Guinea Bissau Region (16th to 20th century)" (forthcoming).

6. On the signares, see George E. Brooks "The Signares of St. Louis and Gorée: Women Entrepreneurs in Eighteenth Century Senegal," in *Women in Africa: Studies in Social and Economic Change*, ed. Nancy Hafkin and Edna Bay (Stanford: Stanford University Press, 1976), 19–44; Amanda Sackur, "The Development of Creole Society and Culture in St. Louis and Gorée, 1719–1817," (PhD diss., University of London, 1999).

7. António Carreira, *Cabo Verde: Formação e extinção de uma sociedade escravocrata (1460–1878)* (Bissau: Centro de Estudos da Guiné Portuguesa, 1972).

8. See Havik, *Silences and Soundbites*, 263–64.

9. Arquivo Histórico Ultramarino (Lisbon) (hereafter AHU), Cape Verde, P. 13/67, C. J. Nozolini, 14 April 1848.

10. Apparently because the poorer Kriston women without good connections continued to be viewed as jezebels; see Havik, *Silences and Soundbites*, 305–9.

11. Jean Boulègue, *XVIè–XIXè siècles* (Lisbon: Instituto de Investigação Científica Tropical, 1989), 65–67; George E. Brooks, *Eurafricans in Western Africa: Commerce, Social Status, Gender, and Religious Observance from the Sixteenth through the Eighteenth Century* (Athens: Ohio University Press, 2003); Philip J. Havik, "A dinâmica das relações de género e parentesco num contexto comercial: Um balanço da produção histórica sobre a região da Guiné Bissau (séculos XVII e XIX)," *Afro-Ásia* (Centro de Estudos Afro-Orientais) 27 (2002): 79–120; Havik, *Silences and Soundbites*, 193–98, 243–53.

12. See Sackur, "Creole Society and Culture," ch. 7, 270–89.

13. In the Senegambia, "men (outsider-traders) could accede to a certain political position by marrying king's daughters." Boulègue, *Luso-Africains*, 67.

14. In accordance with the slave census of 1856, on the island of Santiago women formed 181 out of a total of 549 slave owners, while on the island of Fogo, 89 out of total of 281 slave holders were women. Carreira, *Cabo Verde*, 512–36.

15. Public Record Office, National Archives, Kew, London (hereafter PRO), FO84/117, 17 May 1831.

16. António Carreira, *O tráfico de escravos nos Rios de Guiné e Ilhas de Cabo Verde (1810–1850): Subsídios para o seu estudo* (Lisbon: Junta de Investigação Científica Ultramarina, 1981), 42.

17. J. J. Lopes de Lima, *Ensaio sobre a estatística das Ilhas de Cabo Verde no Mar Atlântico e suas dependências na Guiné Portuguesa ao norte do ecuador* (Lisbon: Imprensa Nacional, 1844).

18. Bertrand Bocandé, "Sur la Guinée Portugaise ou Sénégambie Méridionale," *Bulletin de la Société de Géographie de Paris*, 3rd series, 1 (1849): 265–350; 12:57–93; 315.

19. José Conrado Carlos de Chelmicki and Francisco Adolfo de Varnhagen,

Corografía cabo-verdiana; ou, Descripção geographico-histórica da província das Ilhas de Cabo-Verde e Guiné (Lisbon: Typ. de L. C. da Cunha, 1841), 109.

20. Chelmicki and Varnhagen, *Corografía cabo-verdiana*, 184.

21. Walter Hawthorne, *Planting Rice and Harvesting Slaves: Transformations along the Guinea Bissau Coast, 1400–1900* (Portsmouth, NH: Heinemann, 2003). For contemporary references to these varieties, see Lopes de Lima, *Ilhas de Cabo Verde*, 25; Havik, *Silences and Soundbites*, 229.

22. Arquivo Histórico Nacional (Bissau) (hereafter AHN), SGG, A6/9, Cx.437, 2 November 1845.

23. ANTT, Fundo MNE, Cx. 122, 30 April 1836.

24. AHU, Fundo do Governo da Guiné (FGG), L. 35, 31 January 1857.

25. AHU, FGG, L. 35, 31 January 1857.

26. Relations of matronage are defined here as "networks of female and male support, heading residential kin-aggregates and acting as heads of households themselves while controlling resources of social, economic and political importance." Havik, *Silences and Soundbites*, 29–30. The concept was first applied by Joke Schrijvers in *Mothers for Life: Motherhood and Marginalization in the North Central Province of Sri Lanka* (Delft: Eburon, 1985).

27. For a first approximation to her life, see George E. Brooks, "A Nhara of the Guinea Bissau Region: Mãe Aurélia Correia," in *Women and Slavery in Africa*, ed. Claire C. Robertson and Martin A. Klein (Madison: University of Wisconsin Press, 1983), 293–319. The following account is based on Havik, *Silences and Soundbites*, ch. 5.

28. Contrary to the information supplied by many secondary sources, Aurélia and Nozolini did not marry in church but rather *à la mode du pays*.

29. Being the second in line, after his elder brother José, who inherited the title to the family estate (*morgado*), Caetano, like many of his male contemporaries, opted for a military career; also see Brooks, "Nhara," 303.

30. AHU, Guiné, Cx. 23, 10 January 1828. Under Anglo-Portuguese treaties, masters were allowed to transport only their "domestic slaves."

31. PRO, FO84/117, 25 April 1831.

32. George E. Brooks, "Peanuts and Colonialism: Consequences of the Commercialization of Peanuts in West-Africa, 1830–1870," *Journal of African History* 16 (1975): 29–54.

33. AHN, SGG, A/21, Aurélia Correia, 11 December 1838.

34. PRO, FO97317, Governor Macdonald to Lord Stanley, 14 March 1842.

35. M. M. de Barros, "A Mancarra," *Revista portuguesa colonial e marítima* 1, 2 (1897–98), 798.

36. AHU, CV, P. 13, 27 January 1848.

37. PRO, FO97317, 1 March 1847; Co879/1/27, 4 April 1850). The governor of Sierra Leone reported in 1850 that "several free grumetes" were among those working the "plantations" on Bolama; see PRO/ Co879/1/27, 4 April 1850.

38. PRO, FO97317, 1 March 1847; Co879/1/27, 4 April 1850.

39. PRO, FO97317, 8 March 1859.

40. J. da G. Correia e Lança, *Relatório da Província da Guiné Portuguesa, referido ao anno económico de 1888–1889* (Lisbon: Imprensa Nacional, 1890), 17.

41. PRO, FO, 97317, August-September 1858, Commander Close of HMS Trident to Rear Admiral Sir Grey; FO to Admiralty, 2 February 1859.

42. J. C. de Almeida, *Um mez na Guiné* (Lisbon: Typographia Universal, 1859), 18–19.

43. PRO, CO879/1/27, 4 April 1850.

44. AHU, CV, P. 6/58, Francisco Paula Bastos, 23 December 1843.

45. Ibid.

46. AHU, CV, P. 23, 9 October 1857.

47. AHN, Guiné, Cx. 349, 20 September 1865.

48. AHU, FGG, L: 68, HPB, 6 September 1854.

49. AHU, FGG, L: 36.

50. AHU, FGG, L: 37, 38.

51. AHU, FGG, L: 37, 38.

52. Instituto Nacional de Estudos e Pesquisa (INEP), Bissau, Fundo Bolama, C15/C95, 29 May 1874.

53. AHN, F1/1, Governor CV to Governor Cacheu, 2 December 1817.

54. AHU, Guiné, Cx. 22, Joaquim António de Mattos to Lisbon, 29 April 1819.

55. H. Pereira Barreto, *Memória sobre o estado actual de Senegambia portugueza: Causas da sua decadência, e meios de a fazer prosperar* (Lisbon: Typographia Viuva Coelho, 1843), 45.

56. AHU, Guiné, Cx. 22, Joaquim António de Mattos, 29 April 1819.

57. AHU, FGG, L. 59, Joaquim António de Mattos in Bissau to Manuel António Martins in Praia, Cape Verde, 26 March 1834.

58. C. J. de Senna Barcellos, *Subsídios para a história de Cabo Verde e Guiné*, 7 vols. (Lisbon, Typographia da Academia Real das Ciências, 1899–1913), 2:300.

59. Ibid. 2:159.

60. Chelmicki and Varnhagen, *Corografía cabo-verdiana*, 107.

61. Lopes de Lima, *Ilhas de Cabo Verde*, 106.

62. Senna Barcellos, *História de Cabo Verde*, 3:2.

63. AHU, CV, P. 19/71, Manuel Felicissimo Louzada d'Araujo d'Azevedo, 9 June 1852.

64. Correia e Lança, *Província da Guiné Portuguesa*, 18.

65. António Carreira, pers. comm., in Brooks, "Nhara," 298.

66. Avelino Teixeira da Mota, *Um luso-africano: Honório Pereira Barreto* (Lisbon: Agência Geral do Ultramar, 1959), 394. A similar approach is adopted in a number of biographical sketches of her son Honório published in the 1930s.

67. Significantly, unlike her partner, Nozolini, Mãe Aurélia's name is not even mentioned in the document prepared by the Portuguese government that defended Portugal's rights to the island of Bolama in the dispute with Britain.

68. On their children, see Brooks, "Nhara," 315–17.

69. PRO, FO84/117, 2 July 1831.

70. Recent research has shown that domestic politics and public opinion in Portugal at the time were, generally speaking, little concerned about the monarchy's

subjects' involvement in the slave trade until the 1860s. See João Pedro Marques, *Os sons do silêncio* (Lisbon: Instituto de Investigação Científica Tropical, 2000).

71. The debate on the concept of personhood and gender relations was initiated by the anthropologist Marilyn Strathern in *The Gender of the Gift* (Berkeley: University of California Press, 1988), based on her fieldwork in Melanesia. She contrasted local society's view of a person as a multilayered microcosm to Western ideas on the status of the individual. For recent trends on Africa, see John and Jean Comaroff, "On Personhood: An Anthropological Perspective from Africa," *Social Identities* 7, no. 2 (2001): 267–83.

72. A. Teixeira da Mota, (Lisbon, Agência Geral do Ultramar, Divisão de Publicações e Biblioteca, 1954); Brooks, "Nhara."

View of Cape Town in the late eighteenth century, showing
Platteklip Stream and washing place Area F. Panorama drawn by
Johannes Schumacher, ca. 1778. Reprinted in Nigel Worden,
Elizabeth van Heningen, and Vivian Bickford-Smith, *Cape Town:
The Making of a City* (Cape Town: David Philip, 1998), 47.

14

IT ALL COMES OUT IN THE WASH

Engendering Archaeological Interpretations of Slavery

ELIZABETH GRZYMALA JORDAN

When walking along the banks of the Platteklip Stream, Otto Mentzel, a Prussian soldier stationed at the Cape of Good Hope in the 1730s, encountered "more than one hundred slave women busy with the family washing." Intrigued by what he saw, he spent some time with these women, later commenting on the peculiar way they washed clothes: "At first, all the washing is placed in the flowing stream and held down by stones until it has become thoroughly soaked. Next, each piece is pounded against a rock so as to knock the dirt out of it. . . . Thereafter soap is rubbed on the articles which are then spread out on the grass to bleach in the sun. . . . After a couple of hours, the washing is immersed once more in the stream, and each piece is beaten against the stones to cleanse it of the soap; there is a final rinsing and then each piece is once more spread out and allowed to dry in the sun."[1]

More than a century later, in 1861, washerwomen along the Platteklip again captured the attention of another visitor to Cape Town. From the account of "A Lady" we learn that the women who washed there were

The information presented in this chapter is derived from the archaeological, archival, and oral historical research conveyed in my dissertation, "From Time Immemorial: Washerwomen, Culture, and Community in Cape Town, South Africa" (Rutgers University, 2006). I thank Fulbright IIE for funding my doctoral research, Dr. Carmel Schrire for supervising this project, and Elliott Jordan for helping to bring it all to fruition.

"obliged to be up very early indeed in the morning to secure the best pools for washing" and that in order to do so, they would on occasion, walk "sometimes three miles upstream," where they spent "the livelong day in the open air up to their knees in the water . . . accompanied by their little ones and by a tame goat." At the end of the long workday, they returned to town "with enormous bundles on their heads, their hands on hip, their faces hidden under their yielding burdens, but their tongues going at a merry pace."[2]

These two accounts are among a handful of historical references to women washing in the Platteklip Stream. When pieced together, they provide a narrative framework that spans three centuries, straddles the transition from slavery to freedom, and extends well into the modern era. To date, however, the washerwomen's story has received little attention from social historians.[3] This oversight of the work of women slaves is not specific to Cape historiography but is symptomatic of studies of female slavery generally. Race, class, and gender have rendered slave women all but invisible in the documentary record, thereby creating a serious impediment for the writing of their history.[4] Archaeology, however, offers a partial solution to this shortage of written sources.[5]

Over the past thirty years, archaeologists have explored a variety of topics relating to slavery in a number of different geographical regions, including North America, the Caribbean, and South Africa.[6] While this work has greatly enhanced historical understandings of slave culture and life, until recently there have been few attempts to engender these interpretations.[7] As a result, the female slave experience and the social, cultural, and economic significance of their work have remained largely unexplored.[8]

To begin to fill the gaps cited above, the women who spent their working lives in and along the Platteklip Stream were chosen as the subjects of a comprehensive historical archaeological investigation. Excavations conducted at the site of a former washing place in Cape Town, South Africa, resulted in the recovery of thousands of artifacts, many of which constitute the material signature of washing. In this chapter, it is argued that clothing-related artifacts, such as buttons, buckles, and beads, should not be viewed merely as objects of personal adornment but rather more broadly as the by-products of women's labor. When considered as such, these artifacts not only help to engender archaeological interpretations of slavery but also can be used to explore the social, cultural, and economic significance of slave women's work.

Figure 14.1. Modern Cape Town. Table Bay is in the foreground. Table Mountain is in the background. The arrow marks the upper reaches of the Platteklip Stream.

SLAVE WOMEN IN CAPE TOWN

The first European settlement at the Cape of Good Hope was established in 1652 by the Dutch East India Company (VOC) at the site of present-day Cape Town.

The first slaves were imported to the Cape by the Dutch in 1658, when two shiploads were landed on the shores of Table Bay. The first contained 228 West Africans captured clandestinely by VOC traders in Dahomey, while the second, a captured Portuguese slaver, carried 174 Angolans, the majority of whom were women and children.[9] Some of these individuals were sent on to Batavia in the Dutch East Indies, but most were retained for company service. Journal entries for this year show that over half the population at the Cape consisted of slaves and that most of these individuals were held by the VOC and housed in its Lodge.[10] This reliance on the efforts of enslaved people continued throughout British rule until 1838, when slaves at the Cape, as in every other British colony, were officially emancipated.[11]

While the colonial slave society that developed at the southern tip of the African continent was in many ways similar to the slave colonies of the New World, it differed from them in three respects. First, whereas the majority of individuals enslaved in the New World originated in West

Africa, most Cape slaves came from the east—India, the East Indies, East Africa, and Madagascar. Second, Cape slavery, unlike that of much of the New World, was largely service oriented and decidedly urban in nature, with many of the enslaved living and working in Cape Town.[12] In 1731 slaves accounted for 42 percent of Cape Town's population, and as late as 1767, more than 40 percent of all the colony's slaves resided in the urban center.[13] Finally, whereas women were regularly put to work in the fields of the New World, Cape slave owners acknowledged, reproduced, and imposed a European gendered division of labor on those they enslaved.[14] This gendered division of labor is particularly clear in the context of colonial Cape Town.

Historian Andrew Bank provides a functional analysis of the types of work done by slaves in Cape Town, breaking their occupations down into two categories: services and production. While the former includes tasks that slaves performed to meet the basic needs of the city's ruling class, such as retail, transport, and domestic service, the latter category involves the transformation or processing of raw materials, including building, clothing manufacture, and a variety of crafts.[15] Based on the diversity of the occupations he identified, high levels of specialization, and extensive physical mobility, Bank concludes that urban slaves in Cape Town during the early nineteenth century enjoyed a "far greater degree of social space and freedom from owner surveillance" than either their rural or New World counterparts.[16]

When slaves are considered as an undifferentiated class, this conclusion does in fact seem true, but when Bank's argument is broken down

Table 14.1. Occupations assigned exclusively to slave women in Cape Town, 1816–34

"Housemaids"	2,500
Wash "maids"	233
Seamstresses	191
Nursery "maids"	99
Laundresses	98
Knitting "maids"	59
Scullions	7
Shepherdess	1
Garden "maid"	1
Total	3,189

Source: Bank, Decline of Urban Slavery, appendixes 6 (237–39) and 7 (240–42).

Table 14.2. Domestic occupations
assigned exclusively to slave men in Cape Town, 1816–34

House "boys"	657
Gardeners	131
Musicians	5
Butlers	3
Billiard markers	3
Wash "boys"	3
Total	802

Source: Bank, Decline of Urban Slavery, appendixes 6 (237–39) and 7 (240–42).

along sex lines, a very different picture emerges. Of the seventy-two discrete slave occupations identified by Bank, nine were exclusive to women, with the other sixty-three reserved for slave men.[17] While Bank presents domestic service as an equal opportunity employer, 92 percent of the slave women in his sample would have worked within their masters' homes, whereas only 14 percent of slave men would have done the same.

Furthermore, although Bank suggests that the washing of clothes offered urban domestics "the greatest potential for physical mobility," his sample lists only 233 wash "maids" and 98 "laundresses." Given that twenty-five hundred slave women were engaged as "housemaids," it appears that far more domestics were confined to the household than were able to escape it.

The physical mobility open to slaves not only allowed them to create zones of "personal autonomy" but often put them in direct contact with others on a daily basis.[18] In general, the work of slave men carried them into the streets of Cape Town, thus facilitating their integration into its broader underclass community consisting of free blacks, Chinese merchants, European sailors, and soldiers stationed there.[19] While participation in this underclass world helped slave men blur lines between slavery and freedom daily—and even over the course of a lifetime—the everyday experiences of their female counterparts were far more circumscribed. Isolated within their masters' homes, slave women were subject to close supervision and endless workdays, as well as physical and sexual abuse.[20]

The domestic work assigned to most slave women limited not only their physical mobility but their economic opportunities as well. As

Bank writes, "skilled slaves had far greater earning potential (and there-fore greater opportunity for capital accumulation) than their unskilled fellows."[21] While some women may have been "rented out" by their mas-ters to others in Cape Town, they would have derived few, if any, fi-nancial benefits from this working arrangement. In contrast, the work of male slaves, which included most "skilled" trades, provided them with opportunities not only to earn money but also to choose their employers, secure independent housing, and even purchase freedom.[22] Clearly then, the occupational diversity, high level of specialization, and physical mo-bility that made the urban working experience of Cape slaves distinct were highly gendered in favor of men.

Consequently, as "unskilled laborers" few slave women achieved the physical, social, or economic freedoms enjoyed by slave men. Washer-women, however, seem to have been an exception, as they carried out their tasks in and along the freshwater streams on the slopes of Table Mountain, rising above the city. Through the routine public perfor-mance of their duties, washerwomen became fixtures on the landscape. Over time their presence went unnoticed and their activities unques-tioned.[23] As such, they could partake in any number of diversions simul-taneously with their work, as long as they looked busy and brought home clean linen at the end of the day. Therefore, the washing places provide a unique opportunity to explore the shared experiences of urban slave women.

THE MATERIAL SIGNATURE OF WASHING

The washing places along the Platteklip Stream have recently been the focus of a comprehensive historical archaeological investigation. Today, the upper reaches of this stream are preserved within Van Riebeeck Park, which is managed by the South African national parks system. A recent walking survey revealed extant washing features, including a set of con-crete washtubs built by the Cape Town city council in 1877 and the Plat-teklip Municipal Washhouses, opened to the public in 1888.[24] In addi-tion, small boulder-lined pools resembling the washing pools depicted in historical sketches were observed in the Platteklip itself. While mate-rial indicators of the washerwomen's work were easily traced above-ground, locating them in the archaeological record required more sys-tematic excavation.

In May 2001 a total of 313 shovel test pits were dug throughout the Platteklip Stream valley. Although most of the areas tested were either

Figure 14.2. Aerial view of Van Riebeeck Park showing the location of Area F, just below the Platteklip Municipal Washhouses.

disturbed or devoid of historic period artifacts, shovel tests in a location (Area F) just downstream from the municipal washhouses produced an assortment of clothing-related items.

Additional testing here yielded more than one hundred ceramic fragments, buttons, shirt studs, and an earring, as well as a coin dated 1797. Importantly, these archaeological deposits were intact. Two years later, Area F was the focus of a six-week archaeological excavation during which a number of unexpected discoveries were made, the most significant of which was a buried streambed containing a series of cascading and interconnected washing pools.

The bottom layers (Mo10) of these pools were laden with eighteenth- and nineteenth-century artifacts, revealing more than one hundred years

Figure 14.3. The excavated streambed, facing south. Table Mountain is in the background, and the modern course of the Platteklip Stream is to the far left.

of intensive use. More than twenty thousand artifacts were recovered during excavations in Area F, the majority of which were found in and along the banks of the abandoned stream. These artifacts, recovered from in situ, washing-place period layers, represent the by-products of women's labor and the residues of their daily lives and constitute the material signature of washing, an archaeological pattern that can be used to identify women's work in archaeological contexts elsewhere.

This material signature of washing reflects a multitude of cultural processes that have been broadly grouped into four categories: off of clothing, out of pockets, personal items, and ancillary activities. In Area F, off of clothing artifacts constitute 20.9 percent of the total assemblage, a proportion that clearly points to site specialization.[25] Out of pocket artifacts comprise 2.5 percent of the total, and "personal items" a mere 0.1 percent. Ancillary artifacts constitute the bulk of the assemblage (76.5 percent), with those related to food sharing comprising 74.9 percent of the total. Other on-site activities included in this category are healthcare (1 percent), recreation (0.4), childcare (0.1), and sewing (0.1), all of which make but a faint impression in the archaeological record.

Given the rough manner in which washing was done at the Cape, it is not surprising that a large portion of the artifacts recovered during excavations were banged off clothing during the washing process. Of the more than 4,500 artifacts in this category, 97 percent were used to fasten clothing and 3 percent to adorn it; buttons predominate. A total of 2,167 buttons were recovered from the washing place, 56 percent of which were made of metal, 30 percent of ceramic, and 13 percent of glass. Bone, shell, pottery, and wood buttons were also found, but they constitute less than 1 percent of the total. Fifty-four percent of buttons in the assemblage were fragmented, and 53 percent of the metal buttons exhibited bent faces and broken shanks, indicative of damage caused by rough washing on the rocks of the streambed. Interestingly, of the

Table 14.3. The material signature of washing, washing-place period, Area F[1]

	AREA F	%	IN SITU CONTEXTS	%	MO10[2]	%
Off of clothing	4,556	20.9	3,760	39.7	3,468	57.6
Out of pockets	546	2.5	294	3.1	195	3.2
Personal items	29	0.1	14	0.1	12	0.2
Ancillary activities	16,708	76.5	5,420	57.1	2,349	39.0
Food sharing	16,360	74.9	5,247	55.4	2,270	37.7
Healthcare	226	1.0	99	1.0	44	0.7
Recreation	93	0.4	52	0.5	22	0.4
Childcare	16	0.1	13	0.1	9	0.1
Sewing	13	0.1	9	0.1	4	0.1
Total	21,839	100.0	9,488	100.0	6,024	100.0

[1]Nearly 24,000 artifacts were recovered during excavations in Area F; however, only those dating to the washing-place period (1700–1888) are accounted for in this table.
[2]Mo10 is the master context for the bottom layer of the washing pools, consisting of poorly sorted river gravels.

thirty-three patterns of molded glass buttons discerned, only two repeat, suggesting that multiple button loss from the same garment was relatively uncommon.

While most of the buttons recovered from the washing place were once used to fasten men's clothing, a variety of women's clothing fasteners were also recovered, including 1,248 straight pins, 242 clothing hooks, 42 clothing eyes, 30 corset eyes, and 1 belt fastener. According to Daphne Strutt, pins were "a necessary accessory" for South African women, who used them to fasten their caps, fichus (triangular scarves worn over the shoulders), apron bibs, and bodices.[26] In addition to buttons, a wide assortment of dress accessories were also found, including collar studs, cuff links, watch fobs, and decorative ornaments such as beads.

The second category of artifacts includes items that appear to have fallen out of the pockets of clothing when washed, such as coins, pencils, gunflints, eyeglasses, and pocket knives. Collectively these artifacts comprise a very small portion of the total assemblage, suggesting that either owners or, more likely, washerwomen were careful to check pockets before subjecting them to the washing process. Coins and slate pencils provide archaeological support for this. Whereas the bottom layers of the washing pools yielded only thirty-five coins spanning the washing place's period of most intensive use (1797–1884), 126 slate pencils, nearly all of which were fragmented, were found in the same layers. The small quantities of coins, having obvious exchange value to washerwomen, suggest that the women collected them from pockets before garments made their way into the washing pools. Pencils, however, evidently lacked both exchange and use value among this group of women and so remained in pockets and were broken when banged against rocks. This discriminating behavior, as evidenced in the archaeological record, not only provides insight into the washerwomen's decision-making process but also suggests that checking pockets for items of value or use may have proved a lucrative sideline of this occupation.

While archaeologists of American slavery often interpret many of the artifacts in this and the previous category as direct evidence of slave consumerism, literacy, and hunting practices, considerations of historical context and formation processes, including uselife, damage, discard, and loss, preclude the same conclusions being reached here.[27] Although washerwomen were ultimately responsible for the deposition of these objects, there is little indication that they used or owned them. As such, the artifacts likely represent the possessions and activities of those for whom these women worked, rather than of the washerwomen themselves.

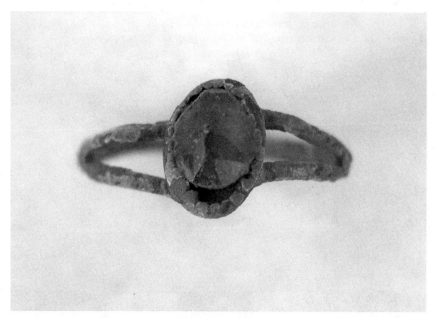

Figure 14.4. A copper-alloy ring with a green glass stone excavated from one of the washing pools.

The third and smallest category includes personal items, artifacts that may have once belonged to individual washerwomen. These include rings, bracelets, pierced coins, and pendants that could have easily slipped off the washerwomen's fingers, wrists, and necks while they worked, knee-deep, in the cold mountain stream. Since so few of these items were incorporated into the archaeological record, it seems likely that when they were dropped or noticed missing, washerwomen attempted—often successfully—to retrieve them.

The last category of artifacts contains those from which ancillary or nonwork activities can be inferred. Prominent among these are ceramic fragments, representing a minimum of 1,673 vessels, 466 of which date to the late slave period.[28] With the exception of willow pattern—which is ubiquitous at nineteenth-century sites at the Cape—and factory slip-wares, there is no discernible overlap in the patterns of the slave-period vessels. So hypothetically, if each of these discretely patterned vessels came from a single residence, then no fewer than 249 Cape households are represented in the washing place assemblage.

Given that the washing place was a work space and not a domestic residence, the presence of so many ceramics on site warrants an explanation. The most plausible interpretation is a modified system of pan toting,

Figure 14.5. A gaming piece fashioned on site from a broken piece of ceramic. The scale represents 5 centimeters.

through which slave women carried food from the homes where they lived to the places where they worked, in ceramics to which they had access but most probably did not own.[29] Once at the washing places, the women working there consumed and likely shared food among themselves. The ceramics themselves would have been used until broken and ultimately discarded along the banks of the Platteklip Stream.[30] Food sharing would have ensured the daily survival of individual washerwomen and their families, while at the same time drawing them into cooperative networks of support, reinforced and maintained through reciprocal obligation and exchange.[31] As such, these ceramics may provide some of the earliest material evidence of occupational solidarity and community among washerwomen.

The recovery of wine and beer bottle glass, in conjunction with gaming pieces fashioned on site from broken pieces of ceramic, may indicate that the "tavern culture" of the town was not confined to the streets of the urban center.[32]

Unusual and valuable objects such as a silver-plated writing pen and a copper-alloy salt spoon may point to petty theft by washerwomen or to their involvement in illicit trading networks. As much of Cape Town's black market trade was in "clothing and accoutrements," slave washerwomen would have been positioned perfectly to participate in it.[33] Not only did they have easy and direct access to goods, but the large bundles they routinely carried on their heads also provided convenient means for secretly conveying items to the washing places, where they could be sold or exchanged.

In addition, artifacts such as thimbles and pins suggest that women may have repaired some of the clothes they damaged in the wash or, alternatively, that they might have sewed in their spare time as a source of income. Finally, marbles, doll parts, and fragments of miniature tea sets remind us that the ability to care for one's own children would have been a substantial benefit of this line of work.[34]

In summary, the excavation of a washing place along the Platteklip Stream in Cape Town resulted in the recovery of thousands of artifacts detailing the lives and labors of slave women and their descendants over more than a century. Although many of the artifacts recovered from the washing place seem to tell us more about the people for whom these women washed than about the washerwomen themselves, when considered together they offer unprecedented insight into the daily lives of urban slave women. Large quantities of clothing-related items attest to the difficulty and intensity of their daily labors, while fragments of ceramics, bottle glass, and toys remind us that work was not the sum total of their daily existence.

In Cape Town, it is clear not only that washing provided these women with a means to assert control over a portion of their daily lives but also that the washing places themselves served as important loci for the transmission of culture and the maintenance of community. Here among peers women resisted domination and reclaimed some of the dignity lost to their enslavement. Significantly, while washing along the Platteklip Stream they created networks that transcended their enslavement and strengthened considerably over time.[35]

BUTTONS, BUCKLES, AND BEADS RECONSIDERED

Many of the artifacts that constitute the material signature of washing have been found also in New World sites once occupied by slaves. In North America buttons in particular have been recovered in such great quantities and with such regularity that they are often considered one of several "ethnic markers" indicative of African American presence.[36] While archaeologists have interpreted these artifacts in a number of different ways, most emphasize the African roots of African

American culture.[37] This emphasis is particularly evident in the following examples.

During excavations at Thomas Jefferson's Poplar Forest (Virginia), a large quantity and diversity of buttons were recovered from the slave cabins.[38] As many of these buttons mirrored contemporary fashions in men's clothing, Barbara Heath attributes this pattern to the "episodic purchase" and "piecemeal" acquisition strategies of fashion-minded male slaves.[39] Basing her argument on descriptions of runaway slaves and store records, as well as the archaeological evidence, she concludes that the Poplar Forest slaves, much like their African ancestors, "valued clothing accessories and jewellery as important tools of self-expression and community identity." For Heath, then, buttons, buckles, and beads underscore the important symbolic role that clothing played in the slave community, helping slaves—in particular slave men—"to cross the lines between work and leisure, routine and holiday, secular and sacred."[40]

A similar pattern of button distribution was encountered by Laurie Wilkie in her excavations at Clifton Plantation in the Bahamas.[41] Here the greatest quantity and most expensive buttons were found at the slave quarters. Whereas Heath's interpretations are rooted in historical accounts of a particular slave community, Wilkie's stem from generalized notions of African cultural practices,[42] leading her to conclude that the slaves of Clifton Plantation may have used buttons "as visual symbols of status, much like beads and scarification were used to denote status, gender, and stage of life among many West African groups" or perhaps even as components in Kongo nkisi charms.[43]

In light of the material signature of washing developed from the Platteklip Stream, I offer an alternative explanation for the presence of buttons on these sites: they are the by-products of women's labor, specifically, of washing. Moreover, I suggest that their ubiquity reflects a gendered experience of enslavement, rather than a shared cultural heritage. Slave women worked, and they worked hard.[44] They worked for their masters as well as their families. They worked for their survival as well as their freedom. They worked in Virginia, they worked in the Bahamas, and they worked at the Cape of Good Hope. Yet, in placing so much emphasis on ethnicity, archaeologists have not only homogenized the in-fact varied experiences of enslaved men and women but also inadvertently obscured slave women's labor. When freed from the analytical category of personal adornment and the interpretive constraints of the culturalist paradigm, artifacts such as buttons, buckles, and beads can be used to expand historical understandings of the female slave experience worldwide.

One area in which archaeology can make a particular contribution is that of slave women's paid overwork.[45] The buttons recovered from Poplar Forest and Clifton Plantation, when considered to be the by-products of female industry, may not only indicate slave women's work for their masters but also their efforts to generate incomes of their own. Washing was not merely a domestic chore but also a trade through which women created access "to material and social capital within the bounds of slavery."[46] As Jillian Galle has shown in her work on seamstresses at the Hermitage (Tennessee), these earnings provided many enslaved families with goods that their masters did not, including clothing, medicine, and a variety of nonessential or "luxury" items.[47] Similarly, Carter G. Woodson, one of the founders of African American history in the United States, noted that money earned through washing ensured the survival of many slave families and in some cases was used to purchase freedom.[48]

Women's labor, however, proved essential not only for surviving enslavement but also helped many African American families make the difficult transition from slavery to freedom. This point, too, is evident in the archaeological record. For example, Wilkie's excavations at Oakley Plantation in Louisiana provided insight into the postemancipation experiences of Silvia Freeman and her daughters, who collectively worked for the planters there from the mid-1880s to the 1930s.[49] As Wilkie points out, this era was a turbulent and uncertain time for many African American families, and there were definite benefits to be derived from steady employment in the big house. Excavations revealed some of these benefits at the Freemans' cabin: fragments of ceramics and glassware matching those owned by the planter. Wilkie explains this material connection in terms of pan toting, petty theft, gift giving, and favoritism, all of which helped the Freemans to meet their daily needs.[50]

Given the Freemans' modest socioeconomic and marital status, and their access to employment in the big house, it is not surprising that large quantities of buttons and other clothing-related items were recovered from their home. What is surprising, however, is Wilkie's failure to make any connection between these artifacts and washing, especially since it was an activity known to occupy "much of black women's time and energy as they transformed their slave skills into paid labor."[51] Instead, buttons lead Wilkie to the conclusion that the African American tenants of Oakley Plantation, much like the slaves at Clifton Plantation, "took pride in ornamenting their clothing with lace, feathers, beads and the finest possible buttons."[52] In this case, however, the privileging of ethnicity over economy not only renders the Freeman women passive but also leaves their efforts seemingly trivial.

While washing may not account for all the clothing-related items recovered from slave-related archaeological contexts, it is an activity that deserves more careful consideration. For as Woodson wrote of washerwomen more than seventy years ago, "whether as a slave or a free woman of color in the antebellum period or a worker in the ranks of an emancipated people, her life without exception was one of unrelenting toil for those whom she loved."[53] The archaeological record is replete with the by-products of women's "unrelenting toil." The task for archaeologists, then, is to recognize artifacts as such and to seize the interpretative possibilities they present.

In a recent publication, Amy Young discusses the ways in which some slave women in the American South were able to capitalize on the gender and kinship responsibilities assigned to them by their masters for the protection and provision of their own families.[54] She suggests that kin terms, such as Mammy or Auntie, not only entailed familial obligations but also structured relationships in ways that slave women could use to their own advantage. A parallel argument can be made with regard to Cape Town's washerwomen, who worked within the parameters of the master-slave relationship, on the periphery of the urban center, to create lives for themselves and their families.[55]

Although laundry has long been considered one of the most difficult and arduous of all household chores, it had its benefits.[56] It was one of the few domestic tasks that slave women could perform outside their owners' homes, affording washerwomen an unprecedented degree of independence. It required no special skills or tools, just strength and determination. As such, it was one of the few occupations through which slave women could have gained access to capital.[57] Significantly, washing was something that could be done over the course of a lifetime, or at any of its various life stages. Single women often washed until married, and widows turned to it after their husbands had passed on.[58] Importantly, slave women could care for children while washing and even involve them in the process. It was not uncommon for small children to haul water, collect firewood, and deliver fresh linen. Finally, laundry "encouraged women to work together in communal spaces within their neighborhoods, fostering informal networks of reciprocity that sustained them through health and sickness, love and heartaches, birth and death."[59]

In Cape Town washing places were sanctioned work spaces where large groups of women gathered to lather, wring, and pound the family linen clean. But as the archaeological record clearly demonstrates, the Platteklip Stream also served as a meeting place where slave women—and later their descendants—exchanged news, information, goods, and services, and shared the responsibilities of childcare. Such washing places provided these women with opportunities to establish and maintain the ties of friendship and community essential for surviving their enslavement.

Since it appears that washing sustained generations of slave women and their families in Cape Town, the buttons, buckles, and beads found at the washing place not only represent the by-products of this industry but also serve as tiny testaments to the social, cultural, and economic significances of this work. When considered as such, these artifacts can be used by archaeologists to explore and expand historical understandings of the female slave experience worldwide.[60]

NOTES

1. Otto Friedrich Mentzel, *A Geographical and Topographical Description of the Cape of Good Hope . . .* , pt. 3 (vol. 2 of German ed.), trans. G. V. Marais and J. Hoge, rev. ed. (Cape Town: Van Riebeeck Society, 1944) 141.

2. Lady, *Life at the Cape a Hundred Years Ago* (Cape Town: Centaur, 1983), 27.

3. In the past couple of decades some excellent works have been written on Cape slavery. See Andrew Bank, *The Decline of Urban Slavery at the Cape, 1806 to 1843* (Cape Town: Centre for African Studies at the University of Cape Town, 1991); John Edwin Mason, *Social Death and Resurrection: Slavery and Emancipation in South Africa* (Charlottesville: University Press of Virginia, 2003); Robert Ross, *Cape of Torments: Slavery and Resistance in South Africa* (Boston: Routledge and Kegan Paul, 1983); Robert C.-H. Shell, *Children of Bondage: A Social History of the Slave Society at the Cape of Good Hope 1652–1838* (Hanover, NH: Wesleyan University Press, 1994); Patricia Van der Spuy, "Slave Women and the Family in 19th Century Cape Town," *South African Historical Journal* 27 (1992): 50–74; Nigel Worden, *Slavery in Dutch South Africa* (Cambridge: Cambridge University Press, 1985); Nigel Worden, Elizabeth Van Heynigen, and Vivian Bickford-Smith, *Cape Town: The Making of a City* (Cape Town: David Philip, 1998); Nigel Worden and Clifton Crais, eds., *Breaking the Chains: Slavery and Its Legacy in the Nineteenth-Century Cape Colony* (Johannesburg: Witwatersrand University Press, 1994).

4. For a good discussion of this source problem, as well as for an excellent example of slave women's history, see Deborah Gray White, *Ar'n't I a Woman? Female*

Slaves in the Plantation South (New York: Norton, 1985). See also Jennifer L. Morgan, *Laboring Women: Reproduction and Gender in New World Slavery* (Philadelphia: University of Pennsylvania Press, 2004); Hilary McD. Beckles, *Natural Rebels: A Social History of Enslaved Black Women in Barbados* (New Brunswick, NJ: Rutgers University Press, 1989).

5. For an excellent discussion of archaeology's potential to contribute to historical understandings, see James Deetz, *In Small Things Forgotten: An Archaeology of Early American Life* (New York: Anchor, 1996).

6. The field of African American archaeology has burgeoned over the past thirty years. For a comprehensive overview and bibliography of this work, see Theresa A. Singleton and Mark Bograd, *The Archaeology of the African Diaspora in the Americas*, Guides to the Archaeological Literature of the Immigrant Experience in America, no. 2 (Glassboro, NJ: Society for Historical Archaeology, 1995). For specific studies in South Africa, see Ann Markell, Martin Hall, and Carmel Schrire, "The Historical Archaeology of Vergelegen, an Early Farmstead at the Cape of Good Hope," *Historical Archaeology* 29, no. 1 (1995): 10–34; Glenda Cox, Judith Sealy, Carmel Schrire, and Alan Morris, "The Isotopic Signature of the Underclass at the Colonial Cape of Good Hope in the 18th–19th Centuries," *World Archaeology: The Archaeology of Slavery* 3, no. 1 (2001): 73–97; Jordan, "From Time Immemorial"; Elizabeth Grzymala Jordan and Carmel Schrire, "The Historical Archaeology of Cape Town's Washerwomen: Preliminary Findings," *Quarterly Bulletin of the National Library of South Africa* 58, no. 4 (2004): 147–58.

7. For recent work on the engendering of the slave experience, see Jillian E. Galle and Amy L. Young, eds., *Engendering African American Archaeology: A Southern Perspective* (Knoxville: University of Tennessee Press, 2004).

8. An excellent exception is the work of Jillian E. Galle, "Designing Women: Measuring Acquisition and Access at the Hermitage Plantation" in Galle and Young, *African American Archaeology*, 39–72. See also Amy Young, "Risk and Women's Roles in the Slave Family," in Galle and Young, *African American Archaeology*, 133–50; Laurie Wilkie, "Granny Midwives: Gender and Generational Mediators of the African American Community," in Galle and Young, *African American Archaeology*, 73–100.

9. James Armstrong and Nigel Worden, "The Slaves, 1652–1838," in *The Shaping of South African Society, 1652–1840*, ed. Richard Elphick and Hermann Giliomee (Middletown, CT: Wesleyan University Press, 1988), 107–83.

10. For an excellent discussion of company slaves and life in the Lodge, see Shell, *Children of Bondage*, 172–205. According to Shell, from 1652 to 1695 more slaves lived in the Lodge than in all other private households combined (172). Although it is likely that slave women from the Lodge washed along the Platteklip Stream, my discussion is largely concerns privately owned slaves. See also Worden, Van Heynigen, and Bickford-Smith, *Cape Town*, 26.

11. It is estimated that between forty thousand and sixty-three thousand individuals entered the Cape as slaves. For an excellent demographic overview of Cape slavery, see Armstrong and Worden, "Slaves"; Shell, *Children of Bondage*, 40–65.

12. For a discussion of the urban nature of Cape slavery, see Shell, *Children of Bondage*, 138–43; Bank, *Decline of Urban Slavery*.

13. Worden, Van Heynigen, and Bickford-Smith, *Cape Town*, 60; Shell, *Children of Bondage*, 139.

14. Bank, *Decline of Urban Slavery*; Worden, Van Heynigen, and Bickford-Smith, *Cape Town*; Van der Spuy, "Slave Women."

15. Bank, *Decline of Urban Slavery*, 26–35.

16. Ibid., 28.

17. Ibid., app. 6, "Inventory of the Slave Population of Cape Town and the Cape District by Occupation, 1816–1834"; app. 7, "Tree Diagram of the Service-Production Divide, Cape Town and Cape District, 1816–1834."

18. For a discussion of "zones of personal autonomy," see Mason, *Social Death*, 118–23. For a good discussion of gendered mobility, see Stephanie M. H. Camp, *Closer to Freedom: Enslaved Women and Everyday Resistance in the Plantation South* (Chapel Hill: University of North Carolina Press, 2004), 28–34.

19. For a discussion of slave and underclass culture and community in Cape Town, see Bank, *Decline of Urban Slavery*, 98–141. For a feminist critique of Bank's interpretation, see Jordan, "From Time Immemorial," 32–36.

20. The hazards and abuses of domestic servants are described in Faye E. Dudden, *Serving Women: Household Service in Nineteenth-Century America* (Middletown, CT: Wesleyan University Press, 1983); Tera W. Hunter, *To 'Joy My Freedom: Southern Black Women's Lives and Labors after the Civil War* (Cambridge, MA: Harvard University Press, 1997); David M. Katzman, *Seven Days a Week: Women in Domestic Service in Industrializing America* (Chicago: University of Illinois Press, 1978); Patricia E. Malcolmson, *English Laundresses: A Social History, 1850–1930* (Chicago: University of Illinois Press, 1986); White, *Ar'n't I a Woman?*

21. Bank, *Decline of Urban Slavery*, 43.

22. Ibid., 39

23. Bernard Herman refers to servants as "props in the world of colonial sociability," 97. It is argued that washerwomen are seen in a similar light by Cape elite. Herman, "Slave and Servant Housing in Charleston, 1770–1820," *Historical Archaeology* 33, no. 3: 88–101. For how washerwomen may have used this to their advantage, see James Scott, *Domination and the Art of Resistance: Hidden Transcripts* (New Haven: Yale University Press, 1990), 120–24.

24. The initial walking survey was conducted in July 1999.

25. See Stanley South, *Method and Theory in Historical Archaeology* (New York: Academic, 1977).

26. See Daphne H. Strutt, *Fashion in South Africa, 1652–1900: An Illustrated History of Styles and Materials for Men, Women, and Children, with Notes on Footwear, Hairdressing, Accessories, and Jewellery* (Cape Town: A. A. Balkema, 1975), 77.

27. For a discussion of artifacts commonly found on African American sites, see Theresa A. Singleton, "The Archaeology of Slave Life," in *Before Freedom Came: African American Life in the Antebellum South*, ed. Edward D. C. Campbell III (with Kym S. Rice) (Charlottesville: University Press of Virginia, 1991): 155–57. For a

detailed discussion of cultural deposition with specific reference to uselife, loss, and discard, see Michael B. Schiffer, *Formation Processes of the Archaeological Record* (Salt Lake City: University of Utah Press, 1987), 47–98.

28. For a discussion of Cape ceramics, see Jane Klose and Antonia Malan, "The Ceramic Signature of the Cape in the Nineteenth Century, with Particular Reference to the Tennant Street Site, Cape Town," *South African Archaeological Bulletin* 55, no. 171 (2000): 49–59.

29. In this chapter, the term *pan toting* is used to describe the practice of removing leftover food from the master's kitchen for consumption by the slave family, with or without their master's consent. This practice became well established among enslaved house servants, and continued after emancipation among many domestic workers. For a discussion of pan toting among domestic workers in South Africa, see Jacklyn Cock, *Maids and Madams: A Study in the Politics of Exploitation* (Johannesburg: Ravan, 1980), 33–35. For a discussion of pan toting among African American domestic workers, see Hunter, *My Freedom*, 60–61; Katzman, *Seven Days*, 198; Ethel Waters, *His Eye Is on the Sparrow* (New York: Doubleday, 1951), 21–22.

30. For discussions of food sharing and commensality, see Carole M. Counihan, *The Anthropology of Food and Body: Gender, Meaning, and Power* (New York, Routledge, 1999), 13; Dimitra Gefou-Madianou, *Alcohol, Gender, and Culture* (New York: Routledge, 1992), 15–16; Deborah Lupton, *Food, the Body, and the Self* (London: Sage, 1996), 25–27.

31. See Carol Stack, *All Our Kin: Strategies for Survival in a Black Community* (New York: Harper and Row, 1974). According to Stack, domestic networks are groups of cooperating kinsmen (including fictive kin) who pool resources in order to meet the everyday needs of its members. For an archaeological analysis of domestic networks, see Amy Young, "Gender and Landscape: A View From the Plantation Slave Community," in *Shared Spaces and Divided Places: Material Dimensions of Gender Relations and the American Historical Landscape*, ed. Deborah L. Rotman and Ellen-Rose Savulis (Knoxville: University of Tennessee Press, 2003): 104–34.

32. Bank coined the term *tavern culture* to describe an underclass culture at the Cape characterized by "drinking, gambling, street-brawling and music-making that thrived on the weekends, outside of places of work." Bank, "The Erosion of Slavery at the Cape," in Wurden and Crais, *Breaking the Chains*, 91; see also Bank, *Decline of Urban Slavery*, 127. Van der Spuy criticizes Bank for failing to engender his interpretation. As she rightly points out, this reconstruction of culture is male centered and holds little for slave women, for whom childcare was often a major concern. Van der Spuy, "Slave Women and the Family."

33. According to Shell, the most frequently promulgated regulations at the Cape forbid company soldiers and slaves from buying "clothing and accoutrements" from slaves. Shell, *Children of Bondage*, 184–85. Interestingly, Shell refers to this black market trade as a "button economy."

34. Childcare is often cited as one of the greatest benefits of laundry work. See James Borchert, *Alley Life in Washington: Family, Community, Religion, and Folklife in the City, 1850–1970* (Chicago: University of Illinois Press), 169; Hunter, *My Freedom*, 62–63; Katzman, *Seven Days*, 83–86.

35. In Jordan, "From Time Immemorial," I trace the washerwomen's narrative of economic survival from slavery to modern times.

36. John Solomon Otto was one of the first archaeologists to suggest a correlation between buttons and African American presence. Citing historical anecdotes describing slave dress, and noting that many of the buttons found at the slave quarters were of the type found on work clothes, he attributes their ownership and use to slaves for fastening their clothing. This assumption has remained virtually unchallenged since the publication of Otto, Cannon's Point Plantation, 1794–1860: Living Conditions and Status Patterns in the Old South (New York: Academic, 1984).

37. Many archaeological works place emphasis on the role of African heritage in the shaping of African American culture. For example, see Leland Ferguson, Uncommon Ground: Archaeology and Early African America, 1650–1800 (Washington, DC: Smithsonian Institution Press, 1992); Theresa A. Singleton, ed., "I, Too, Am America": Archaeological Studies of African American Life (Charlottesville: University Press of Virginia, 1999). For specific interpretations of buttons within the culturalist paradigm, see William M. Kelso, Archaeology at Monticello: Artifacts of Everyday Life in the Plantation Community (Charlottesville: Thomas Jefferson Memorial Foundation, 1997), 94; Patricia Samford, "The Archaeology of African American Slavery and Material Culture," William and Mary Quarterly, 3rd ser., 53, no. 1 (1996): 87–114; Laurie Wilkie, "Methodist Intentions and African Sensibilities: The Victory of African Consumerism over Planter Paternalism at a Bahamian Plantation," in Island Lives: Historical Archaeologies of the Caribbean, ed. Paul Farnsworth (Tuscaloosa: University of Alabama Press, 2001), 272–300; Laurie Wilkie, Creating Freedom: Material Culture and African American Identity at Oakley Plantation, Louisiana, 1840–1950 (Baton Rouge: Louisiana State University Press, 2000), 154–65.

38. A total of 122 buttons were found during excavations; most were metal. Significantly, many of the metal buttons had broken or missing shanks, which would have rendered them "unusable," like many of those recovered from the washing pools in Cape Town. For more on the archaeological excavations and finds at Poplar Forest, see Barbara Heath, Hidden Lives: The Archaeology of Slave Life at Thomas Jefferson's Poplar Forest (Charlottesville: University Press of Virginia, 1999); Heath, "Buttons, Beads, and Buckles: Contextualizing Adornment within the Bounds of Slavery," in Historical Archaeology, Identity Formation, and the Interpretation of Ethnicity, ed. Maria Franklin and Garrett Fesler (Williamsburg, VA: Colonial Williamsburg Research Publications, 1999), 47–69.

39. Heath, "Buttons, Beads," 62; Heath, "Engendering Choice: Slavery and Consumerism in Central Virginia," in Galle and Young, African American Archaeology, 19–38. In this publication Heath expands on previous work, providing a detailed analysis of the consumer patterns of male and female slaves. Although she links the purchase of cloth and clothing-related items to sewing, the broader economic implications of this work are not explored. Significantly, gendered mobility, which would have affected the consumer patterns of slave men and women, is not addressed.

40. Heath, Hidden Lives, 53.

41. Wilkie, "Methodist Intentions."

42. For a discussion of the "pitfalls" of using African ethnography and history in this way, see Christopher R. DeCorse, "Oceans Apart: Africanist Perspectives on Diaspora Archaeology," in Singleton, "I, Too, Am America," 132–55.

43. Wilkie, "Methodist Intentions," 298.

44. For discussions of slave women's labor and the central role they played on colonial plantations in the New World, see Beckles, Natural Rebels; White, Ar'n't I a Woman?

45. In addition to the examples discussed in this chapter, the large quantity of military buttons found during the excavations of the slave quarters at Kingsmill Plantation near Williamsburg may also be evidence of slave women's paid overwork. Kelso attributes the presence of these buttons to the distribution of surplus uniforms to slaves after the American Revolution. However, these buttons may reflect the business dealings of slave women and soldiers. See William M. Kelso, Kingsmill Plantations, 1619–1800: Archaeology of Country Life in Colonial Virginia (New York: Academic, 1984), 200–204.

46. Galle, "Designing Women," 67.

47. Ibid., 61.

48. Carter G. Woodson, "The Negro Washerwoman, a Vanishing Figure," Journal of Negro History 15, no. 3 (1930): 269–77.

49. Wilkie, Creating Freedom, 98.

50. Ibid., 122–33.

51. Hunter, My Freedom, caption beneath photo of washerwoman at work with her family, between pp. 144 and 145 (no pagination). For discussions regarding the importance of washing for sustaining African American families after emancipation in the South, see Borchert, Alley Life, 169–73; Katzman, Seven Days, 24–25, 60–62; Paul R. Mullins, Race and Affluence: An Archaeology of African America and Consumer Culture (New York: Kluwer Academic/Plenum, 1999), 137–40. Significantly, Mullins makes an archaeological connection between buttons and laundresses' labor within the context of an African American working-class neighborhood in Annapolis, Maryland.

52. Wilkie, Creating Freedom, 231.

53. Woodson, "Negro Washerwoman," 270.

54. Young, "Risk and Women's Roles."

55. In Cape Town space played an integral role in the washerwomen's ability to create independent lives for themselves and their families. The washing places therefore provide a good example of "rival geography," as described by Camp in Closer to Freedom, though in an urban context.

56. For a discussion of benefits of laundry work, see Dudden, Serving Women; Hunter, My Freedom; Katzman, Seven Days; Malcolmson, English Laundresses.

57. Woodson, "Negro Washerwoman." See also Camp, Closer to Freedom, 98. For a discussion of the postemancipation experiences of laundresses, see Borchert, Alley Life, 68–74; Katzman, Seven Days, 184–222; Mullins, Race and Affluence, 137–40.

58. This was evident in my own research with regard to washerwomen at the turn of the twentieth century. Although some women washed over the entire course of

their lives, many left it and came back to it when money was needed. For discussion of washing, domestic service, and life cycle, see Katzman, *Seven Days*, 80–87.

59. Hunter, *My Freedom*, 62; also 57.

60. In addition to the examples provided in this chapter, there is substantial documentary evidence indicating that washing laundry in streams was fairly widespread, practiced in the former slave societies of Saint Vincent, Panama, Brazil, and Mauritius. In all cases, it appears to have been a communal activity. For communal washing at public fountains in Rio de Janeiro, see Sandra Lauderdale Graham, *House and Street: The Domestic World of Servants and Masters in Nineteenth-Century Rio de Janeiro* (Austin: University of Texas Press, 1988).

15

FREE WOMEN OF COLOR AND SOCIOECONOMIC MARGINALITY IN MAURITIUS, 1767–1830

RICHARD B. ALLEN

The central premise underlying modern studies of free populations of color is that these *gens de couleur libres* were an "unappropriated" people—neither slave nor free—in societies defined by white-minority domination of large slave populations of African origin or ancestry.[1] The marginal status of gens de couleur in such two-tier societies is usually traced to the racism endemic in the slave plantation world, and especially to white monopolization of violence and control over avenues of socioeconomic mobility.[2] This emphasis on the legal and quasilegal dimensions of slave plantation life has shed much light on some aspects of the free colored experience. However, it has also limited our knowledge of how and why these populations developed the way they did, the extent to which they remained marginalized, and their role in shaping local social, economic, and political developments both before and after slave emancipation. Moreover, a propensity to minimize the complexity of social and economic relationships in slave plantation systems, to view free colored populations as static rather than dynamic entities, and to ignore the larger socioeconomic contexts within which they arose has further limited our understanding of the free colored experience.[3] These limitations have, in turn, restricted the comparative study of these populations and the societies of which they were an integral part.

While some previously ignored aspects of free colored social and economic life in the Americas are now being explored,[4] three issues central to understanding the history of these populations have yet to be addressed in meaningful ways. Firstly, assertions that free colored populations

played a "special," if not "pivotal," role in the evolution of slave plantation societies remain largely unexplored.[5] Most studies of these societies
make little substantive reference to the range or impact of free colored
economic activity in the many colonies that entered a period of pro-
longed economic crisis during the late eighteenth century.[6] Little attention has likewise been paid to the changing patterns of social, economic,
and cultural interaction between gens de couleur and local white and
slave populations or the reasons why these patterns changed.

The role of gens de couleur in the development of "Creole" societies is
a second area of concern. In his classic study of Jamaica, Edward Brathwaite held that the creation of such societies rested on the juxtaposition
between master and slave, elite and laborer, with free persons of color
playing no substantive role in this process.[7] However, the fact that gens
de couleur often comprised 20 to 25 percent of colonial populations by
the late 1820s and early 1830s, together with their frequent possession of
significant economic resources and the widely acknowledged role of
women as cultural entrepreneurs in slave plantation societies, suggest
that the dynamics of Creole identity formation need to be reconsidered.

The extent to which free colored women functioned as actors on
colonial stages is a third unexplored topic. As others have noted,[8] the expanding research on slave women in Africa and the Americas has not
spurred a corresponding interest in recovering the history of *femmes de
couleur* or assessing their place in free colored and colonial history. Recent work on gender and slavery in the Americas[9] highlights the importance of doing so, as does work on gender issues after slave emancipation[10]
and studies of women in modern multicultural plantation societies.[11]
Women regularly outnumbered men in most free populations of color,
and our continuing ignorance about these women and their relationships with free men of color, local whites, and slaves is a major impediment to a fuller understanding of pre- and postemancipation colonial
plantation life.

The tantalizing glimpses that we have into the activities of Mauritian
femmes de couleur underscore the need to examine the ways in which
these women shaped the contours of life in the late-eighteenth- and
early-nineteenth-century slave plantation world. These women's careers
raise three issues of particular importance. In the first instance, despite
their demographic prominence in many colonies by the early nineteenth
century, studies of gens de couleur have not considered the impact of
gender on free colored socioeconomic status. In short, the fundamental
question of the extent to which a substantial female presence influenced

the degree to which gens de couleur were, or continued to be, "unappropriated" peoples remains unexplored.

Secondly, while some gens de couleur accumulated substantial wealth, free populations of color nevertheless continue to be viewed as monolithic entities defined largely, if not exclusively, by race. The careers of Mauritian femmes de couleur indicate, however, that class and ethnicity, as well as race and gender, figured prominently among the criteria that shaped social and economic relationships among gens de couleur and between free persons of color, colonial whites, and local slaves. The subtle and complex interplay between these variables may ultimately be the key to understanding not only the nature and dynamics of the Mauritian free colored experience, but also that of gens de couleur elsewhere in the colonial plantation world.

Lastly, what we know about the careers of individual Mauritian femmes de couleur points up the need to situate free populations of color firmly within their larger social, economic, and political contexts. The consequences of failing to do so are readily apparent in recent studies of gender and slavery that dwell at length on the ideology of master-slave, black-white gender relationships but do not consider the extent to which these ideological constructs mirrored, or were framed by, local socioeconomic realities. Attempts to analyze the status and condition of black women after slave emancipation, for example, invariably emphasize the agency of white men (and occasionally of black men), with no consideration of the way(s) in which the existence of large, well-established free populations of color and the presence of manifestly successful hommes and femmes de couleur influenced the world view of both these new freedmen and their former masters.

FEMMES DE COULEUR IN MAURITIUS

The origins of the Mauritian free population of color date to 1729, when the first of a small but steady stream of free artisans and craftsmen recruited in India reached the island. One hundred and ninety of these Indian immigrants landed on the island by 1735,[12] at least a few of whom were women, as the marriage between Ignace and Anne, *noirs indiens libres de Pondichéry*, on 22 January 1736 attests.[13] The island also soon housed free Indian and Malay sailors, as well as free colored immigrants from elsewhere in the French colonial empire, such as St. Domingue and Grenada. Manumitted slaves constituted another important component of this population. The exact number of men and women who secured their freedom from servitude remains somewhat problematic, but normally no more than 0.2 percent of the island's slave population could expect to be emancipated each year during the late eighteenth and early nineteenth centuries.[14]

As in the Americas, the Mauritian free population of color was initially too small to be of much consequence; a population of 342 persons in 1740 increased to only 587 in 1767.[15] During the last decades of the eighteenth century, however, these numbers rose steadily, to 2,456 in 1788 and then to 7,154 by 1806. The early nineteenth century witnessed further sustained free colored population growth. Mauritius housed 14,831 gens de couleur in 1825. Five years later, the 18,019 free colored men, women, and children on the island comprised two-thirds of its non-slave residents and one-fifth of its total population.[16] The large number of children enumerated in colonial censuses indicates that high rates of natural reproduction, rather than immigration and manumission, underpinned this demographic expansion.[17]

The Mauritian free population of color, like those in the Americas, was characterized by a marked imbalance between the sexes. Adult women outnumbered adult men by a substantial margin by the early 1780s, and continued to do so throughout the remainder of the period under consideration. Femmes de couleur also comprised an overwhelming majority of all free adult women on the island and a large percentage of the island's total free adult population during the early nineteenth century (see table 15.1). These data underscore the importance of demographic factors in determining the extent to which gens de couleur were "unappropriated" peoples. Recent work on pre- and postemancipation slave societies has emphasized that these societies were strongly patriarchal, so much so that even white women, who enjoyed high social status because of their color, usually had little independent standing in law.[18] As such, there can be little doubt that the demographic prominence of femmes de couleur contributed significantly to the marginal status of free colored populations, especially in societies that also regularly circumscribed the social, economic, and political arenas in which even hommes de couleur might function.

The importance of gender in defining the parameters of free colored marginality is confirmed by what we know about Mauritian free colored social structure. Census data indicate, for example, an increasing proclivity toward matrifocal forms of social organization among the island's gens de couleur. In 1776, 35.8 percent of 499 free colored households in the colony were headed by women or composed of individual women.[19] Four

Table 15.1. Femmes de couleur and the Mauritian population, 1776–1830

Year	FREE PERSONS OF COLOR		FEMMES DE COULEUR		
	Adult men	Adult women	% all adult GDC[a]	% all adult free women	% all free adults
1776	318	298	48.4	32.1	11.6
1780	302	397	56.8	34.9	12.5
1788	435	726	62.5	46.5	19.2
1806	996	2,157	68.4	62.2	30.1
1814	1,951	2,653	57.6	66.3	30.9
1819	1,561	2,791	64.1	64.6	33.7
1825	2,599	3,169	55.9	63.0	31.0
1830	4,409	5,792	56.8	70.5	36.8

Sources: CAOM, G¹ 473—Recensement général de l'Isle de France, 1776; G¹ 474, Recensement général de l'Isle de France, 1780; G¹ 505, no. 9, Relevé du cadastre général de l'Isle de France fait pour l'année 1809 . . .; R. R. Kuczynski, *Demographic Survey of the British Colonial Empire*, 2 vols. (London: Oxford University Press, 1949), 2:760, 768, 773.
[a] Gens de couleur

years later, a census of Port Louis reveals that 47.5 percent of the 360 households situated in areas set aside for the city's free colored residents were headed by women or composed of individual women.[20] Later censuses confirm this trend. Women headed three-fifths of 238 free colored households in Plaines Wilhems district in 1826,[21] and may have headed some 55 percent of such households two years later in Port Louis.[22]

This development is not unexpected. Female slaves were manumitted in substantially larger numbers than were male slaves.[23] Twice as many women as men received their freedom between 1768 and 1789,[24] a ratio that increased between 1789 and 1810.[25] Despite the absence of comprehensive data on manumissions after 1810, there is every reason to believe that this pattern persisted until the abolition of slavery on 1 February 1835. Female manumittees outnumbered male manumittees by a margin of three to two between 1808 and 1822.[26] Of the 418 slaves manumitted between 1 January 1821 and 1 June 1826 whose age and sex can be ascertained, adult women outnumbered adult men two to one.[27]

If these data point to the increasing matrifocality of free colored society during the late eighteenth and early nineteenth centuries, other data indicate that free colored social structure was actually more complex than might otherwise be supposed. The establishment in the early 1770s of several camps on Port Louis's outskirts, where gens de couleur of the appropriate cultural or ethnic background were expected to reside, highlights the importance of ethnicity in shaping the contours of free colored society.[28] A marked disparity in the number of male- and female-headed households in the Camp des Noirs Libres and the Camp des Malabars in 1780 suggests that patrifocal forms of social organization tended to prevail among gens de couleur of Indian origin or ancestry while matrifocal forms predominated among gens de couleur of African or Malagasy origin. Grants and sales of public land to free persons of color provide indirect corroboration of these trends. Individual women received 56.5 percent of the 214 properties granted or sold to "black" gens de couleur between 1770 and 1810, a pattern generally consistent with the previously noted propensity toward matrifocality among gens de couleur of African or Malagasy origin. A tendency toward patrifocality among gens de couleur of Indian ancestry or origin may be likewise be inferred from the fact that individual men received 64.6 percent of the eighty-two grants and sales made to members of this particular subpopulation.[29]

These data also point, however, to a certain fluidity in these social organizational foci over time. The almost equal distribution of public land grants and sales between black "Creole" (locally born) hommes and femmes de couleur before 1810 can be interpreted as evidence of an increasing trend toward patrifocality among second-generation gens de couleur of African or Malagasy descent or, more probably, the establishment of both matri- and patrifocal forms of social organization within this segment of the free population of color.[30] The large number of grants and sales to Indian Creole men, on the other hand, suggests that the tendency toward patrifocality among first generation Indian gens de couleur became more pronounced with the passage of time even though Indian femmes de couleur continued to outnumber Indian hommes de couleur by a substantial margin.

These data suggest that gens de couleur of Indian origin or ancestry may have enjoyed a greater degree of social structure stability than other major subpopulations within the larger free population of color. Such a conclusion is admittedly speculative and problematic in light of the linguistic, religious, and cultural diversity among the island's Indian slave and free residents,[31] the small samples in question, and the sustainability of the assumption on which such an interpretation rests. Scattered references to Indian social and religious life nonetheless suggest that such a conclusion is not completely unfounded. Contemporary observers of Mauritian life reported, for instance, that the annual "Yamsey" festival united all the island's Indians and other "oriental" residents.[32] A desire to maintain a sense of Indian identity or community (or both) may also be inferred from the marriage contracts, wills, and other notarial acts that gens de couleur of Indian origin or ancestry executed to formalize various social relationships.

The extent to which ethnicity and gender influenced free colored social structure stability must remain open to question pending an examination of local marriage and inheritance patterns. There can be little doubt, however, that gender influenced the ability of Mauritian gens de couleur to accumulate property. Femmes de couleur, for example, received a disproportionately small number of the grants of public land made to free persons of color between 1770 and 1789. They were also much more likely to receive small plots suitable only for the erection of a modest dwelling or the establishment of a small garden or both. The subdivision and sale of the Grand Réserve between 1807 and 1809 graphically illustrates this fact of socioeconomic life; only seven of the twenty-four tracts purchased by gens de couleur were acquired by or for women. A similar pattern characterizes free colored purchases of privately owned land. In a sample of 356 properties purchased by femmes de couleur between 1769 and 1823, more than half encompassed less than an arpent.[33]

The importance of gender in the distribution of economic resources among Mauritian gens de couleur is also readily apparent in patterns of free colored slave ownership. Available data suggest that many female-headed free colored households relied more heavily on slaves for their economic survival than did those headed by hommes de couleur (see table 15.2). The demographic characteristics of the slaves held by Port Louis's free colored residents indicate, moreover, that slave ownership could be as much a liability as it was an asset for some femmes de couleur. Many of the city's gens de couleur, a substantial majority of whom were women, made their living or supplemented their income by renting out their slaves, 60 percent of whom were women and children, who commanded lower rents than did adult male slaves. That these slaves could be an economic resource of potentially limited value to their owners is underscored by the fact that a great majority of the city's free colored slave-owning households held only one or two bondmen, and that not infrequently these slaves were family members whose labor could not be exploited unconditionally. These slaves could be children, siblings, or other relatives whose liberty had not been secured because their parents or other relatives lacked the economic resources either to purchase them

Table 15.2. Property ownership by free colored households, 1806–26 (percent)

	NO SLAVES/ NO PROPERTY[a]	SLAVES ONLY	SLAVES AND PROPERTY	PROPERTY ONLY	NUMBER
Port Louis, 1806					
Total households	29.5	30.7	29.8	10.0	1,666
Plaines Wilhems, 1826					
Distribution among households					
Male-headed	20.7	16.3	52.1	10.9	92
Female-headed	15.1	34.2	44.5	6.2	146
Total/average	17.2	27.3	47.5	8.0	238
Comparison between households					
Male-headed	46.3	23.1	42.3	52.6	
Female-headed	53.7	76.9	57.7	47.4	
Number	41	65	113	19	

Source: MA, KK 5, Recensement des impositions de l'an XII, populations blanche et libre (25 mars 1806); KK 15, Cadastre des Plaines Wilhems. Populations blanche et libre, 1826.
[a]Real estate and/or buildings in Port Louis; real estate only in Plaines Wilhems.

from their legal owner or to guarantee that they would not become a public charge after having been manumitted.[34]

Tax records provide further insight into the economic condition of the island's gens de couleur during the early nineteenth century. The 1806 Port Louis tax register reveals, for example, that the city's free colored residents owned real property valued at 247,879 piastres ($), and that 59 of 70 gens de couleur with real property valued at one thousand piastres or more were women.[35] Twenty-two years later, the assessed value of immovable property in the city's former Camp des Malabars and Camp des Noirs Libres had increased to $638,300, while the number of gens de couleur with property valued at one thousand piastres or more had tripled to 210, almost three-fifths of whom were women.[36]

The 1828 Port Louis census illustrates the continuing importance of gender in the distribution of economic resources (see table 15.3). It likewise suggests that ethnicity continued to be an important socioeconomic variable even in an increasingly creolized society. More specifically, the census reveals a marked disparity in the value of property owned by the residents of the city's two principal suburbs; 70.6 percent of those in the

Table 15.3. Valuation of free colored property in Port Louis, 1828 (percent)

	PROPERTY VALUATION			
	$1–499	$500–999	$1,000+	Number
Distribution among:				
Males	63.3	17.5	19.2	371
Females	56.2	17.3	26.5	452
Total/average	59.4	17.4	23.2	823
Distribution between:				
Males	48.1	45.5	37.2	
Females	51.9	54.5	62.8	
Number	489	143	191	

Source: MA, KK 20, Recensement des populations blanche et libre, Port Louis, 1828–29.

western suburb (the former Camp des Noirs Libres) either owned no real property or held property deemed to be of no taxable value, compared to 55 percent of those living in the city's eastern suburb (the former Camp des Malabars). Other data, however, illustrate the problems of attempting to correlate residence with ethnicity, especially by the late 1820s. More specifically, 14.6 percent of 1,056 western suburbanites claimed India as their place of birth.[37] The fact that three-fifths of the city's free colored residents with property valued at five hundred piastres or more lived in the old Camp des Noirs Libres rather than the former Camp des Malabars underscores the need to treat any such correlation with care.

FEMMES DE COULEUR AND FREE COLORED MARGINALITY

When viewed in their totality, these data demonstrate the importance of gender in assessing the extent to which gens de couleur were an "unappropriated" people. There can be little doubt that the continuing presence of disproportionately large numbers of femmes de couleur and a propensity toward matrifocal forms of social organization in a sociolegal system that relegated any free woman, regardless of her race, to second-class citizenship, had a marked impact on the status and standing of the Mauritian free colored population as a whole. The importance of gender, either as an independent variable or in tandem with ethnicity, in shaping patterns of free colored land and slave ownership is also readily apparent.

On Mauritius, at least, there is every reason to believe that the ability of gens de couleur to acquire or mobilize economic resources rested in part on the degree to which matri- or patrifocal forms of social organization prevailed not just within the free colored population as a whole, but also within its major subpopulations.

If these data give substance to the characterization of gens de couleur as an unappropriated people, they also indicate that any such attribution must be qualified with the passage of time. There is abundant evidence that the economic condition of the Mauritian free population of color as a whole improved steadily after 1770. Gens de couleur owned 13.4 percent of all inventoried land and 17.8 percent of all livestock on the island in 1828–29, compared to 1.3 percent of all land and 2.2 percent of all livestock in 1776.[38] Figures on colonywide slave ownership by free persons of color are unavailable after 1809, but that year gens de couleur owned 14.7 percent of all slaves on the island, compared to 2.5 percent in 1776.[39] Other indices of their growing economic importance include free colored cultivation of ever-larger percentages of the arpentage devoted to foodstuffs and their growing involvement in spice and sugar cultivation.[40] By about 1830 gens de couleur controlled perhaps 16 to 20 percent of the island's agricultural and related wealth, compared to less than 10 percent of such wealth in 1806.[41]

Their ability to accumulate economic resources of this magnitude must necessarily challenge characterizations that gens de couleur remained an "unappropriated" people as the early nineteenth century progressed. Contemporary observers of colonial life did not hesitate to do so. The Commission of Eastern Enquiry, which investigated local conditions from 1826 to 1828, noted that "although the property of the colored class is far inferior to that of the Whites, it is still considerable in Land and Slaves" and observed that a distinct sense of corporate social identity existed among the island's free colored inhabitants.[42] This social consciousness had first manifested itself earlier in the decade when gens de couleur began agitating for the removal of the local color bar. Even some local whites appreciated, if only implicitly, that the island's free population of color had become an entity of some socioeconomic consequence. Mr. Delaville, for one, advised the commissioners that it would be much more beneficial to the colony if gens de couleur keeping shops in Port Louis were dispersed about the countryside.[43] Additional proof of free colored economic clout would come during the late 1830s and early 1840s, when gens de couleur not only provided many former apprentices with viable alternatives to wage labor on the Island's sugar estates but also participated actively in the subdivision and sale of these estates and other properties precipitated by the suspension of the indentured Indian labor trade to the island late in 1838 and the collapse of the apprenticeship system several months later.[44]

The fact that femmes de couleur continued to outnumber their male counterparts during this period invariably raises questions about the role of these women in transforming a "marginal" people into a community possessing a distinct sense of social identity. Addressing this issue requires looking beyond traditional notions that these populations were largely undifferentiated socioeconomic entities and considering issues of class and class formation.

Early-nineteenth-century reports attest to growing socioeconomic differentiation within the Mauritian free population of color.[45] In the same year that Delaville suggested that free colored shopkeepers should be dispersed about the island, Mr. Marcenay advised the Commission of Eastern Enquiry that the colony housed a "very numerous class" of indigent gens de couleur who eked out a miserable existence by hunting and fishing or dealing in the goods and foodstuffs that slaves stole from their masters.[46] Census data substantiate his observations. In 1806, 30 percent of Port Louis's free colored households owned both slaves and real property, compared to the 40 percent that owned either land or slaves and the 30 percent that owned neither land nor slaves (table 15.2). As noted earlier, a substantial majority of the city's suburban residents in 1828 likewise owned either no real property whatsoever or held real property of no taxable value.

Given their continuing demographic prominence during the early nineteenth century, there can be little doubt that many of these impoverished gens de couleur were women. Occupational patterns provide indirect confirmation of this state of affairs. One hundred of the 123 femmes de couleur in Port Louis with a declared occupation in 1776 reported that they were seamstresses or dressmakers, while another twenty were washerwomen.[47] Free colored women continued to depend on the local service sector for their livelihood; in 1805 the city housed 779 seamstresses and washerwomen among its 833 femmes de couleur with a reported occupation.[48] This pattern continued with the further passage of time; the 722 dressmakers in Port Louis's suburbs accounted for 87.9 percent of all female suburbanites with a declared occupation in 1828.[49]

If many femmes de couleur hovered on the edge of penury, if not outright destitution, it is also clear that significant numbers found their way into the free colored elite that began to develop in earnest during the early nineteenth century. Census data from the 1820s reveal that female-headed households in Plaines Wilhems often outstripped male-headed households in terms of general slave and property ownership (table 15.2) and that women outnumbered men among free colored residents of Port Louis with real property with an assessed value of one piastre or more (table 15.3). Other indices include the growing number of female estate owners. Plaines Wilhems alone housed as many as forty-eight such proprietors by 1810–12,[50] compared to only thirteen on the entire island in 1776.[51] A similar, albeit less pronounced, trend can also be discerned in the world of commerce. Port Louis housed just one free colored female merchant in 1776; three decades later the city sheltered seven such merchants as well as twelve market women and a female fishmonger.

There is no simple explanation how or why some femmes de couleur managed to improve their standing in a society that was, by most accounts, overtly patriarchal and blatantly racist. There can be no doubt that some did so by virtue of their talents and the sweat of their brow. Baron d'Unienville, for one, held that freedwomen were much harder workers than their male counterparts.[52] The notarial record attests to the entrepreneurial skills of women such as the washerwoman Marie Louise, called Henriette, who realized a 2,800-livre profit in August 1793 on the eight-arpent property she had purchased less than four months earlier.[53] Nor did dependence on the local service sector necessarily impede a free colored woman's ability to improve her economic fortunes; seventeen of the thirty-two gens de couleur in Port Louis who owned ten or more slaves in 1805 reported their occupation as dressmaker or seamstress.[54] Almost a quarter of a century later, seventeen such *couturières* were among the city's eighty-four suburban residents with both a declared occupation and property valued at one thousand piastres or more.[55]

In other instances, femmes de couleur clearly benefited from their close personal relationships with local whites. A great majority of the slave women manumitted between 1768 and 1789 had been their masters' concubines,[56] and the same undoubtedly held true for many of those freed after 1789. Manumitted slaves had to be provided with adequate means of subsistence by their former owners and, as the notarial record demonstrates, substantial sums of money or property could be involved. On 28 December 1763, to cite an early example, François Desveau bequeathed twenty thousand livres to Hélène, the emancipated daughter of Roze, *négresse de caste indienne*.[57] The following year, Nicolas Auclair's last will and testament stipulated that Susanne, *négresse de caste malgache*, and her six children were to be freed on the day of his death, and that Susanne was to receive his estate at Rivière des Lataniers, together with all his slaves, livestock, furniture, and other possessions.[58] In some instances, freedwomen's fortunes were linked to their continuing association with local whites. On the same day that Marie Rozette consigned 63,000 livres (a sum equal to the purchase price of forty to fifty slaves) to Jean Victor Galdemar to hold for her or her heirs for twenty years, she also designated Galdemar as executor of her estate.[59] Marie's involvement with prominent local whites would continue for the rest of her life. Shortly before her death in 1804, for instance, she gave the civil commissioner for Rivière du Rempart District full power of attorney over her affairs and designated him as her testamentary executor.[60]

Many gens de couleur undertook to secure their property legally and free colored women were no exception. The notarial record reveals that some femmes de couleur clearly benefited from their parents' accomplishments and foresight, or that of other relatives. Since she was childless, Jeanneton sought not only to provide for the economic well-being of her heirs but also to ensure that her property remained within her extended family. In addition to bequeathing four arpents and a slave to her nephew, Jean Marie, and his sister, Louison, and her house with all its furnishings, two arpents of land, and a slave to her other nieces, Louise and Angélique, Jeanneton mandated that should Jean Marie and Louison die without marrying, the property left to them was to go to their cousins.[61] Quasifamilial ties could be equally strong. Because she had no living blood relatives, Marie Gassin set about guaranteeing her godchildren's future. In 1808 she gave her five-month-old godson, Jean François, fifteen arpents of land that she had purchased six weeks earlier for five hundred piastres.[62] Five and a half years later, she gave him another nine arpents.[63] Early in 1817, Marie stipulated in her will that Jean François was to receive the ten slaves she had purchased one week earlier for nine hundred piastres, while her eight-year-old goddaughter, Elise Gigette, was to inherit the balance of her estate, including all land, slaves, livestock, silver, and linens.[64] The importance Marie assigned to these "familial" relationships is further attested to by her designation of Elise's maternal uncle as executor of her estate. Other notarial acts likewise attest to the importance that many hommes and femmes de couleur assigned to socioeconomic undertakings with others of their kind.

The Mauritian case study demonstrates that a fuller understanding of the nature and dynamics of the late-eighteenth and early-nineteenth-century slave plantation experience requires careful consideration of the role that gens de couleur, and free women of color in particular, played in shaping that experience. It is clear that free populations of color were usually entities of little consequence during the late eighteenth century, a state of affairs that in part reflected the demographic prominence of femmes de couleur in social, economic, and political contexts defined by racist and patriarchal ideologies. The Mauritian case study also reveals, however, that the free colored experience was a complex one, and that the standing of these populations in the colonial order could and did change over time. Contemporary observers of colonial life, unlike many of their modern counterparts, appreciated as much. The Commission of Eastern Enquiry observed in July 1828 that although the island's "coloured class" still had to contend with "the prejudices of Colonial Society," the Mauritian government could nevertheless "look forward to a large and increasing portion of th[is] Community becoming progressively more useful to the Country, by finding themselves no longer in the condition of a degraded Caste."[65] As the commissioners understood only too well, the ability of gens de couleur to do so stemmed from their demonstrated capacity to acquire significant amounts of land, substantial numbers of slaves, and other capital resources over the years.

Femmes de couleur were not insignificant players in this transformation of an "unappropriated" people into a community that would have a marked impact on Mauritian life during the early nineteenth century. However, to acknowledge free colored women's role in this transformational process is one thing; to explain how individuals who were supposedly severely constrained by racist and patriarchal dicta could wield such influence is something else. Recent work on slavery and gender offers no substantive clues to answering this question; neither does the substantial body of scholarship on free populations of color in the Americas. Under such circumstances, coming to terms with this question requires reconsidering at least some of the ways in which the free colored experience has been approached and conceptualized.

A first step in any such process must include a greater willingness to acknowledge that dominant ideologies and their attendant legal or quasi-legal manifestations are not necessarily accurate guides to what actually happened on the ground. The literature on slave plantation systems is replete with examples of individuals who modified or ignored the rules that were supposed to govern black-white relations to suit their own purposes and further their own ends. The willingness of white men throughout the slave plantation world to cohabit with or marry femmes de couleur and provide for their partners' future welfare illustrates that socioeconomic realities did not necessarily conform to ideological dicta. The careers of women such as Marie Rozette are additional striking examples of the fact that free persons of color engaged in activities and cultivated relationships that flew directly in the face of racist and patriarchal norms, and that local whites would also readily bend, if not break, the normative rules in which they supposedly had a vested interest.

The depth of white involvement with the island's gens de couleur, together with the steady improvement in this population's socioeconomic condition, highlights the increasingly complex structure of Mauritian society by the early nineteenth century, and indicates that the standard characterization of slave plantation societies as two-tier systems and of free colored populations as little more than marginal peoples in such systems needs, at a minimum, to be carefully qualified. The necessity of doing so is demonstrated by the simple fact that the composition and structure of Mauritian society changed over time. Gens de couleur comprised one-fifth of the island's total population and accounted for more than two-thirds of its free inhabitants in 1830, demographic realities that point to the development of at least a three-tier society in which free persons of color constituted a truly intermediate, if not pivotal, group between the black slave majority and the white minority.

Although more representative of change through time, any such model will also be problematic if it too emphasizes race as the sole definitive criterion around which Mauritian society, or that of other colonies with large free populations of color, was organized. While the importance of race in structuring slave plantation social relations cannot be denied, focusing on race to the exclusion of other organizational foci serves only to obscure the increasingly complex social and economic life that is a hallmark of many early-nineteenth-century slave plantation colonies. There is compelling evidence that both Mauritian whites and gens de couleur challenged racially defined social boundaries throughout the period under consideration. The Commission of Eastern Enquiry noted that interracial marriages during the era of the French Revolution had "placed the Descendants of some coloured people amongst the class of Whites," the members of which were "really darker in complexion than many who are now rigorously excluded [from white society]." The commissioners also observed that the establishment of separate registers for the colony's white and free colored inhabitants had served only to induce "connections of concubinage to be formed between males of the white, and females of the coloured Class, when, but for this prohibition, the parties would willingly enter into relations of marriage."[66]

The willingness of both whites and gens de couleur to contest racial boundaries underscores the growing importance of class in shaping the

contours of Mauritian society as the eighteenth century gave way to the
nineteenth. We currently know relatively little about white social structure on the island, but the distinction between *grand* and *petit blancs* that
marked early Réunionnais society[67] also probably prevailed on Mauritius.
Census data suggest, however, that this distinction became more nuanced
as the social boundaries between at least some whites and free coloreds
became increasingly blurred during the early nineteenth century. The
changing composition of the island's working class implies as much. In
1828, Port Louis's eastern and western suburbs supplied 67.2 percent of
the city's skilled craftsmen and artisans and 63.6 percent of its bakers,
butchers, cooks, and so on, compared to 35.5 percent and 23.9 percent,
respectively, of such workers in 1805.[68] The importance of class considerations among free persons of color themselves may likewise be inferred from
early-nineteenth-century reports that emphasize the depth of free colored
prejudice against the island's slaves.[69]

These developments indicate that descriptions of gens de couleur as essentially marginal socioeconomic entities in the late-eighteenth and early-
nineteenth-century slave plantation world can be at least something of a
misnomer. At a minimum, they point up the dangers inherent in ignoring or oversimplifying the complex patterns of social, economic, and cultural interaction that were an integral part of life in any such system. If
Mauritian gens de couleur, like their counterparts in the Americas, were
initially an unappropriated people, they did not remain so.[70] That
femmes de couleur participated actively in improving free colored fortunes attests to the fact that, racist and patriarchal norms notwithstanding, gender was not necessarily a barrier to free colored socioeconomic
advancement. Further research may reveal that femmes de couleur played
a more important role in this process than hitherto supposed, and that
their ability to do so stemmed the fact that the marginal status conferred
upon them by their gender provided at least some of these women with
opportunities that were normally denied both to hommes de couleur and
their white female counterparts.

NOTES

Abbreviations

CAOM	Centre des Archives d'Outre-Mer, Aix-en-Provence
CO	Colonial Office records, British National Archives, Kew
MA	Mauritius Archives
PP	British Parliament Sessional Papers

1. David W. Cohen and Jack P. Greene, eds., *Neither Slave nor Free: The Freedmen of African Descent in the Slave Societies of the New World* (Baltimore: Johns Hopkins University Press, 1972); Jerome Handler, *The Unappropriated People: Freedmen in the Slave Society of Barbados* (Baltimore: Johns Hopkins University Press, 1974).

2. Orlando Patterson, *Slavery and Social Death: A Comparative Study* (Cambridge, MA: Harvard University Press, 1992); Arnold Sio, "Marginality and Free Coloured Identity in Caribbean Slave Society," *Slavery and Abolition* 8, no. 2 (1987): 166–82.

3. Sidney W. Mintz and Richard Price, *An Anthropological Approach to the Afro-American Past: A Caribbean Perspective*, ISHI Occasional Papers in Social Change, no. 2 (Philadelphia: Institute for the Study of Human Issues, 1976).

4. John D. Garrigus, "Blue and Brown: Contraband Indigo and the Rise of a Free Colored Planter Class in French Saint-Domingue," *Americas* 50 (1993): 233–63; Garrigus, "Colour, Class and Identity on the Eve of the Haitian Revolution: Saint-Domingue's Free Coloured Elite as *Colons américains*," *Slavery and Abolition* 17, no. 1 (1996): 20–43; Kimberly S. Hanger, "Patronage, Property and Persistence: The Emergence of a Free Black Elite in Spanish New Orleans," *Slavery and Abolition* 17, no. 1 (1996): 44–64; Paul Lachance, "The Limits of Privilege: Where Free Persons of Colour Stood in the Hierarchy of Wealth in Antebellum New Orleans," *Slavery and Abolition* 17, no. 1 (1996): 65–84; Wilma King, *The Essence of Liberty: Free Black Women during the Slave Era* (Columbia: University of Missouri Press, 2006).

5. Laura Foner, "The Free People of Color in Louisiana and St. Domingue: A Comparative Portrait of Two Three-Caste Slave Societies," *Journal of Social History* 3, no. 4 (1969–70): 415; David W. Cohen and Jack P. Greene, introduction to Cohen and Green, *Neither Slave nor Free*, 3.

6. David Watts, *The West Indies: Patterns of Development, Culture, and Environmental Change since 1492* (Berkeley: University of California Press, 1987), chs. 6, 7, 9; J. R. Ward, *British West Indian Slavery, 1750–1834: The Process of Amelioration* (Oxford: Oxford University Press, 1988), 38–60.

7. Edward Brathwaite, *The Development of Creole Society in Jamaica, 1770–1820* (Oxford: Oxford University Press, 1971).

8. Adele Logan Alexander, *Ambiguous Lives: Free Women of Color in Rural Georgia, 1789–1879* (Fayetteville: University of Arkansas Press, 1991), 7; David P. Geggus, "Slave and Free Colored Women in Saint Domingue," in *More Than Chattel: Black Women and Slavery in the Americas*, ed. David Barry Gaspar and Darlene Clark Hine (Bloomington: Indiana University Press, 1996), 259–78; Susan M. Socolow, "Economic Roles of Free Women of Color of Cap Français," in Gaspar and Hine, *More Than Chattel*, 279–97.

9. Verene Shepherd, Bridget Brereton, and Barbara Bailey, eds., *Engendering History: Caribbean Women in Historical Perspective* (New York: St. Martin's, 1995); Hilary McD. Beckles, *Centering Woman: Gender Discourses in Caribbean Slave Society* (Princeton: Markus Wiener, 1999).

10. Leslie A. Schwalm, "'Sweet Dreams of Freedom': Freedwomen's Reconstruction of Life and Labor in Lowcountry South Carolina," *Journal of Women's History* 9, no. 1 (1997): 9–38; Pamela Scully, *Liberating the Family? Gender and British Slave Emancipation in the Rural Western Cape, South Africa, 1823–1853* (Portsmouth, NH:

Heinemann, 1997); Bridget Brereton, "Family Strategies, Gender, and the Shift to Wage Labour in the British Caribbean," in *The Colonial Caribbean in Transition: Essays on Postemancipation Social and Cultural History*, ed. Brereton and Kevin A. Yelvington (Gainesville: University Press of Florida, 1999), 77–107; Amy Dru Stanley, ""We Did Not Separate Man and Wife, but All Had to Work": Freedom and Dependence in the Aftermath of Slave Emancipation," in *Terms of Labor: Slavery, Serfdom, and Free Labor*, ed. Stanley L. Engerman (Stanford: Stanford University Press, 1999), 188–212; Melanie Newton, "'New Ideas of Correctness': Gender, Amelioration and Emancipation in Barbados, 1810s–50s," *Slavery and Abolition* 21, no. 3 (2000): 94–124; Sheena Boa, "Experiences of Women Estate Workers during the Apprenticeship Period in St. Vincent, 1834–38: The Transition from Slavery to Freedom," *Women's History Review* 10, no. 3 (2001): 381–407.

11. Janet Momsen, ed., *Women and Change in the Caribbean: A Pan-Caribbean Perspective* (London: James Currey, 1993).

12. Philip Baker, "On the Origins of the First Mauritians and of the Creole Language of Their Descendants: A Refutation of Chaudenson's 'Bourbonnais' Theory," in *Isle de France Creole: Affinities and Origins*, ed. Philip Baker and Chris Corne (Ann Arbor: Karoma, 1982), 193.

13. Harold Adolphe, *Les archives démographiques de l'Ile Maurice (1721–1810)* (Port Louis: R. Coquet, 1966), 80–81.

14. Richard B. Allen, *Slaves, Freedmen, and Indentured Laborers in Colonial Mauritius* (Cambridge: Cambridge University Press, 1999), 83.

15. Huguette Ly-Tio-Fane Pineo, *Ile de France, 1747–1767* (Moka, Mauritius: Mahatma Gandhi Institute, 1999), 221; R. R. Kuczynski, *Demographic Survey of the British Colonial Empire*, 2 vols. (London: Oxford University Press, 1949), 2:758.

16. CAOM, G^1 473, Recensement général de l'Isle de France, 1776; G^1 474, Recensement général de l'Isle de France, 1780; G^1 505, no. 9, Relevé du cadastre général de l'Isle de France fait pour l'année 1809 . . . ; Kuczynski, *Demographic Survey*, 758, 760–61, 768–89, 773.

17. Allen, *Slaves, Freedmen*, 84–85.

18. Scully, *Liberating the Family*; Beckles, *Centering Woman*, xv; Stanley, "'We Did Not Separate,'" 202; Schwalm, "'Sweet Dreams of Freedom,'" 12; Brereton, "Family Strategies," 78, 102ff.; Momsen, *Women and Change*, 6.

19. CAOM, G^1 473.

20. CAOM, G^1 474.

21. MA, KK 15, Cadastre des Plaines Wilhems, Populations blanche et libre, 1826.

22. MA, KK 20, Recensement des populations blanche et libre, Port Louis, 1828–29.

23. On female slaves in Mauritius, see Vijaya Teelock, *Bitter Sugar: Sugar and Slavery in 19th Century Mauritius* (Moka: Mahatma Gandhi Institute, 1998), passim; Megan Vaughan, *Creating the Creole Island: Slavery in Eighteenth-Century Mauritius* (Durham: Duke University Press, 2005).

24. Musleem Jumeer, "Les affranchissements et les libres à l'île de France à la fin de l'ancien régime (1768–1789)" (Mémoire de maîtrise, Faculté des Sciences Humaines, Université de Poitiers, 1979), 26.

25. Pritilah Rosunee, "Manumission in Isle de France during the Revolutionary and Post Revolutionary Years from 1789 to 1810" (MA thesis, University of Cape Town, 2002), 73.

26. PP 1823 XVIII [89], 125, Return of all Manumissions effected by Purchase, Bequest or otherwise, since the 1st of January 1808. . . .

27. PP 1828 XXV [204], 58–75, Return of the Number of Manumissions effected by Purchase, Bequest or otherwise . . . from 1st January 1821 to 1st June 1826.

28. Five such camps—des malabars et lascars, des iolofs, des malgaches, des bambara, and des noirs libres—existed in the early 1790s. MA, B1A/A.31/22, Plan de la Ville de Port Louis dans l'Ile de France par Douville, 1791.

29. Richard B. Allen, "Lives of Neither Luxury nor Misery: Indians and Free Colored Marginality on the Ile de France, 1728–1810," *Revue française d'histoire d'outre-mer* 78 (1991): 352–53.

30. A similar pattern exists among modern Mauritians of African descent. Linda Sussman, pers. comm., 16 June 1984.

31. Cf. Baron Grant, *The History of Mauritius, or the Isle de France, and the Neighbouring Islands* . . . (London: W. Bulmer and Co., 1801), 73–77, 297–98; J.-H. Bernardin de St. Pierre, *Voyage à l'île de France* (Paris: Armand-Aubrée, 1834), 121; M. J. Milbert, *Voyage pittoresque à l'Ile de France, au Cap de Bonne-Espérance et à l'Ile de Ténériffe*, 2 vols. (Paris: A. Nepveu, 1812), 1:169–70.

32. Milbert, *Voyage pittoresque*, 2:187–88; James Holman, *A Voyage Round the World, including Travels in Africa, Asia, Australasia, America, Etc., Etc, from 1827 to 1832*, 4 vols. (London: Smith, Elder, and Co., 1834–35), 2:416–18.

33. One arpent equals 1.043 acres.

34. Allen, *Slaves, Freedmen*, 93, 95.

35. MA, KK 5, Recensement des impositions de l'An XII, populations blanche et libre (25 March 1806).

36. MA, KK 20.

37. Only 3.1 percent of 1,143 eastern suburbanites, on the other hand, reported being been born in Africa or Madagascar.

38. CAOM, G¹ 473; Baron d'Unienville, *Statistique de l'île Maurice et ses dépendances suivie d'une notice historique sur cette colonie et d'un essai sur l'île de Madagascar*, 2nd ed., 3 vols. ([Ile] Maurice: Typographie *Merchants and Planters Gazette*, 1885–86), 1:52–228.

39. CAOM, G¹ 473; G¹ 505, no. 9, Relevé du cadastre général de l'Isle de france fait pour l'année 1809. . . .

40. Allen, *Slaves, Freedmen*, 98–99.

41. Ibid., 96.

42. CO 167/43, Report of the Commissioners of Inquiry upon the condition of the Free People of Colour at Mauritius, 15 July 1828.

43. CO 415/11/B.5 (no. 10), Statement of Mr. Delaville . . . respecting the number of Free people of Colour in Port Louis, and the encouraging [of] them to reside in the Country . . . , [21 March 1827].

44. Allen, *Slaves, Freedmen*, ch. 5.

45. For comparable developments in the Caribbean, see Bernard Marshall, "Social Stratification and the Free Coloured in the Slave Society of the British Windward

Islands," *Social and Economic Studies* (Jamaica) 31, no. 1 (1982): 1–39; Jay Kinsbruner, "Caste and Capitalism in the Caribbean: Residential Patterns and House Ownership among the Free People of Color of San Juan, Puerto Rico, 1823–46," *Hispanic American Historical Review* 53, no. 3 (1990): 435–46.

46. CO 415/19/Q.3, "Exposé" of Mr. Marcenay relative to the Cultivation of Land by Free Persons of Colour . . . , [12 October 1827].

47. CAOM, G¹ 473.

48. MA, KK 3, Recensement des populations blanche et libre, Port Louis (1805).

49. MA, KK 20.

50. MA, KK 7, Recensement des populations blanche et libre, Plaines Wilhems (1810–12).

51. CAOM, G¹ 473.

52. D'Unienville, *Statistique*, 1:237.

53. MA, NA 43/1/27, 4 May 1793; NA 33/23/41, 28 August 1793.

54. MA, KK 3.

55. MA, KK 20.

56. Jumeer, "Affranchissements," 16–17.

57. MA, NA 15/1B/70, 28 December 1763.

58. MA, NA 15/2D/141, 20 December 1764.

59. MA, NA 22/21/27, 28 August 1790; NA 22/21/28, 28 August 1790.

60. MA, NA 43/6/81, 15 messidor, An XII; NA 43/6/83, 24 messidor, An XII.

61. MA, NA 43/14, 5 September 1811.

62. MA, NA 43/8/75, 5 May 1808.

63. MA, NA 43/16a, 29 November 1813.

64. MA, NA 43/16b, 17 February 1817.

65. CO 167/143, Report of the Commissioners of Inquiry upon the condition of the Free People of Colour at Mauritius, 15 July 1828.

66. Ibid.

67. André Scherer, *Histoire de La Réunion* (Paris: Presses Universitaires de France, 1974), 37–39, 62–66; Deryck Scarr, *Slaving and Slavery in the Indian Ocean* (London: Macmillan; New York: St. Martin's, 1998).

68. MA, KK 3, KK 20. See also Allen, *Slaves, Freedmen*, 95.

69. A Lady, *Recollections of Seven Years Residence at the Mauritius, or Isle of France* (London: James Cawthorn, 1830), 154–56; James Backhouse, *A Narrative of a Visit to the Mauritius and South Africa* (London: Hamilton, Adams, and Co., 1844), 17; Charles Pridham, *An Historical, Political and Statistical Account of Mauritius and Its Dependencies* (London: T. and W. Boone, 1849), 172.

70. See also Allen, *Slaves, Freedmen*, ch. 4.

CONTRIBUTORS

SHARIFA AHJUM (sharifaahjum@optusnet.com.au) currently tutors in the humanities at Murdoch University. Her doctoral thesis involved looking at the implications of French feminist theories of the feminine and the maternal, with regard to the law of uterine descent for slaves, for the representational status of Cape slave women. It thus shifts the analytic focus away from a masculine-centered conceptualization of slavery and underlines the central role of slave women in the delineation of power in Cape slave society.

RICHARD B. ALLEN (rallen@frc.mass.edu) is the author of *Slaves, Freedmen, and Indentured Laborers in Colonial Mauritius* (1999) and numerous articles on the social and economic history of Mauritius. He is currently working on a book-length manuscript on African and Asian free men and women of color and the development of a Creole society in Mauritius between 1721 and 1835.

KATRIN BROMBER received her PhD in African linguistics from the University of Leipzig (Germany). She specializes in Swahili studies with a methodological preference for text linguistics. Currently she works as a research fellow at the Centre for Modern Oriental Studies in Berlin (katrin .bromber@rz.hu-berlin.de). Her books include *The Jurisdiction of the Sultan of Zanzibar and the Subjects of Foreign Nations* (2001), *Kala Shairi: German East Africa in Swahili Poems* (coedited with Gudrun Miehe, Said Khamis, and Ralf Großerhode, 2003), and *Globalisation and African Languages: Risks and Benefits* (coedited with Birgit Smieja, 2004).

GWYN CAMPBELL holds a Canada Research Chair and is the director of the Indian Ocean World Centre in the Department of History, McGill University (gwyn.campbell@mcgill.ca). Born in Madagascar and raised in Wales (where he worked as a BBC radio producer in English and Welsh), he holds degrees in economic history from the universities of

Birmingham and Wales. He has taught in India, Madagascar, Britain, South Africa, Belgium, France, and Canada and served as an academic consultant to the South African government in the lead-up to the 1997 formation of an Indian Ocean regional association. He has organized a series of international conferences on slavery following the "Avignon format" (after the place where they were inaugurated), the latest—"Sex, Power, and Slavery" at McGill University in 2007—to mark the bicentenary of the British Anti-Slave Trade Act. As author, editor, or coeditor, he has more than one hundred publications, a significant proportion of which are on the theme of unfree labor and slavery.

CATHERINE COQUERY-VIDROVITCH (catherine. vidrovitch@orange.fr) is a professor emeritus of modern African history, University Diderot-Paris-7, and was an adjunct professor at Binghamton University, SUNY (1981–2005). Three of her books are translated into English: *Africa South of the Sahara: Endurance and Change* (1987), *African Women: A Modern History* (1998), and *The History of African Cities South of the Sahara* (2006; selected by *Choice* as an outstanding academic book). A fourth one is in translation as *Africa and the Africans in the 19th century*. Her latest book is *Les Noirs et l'Allemagne dans la première moitié du XXe siècle* (2007). She received the 1999 ASA Distinguished Africanist Award.

JAN-GEORG DEUTSCH (PhD London) is University Lecturer in Commonwealth History at the University of Oxford (jan-georg.deutch@stx.ox .ac.uk). He is working on the social and economic history of West and East Africa in the nineteenth and twentieth centuries. His recent publications with regard to slavery in Africa comprise *Emancipation without Abolition in German East Africa, c. 1880–1914* (2006) and "Absence of Evidence Is No Proof: Slave Resistance under German Colonial Rule in East Africa," in *Rethinking Resistance: Revolt and Violence in African History*, edited by Jon Abbink, Mirjam de Bruijn, and Klaas van Walraven (2003).

TIM FERNYHOUGH spent his childhood years in Ethiopia, trained in history in Great Britain, and earned his PhD in African history at the University of Illinois at Urbana-Champaign. He taught at the University of Florida and at Brunel University (London) until his untimely death in 2003. His research focused on serfdom, slavery, and other aspects of labor history in nineteenth- and twentieth-century Ethiopia and on related contemporary issues of human rights. He left a manuscript, "Slaves, Serfs, and Shifta: Modes of Production and Resistance in Pre-revolutionary Southern Ethiopia," now being reviewed for publication.

PHILIP J. HAVIK (havik@mail.telepac.pt) obtained his PhD in social sciences at the University of Leiden in The Netherlands and specializes in the anthropology and history of West Africa, and Guinea-Bissau in particular. He is currently a researcher at the Institute for Tropical Research in Lisbon and guest lecturer at the History Department of the University of Brasilia. His recent publications include *Creole Societies in the Portuguese Colonial Empire*, edited with Malyn Newitt (2007), and "Les Noirs et 'les Blancs' de l'ethnographie coloniale: Discours sur le genre en Guinée Portugaise" in *Lusotopie* 12, nos. 1–2 (2005), special issue on Gendered Social Relationships.

ELIZABETH GRZYMALA JORDAN (PhD Rutgers, The State University of New Jersey) is a historical archaeologist whose research interests include gender, colonial slavery, and the African diaspora. Her doctoral research, upon which her chapter is based, was funded by Fulbright IIE, and her dissertation, *From Time Immemorial: Washerwomen, Culture, and Community in Cape Town, South Africa*, was recently awarded the Society for Historical Archaeology's 2007 Dissertation Prize. Currently, she is a principal investigator for archaeology with Gray & Pape, Inc.

MARTIN A. KLEIN is a professor emeritus from the University of Toronto (martin.klein@utoronto.ca). He has been doing research on slavery and the slave trade in West Africa for thirty-five years and has recently branched out to study comparative slavery. His best-known book is *Slavery and Colonial Rule in French West Africa*. He is also the editor of *Breaking the Chains: Slavery, Bondage and Emancipation in Modern Africa and Asia* and, with Claire Robertson, of *Women and Slavery in Africa*.

GEORGE MICHAEL LA RUE is a professor of history at Clarion University of Pennsylvania (glarue@clarion.edu). He conducted field research in Dar Fur province of Sudan on the *hakura* system (a precolonial land tenure system). He has written on trans-Saharan trade from Bagirmi and Dar Fur. Most recently, he has been using French medical sources to investigate African slavery in nineteenth-century Egypt, and gathering slave narratives and biographical material.

PAUL E. LOVEJOY FRSC, Distinguished Research Professor, Department of History, York University (plovejoy@yorku.ca), holds the Canada Research Chair in African Diaspora History and is the director of the Harriet Tubman Institute for Research on the Global Migrations of African Peoples (see www.yorku.ca/tubman). His recent publications include *Slavery*,

Commerce and Production in West Africa: Slave Society in the Sokoto Caliphate (2005); *Ecology and Ethnography of Muslim Trade in West Africa* (2005); *The Biography of Mahommah Gardo Baquaqua: His Passage from Slavery to Freedom in Africa and America* (2nd ed., 2006); and *Pawnship, Slavery and Colonialism in Africa* (2003). He has edited or coedited volumes on the African diaspora, including *Trans-Atlantic Dimensions of Ethnicity in the African Diaspora* (2004), *Enslaving Connections: Western Africa and Brazil during the Era of Slavery* (2004), *Slavery on the Frontiers of Islam* (2004), and *Studies in the History of the African Diaspora—Documents (SHADD)*. He is coeditor of the journal *African Economic History*. Professor Lovejoy is a member of the UNESCO "Slave Route" Project and holds an appointment as Research Professor, Wilberforce Institute for the Study of Slavery and Emancipation (WISE), University of Hull (UK).

SUZANNE MIERS is a professor emerita of history at Ohio University. She is the author of *Slavery in the Twentieth Century* and coeditor of *The End of Slavery* and other books. For further biographical details, see "A Tribute to Suzanne Miers" in this volume.

JOSEPH C. MILLER is the T. Cary Johnson Professor of History at the University of Virginia, where he has taught since 1972. He is a historian of early Africa with training at the University of Wisconsin–Madison under Jan Vansina and Philip D. Curtin. His early research on oral traditions in Angola led to Atlantic-scaled interests in the Angola-Brazil trade in slaves and a 1988 monograph, *Way of Death: Merchant Capitalism and the Angolan Slave Trade, 1730–1830*; to a comprehensive bibliography of slavery and slaving throughout the world about to appear (sponsored by the Virginia Center for Digital History) in searchable online format; and to a long-term effort to historicize the study of slavery on a global scale, developed significantly through his participation in the series of Avignon conferences that have led to the current, and other, volumes of papers. Further details are available at www.virginia.edu/history/faculty/miller.html.

FRED MORTON (fred.morton@loras.edu), retired professor of history of Loras College and residing in Botswana, has published on East African and South African slavery, and on the nineteenth-century western Transvaal and eastern Botswana. His titles include *Children of Ham: Freed Slaves and Fugitive Slaves on the Kenya Coast, 1873–1907* (1990), *Slavery in South Africa: Captive Labor on the Dutch Frontier* (with Elizabeth Eldredge,

1994), and *"To Make Them Serve" — The 1871 Transvaal Commission on African Labour* (with Johan Bergh, 2003).

RICHARD ROBERTS is a professor of African history and the director of the Center for African Studies at Stanford University. He has written widely on the social history of French West Africa, and his two more recent books are *Litigants and Households: Colonial Courts and African Disputes in the French Soudan, 1895–1912* (2005) and *Intermediaries, Interpreters, and Clerks: Africans in the Making of Modern Africa* (2006), edited with Benjamin Lawrance and Emily Osborn. He is currently collaborating with Martin Klein on a general history of Africa in the twentieth century.

KIRSTEN A. SEAVER, a native of Norway, is an independent scholar with research privileges at Stanford University. Her field is early North Atlantic exploration and colonization, with a special focus on the medieval Norse and on early maps. She has published a number of books and articles, including *The Frozen Echo: Greenland and the Exploration of North America ca. A.D. 1000–1500* (1996) and *Maps, Myths, and Men: The Story of the Vinland Map* (2004).

INDEX

Women and Slavery, Volume I

WOMEN AND SLAVERY

VOLUME TWO

The Modern Atlantic

CONTENTS